The Essence of Liberty

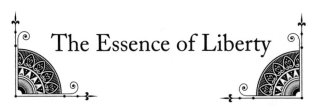

The Essence of Liberty

FREE BLACK WOMEN DURING THE SLAVE ERA

Wilma King

University of Missouri Press   Columbia and London

Copyright © 2006 by
The Curators of the University of Missouri
University of Missouri Press, Columbia, Missouri 65201
Printed and bound in the United States of America
All rights reserved
5 4 3 2 1   10 09 08 07 06

Library of Congress Cataloging-in-Publication Data

King, Wilma, 1942–
    The essence of liberty : free black women during the slave era / Wilma King.
        p.   cm.
    Summary: "King uses a wide range of sources to examine the experiences of free
black women in both the North and the South, from the colonial period through
emancipation, showing how they became free, educated themselves, found jobs,
maintained self-esteem, and developed social consciousness—even participating
in the abolitionist movement"—Provided by publisher.
    Includes bibliographical references and index.
    ISBN-13: 978-0-8262-1657-1 (hard cover : alk. paper)
    ISBN-13: 978-0-8262-1660-1 (paperback : alk. paper)
    1. Free African Americans—History.   2. African American women—History.
3. Free African Americans—Social conditions.   4. African American women—
Social conditions.   5. Free African Americans—Intellectual life.   6. African
American women—Intellectual life.   7. United States—Race relations.
8. Liberty—History.   I. Title.
    E185.18.K56   2006
    305.48'896073—dc22   2005037309

♾TM This paper meets the requirements of the
American National Standard for Permanence of Paper
for Printed Library Materials, Z39.48, 1984.

Designer: Jennifer Cropp
Typesetter: Phoenix Type, Inc.
Printer and binder: The Maple-Vail Book Manufacturing Group
Typefaces: Palatino and Caslon

For Alvin Russel "Chief" Hunter

They also serve who . . .
stand and wait.

John Milton

Tell us no more of southern slavery;
for with few exceptions, although I may be
very erroneous in my opinion, yet I consider
our condition but little better than that.

Maria W. Stewart

Contents

List of Illustrations

List of Tables

Acknowledgments

As usual I have accumulated debts that I cannot repay adequately. Several colleagues and friends read the manuscript during various stages of its completion. Their probing questions and trenchant comments demanded rethinking many ideas. Lois Virginia Mecham Gould, Karen V. Hansen, Michelle A. Krowl, and Steve Whitman graciously forwarded unpublished research findings that enriched my own work. Angela Boswell, Anita Bunkley, Darlene Clark Hine, Michael P. Johnson, Randall Miller, Ronnie Nichols, Charmaine Flemming, Daina Ramey Berry, and Ruthe Winegarten contributed valuable citations that I was certain to miss. Andrew Phillips, an undergraduate in the spring 1998 African American History 311 course at Michigan State University, won my gratitude for his assistance in verifying a citation that evaded me. Michael Moran of Cane River, a descendant of Marie Thérèze Coincoin and Claude Metoyer, offered a brief but invaluable lesson in searching the public records for free women of color in Natchitoches, Louisiana. And Scotti Cohn was kind enough to provide copies of the Crowder-Starrs correspondence from her own files when the originals, probably misfiled, could not be located at the National Archives.

Among the librarians and archivists to whom I am especially indebted are Natalie A. Caldwell, City Archives of Philadelphia, Philadelphia, Pennsylvania; Brenda Square, Amistad Research Center, Tulane University, New Orleans, Louisiana; Mary W. Miller, Historic Natchez Foundation, Natchez, Mississippi; and Anita Marshall, formerly of Michigan State University Library, East Lansing, Michigan; along with the staffs at the Arkansas History Commission, Little Rock, Arkansas; Connecticut Historical Society, Hartford, Connecticut; Pennsylvania Historical Society, Philadelphia, Pennsylvania; Hampton University Archives, Hampton, Virginia; Howard University, Washington, D.C.; North Carolina Department of Archives and History, Raleigh, North Carolina; Special Collections,

College of Charleston, Charleston, South Carolina; University of Texas, Austin, Texas; Texas Department of Archives and History, Austin, Texas; and the Louisiana and Lower Mississippi Collection, Louisiana State University, Baton Rouge, Louisiana. The staff at Ellis Library, University of Missouri–Columbia, especially Rhonda Whithaus and Geoffrey D. Swindells, assisted with acquiring U.S. Census data.

I owe much to the University of Houston's African American Studies Visiting Scholars program under the direction of Linda Reed for awarding me a 1995–1996 residency at the University of Houston. It provided the time for completing much of the research for and to draft chapters of *The Essence of Liberty* in a hospitable environment. A 1995 Andrew W. Mellon Grant for a month-long stay at the Library Company of Philadelphia and a 1997 faculty research grant from Michigan State University were valuable and much appreciated.

Finally, a general heartfelt thank you is directed toward the reviewers and colleagues in the field who scrutinized the manuscript and offered useful suggestions for honing the study. Without the assistance of these persons, named and unnamed, this study would not be a reality.

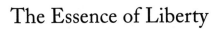

The Essence of Liberty

Introduction

By the onset of the Civil War, women constituted slightly more than 50 percent of the free black population, and a prevailing interest in free blacks during the slave era in North America is responsible for numerous dissertations, monographs, and chapters in general texts appearing as early as the turn of the twentieth century. Despite long-standing interests in the free black population, women in that general population were largely invisible. The advent of a "new" history following the social, economic, and political upheaval of the 1960s resulted in shifting greater attention to women's history, past and present.

The time is now ripe for reconstructing the lives of ordinary and extraordinary free black women from a historical perspective. Selected free women, unlike the majority of their enslaved sisters, left a cornucopia of legal documents, manuscripts, newspaper commentaries, poems, diaries, letters, and autobiographies. Statistical reports and registers containing data about free blacks are also available. These are wonderful sources, but they rarely, if ever, offer rich personal details that reflect the women's inner thoughts. Furthermore, the primary sources are uneven across geographical regions and biased in favor of literate resourceful women east of the Mississippi River.[1]

The Essence of Liberty is a general overview of the disparate body of literature designed to offer a more comprehensive view of free black women during the slave era. Slavery and freedom coexisted tenuously in an environment that made it possible for enslaved women to become free and for liberated women to lose their freedom. Furthermore, economic depravation and draconian legislation threatened to make a mockery of their freedom. Nevertheless, many free women fought to maintain their liberty and make it more than an illusive spirit or fleeting ephemeral sense of liberty. To be sure, the freedom of many black women was not comparable to that enjoyed by their white contemporaries, yet it was not slavery.

Experiences in freedom, like those in bondage, were not monolithic. Recent studies of the slave community point to the agency or determination exuded by women and men, in their own time, to forge a meaningful life for themselves and their loved ones. Their resourcefulness assured survival. In a similar vein, free persons, many of whom had been enslaved, were also resourceful and resilient. Pernicious legislation could have reduced them to slaves without owners, but their agility in developing survival techniques while protecting themselves from the furies of racism points to their will to make their freedom meaningful.[2]

There were nuances between the effervescence of liberty and the destruction of that state by legislative action, social customs, and personal vindictiveness. In some instances, black women exercised autonomy in supporting themselves, and in other cases a few economically deprived women entered slavery voluntarily. Certainly, the majority of free women enjoyed neither a completely liberating euphoria nor the degradation of the same. The extent to which black women found balance—economically, spiritually, and mentally—or enjoyed their freedom is most evident through an examination of the relationships they shared with others as they formed families, worshiped, worked, enjoyed leisure moments, and fought for rights to improve their lives and the lives of their people.

This study recognizes the gulf between rhetoric and reality, or the ideal and the real nature of freedom during the slave era. Therefore, it examines the intellectual along with the social, political, and economic history of a selected group of women. In so doing, it addresses several questions: How did free women maintain self-esteem and by what standards did they judge themselves? Did southern free women separate themselves from their enslaved female contemporaries to secure their own freedom, and did their northern contemporaries meld their interests with those of enslaved women to help them gain freedom? Color, class, and gender distinctions were often blurred.

After reading an earlier draft of this manuscript, Richard Blackett suggested that I ground it within the New World context to determine the extent to which the lives of free women in the United States were similar to or differed from their contemporaries elsewhere in the diaspora. I turned immediately to monographs and scholarly essays for a larger view and the place of free women in the black Atlantic before emancipation. The literature generally fell into two categories. The older studies ignored women while newer ones focused more specifically on enslaved women. Free women, like Deborah Gray White's enslaved women as she began the initial research for *Ar'n't I a Woman?* "were everywhere, yet nowhere."[3]

African women had come to the New World in smaller numbers than men, yet a greater percentage of women were free. This raises questions about their lives within slave societies. Did they form families? What kinds of activities consumed their days? How did they support themselves and spend their leisure moments? Moreover, did they maintain associations with their enslaved sisters and fight for their freedom? Or did they hold themselves aloof from their bonded contemporaries to better secure their own liberty?

The literature necessary for answering these questions is uneven at best. Similarly, the absence of systematic studies about the behavior of free black women, especially in Saint Domingue, has fortified long-standing stereotypes. For example, Moreau de Saint-Mery's *Description topographique, physique, civile, politique et historique de la partie francaise de l'isle de Saint-Domingue* (1797) asserts that free women were overwhelmingly prostitutes who spent their earnings on lavish clothing and jewelry. Such a conclusion remained largely unchallenged until the 1990s when Susan M. Socolow used notarial records to test the validity of de Saint-Mery's findings. It was not surprising to learn that free women in Cap Francais, Saint Domingue, like free women in English-speaking North America, engaged in a variety of occupations. As active participants in the interest of their own economic well-being, the women also bought and sold personal and real property. And on rare occasions, they freed slaves. In short, their lives were more nuanced than de Saint-Mery claimed.[4]

In the 1990s, Arlene J. Diaz examined 254 ecclesiastical, civil, and criminal cases to study gender roles among women and men in Caracas, Venezuela, between 1835 and 1840. Diaz concluded that the women, without regard for color and class, wanted fair treatment within their families and equitable protection under the law. Ironically, as women worked outside their homes, they experienced social and economic liberties, but their spouses insisted that these increasingly independent women remain subordinate to their wills. The tensions created between women and men often resulted in litigation.[5]

As the women struggled for liberty and equality in their own domestic relationships and in the courts, their enslaved contemporaries were fighting to win their freedom. This situation is not unlike others in the United States when free women displayed independence in challenging accepted conventions. The differences are in the degrees to which free women set aside their personal ambitions in the interest of their sisters and brothers in bondage.

Even a cursory review of the New World literature suggests that much extensive research is needed before a finely nuanced portrayal of free women in the Americas will emerge. The same is true of free women in the urban and rural areas of the North, Upper South, and Lower South. One historian suggested framing this study by comparing similarities and differences in a half dozen selected communities of the North, Upper South, and Lower South to determine regional distinctions in the women's lives. Such an investigation would take this work in a different direction from its original intent and produce six comparative mini-studies.

The Essence of Liberty examines the myriad founts of freedom for black women in the United States and argues that the sources of liberty and the amount of time spent in slavery before emancipation shaped the meanings of freedom. *The Essence of Liberty* also raises questions about whether free women were bound to or liberated from gender conventions of their day. Issues related to how free women earned a living, educated themselves, and developed a social consciousness are no less important.

An examination of the autobiographical writings of selected nineteenth-century black women spiritualists reveals the complex dilemma they faced when they took a stand against men—even black ones—in order to follow their calls to serve a superior being. Freedom from gender oppression within the religious setting was as important as physical and economic freedom. The spiritualists labored to extricate themselves from institutional fetters and sought legitimacy in a profession ordinarily closed to them. In the great struggle to set their souls free, the spiritual auto-biographers called attention to sexism within their own churches while black Catholic women encountered racism in theirs. It is in the religious setting where black women were most adamant in opposing gender conventions that inhibited self-actualization.

Free women faced fewer objections from society when they assisted in abolishing slavery. The fact that so many free persons had been enslaved or had relatives and friends remaining in bondage made opposition to their participation imprudent. Many free women, like free black men and white women and men, supported the abolitionist movement and helped newly freed women and men shape their liberty and give meaning to their new status following the Civil War.

Finally, this study concludes that the *essence of liberty*, the heart, soul, and core of freedom, liberty, independence, or autonomy is complex in that the absence of physical, social, and spiritual shackles was as important as relief from racial discrimination and independence in making decisions leading to one's economic well-being. The final linkages in making the *true* essence of liberty a reality for free women emerged when their enslaved people were also free.

"Full Liberty to go and live with whom
& Where She may Chuse"

Founts of Freedom

It is said Master is in want of money. If so, I know not what time he may sell me, And then all my bright hopes of the futer are blasted, for their has been one bright hope to cheer me in all my troubles, that is to be with you.

Harriet Newby

"In every Breast God has implanted a Principle, which we call Love of Freedom, it is impatient of oppression and pants for Deliverance," wrote the African-born Phillis Wheatley following her manumission by John Wheatley in 1773. As a Boston resident during the Revolutionary era, the young poet was cognizant of the surrounding tumult. Her writing reflects the apprehension of liberty-loving colonists who feared enslavement by tyrannical British leaders and their colonial minions.[1]

This chapter calls attention to myriad sources of freedom before 1865 while recognizing the lack of clarity in the status of twenty Africans arriving in Virginia aboard a Dutch frigate in 1619. In all probability, they blended in with other indentured servants and worked several years to satisfy obligations. Once indentures ended, servants were free; however, after 1660 the majority of Africans were enslaved. As a result, enslaved and emancipated Africans coexisted in colonial America. Such circumstances raise several questions, among which two will be discussed here. What did it mean to be free in a slave society? Did liberated women interact freely with those in bondage?

At the outset of the American colonial experience, there were fewer African women, enslaved and free, than men, and the reasons continue to defy a satisfactory explanation. One argument claims men were more desirable for performing heavy work. Another theory suggests that price differentials along with supply and demand created the disparity. Finally, some historians assert that Africans limited the number of women sold into slavery because they were highly prized agricultural workers. Whatever the cause, the resulting gender disparities combined with uneven population distributions made it difficult for African men in the New World to find partners of African descent, if they desired.[2]

By 1623, there were twenty-three Africans in Virginia. Among them were Mary and Anthony Johnson, a free black couple, and they stand out in this regard. He had come to the colony aboard the *James* in 1621, and she arrived on the *Margarett and John* in 1622. They married and established a home near the Pungoteague River for themselves and their four children. They acquired land in the 1640s and owned more than 250 acres by 1651. Property helped them to protect and enjoy their liberty. In fact, in 1645 when Anthony Johnson and Philip Taylor, a white neighbor, ended a joint interest in cultivating corn, Johnson was not disappointed. "Hee finds fault with me that I doe not worke," said Johnson of Taylor's scrutiny, "but now I know myne owne ground and I will worke when I please and play when I please." Dissolving the partnership had little impact on the Johnsons, whom local officials recognized for their "hard labor and known service."[3]

The Johnsons lived in Northampton County where the black female-to-male ratio remained fairly even during the seventeenth century. In 1664, there were twenty-nine females, twenty-eight males, and five persons whose gender was not recorded. Ten years later, there were thirty-eight women and thirty-six men. Only one person's gender was not identified. By contrast, the ratio in Surry County was uneven throughout the same period. The 1674 population included ten women and eighteen men along with twelve persons of unidentified gender. The disparities became even greater at the end of the century when the black population included forty-seven females and 104 males. The number of unidentified persons declined to four. Admittedly, the figures are not representative, but the fact remains that uneven gender ratios and population patterns in colonial Virginia made finding partners of African descent, if desired, difficult in some areas.[4]

Africans had no monopoly on Virginia's population imbalance. Nearly twenty years after the first settlers arrived, the white population reached 1,292. Of that number, only 244 were women of all ages, and their numbers remained significantly smaller than the number of men throughout the seventeenth century. Incidentally, the pattern was no different in colonial Maryland where the ratio was two to three at the turn of the century.[5]

It is not surprising that miscegenation occurred and was probably more extensive in colonial America than at any other time before slavery ended. Consequently, the status of children, called the "spurious issue," of Africans and Europeans was a concern that ultimately resulted in sexual circumscription or acts of "racing sex and sexing race." In 1662, the Virginia Assembly declared that "all children born in this country shall be held bond or free only according to the condition of the mother." The children of European women and African men were free but considered black.[6]

At least two centuries after codifying the law, Elizabeth Keckley, a slave-born mother, asked, *"Why should my son be held in slavery? . . .* Anglo-Saxon blood as well as the African flowed in his veins; the two currents commingled . . . *Why should not the Anglo-Saxon triumph*—why should it be weighed down with the rich blood typical of the tropics? Must the life-current of one race bind the other race in chains as strong and enduring as if there had been no Anglo-Saxon taint?" Keckley's word choices lend themselves to interpretations about the real meaning of her inferences. Ordinarily, Anglo-Saxon interests prevailed over Africans' and "weighed them down." But, in defining the "race" of mixed persons in British North America, the Anglo-Saxon "taint" was, if not insignificant, open to the judgment of the white community or court.[7]

Virginia's statute was contradictory to English common law that based status on the condition of fathers but was in keeping with British notions about property rights. The law, which was reflective of racialized sex, relieved white men of financial and legal responsibilities for mixed offspring and robbed children of their rightful heritage and legacy. Also, the 1662 statute dissuaded intimacy between blacks and whites by imposing double penalties on whites guilty of fornication or adultery with blacks. The statute entreated white women to marry white men or suffer consequences, such as heavy fines and five years of indentured service, for "sexual transgressions." The law reduced the number of white women bearing black children whom the courts could bind out until they reached thirty years of age.[8]

Along with the decline of free-born blacks were organized efforts to abolish slavery, thereby increasing the number of free persons. The Society of Friends, or Quakers, in the North began such a move with their 1688

Germantown, Pennsylvania, protest addressing the hypocrisy of slavery. They asked, "Have these negers not as much right to fight for their freedom, as you have to keep them slaves?" The question focused on civil and property rights along with race relations within the context of labor shortages. The issues were complex, yet the Quakers and others persisted. Their arguments coupled with Enlightenment beliefs reinforcing ideas about the possibilities of human progress and social reform further encouraged abolition. Several New England and middle colony legislatures received petitions to end the slave trade or to lift manumission restrictions. And residents of Massachusetts, including some blacks, asked lawmakers to influence the General Court to abolish slavery.[9]

These early efforts brought few tangible results except in Rhode Island and Connecticut, where legislatures ended the slave trade. By contrast, the intangible results were notable since antislavery activities sensitized the public to the extent that challenges to slavery were the norm in the northern colonies.[10]

Bondage was not compatible with the natural rights ideology. Well-read colonists were familiar with condemnations of slavery in Charles Baron de Montesquieu's *Spirit of the Laws* (1748) and Adam Smith's *Theory of Moral Sentiments* (1764). Both works influenced the Harvard-educated attorney James Otis, author of a widely read pamphlet published in 1764. It asserted that men (read *human* to include women) "are by the law of nature free born, as indeed all [wo]men are, white or black." The politically sagacious Otis asked, "Does it follow that tis right to enslave a [wo]man because [s]he is black? Will short curl'd hair like wool, instead of christian hair, as this called by those whose hearts are as hard as the nether millstone, help the argument? Can any logical inference in favor of slavery be drawn from a flat nose, a long or a short face?" Otis's *Rights of the British Colonists* (1768) points to the fallacy of linking phenotypes to one's fate. "It was not *right*," Otis concluded, and he was not alone in decrying the inconsistencies. "Let us either cease to enslave our fellow-[wo]men," wrote one pamphleteer, or "let us cease to complain of those that would enslave us." Similarly, Abigail Adams pointed to the incongruence: "It always appeared a most iniquitous scheme to me to fight ourselves for what we are daily robbing and plundering from those who have as good a right to freedom as we have."[11]

Phillis Wheatley's awareness of the disjuncture is evident in her "To the Right Honorable William, Earl of Dartmouth," a poem included in her *Poems on Various Subjects* (1773). With reference to England's iron grip on the colonies, she wrote:

No more, America, in mournful strain
Of wrongs, and grievance unredress'd complain,
No longer shall thou dread the iron chain,
Which wanton Tyranny with lawless hand
Had made, and with it meant t'enslave the land.

The poet's allusion to America loathing the "iron chain" suggests the shackles restraining Africans. Further cementing the connection between her understanding of liberty and bondage, Wheatley asked if the Earl wondered "from whence [her] love of *Freedom* sprung." She answered, "I [when] young in life . . . was snatchd from *Afric's* fancy'd happy seat." Wheatley imagined her parents' sorrow when they knew their "babe belov'd" had been kidnapped. "And can I then but pray," wrote Wheatley, that "others may never feel tyrannic sway." She understood the true essence, personal and political, of freedom.[12]

Ultimately, the Revolutionary War ideology was responsible for the largest increase in the free population when states north of Delaware either ended slavery or made provisions for gradual abolition. Initially, it appeared that the revolutionary spirit flowed generously from newly independent lawmakers to enslaved persons beneath them. For example, the preamble to Pennsylvania's 1780 emancipation bill recounted both the horrors of British occupation and the "grateful sense of the manifold blessings" upon the citizens when they evacuated. "We conceive that it is our duty," declared the legislators, "to extend a portion of that freedom to *others*, which hath been extended to us, and a release from that state of thralldom." Based on this premise, they passed a bill, effective March 1, 1780, which won the distinction of being the first of its kind in North America. However, it did not free anyone instantly. Persons born before March 1, 1780, remained in bondage while those born afterward were freed at twenty-eight years of age.[13]

Between 1777 and 1804, other states adopted similar statutes. New York granted unconditional freedom to blacks born before 1799, but girls born afterward were bound to service until they reached twenty-five years of age. Boys remained enslaved until they were twenty-eight years old. Laws in New Jersey, Rhode Island, and Connecticut granted freedom to children at eighteen years of age. Such laws actually rendered free-born children unfree until they reached specified ages. In the meantime, their service to "masters" varied little from the servitude of slaves. Despite complications and the tardiness of gradual abolition laws, northern slavery had disappeared before the Civil War.[14]

Table 1.1
Abolition of Slavery Prior to Ratification of Thirteenth Amendment, December 1865

1777	Vermont	State Constitution
1780	Pennsylvania	Gradual Abolition Act
1781	Massachusetts	Judicial Decision
1783	New Hampshire	Interpretation; 1857 legislative act
1784	Connecticut	1797—Gradual Abolition Act
1784	Rhode Island	Gradual Abolition Act
1787	Illinois	Prohibited by Northwest Ordinance; State Constitution, 1818
1787	Indiana	Prohibited by Northwest Ordinance; State Constitution, 1816
1787	Michigan	Prohibited by Northwest Ordinance
1787	Ohio	Prohibited by Northwest Ordinance; State Constitution, 1802
1787	Wisconsin	Prohibited by Northwest Ordinance
1799	New York	1799 and 1827—Gradual Abolition Act; Abolition
1804	New Jersey	Gradual Abolition Act
1850	California	State Constitution
1861	Kansas	State Constitution
1862	Washington, DC	U.S. Congress
1863	West Virginia	State Constitution
1864	Maryland	State Constitutional Amendment
1864	Missouri	State Constitutional Amendment

By contrast, bondage became more entrenched in the South following the Revolutionary War, but the possibilities of freedom remained open and varied. For example, the French Revolution (1789–1799), which touted "Liberty, Equality, and Fraternity," was also responsible for growth in the free black population in the United States. Two years after the Revolution began, its fervor reached Saint Domingue, a French colony sometimes called the "pearl of the Antilles and the pride of France," the wealthiest of the slave colonies in the Caribbean. The small country's agricultural yields, including sugar and coffee, furnished two-thirds of France's overseas trade, and the island was the largest single market for the Atlantic slave trade.[15]

Perhaps the colony was a "jewel in the crown," but unrest among whites, free blacks, mulattoes, and slaves eventually turned it into a multiplicity of thorns. The minority of white slaveholders began complaining about their lack of representation in the French General Assembly. By 1788, they were demanding a voice in the government along with an end to "ministerial despotism" from the French crown. The objectives of whites did not include free blacks and mulattoes. While in France, the mulattoes enjoyed rights and privileges of free persons, but when they returned to Saint Domingue they did not have comparable rights. This was especially galling to affluent mulattoes, who thirsted for freedom from racial and political discrimination.[16]

When political equality was not forthcoming, supporters of the mulatto cause organized a common front against the "forces of white supremacy," which quelled their rebellion quickly. Amid further political wrangling, the free mulattoes gained political rights. Meanwhile, the enslaved masses were not content, and it was impossible to shield them from the revolutionary rhetoric and news of events in France. Given the enslaved women and men's disaffection, it is not surprising that an insurrection against slaveholders began in August 1791 and continued until the emancipation of Haiti in 1804.[17]

Many white slaveholders, sometimes accompanied by free black servants, migrated to the United States to escape bloodshed. Thousands of free mulattoes fled to avoid persecution because of support for or personal relationships with whites. The black emigrants added to the free population, especially in New York, Philadelphia, Baltimore, Norfolk, Charleston, and New Orleans.[18]

Concomitant with the French and Haitian revolutions, France and Spain signed the secret Treaty of San Ildefonso in 1800 agreeing to the retrocession of Louisiana to France. Spain had granted the United States the right to navigate the Mississippi River in the Pinckney Treaty negotiated in 1795, but the transfer of Louisiana to France was foreboding, the "embyro of a tornado." In 1802, President Thomas Jefferson wrote, "There is on the globe one single spot, the possessor of which is our natural and habitual enemy. It is New Orleans, through which the produce of three-eighths of our territory must pass to market."[19]

Spanish possession of Louisiana was "most favorable to our interests," wrote President Jefferson in 1801. "Any other nation substituted for them," he continued, would be seen as "an extreme pain" to the United States. Rather than "marry ourselves to the British fleet and nation," as a bulwark against the French, the president authorized negotiations to buy New Orleans to solve the right-to-deposit problem. Once Toussaint L'Ouverture and his soldiers defeated the French and declared Saint Domingue an independent nation, which the United States did not yet recognize, Napoleon's plan was inconsequential. The French decided to sell all of Louisiana for $15 million. The purchase added 825,000 square miles of land to the United States along with 10,500 free women and men.[20]

Many of the free blacks had bought themselves and loved ones through *coartacion* under the Spanish between 1763–1803. By the terms of *coartacion*, enslaved women and men had a right to freedom since the Spanish *Las Siete Partidas* declared "a rule of law that all judges should aid liberty for the reason that it is a friend of nature, because not only [wo]men, but all animals love it." The *coartacion* made self-purchase possible, and the number of transactions reached fifty per year in Spanish New Orleans between 1800 and 1803. During the entire period of Spanish rule in the city, 1,490 women and men purchased themselves.[21]

In English-speaking North America, self-purchase was possible, but no state or national statute declared a person entitled to such a right or encouraged its execution. However, some women did buy themselves or their children. A northern-born white woman living in Alabama described the process used by an industrious enslaved woman:

> I believe she paid $2. per week [to her owner] besides $3 or 4 00 for herself...She sells cakes and pies in the street Every day she takes a large waiter full of cakes on her head and her knitting in her hand marches through the town She frequently buys eggs and butter [from] private families [to sell] They all go on the waiter...She often "toats" much more than I can lift How often when I've seen her turn her head to answer some one calling to her have I trembled lest eggs butter pies and cakes should form a useless compound with the dust of the earth But she always keeps the balance perfectly...

Of more importance than balancing the goods, the woman earned enough money to liberate herself.[22]

Ordinarily, enslaved women's wages were so meager they barely eked out an existence after satisfying financial obligations to owners. Few skilled women managed to purchase themselves without aid from others. Elizabeth Keckley's quest for independence is exceptional and illustrative. While enslaved, she "kept bread in the mouths of seventeen persons for two years and five months." Even so, Keckley, as a dress maker, did not earn enough to buy herself and her son. She succeeded only through an arrangement with patrons in Missouri who loaned her $1,200. The meaning of self-purchase is best explained by Keckley's own words: "Free, free! what a glorious ring to the word. Free! the bitter heart-struggle was over."[23]

Examples abound, but the one of Marie Thérèze, nee Coincoin, is most informative, for she played a significant role in buying and emancipating her children. She was a slave-born mother of fourteen children, and in 1786, the nearly twenty-year union with Claude Thomas Pierre Metoyer, a Frenchman who had owned her and fathered ten of her younger children, ended. Six of the children born prior to Metoyer's emancipation of Coincoin were technically enslaved and owned by their father. The liberation of these children along with the older ones took nearly thirty years and involved the personal sacrifices of a single parent in her declining years. Coincoin forfeited an annual stipend from Metoyer in exchange for their emancipation. Beyond the financial costs, there were emotional liabilities in having several children freed by Metoyer in a niggardly fashion. It must have been difficult to see Nicholas Augustine, born in 1768 and freed in 1792, while his twin sister, Marie Suzanne, remained enslaved nearly twenty-five years longer. In buying and emancipating her children, Coincoin acted with determination and finesse. No doubt her own liberty was more meaningful once her children were also free.[24]

Marie Thérèze Coincoin may be compared to Alethia Tanner. Coincoin was a planter in Natchitoches, Louisiana, a Lower South farming community, while Tanner was a market woman in Washington, D.C., an urban center in the Upper South. They were similar in business acumen, which was responsible, in part, for their successes. After a self-purchase in 1810, Tanner bought and liberated twenty-two persons. Among them was her sister, Laurena Cook, and her five offspring. The price of emancipation certificates increased from twenty to fifty dollars in 1851, thus making freedom more costly. Perhaps Tanner, like Coincoin, received assistance from others in her effort.[25]

Coincoin, Tanner, and other free women with resources helped to free loved ones. In the Washington, D.C.–Georgetown area where Tanner lived, relatives manumitted 10 percent of the recorded deeds in 1856, 1858, and 1860. Tanner was unusual because of the large number of manumissions. This was more difficult for ordinary free women because of their general poverty.[26]

Aside from purchases, public and private manumissions increased the free population. Well-known slaveowners including George Washington, Robert Carter, George Wythe, and John Randolph freed hundreds of blacks. Others, such as Thomas Jefferson, liberated only a few. Less well-known slaveholders who emancipated women and men include Samuel Gist, of Hanover, Virginia, who emancipated 263 men, women, and children in 1819; and Thomas Sewall, a doctor practicing in Washington, D.C., who purchased four blacks, a forty-year-old woman and her three children, in 1839 with the intent to free them. Sewall said they were to "go to Massachusetts to join David a colored man the husband of Celia & the father" of her children. The children's freedom hinged on subjection "to the parental care & authority of their father & mother, until they shall become of age," by Massachusetts law.[27]

Many manumissions were without encumbrances, while others were complex. The 1813 manumission of Franky, a woman owned by James McCary, a white craftsman in Natchez, Mississippi, is riddled with convolutions. McCary manumitted Franky and her daughter and son, Kitty and Robert, presumably children he fathered, while the status of Franky's third child, Warner, remained unchanged. McCary's will stipulated that Warner "and his progeny were 'to be held as slaves during all and each of their lives'" for the benefit of Kitty and Robert. This illuminates the tangled roots of kinship and slavery in households where relatives, black or white, owned their own folk.[28]

Warner's fate reflects McCary's disaffection with Franky. Seemingly, McCary was interested in punishing his unfaithful lover by elevating their mulatto children to a higher level than Franky's two-year-old dark-skinned son. McCary punished Warner for the "sins" of his mother and established the foundation for strife and confusion within the freed-woman's family. There were two certainties: Warner was to remain enslaved, and McCary's will could not assign status to the boy's progeny. Warner's offspring would follow the status of their mother(s). The children—whether enslaved or free—owed no service to their uncle and aunt unless they also owned their half-brother's partner(s). In all probability, this quagmire prevented Franky from enjoying her liberty as a freedwoman.

Intimacy between slaveholding men, like McCary, and enslaved women, like Franky, did not guarantee freedom, yet women were more likely than men to gain freedom based on intimacy for two reasons. First, fewer women owned real and personal property than men; consequently, fewer women were at liberty to dispose of holdings—land and slaves—through sales, wills, or manumissions. Second, slaveowners, male or female, were within their legal rights to engage in sex with persons they owned. However, society's double standard restrained white women from intimate relationships with blacks that might lead to the men's freedom.[29]

After the eighteenth century, social conventions and class dimensions shrouded possibilities of miscegenation between white women and black men. Yet it is reasonable to ask if the Virginian Esther Russell gave Sam his freedom, land, and several young slaves in 1821 because he was her lover. Was Sally Taylor's 1853 will providing for William Henry's emancipation and a legacy of $100 to leave Amherst County, Virginia, due to intimacy? Did a personal attraction prompt Sarah Robinson to free Elias and give him the use of her dray and team? Folk wisdom suggests that white women freed black men due to their goodwill or "maternalism" toward industrious or faithful servants.[30]

Questioning the route to freedom of black men calls attention to uneven standards of social acceptability, regional variations, and laws that forbade sex or love across the color line. Received wisdom suggests that intimacy between white women and black men "involved women with defective notions of their social positions," aside from those who were possibly "mentally retarded," had poor self-images, or were social deviants with little or no property, real or personal. It was assumed that respectable propertied white women with class standing would never become intimate with enslaved men. This assumption hinders investigations into different possibilities. Additionally, scholars have yet to examine the possible linkages between homoeroticism and the emancipation of enslaved men. Nevertheless, the actual number of blacks, male and female, emancipated due to intimacy with whites, male and female, is unknown. The absence of recorded details is less concrete than biological results, the offspring of intimacy between persons of different colors.[31]

Progeny of mixed parentage were present in the seventeenth century, but the U.S. Census did not include a separate category for mulattoes until 1850. And it was the enumerator's observation, which was imprecise at best, that determined who belonged in this category. According to the 1850 census, there were 159,095 free mulattoes, more than 40 percent of the total of free persons of color, and 246,656 enslaved mulattoes constituting nearly 9 percent of the entire enslaved population. Some enslaved mulattoes were the offspring of owners with the option to free them. Other mulattoes were the children of owners' relatives, overseers, friends, or persons without legal authority to emancipate another person's chattel.[32]

The slaveholder's status, marital and financial, was tangential to the possibilities of emancipation prior to an owner's death. Unmarried or widowed owners of means were more likely to free lovers than persons of means with legally recognized spouses and children, or an interest in avoiding scandals. Emancipations by wills, regardless of the deceased owners' marital status, were subject to challenges by money-hungry or poverty-stricken heirs or relatives. It was not unusual for courts to overturn manumission decrees. Such trials often reveal specific reasons for emancipations whereas references in recorded manumissions, wills, and county order books do not always provide details. According to a November 22, 1843, document in the St. Louis Circuit Court, Nathaniel E. Janney manumitted the thirty-one-year-old Nance, his twenty-nine-year-old wife, Fanny, and their four children ranging in age from two to nine years of age for "diverse good causes and considerations."[33] Exactly why Janney or other slaveholding men liberated men or women and why the few slaveowning women freed men or women is often impossible to determine.

Of course, specifics regarding intimacy do appear occasionally. For example, the April 11, 1789, will of William Barland, a white slaveowner of means, in Natchez, Mississippi, contains clauses referring to the slave-born Elizabeth. Barland describes her as his "friend and companion" and acknowledges paternity of three children. Another example involves Andrew, a black man, who appeared before a Barnwell District, South Carolina, official, Nicholas Powers, on April 22, 1803, to emancipate his wife and "her four children." He said the act was "in consideration of . . . Goodwill and Affection" for his "Loving Wife." "Love and affection" prompted John Dipper, a freedman, to purchase and emancipate Edey in 1818. And "diverse good considerations" caused Russell Davis, a free black man, to emancipate Eliza, his wife. The men's color was less important than their love for and concerns about their partners and children's well-being.[34]

Intimacy was far from the sole cause of emancipations. Many women and men in Maryland received freedom between 1796 and 1830 due to "diverse good causes and consideration," a generic explanation covering a multitude of reasons. The state's permissive attitude regarding black Revolutionary War service and economic considerations further explain the size of the free population. The decreasing importance of tobacco as a cash crop, soil exhaustion, the reduced need for slave labor, and the Panic of 1819 also contributed to the decline of slavery in Maryland.[35]

A study of emancipations in Washington, D.C., between 1850 and 1860 concludes that "slaveholders used manumissions to divest themselves and their families of slaves who were unable to contribute wages or services to their households." Teenaged females were three times more likely to receive manumissions than their male contemporaries. It appears that the owners were unwilling to underwrite the cost of child care during the women's fecund years and allowed them to buy themselves. If owners maintained the women through their reproductive years, they were less likely to manumit them afterward since the women's productivity increased when unencumbered by childbirth and child care.[36]

Although some blacks were manumitted privately, promises of emancipations sometimes went awry with changes in owners' commitments, economic status, or legal statutes forbidding manumissions. There are multitudes of examples of unfulfilled promises and derailed dreams, but enslaved women did not depend solely on others for their freedom. On occasions, they entered judicial proceedings, which like private

Table 1.2
Black and Mulatto Population of the United States, 1850

States	Free			Slaves		
	Black	Mulatto	Total	Black	Mulatto	Total
New England						
Connecticut	5,895	1,798	7,693	. . . . .	. . . . .	. . . . .
Maine	895	461	1,356	. . . . .	. . . . .	. . . . .
New Hampshire	336	184	520	. . . . .	. . . . .	. . . . .
Massachusetts	6,724	2,340	9,064	. . . . .	. . . . .	. . . . .
Rhode Island	2,939	731	3,670	. . . . .	. . . . .	. . . . .
Vermont	512	206	718	. . . . .	. . . . .	. . . . .
Middle Atlantic						
New Jersey	20,113	3,697	23,810	232	4	236
New York	40,930	8,139	49,069	. . . . .	. . . . .	. . . . .
Pennsylvania	38,285	15,341	53,626	. . . . .	. . . . .	. . . . .
North Central						
Illinois	2,930	2,506	5,436	. . . . .	. . . . .	. . . . .
Indiana	5,941	5,321	11,262	. . . . .	. . . . .	. . . . .
Iowa	178	155	333	. . . . .	. . . . .	. . . . .
Michigan	1,465	1,118	2,583	. . . . .	. . . . .	. . . . .
Ohio	11,014	14,265	25,279	. . . . .	. . . . .	. . . . .
Wisconsin	338	297	635			
Upper South						
Delaware	16,425	1,648	18,073	2,207	83	2,290
Kentucky	7,381	2,630	10,011	181,252	29,729	210,981
Maryland	61,109	13,614	74,723	82,479	7,889	90,368
Missouri	1,687	931	2,618	74,187	13,235	87,422
North Carolina	10,258	17,205	27,463	271,733	16,815	288,548
Tennessee	2,646	3,776	6,422	219,103	20,356	239,459
Virginia	18,857	35,476	54,333	428,229	44,299	472,528
Washington, DC	6,783	3,276	10,059	2,885	802	3,687
Lower South						
Alabama	567	1,698	2,265	321,239	21,605	342,844
Arkansas	201	407	608	40,739	6,361	47,100
Florida	229	703	932	36,288	3,022	39,310
Georgia	1,403	1,528	2,931	359,013	22,669	381,682
Louisiana	3,379	14,083	17,462	224,974	19,835	244,809
Mississippi	295	635	930	290,148	19,730	309,878
South Carolina	4,588	4,372	8,960	372,482	12,502	384,984
Texas	140	257	397	50,458	7,703	58,161
West						
California	875	87	962	. . . . .	. . . . .	. . . . .

States	Free			Slaves		
	Black	Mulatto	Total	Black	Mulatto	Total
Territories						
Minnesota	16	23	39	. . . . .	. . . . .	. . . . .
New Mexico	6	16	22	. . . . .	. . . . .	. . . . .
Oregon	45	162	207	. . . . .	. . . . .	. . . . .
Utah	15	9	24	9	17	26+
Totals	275,400	159,095	434,495	2,957,657	246,656	3,204,313 +transients

Source: J. D. B. DeBow, *Statistical View of the United States, being a Compendium of the Seventh Census* (Washington, DC: A. O. P. Nicholson, 1854), 83.

manumissions, date back to the colonial period. Such actions often involved the collaboration of white supporters as in the case of Elizabeth "Mumbet" Freeman, an illiterate woman in Massachusetts, who listened to the conversations of visitors in her owner's home during the American Revolution. Discussions about the 1780 constitution saying all persons were "born free and equal" piqued her desire for liberty. She and another bondservant solicited the help of Theodore Sedgwick who filed *Brom and Bett v. John Ashley* (1781) on their behalf.[37]

Sedgwick argued that the state never gave legal sanction to bondage and the constitution's first article nullified it. The enslaved woman and man won their freedom, and Bett probably added the surname "Freeman" to signify her new status. Of his client, Sedgwick wrote, "If there could be a practical refutation of the imagined superiority of our race to hers, the life and character of this woman would afford that refutation." The case set the precedent for destroying slavery in the Bay State.[38]

Plaintiffs elsewhere based arguments on detention after promises of freedom, detention after expiration of apprenticeships, sale after promises to manumit, and the birth of a child pending the manumission of the mother. *Maria v. Surbaugh* (1824) is one suit that exemplified the complexities associated with acquiring freedom. It began in 1790 when Virginian William Holliday bequeathed Mary to his son William "with a declaration, that she shall be free as soon as she arrived at the age of thirty-one years." Fourteen years later, William Holliday ignored the will and sold Mary to a buyer known only as White, who then sold her to Gilkeson. There was yet another sale to Carman. Ultimately, Surbaugh bought Mary and an infant, Maria, for whom the case is named. Maria and siblings, Nancy, Solomon, and Samuel, were born prior to their mother's thirty-first birthday, September 1, 1818. Mary, who was entitled to freedom but held in bondage, sued for her freedom and that of her four children.[39]

When hearing *Maria v. Surbaugh*, the court reviewed details of *Pleasant v. Pleasant* (1799), a similar case wherein John Pleasant bequeathed chattel to his son, Robert, and stipulated that they be free at thirty years of age. The same applied to any children born to the women prior to their thirtieth birthday. Based on the *Pleasant* decision, the judge in *Maria v. Surbaugh* declared that Mary's former owner had not made provisions to emancipate her children; therefore, they were to remain in bondage while she was freed.[40]

The *Surbaugh* decision was not the last case in which former slaves sued for the freedom of children born while the mothers awaited emancipation. To rectify the situation, Virginia added a code to its body of laws in 1849, saying, "The increase of any female so emancipated by deed or will hereafter made, born between the death of the testator, or the record of the deed, and the time when her right to the enjoyment of her freedom arrives, shall also be free at that time, unless the deed or will otherwise provides." The law did not benefit Mary's children but guaranteed other women with pending manumissions that their offspring would also be free.[41]

Occasionally, courts awarded plaintiffs freedom based on visual interpretations and core beliefs. A judge's decision in *Hudgins v. Wrights* (1806), a case of several Virginians representing three generations, is informative. The court considered physical characteristics of Africans to determine if the Wrights were entitled to freedom. He posited that a "flat nose and woolly head of hair" were stronger evidence of African ancestry than one's complexion. The women's phenotypical features convinced him that they were "the same with those of whites." In other words, the evidence of "race" was in the eyes of the beholder, and the court freed the women.[42]

Other women gained freedom through suits grounded in the concept of "freedom elsewhere," domicile in a free state, territory, or nation. The unsuccessful but best known of all "freedom elsewhere" cases is *Dred Scott v. John F. A. Sandford* (1857). It received notoriety because the U.S. Supreme Court rendered a decision of greater national importance than the freedom of the plaintiffs, Harriet, Eliza, Lizzie, and Dred Scott. The most significant Supreme Court decision in constitutional history began as *Harriet Scott v. Irene Emerson* (1846) when Harriet Robinson Scott initiated action against the widow of John Emerson, a medical doctor who had owned Dred Scott. The suit began as that of Harriet Robinson Scott and her daughters. That she filed such a complaint was not unusual in the St. Louis courts where women initiated the majority of the freedom suits.[43]

Among Scott's claims to freedom were her residence in Wisconsin Territory where the Northwest Ordinance of 1787 and the 1836 Wisconsin Enabling Act prohibited slavery. Her marriage, a lawful ceremony performed by her owner, Lawrence Taliferro, a government official in the Wisconsin Territory, was an added factor. In the ceremony, Taliferro "gave" Harriet to Dred in marriage and rendered her a free woman as well. As a justice of the peace, he recorded the marriage just as he did other important civil events. Finally, the "freedwoman's" daughter Eliza was born in 1840 aboard the *Gipsey* on the Mississippi River flanked by Illinois on one bank and Wisconsin on the other. Eliza based her claim on place of birth and her mother's manumission at marriage. Lizzie, Scott's second child, was born in a slave state in 1846. Yet she had a claim to freedom based on her mother's status, a free woman after living in free territory and manumission at marriage.[44]

Harriet Scott's claim to freedom was stronger than her husband's. While owned by John Emerson, the Virginia-born Dred Scott lived in Illinois and the Wisconsin Territory. Both the Illinois constitution and Northwest Ordinance of 1787 forbade bondage. Dred Scott's lawyer argued that residency in free lands entitled him to liberty. Harriet Scott's case was subsumed under her husband's once her lawyer moved outside the state, but their cases were not identical.[45]

After eleven years in lower courts, *Dred Scott* reached the U.S. Supreme Court, which was to decide if a state could reverse freedom once granted through the Northwest Ordinance. The Supreme Court, dominated by seven Democrats of whom five were pro-slavery southerners, would also decide whether blacks were citizens and justified in bringing a case before that body. The Court could have avoided the subsequent political confrontation by saying states could decide if sojourners were free on entry and lost it by egress, the precedent established in *Strader v. Graham* (1850), in which Chief Justice Roger B. Taney said "every State has an undoubted right to determine the *status* or domestic condition of the persons domiciled within its territory."[46]

The Supreme Court scuttled the "once free always free" precedent and returned the Scotts to slavery. The Court also said blacks, even free ones, were not citizens and that the 1820 Missouri Compromise was unconstitutional. What began as an individual freedom suit rendered a major decision regarding citizenship and the constitutionality of forbidding slavery in federal territory. The Scotts were probably bewildered at the turn of events as their case became a national political issue. Certainly they were disappointed by the Court's decision but were freed nonetheless: the sons of Peter Blow, Dred Scott's first owner, purchased and emancipated him and his family.[47]

When liberty was not forthcoming through manumissions, purchases, or legal suits, slaves resorted to other acts, including running away. Among the most famous slave-born women who fled from bondage are Harriet Jacobs, Ellen Craft, and Sojourner Truth. The legendary Harriet Tubman not only fled from slavery but was responsible for the escapes of scores of others from involuntary servitude. Based on the number of slaveholders in 1860, one estimate concluded that if one person per owner fled annually, the number of fugitives would be as high as 50,000. Runaways fled to northern states or to crowded southern cities where chances of detection were slim. Fugitives melded easily into anonymity in Baltimore, "an essentially free-labor city," where free blacks outnumbered unfree blacks.[48]

Women with children were less likely to flee because of the difficulties of taking youngsters along and many mothers' refusal to leave them behind. Females in their childbearing years appeared infrequently in advertisements for runaways. Of the notices in the Richmond, Virginia, *Enquirer* between 1804 and 1824, only 15.4 percent of the 1,250 runaways were females. Among the 424 advertisements in selected New Orleans newspapers in 1850, only 136 refer to females. In all probability, women traveling alone attracted more attention and were detained and returned to owners more quickly than men. Without respect for gender, owners failed to end the massive outflow of freedom seekers, of whom many failed to liberate themselves permanently. Yet neither slaves nor slaveowners ever abandoned their efforts.[49]

The most dramatic of all acts to win freedom were armed rebellions. Enslaved women did not lead such uprisings but, like Harriet Newby, would possibly benefit from successful resistance. Newby wrote letters to her partner Dangerfield Newby, a freedman, expressing her desperation with their separation. Her August 16, 1859, letter is telling. "I want you to buy me as soon as possible," she warned; if "you do not get me some body else will." She was anxious about their six children and believed he could free them. "Their has been one bright hope to cheer me in all my troubles," she wrote, and "that is to be with you.... If I thought I shoul never see you this earth would have no charms for me," she added. At the letter's end, she begged, "Do all you can for me, witch [sic] I have no doubt you will."[50]

Newby's partner had worked in the North for the purpose of earning money to buy his family's freedom but chose an alternative. He joined forces with the white zealot John Brown and fifteen to twenty well-armed men involved in the 1859 raid at a federal arsenal in Harpers Ferry, Virginia. Brown's intent was not entirely clear, but it appears that he planned to acquire weapons, rally enslaved persons to the abolitionist cause, and end bondage in the area.[51]

During the assault, Newby was shot in the head yet managed to return fire before dying from a wound in the neck. He must have weighed the efficacy of Brown's plot against other costs, including the time necessary to earn enough to buy seven souls, separation from his family, and possible imprisonment or death if the plan failed. The odds against Brown's success were great, but Newby joined the abolitionist to free his family.[52]

As word of the raid spread, Harriet Newby and her children were probably aware of it since they lived thirty miles from Harpers Ferry. It is also possible that they learned of the "wild and madly excited" mob mutilating the body of their loved one. The raid had terrorized whites and created an atmosphere in which ordinary citizens resorted to savage behavior.[53] It is impossible to know how news of the raid affected Harriet Newby and her children. She probably held herself responsible since her partner's actions reflected a strong sense of family responsibility. In fact, he carried Harriet's letters into Brown's battle for freedom. Although she had declared the "earth would have no charms" without him, Harriet Newby must have been comforted in knowing the extent to which Dangerfield Newby had gone to free her and their children.[54]

The various founts of liberty caused the free population to escalate from 59,466 in 1790 to 487,970 in 1860. It peaked in 1830 at 13.7 percent of the total black population. Afterward the percentages fell to 13.4 percent in 1840, 11.9 percent in 1850, and finally to 11.0 percent in 1860. The growth slowed over the years because whites abhorred the unsettling idea of free persons among their slaves raising their aspirations for freedom. "It was no accident," writes historian Ira Berlin, "that an articulate defense of slavery appeared with the emergence of the free Negro caste." Proslavery arguments figured more prominently in southern intellectual life between 1830 and 1860. Despite the arguments and fears of proslavery advocates, the actual number of free women increased from 123,190 in 1820 to 253,951 in 1860.[55]

Regardless of the manner in which blacks were freed, they were anomalies in a slave society that assumed whites were free and blacks were not. Even greater aberrations were the "quasi-slaves," legally bound persons who lived, worked, and behaved as if they were emancipated.

"We were free," declared Cornelia Smith, a biracial North Carolinian. "We were just born in slavery, that's all." Smith and her three sisters resided in the home of their grandfather, a planter, while their mother and older half-brother lived across the yard in the slave quarters. Smith and others, including Amanda America Dickson, offspring of the enslaved Julia Frances and a wealthy Georgia entrepreneur and scientific farmer David Dickson, and Kentuckians Imogene and Adeline Johnson, daughters of the enslaved mulatto Julia Chinn and Richard Mentor Johnson, vice president of the United States from 1837–1841, were hobbled by similar circumstances, yet they enjoyed unrestricted mobility and suffered little or no interferences from owners. Legal documents made them chattel, "that's all."[56]

Papers granting freedom were not forthcoming for various reasons. The costs of emancipations were prohibitive for some, especially in cases where laws required freed persons to relocate within a specified time or risk re-enslavement. If emancipators could not afford the costs of legal documents or relocating loved ones, they kept them enslaved. If states demanded security in property to assure that freed persons did not become financial liabilities, emancipators did not liberate them. Harriet Jacobs's brother, John, explained, "It may seem rather strange that my grandmother [Molly Horniblow] should hold her son a slave; but the law required it. She was obliged to give security that she would never be any expense to the town or state before she could come in possession of her freedom. Her property in him was sufficient to satisfy the law; he could be sold at any minute to pay her debts, though it was not likely this would ever be the case."[57]

Table 1.3
Free Black Population in States and Territories, 1790–1860

	1790	1800	1810	1820	1830	1840	1850	1860
NEW ENGLAND AND MIDDLE								
Connecticut	2,801	5,330	6,453	7,844	8,047	8,105	7,693	8,627
Illinois	.....	.....	613	457	1,637	3,598	5,436	7,628
Indiana	.....	163	393	1,230	3,629	7,165	11,262	11,428
Iowa	.....	.....	.....	.....	.....	172	333	1,069
Maine	538	818	969	929	1,190	1,355	1,356	1,327
Massachusetts	5,463	6,452	6,737	6,740	7,048	8,669	9,064	9,602
Michigan	.....	.....	120	174	261	707	2,583	6,799

	1790	1800	1810	1820	1830	1840	1850	1860
Minnesota	.....	.....	.....	.....	.....	.....	39	259
Missouri	.....	.....	607	347	569	1,574	2,618	3,572
New Hampshire	630	856	970	786	604	537	520	494
New Jersey	2,762	4,402	7,843	12,460	18,303	21,044	23,810	25,318
New York	4,654	10,374	25,333	29,279	44,870	50,027	49,069	49,005
Ohio	.....	337	1,899	4,723	9,568	17,342	25,279	36,673
Pennsylvania	6,537	14,561	22,492	30,202	37,930	47,854	53,626	56,849
Rhode Island	3,469	3,304	3,609	3,554	3,561	3,238	3,670	3,952
Vermont	255	557	750	903	881	730	718	709
Wisconsin	.....	.....	.....	.....	.....	185	635	1,171
UPPER SOUTH								
Delaware	3,899	8,268	13,136	12,958	15,855	16,919	18,073	19,829
Kentucky	114	741	1,713	2,759	4,917	7,317	10,011	10,684
Maryland	8,043	19,587	33,927	39,730	52,938	62,078	74,723	83,942
N. Carolina	4,975	7,043	10,266	14,612	19,543	22,732	27,463	30,463
Tennessee	361	309	1,317	2,727	4,555	5,524	6,422	7,300
Virginia	12,766	20,124	30,570	36,889	47,348	49,852	54,333	58,042
Wash., D.C.	.....	783	2,549	4,048	6,152	8,361	10,059	11,131
LOWER SOUTH								
Alabama	.....	.....	.....	571	1,572	2,039	2,265	2,690
Arkansas	.....	.....	.....	59	141	465	608	144
Florida	.....	.....	.....	.....	844	817	932	932
Georgia	398	1,019	1,801	1,763	2,486	2,753	2,931	3,500
Louisiana	.....	.....	7,585	10,476	16,710	25,502	17,462	18,647
Mississippi	.....	182	240	458	519	1,366	930	773
S. Carolina	1,801	3,185	4,554	6,826	7,921	8,276	8,960	9,914
Texas	.....	.....	.....	.....	.....	.....	397	355
WEST								
California	.....	.....	.....	.....	.....	.....	962	4,086
Colorado	.....	.....	.....	.....	.....	.....	.....	46
Dakota	.....	.....	.....	.....	.....	.....	.....	.....
Oregon	.....	.....	.....	.....	.....	.....	207	128
Nebraska	.....	.....	.....	.....	.....	.....	.....	67
Nevada	.....	.....	.....	.....	.....	.....	.....	45
New Mexico	.....	.....	.....	.....	.....	.....	22	85
Utah	.....	.....	.....	.....	.....	.....	24	30
Washington	.....	.....	.....	.....	.....	.....	.....	30
Total	*59,466*	*108,395*	*186,446*	*233,524*	*319,599*	*386,303*	*434,495*	*487,970*

Source: J. D. B. DeBow, *Statistical View of the United States, being a Compendium of the Seventh Census* (Washington, DC: A. O. P. Nicholson, 1854), 63; Jos. C. G. Kennedy, *Preliminary Report on the Eighth Census, 1860* 37th Congress, 2d Session, Senate (Washington: Government Printing Office, 1862), 131.

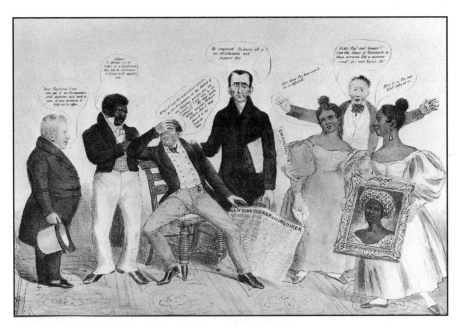

Figure 1.1. "An Affecting Scene in Kentucky" (Richard Mentor Johnson and his slave-born mulatto daughters). Library Company of Philadelphia, Philadelphia, Pennsylvania.

Similarly, extenuating circumstances affected the slave-born April Ellison of Winnsboro, South Carolina. After completing an apprenticeship under the tutelage of William McCreight, Ellison bought his freedom. Once emancipated, he changed his name to William, built a new life as a prosperous cotton gin manufacturer, and purchased his enslaved spouse, Matilda, and their daughter, Eliza Ann. Another daughter, Maria Ann—apparently the offspring of another woman—remained in bondage. Eventually, Ellison bought but never emancipated her because manumissions in South Carolina were illegal by 1830. Ellison asked McCreight to hold the title to his daughter, but she lived as a free woman.[58]

Regardless of her apparent liberty, Maria Ann Ellison remained enslaved, technically and tenuously. Changes in McCreight's life could complicate her own. It is not known how Ellison spent her days, but it is clear that some quasi-slaves lived and worked at a distance from owners while carving out degrees of autonomy for themselves in the process. Sally Thomas, an enslaved washerwoman in Nashville, stands out in this regard. After agreeing to hand over a portion of her earnings to her owner, Thomas hired herself out. The mother of three biracial sons managed to satisfy her obligations and save for her own business. She rented a house, probably her greatest expense, on the corner of a busy intersection in the Nashville business district. Thomas used two rooms for a laundry. The money earned from the painstaking chore was enough to support herself. Of greater importance, Thomas purchased her youngest son's freedom and educated him in a local school. No one circumscribed her liberty or interfered with her decisions.[59]

The quality of life for free and virtually free women had much to do with the region of the country in which they lived. In the North where blacks were presumed to be free, the greatest threats to their liberty were kidnapping and enslavement in the South. Free southerners were in jeopardy of enslavement if they failed to pay taxes, violated laws, or committed crimes.[60]

Due to the tenuous nature of freedom in a slave society, it is appropriate to ask if black women made distinctions among themselves based on skin color and status. The abbreviations "f.w.c.," "f.m.c.," and "f.p.c.," meaning free women of color, free men of color, and free persons of color often appear in legal records without insight about individual perceptions. Descriptors such as "light sambo" are more telling but confusing since not all officials viewed pigmentation in the same way. Over twenty-five descriptors ranging from "very black" to "bright yellow" appear in public records.[61]

To further complicate matters, official records lack uniformity across geographical regions and within states. Georgia's antebellum registers of free persons are informative. The Chatham County Register (1826–1835) recorded names, places of birth, occupations, and guardians without mentioning skin color. Registers for Taliaferro County (1829–1861) and Camden County (1818) noted the complexion of registrants. "Black" and "mulatto" appear in the Camden County records along with "free woman of color." The only measure of consistency is in the use of "black" and "mulatto" on the same page or "free person of color" exclusively. Only one label, "yellow," appears in the Columbia County record, and that was sporadic.[62]

The absence of uniformity is evident in a compilation of "record linkage" in selected areas of Philadelphia from 1850 to 1880. The data indicate that approximately one-third of the sample received different designations over time. Twenty-six percent of those called "black" in 1850 received "mulatto" designations in 1860. A larger shift occurred when the census designated 47 percent of the persons considered "mulatto" in 1850 as "black" in 1860. The changes and lack of uniformity in designations give pause about the significance of skin color in the eyes of the beholder.[63]

There is no corpus of primary sources attributed to free women before 1865 that sheds light on how they viewed their own color. The narratives of former slaves collected by Works Progress Administration (WPA) interviewers in the 1930s contain scattered commentary about color stratification and strife in the slave community. It also suggests that whiter slaves enjoyed privileges that evaded darker ones. If those privileged slaves were the daughters and sons of white owners, it is likely that some of them received preferential treatment. This, of course, encourages queries about their special status—whether color alone set them apart, or familial relationships and class privileges were responsible. Of equal significance is knowing if hostilities were directed at the light-skinned person or the individuals responsible for making differences based on color.[64]

In either case, it seems incongruent to argue that the kinds of color stratification that existed in some slave communities were replicated in free black communities where different household structures existed. The absence of multiple families varying in hues living in one household as existed on a plantation would make it impossible to have color-based strife amongst its members. So if light-skinned free blacks received privileges, was it color alone that elevated them? Or, was it education and class standing that set them apart?

Two free black men's organizations, the Brown Fellowship Society and the Society of the Free Dark Men, in Charleston, South Carolina, illustrate that tensions existed among free persons based on skin color. Color and class were important for the club members who separated themselves from poor enslaved blacks. That Charleston was the location of this documented tension is an important link in the history of blacks from the West Indies where color stratification was obvious. The situation in Charleston was not entirely representative of all free black communities across the United States.[65]

Attention to color among blacks was probably more pronounced in South Carolina where mixed marriages were not illegal until after the Civil War and in Louisiana where *placage*, arranged extralegal unions between European men and women of African descent, primarily mulattoes, quadroons, and octoroons, existed. Furthermore, many planters from the West Indies migrated to South Carolina and Louisiana, states with the largest number of free blacks in the Lower South, and they were less rigid about miscegenation than were white southerners. Furthermore, whites from the West Indies were more inclined to recognize a three-tier system wherein persons of mixed parentage had a higher status than unmixed blacks.[66]

Color stratification did not have the same relevance in the North where some states freed blacks en masse after 1781 or made provisions for gradual abolition. By contrast, many post-Revolutionary emancipations in the Lower South were linked to special circumstances often associated with white lovers, benefactors, or relatives. Whatever black women thought about differences in skin colors, or if they valued one over another, probably had as much to do with the environment in which they lived as with the source of color variations. In either case, if free black women left records about the meaning of color and their perceptions of its importance, they are not readily available.

In the absence of historical data, readers may resort to literary interpretations such as Harriet Beecher Stowe's *Uncle Tom's Cabin*. The novel links color differences to personality traits among several enslaved women ranging from the cultured to the "wild and evil." Stowe describes Eliza as having the "peculiar air of refinement, that softness of voice and manner, which seems in many cases to be a particular gift to the quadroon and mulatto woman." Aunt Chloe, Old Dinah, and Topsy are at the opposite end of the spectrum. The negative treatment of the dark-skinned Topsy, whom Stowe labels as a "heathenish" "thing," or "image," is unparalleled. The suggestion is that persons with whiter skin were more "civilized" than their darker contemporaries. It follows that once Eliza flees from slavery her "refined qualities" will serve her well. This stereotypical rendering is based on the imagination of a white writer and not that of free black women.[67]

Certainly, whiteness could merit privileges for Africans with European phenotypes under specific circumstances as in Louisiana. According to historian John W. Blassingame, who studied race relations in antebellum New Orleans, "The desire of white men for sexual relations with Negro women was so great that special institutions grew up to satisfy it." *Placage* was more complex. Persons acting on the women's behalf exerted some authority in the arrangements that gave the women economic advantages that were unlikely had they married black men. Furthermore, generational linkages to parents in such unions, along with the possibilities of color and class advantages or being accepted by white society, must have had some influence in the choices.[68]

The possibilities of more favorable treatment based on color existed when whites concluded that fair-skinned blacks were more intelligent and trustworthy than dark-skinned blacks. But whiteness alone was not sufficient to secure privileges in states that made little or no distinction among blacks, regardless of the skin tone and legal status.[69]

Within such an environment, one may ask if blacks made distinctions among themselves. The nature of the relationships between free blacks and enslaved blacks had more to do with class and legal status than with color. Based on an extensive study of free blacks in the antebellum South, historian Ira Berlin concluded that successful free persons, many of whom were of mixed blood, separated themselves from their enslaved contemporaries to protect their own liberty. He noted, "Standing a step above the slave, these freemen could see how their status might degenerate and they knew whites needed only the flimsiest excuse to grab their liberty...and they were not willing to surrender...[precious benefits] without a guarantee of something better. Slaves were in no position to offer such an assurance. Freedom within the context of slavery thus pushed freemen and bondmen apart." Free Upper South blacks were in the unenviable position of lacking enough confidence in their own status to lend a hand to their enslaved sisters and brothers. Michael P. Johnson and James L. Roark argued that free blacks in the South remained aloof from their bonded contemporaries largely because free women and men feared the possibilities of losing their own independence. Their freedom, the historians wrote, was "eggshell-thin, and its fragility caused...constant concern."[70]

More recent historical studies focusing on Upper and Lower South cities suggest greater fluidity between enslaved and emancipated women and men. Tommy L. Bogger's findings claim interactions between free and enslaved blacks in Norfolk, Virginia, were common. Whittington B. Johnson's examination of black Savannah, Georgia, asserts that "social lines between free African-Americans and slaves were blurred." Bernard Powers's study of Charleston finds that free blacks and slaves "interacted freely and naturally." Finally, Lois Virginia Meacham Gould's investigation of New Orleans, Pensacola, and Mobile between 1769 and 1860 argues that the conditions under which black women lived in the Gulf ports were flexible enough for slaves to "pass" as free and for fairskinned blacks to "pass" as whites. The location and size of the towns or cities, the number of free and enslaved blacks in the general population, and the economic status of the free persons had much to do with the nature of their actions and interactions. Moreover, hobnobbing with enslaved persons beyond the view of whites brought fewer risks than open associations under the scrutiny of anyone who could have an impact on another's life.[71]

Only a systematic investigation of associations between enslaved and emancipated persons informed by spatial, temporal, and class dimensions

Table 1.4
Relative Rank of Free Population by States, 1790–1860

States	1790	1800	1810	1820	1830	1840	1850	1860
Alabama	....	....	....	22	20	20	22	23
Arkansas	....	....	....	27	28	28	29	33
Calif.	....	....	....	....	....	....	24	19
Conn.	9	8	10	9	10	13	15	15
Delaware	7	5	5	6	8	9	8	8
Florida	....	....	....	....	23	24	25	27
Georgia	13	12	15	17	18	19	19	22
Illinois	....	....	20	23	19	17	17	16
Indiana	....	20	22	18	16	15	10	10
Iowa	....	....	....	....	....	30	32	26
Kentucky	16	15	16	15	14	14	12	11
Louisiana	....	....	9	8	7	5	9	9
Maine	....	....	....	19	21	23	23	24
Maryland	2	2	1	1	1	1	1	1
Mass.	4	6	8	10	12	10	13	13
Michigan	....	....	24	26	27	26	21	18
Minnesota	....	....	....	....	....	....	....	32
Miss.	....	19	23	24	26	22	26	28
Missouri	....	....	21	25	25	21	20	21
N.H.	12	13	18	20	24	27	30	30
N.J.	10	9	7	7	6	7	7	7
N.Y.	6	4	3	4	3	2	4	4
N.C.	5	7	6	5	5	6	5	6
Ohio	....	17	14	12	9	8	6	5
Oregon	....	....	....	....	....	....	....	34
Penn.	3	3	4	3	4	4	3	3
R.I.	8	10	12	14	17	18	18	20
S.C.	11	11	11	11	12	12	14	12
Tenn.	14	18	17	16	15	16	16	17
Texas	....	....	....	....	....	....	31	31
Vermont	15	16	19	21	22	25	27	29
Virginia	1	1	2	2	2	3	2	2
Wisconsin	....	....	....	....	....	29	28	25
Wash., D.C.	....	14	13	13	13	11	11	14

Source: J. B. B. DeBow, *Statistical View of the United States, being a Compendium of the Seventh Census* (Washington, DC: A. O. P. Nicholson, 1854), 65; *Population of the United States in 1860: Compiled from Original Returns of the Eighth Census by Joseph C. G. Kennedy* (Washington, DC: Government Publishing Office, 1864); Eighth Census of the United States.

will yield more nuanced results about the relationships between free and unfree persons. Many were bound by blood or marriage. Also, the distance between enslavement and emancipation is a factor in these relationships since newly freed persons were likely to have more personal ties to and interactions with the slave community than persons who had enjoyed freedom for several generations.[72] Moreover, the extant data suggest that the most meaningful and longest lasting interactions between free and enslaved women in the Upper South and Lower South, regardless of skin tones, have been almost without exceptions based on blood relations.[73]

Beyond family associations, there is virtually nothing that speaks directly about what free black southern women thought. Diaries kept by William Johnson, a prosperous Natchez, Mississippi, barber between 1835 and 1851 reveal much about the relationship between his free apprentices and their enslaved associates, but the manuscripts contain almost nothing about Johnson's wife, Ann Battles, and her interactions with the women he owned. "Fraternization with slaves," Johnson's biographers write, "was out of the question—or so he thought." The barber grumbled about the apprentices' interest in attending "darkey parties," entertainments arranged by slaveholders for their chattel. Ostensibly, Johnson's disparaging description reflects revulsion at the thought of free and enslaved persons socializing. A closer reading of the diaries suggests that his aversion to "darkey parties" was based on his notions about morality. The possibilities of intimacy between young, unmarried persons was more disturbing to him than crossing legal boundaries. Readers must ask if Ann Johnson agreed.[74]

Similar questions remain unanswered regarding the interactions of the South Carolinian Matilda Ellison and the women her husband William owned. Researchers probably wonder if the gender ratio among his slaves concerned the slave-born Matilda. The number of enslaved men always outdistanced that of the women, but the gender bias was more pronounced among children. Of the eight youngsters William Ellison owned in 1840, five were boys. Ten years later, he owned ten children. Only one was a girl. In 1860, fifteen of the twenty enslaved children were boys. The ratios defy explanations related to natural increases, and historical records do not support notions about Ellison liberating or giving the children to his own offspring. It appears that he sold the girls to raise capital to purchase men for use in his shop. If this is true, Matilda Ellison witnessed the separation of mothers and daughters in extraordinary numbers over an extended period of time.[75]

Matilda Ellison, the mother of a five- or six-year-old child when emancipated, was not so far removed from bondage that she was oblivious to the pain involved in separating families. If enslaved women sought Matilda's influence in halting the separations, it was inconsequential since the number of girls remained unusually small between 1840 and 1860. This, of course, is speculation about the relationship between Matilda Ellison, who died in 1850, and the females her husband owned or sold.[76]

Nevertheless, there were two certainties about the coexistence of slavery and freedom. Until bondage ended, free persons resisted enslavement, and unfree persons sought freedom. Of equal importance, blacks were ever vigilant in protecting their liberty and that of their loved ones. Their interest was in defining the essence of their liberty and making freedom more real than ephemeral. The dream of each black woman, with few exceptions, was to enjoy "Full Liberty to go and live with whom & Where She may Chuse.'"[77]

2

"This modest bending of the head"

Gender Conventions, Expectations, and Misrepresentations

The contempt we have been taught to entertain for blacks makes us fancy many things that are founded neither in reason nor in experience.

Alexander Hamilton

"By what strange perversion of reason can it be deemed disgraceful in a white man to marry a black or Mulatto woman, when it is not thought dishonorable in him to be connected with her in the most licentious familiarity?" asked Mary Elizabeth Cogdell, daughter of John Stevens, a British migrant to Georgia in the 1760s, and wife of George Cogdell, a slaveholding merchant in Georgetown, South Carolina. Reading Marcus Rainsford's *An Historical Account of the Black Empire of Hayti* had prompted her to think about the conditions under which her family lived. Cogdell mused, "The Laws of a Country are imperfect allowing such familiarity with impunity, every white man having such connection, should be compell'd by the law of humanity to marry the person, black or Mulatto, with whom such familiaritys have existed." Clearly, issues of color and gender fueled Cogdell's concerns. With another stroke of the pen, she added that these men should "have no intercourse with genteel Society [or] appear in any place of amusement on an equality with other Citizens."[1]

Cogdell's comments are not specific about her reactions to the "familiarity" shared by Sarah Martha Sanders, an enslaved woman, and Richard Walpole Cogdell, her son. Were Cogdell's ideas about the "laws of humanity" applicable to her own son? If so, was she prepared to accept Sarah as a daughter-in-law and have Richard ostracized by polite society? Did Mary Cogdell develop a loving relationship with her grandchildren, Richard and Sarah's ten offspring born between 1832 and 1850? Cogdell did not attempt to explain reasons for what she termed "the most licentious familiarity" nor did she wink at philandering behavior.[2]

By contrast, other whites overlooked the men's behavior but castigated the women as "alluring," seductive "Jezebels" who enticed unwitting victims into illicit relationships. In such cases, the men abused the women, and society ignored it, or blamed the women for their culpability. The use of negative descriptions and objectification when discussing black women's sexuality belongs to what historian Nell Irvin Painter calls "the panorama of American racist caricature." But, says literary scholar Hazel Carby, "Identifying and cataloguing the perpetrators of racist stereotyping . . . [do] not reveal how ideologies actually worked to construct racial and sexual referents."[3]

In the discussion that follows, private letters, diaries, and public records will be used to examine the construction and application of sexual referents about black women before freedom. In these sources, women responded to misrepresentations about their manners and morals. These women shaped and adhered to their own standards of beauty, dress, and behavior in defining womanhood in ways that sometimes challenged society's expectations and beliefs about them.

The private records belonged to women whose education, wealth, and social standing set them apart from the masses of free blacks. The published works by free women are primarily nineteenth-century creations and skewed towards the North where the women had access to publishers willing to make their works available to the public. The available private sources are uneven and not representative of all free black women in the North, Upper South, and Lower South across time. The same is true of the public records, a source of information about women who owned property, received inheritances, ran afoul of the law, or carried complaints to court. Despite the lack of uniformity, the materials are illustrative when taken together.

Slavery shaped dominant ideas about black women to the extent that historical studies prior to the 1980s rarely included substantial discussions of free women before the general emancipation. Stereotypical notions about black women essentialize their experiences and ignore variations across classes, regions, and periods of time. As a result, two overdrawn perceptions of black womanhood emerged and remained vibrant in America's consciousness. First, the Jezebel myth was the timeless conception across geographical boundaries of a naturally promiscuous woman that served to assuage the conscience of people guilty or supportive of the sexual exploitation of black women. Second, the mythical "mammy" was an asexual character diametrically opposed to the sexually alluring Jezebel. The mammy myth helped ex-slaveholders rationalize the evils of slavery. Mammy had a "direct bearing on the history of sexuality in the Old South," writes historian Catherine Clinton. Mammy and Jezebel together made up a "virgin/whore" dichotomy.[4]

Both myths prevented black women from perching alongside selected white women upon a protected and socially constructed pedestal for "true woman." Even if black women adhered to the Victorian standards for the "cult of true womanhood," an ideology about women subscribing to concepts of purity, piety, domesticity, and submissiveness, racial differences made them outcasts. The free-born Maria W. Stewart noted disjunctures and proffered that the morals and manners of black women would be comparable to those of white women if opportunities to develop and perfect them were identical. Stewart pointed to most black and poor women's inability to devote undivided attention to their families, homes, or themselves. When women worked like men, it was incongruent to think they would be delicately submissive or incapable of defining their own ideals. Economic circumstances had made many black women strong in body and constitution. Stewart's observation brims with a rationale for the perceived absence of morals among black women. Most black women were enslaved and could not protect themselves against degradation from owners, overseers, and others. Similarly, free black women had little or no legal protection from white sexual aggression.[5]

Given the parameters of the cult of true womanhood, it is not surprising that large numbers of women did not fit into the imaginary worlds of "ladies" and "true women" due to their class, color, or boldness in defying prescribed conventions. But neither did black women conform to the stereotypical descriptions of "Jezebel," "Mammy," or "nasty wench."[6]

The historical origin of the image of the promiscuous black woman dates back to the initial contact between Europeans and Africans. Ignorance about different cultures and ethnocentricity prompted Europeans to misinterpret traditional African dress, dance, and marriage as promiscuous or lewd. The manner in which Europeans enslaved, transported, and sold Africans added to the misconceptions. Furthermore, poorly clad or unclad black women were punished or sold in North America, thereby fueling notions that they were unusually libidinous. It was unthinkable to have white women exposed in the same way since whites associated public nudity with lascivious behavior. But labels were attached to black women without considering the conditions under which they appeared poorly clad in public or in clothing that was too ragged to cover their bodies properly, especially as they worked.[7]

Historian Kathleen Brown's study of status, class, and color in colonial Virginia helps to explain the categorization of black women as "nasty wenches." "Good wives," a term used by the English settlers, referred to married (white) women, while "nasty wenches" was the designation for poor, unmarried, and unsupervised women. Over time, differentials in laborers—those who were domestic workers or agricultural drudges—along with the layering of "race" changed the meanings of both "good wives" and "nasty wenches." To the class-conscious British, white women were not to toil in fields alongside men; however, they did not object to black women working like men or being used interchangeably with them. Once firmly accepted, the concept hoisted white women into privileged positions and relegated black women into the "lusty drudges" or "nasty wenches" category.[8]

The general society made little or no distinction between black women; therefore, free women could be perceived as chattel and treated accordingly. Free women, unlike their unfree sisters, were not subjected to sexual exploitation by owners, yet the courts offered them little protection from sexual abuse. In several nineteenth-century cases involving the rape of free black Virginians, the courts found the accused—enslaved men—guilty and ordered them transported out of the state. Executing or jailing them was a financial liability for owners, hence their removal. In cases involving the rape of free black women by white men, the courts generally acquitted the men. An exception occurred in 1858 when a Virginia court found Edward B. Ledbetter of Sussex County guilty of raping a twenty-four-year-old free woman and sentenced him to ten years in prison. In the end, however, the jury recommended clemency, and the governor pardoned him. In 1861, the court found Ledbetter guilty of raping another free black woman. The pardon, unlike a ten-year sentence, had not deterred Ledbetter from committing another crime.[9]

Equally arresting was *State v. Sewell* (1855), a North Carolina case, involving a victim identified as "an old free negro woman." Her assailant was charged with shooting her in the "eyes and face with a pistol" and, according to court documents, he "ravished her as she lay insensible." Sewell had a "jug of liquor" in his possession and was in a state of "delirium tremens." Neither his drunkenness nor delirium prevented an indictment for murder. Rape was not an issue, however, and by ignoring it, the court marginalized the violation of black women in keeping with the attitudes of the larger white society.[10]

Black women, enslaved and free, remained unprotected from sexual violation and endured conditions that contributed to the construction of stereotypes about their alleged promiscuity. The idea spilled over into popular culture and surfaced in minstrel songs that caricatured them shamelessly. The erotic lyrics of the popular "Jumbo Jum" (1840) present a "nigger wench" swooning in "a big fit" and "reeling" before she "dropt right down on the floor, in a state of agony" while begging her lover to "do dat agin." Grotesque descriptions in vulgar songs probably overshadowed the women's true qualities.[11]

A close reading of available records makes it abundantly clear that many black women were Christians and adhered to a moral code. In fact, many sought to free themselves of negative sexual referents. Examples abound in the Works Progress Administration (WPA) narratives, collected in the 1930s, wherein former slaves describe their experiences in bondage. There is no parallel corpus of literature about free black women in the slave era. In spite of the dearth of documentation, it is reasonable to think emancipated persons would not abandon their Christian values or moral standards once freed, whether before or after 1865. Harriet Jacobs's *Incidents in the Life of a Slave Girl*, published when she was no longer a slave, is informative. Jacobs says her grandmother, the freedwoman Molly Horniblow, was influential in her moral development. The narrative speaks volumes about teaching and transferring values from one generation to another in slavery or freedom.[12]

Jacobs said enslaved girls lived in an environment of "licentiousness and fear." Possibilities to free themselves of depravity and adhere to moral values existed if they "had religious principles inculcated by some pious mother or grandmother, or some good mistress." As a result, "profligate men [with] power over her may be exceedingly odious," Jacobs continued. Her knowledge of right and wrong was based on the "religious principles" of her grandmother, an influential role model in her life after her own mother died.[13]

A July 1849 letter penned by the enslaved South Carolinian Lavina is pregnant with moral consciousness and the "religious principles" of a "pious mother." Lavina addressed the letter "dear missis" but shifted its supplication to the "master." Ultimately, it was he who made final decisions about the slaves. Lavina's alarm over his allowing Jimmy, her "son-in-law," to abandon his wife, Aggy, for Juddy, "a base woman more worse than Mary Magdalene," precipitated the letter. "If she [Juddy] was a vertous wommun," explained Lavina, "i wold not care but she is one of the vilest of the vile." Lavina, a Christian, said Juddy used her bewitching "art" and "sparklin black Eye[s] [for] caching Other wimmins husbans." It vexed Lavina to know Jimmy would "Take up with A Jezebel."[14]

Lavina's characterization of Juddy falls well within the stereotype of a lusty woman with a devil-may-care attitude. Of importance is Lavina's condemnation of behavior framed against her own understanding of virtue and morality. No doubt Lavina was concerned also about her daughter Aggy's happiness and may have resorted to hyperbole to argue the point more convincingly.[15]

By writing to her owner, Lavina takes the argument beyond the slave community and poses stinging questions reflecting her moral principles. "Do you think it rite," she asked boldly, "in the sight of god" to dissolve the union between Aggy and Jimmy? This was "a cruel thing," she asserted. Slave marriages had no legal standing, but bond servants did not take violations of their unions lightly. In an effort to force her owner to grasp the importance of her argument, Lavina asked him to "view the Matter as u would if they were yore children." She urged him to "take the scales of justice and put . . . this Magdalene [Juddy] In 1 side, and put justice humanity and religion on the other and see wich will sink and wich will rise up."[16]

Lavina continued, "Have they not souls as well as wite [white] people?" She was knowledgeable about Christianity and intelligent enough to manipulate the situation to show the distance between preaching and practicing religion. The letter points to hypocrisy within a Christian setting. It was incongruent for slaves to accept religious principles without applying them to their own lives and that of their children. Lavina worried about the weight of sins on earth and in the afterlife. Therefore, she pled, "Do not allow sutch adultry."[17]

Based on these sources, the autobiographical account written for publication and a personal letter never intended for public view, enslaved and free women had a sense of right and wrong and were knowledgeable about Christian morality. The sources differ in length and style, yet each woman emphasized the importance in her life. It is reasonable to assume that "the pure principles" Harriet Jacobs "inculcated" had been passed on by Horniblow to Jacobs's "pious mother." Perhaps Horniblow also transferred "the pure principles" to her enslaved great-granddaughter and great-grandson while caring for the children during Jacobs's absence for nearly seven of the children's formative years.

Both enslaved and free black women, contrary to the aspersions that they were lascivious, created a value system based on their cultural and religious training along with a recognition of customs in the larger population. The poem "To the Daughters of James Forten," composed by John Greenleaf Whittier, praises the women's "chaste demeanor." The significance is not in the Fortens possessing such characteristic but in a white man's recognition of it rather than assuming that they were unchaste because they were of African descent.[18]

Sojourner Truth's biographer, Nell Irvin Painter, points to differences in perceptions about black women by whites when Truth accompanied two white women reformers in their work among black prostitutes in New York. The slave-born Truth did not fit in as her friends had expected. They saw black women without distinction. By contrast, Truth "did not lump herself with the people at the bottom, poor women and black women who, she knew, were not of her caliber," writes Painter. In fact, as a freedwoman Truth devoted considerable time to presenting herself, especially in photographs, as a respectable gentlewoman, the antithesis of the ordinary portrayal of black women.[19]

Society defined respectable behavior and gender roles. At some point these messages reached many black women through traditions, observations, or the popular media. One black newspaper admonished, "Employ yourself in household affairs. Wait till your husband confides in you, and do not give your advice till he asks it. Always appear flattered by the little he does for you. Never wound his vanity, not even in the most trifling instance. A wife may have more sense than her husband but she should never seem to know it." Aside from whether the advice was followed willingly—some, regardless of race, saw it as confining—gainfully employed women could not give full attention to "household affairs" as suggested. In their struggle for economic survival, these women were probably too exhausted from the rigors of work to submissively coddle their partners and wait until invited to discuss their experiences. Black women and men were often in situations of worker qua worker. Both were exploited.[20]

The historian James Oliver Horton surveyed several black newspapers in antebellum America, including the Colored American, Freedom's Journal, and the North Star, to investigate gender conventions. Readers, primarily free northern blacks, received a steady diet of platitudes such as these in the Colored American:

Man is strong—Woman is beautiful
Man is daring and confident—Woman is deferent and unassuming
Man is great in action—Woman is suffering
Man shines abroad—Woman at home
Man talks to convince—Woman to persuade and please

The structure of the adages cast men into privileged positions, and the statements tell much about the construction of masculinity.[21]

Other maxims touted men's ruggedness, wise judgment, interests in science, and propensity for preventing misery. The paper portrayed women as "soft and tender" sensible "angels of mercy" who relieved pain. When these pithy statements characterized women as antithetical reflections of their male counterparts, they revealed as much about the construction of femininity as they did about the creation of masculinity.[22]

Sojourner Truth challenged the idealized portrayals of women. In doing so, she revealed her understanding of what constituted the expected behavior of working men. Allegedly, when she rose to speak at the 1851 Women's Rights Convention in Akron, Ohio, she drew on her background as a northern slave that was very much like that of other women of her class and station at the time. Free women working in agricultural pursuits probably had similar experiences. In the well-known account, Truth claimed she could work like a man, eat as much, and endure the lash as well, yet no one gave her special treatment because she was a woman. In flexing her muscles and raising her voice, Truth comes across as strong and confident—like a man. The legendary "Ar'n't I a Woman?" speech presents a sharp contrast between Truth's reality and the media's portrayal of women.[23]

Why did black newspapers ignore the truth? Several explanations exist. Black men, many of whom were ministers, owned and edited the newspapers. The lack of resources to investigate and report current news forced them to print fillers. Some presses behaved as "specialized digest magazines, excerpting material" from other sources, especially white publications. In defining acceptable social behavior in this way, the media left women less freedom to make determinations about their beliefs and desires.[24]

Perhaps some readers knew of the papers' limitations and accepted the homilies. This raises questions about the extent to which black women subscribed to the cult of true womanhood. This is impossible to quantify, but it is possible to make assumptions on an individual basis. Pious, submissive women with the wherewithal to devote uninterrupted attention to domestic responsibilities probably had few, if any, qualms about the cult. Less fortunate women could not devote full attention to their families. This does not mean they were not worthy of the true-woman accolade.

Eliza Potter, a free-born hairdresser, articulated her ideals in response to her customers, white women, who had asked for a definition of a lady. Potter explained, "Ladies, I can not tell you what I think constitutes a lady, and keep my seat. I must get up. I do not think all those are ladies who sit in high places, or those who drive round in fine carriages, but those only are worthy [of] the names who can trace back their generations without stain, honest and respectable, that love and fear God, and treat all creatures as they merit, regardless of nations, stations or wealth. These are what I say constitute a lady." Was Potter employing the rhetoric of true womanhood? One could claim the cult of true womanhood influenced her as easily as to say she subscribed to Christian ethics.[25]

A review of late-eighteenth- and early-nineteenth-century black women's societies shows that members concerned themselves with moral codes or social conventions. The organizations, benevolent and literary, were open to all women, and members toed the line or "came forward" at open meetings to "answer to charges" in keeping with the organization's right to "exact the constitution." On June 3, 1823, Philadelphia's Daughters of Africa, founded in 1821, asked a committee to "consider the conduct" of two members accused of "disorderly and improper [behavior] in the extreme." Several months later, the organization resolved that Elizabeth Griffith "ought to be expelled for stealling." The following year, the society's watchdog committee considered the conduct of Frances Williams, Ann Lawrence, and Patty Thomas "immoral" and requested the society to "exact the constitution" against them.[26]

Similarities in the membership rules of several organizations are striking in their notions about womanhood. New York's Abyssinian Benevolent Daughters of Esther refused to admit persons "addicted to inebriety or having a plurality of husbands." Boston's Afric-American Female Intelligence Society's constitution declared that potential members had to be of "good moral character." The Newport, Rhode Island, African Female Benevolent Society expected its members to be "good and moral Characters." The Salem, Massachusetts, Colored Female Religious and Moral Society was of the same ilk. It reserved the right to "advise, caution and admonish" members whenever necessary. According to its constitution, "If any member[s] commit any scandalous sin, or walk unruly, and after proper reproof continue manifestly impenitent, she shall be excluded." If women repented, they were readmitted.[27]

When compared, it is evident that what the club women thought of themselves and each other was of paramount importance. Their vigilance in monitoring members' behavior was a direct reflection of their desire for respectability. The attention to religious principles was the primary influence in their valuing benevolence and modesty in actions, words, and dress.

Among several original and borrowed inspirational writings in a blank book, belonging to Philadelphian Martina Dickerson, is advice offered July 16, 1840, by her friend, Rebecca F. Peterson:

A Lady's Dress

Let your earrings be *Attention* encircled by the pearls of *Refinement;* the diamond of your necklace the *Truth;* and the chain *Christianity* your breast-pin be *Modesty* set with *Compassion,* your bracelets be *Charity* ornamented with the tassels of *Good Humour,* your finger rings be *Attention* set round with the pearls of *Gentleness,* let your thicker garb be *Virtue* and your drapery *Politeness;* let your shoes be *Wisdom* secured by the buckles of *Perseverance.*

The advice was much like the biblical admonition for women to "adorn themselves in modest apparel, with shamefacedness and sobriety; not with braided hair, or gold, or pearls, or costly array." Few free women could afford precious jewels; therefore, it is difficult to tell if ideals such as those listed in "A Lady's Dress" or economic circumstances influenced their taste in clothing.[28]

Despite the economic deprivation of many free blacks, at least two series of graphic racist caricatures, "Life in New York" and "Life in Philadelphia," appeared in the 1820s and ridiculed prosperous free blacks relentlessly. Artists, including David Claypoole Johnston, David Clay, H. R. Robinson, and William Thackera, etched images of overdressed, overweight, poorly educated, childish social climbers. The caricatures captured the imagination of whites in America and Europe who were eager to see the worst in free, educated, prosperous blacks. Black presses decried the misrepresentations but to no avail.[29]

The etchings went beyond anything the free-born teacher Sarah Mapps wanted for her students. Mapps, who came from a prominent Philadelphia family, emphasized chastity, virtue, refinement, and modesty as desirable characteristics in behavior and dress. Modesty was as important in determining what the women wore as it was in governing what they thought about their own physical characteristics. The sources do not always answer questions about how free black women viewed themselves. For example, what were their opinions regarding their own phenotypical features? Did they accept white skin and European features as their standards of beauty?

Differences in literacy rates among black and white women and men before 1865 make collecting the responses of free black women nearly impossible, while whites seemed fascinated with the skin tones of African

Figure 2.1. "A Black Tea Party." Library Company
of Philadelphia, Philadelphia, Pennsylvania.

Americans and commented accordingly. For example, a Civil War soldier from Massachusetts wrote about a New Orleans crowd, mostly
slave-born "nigros of al complexions," including a little girl who was
"blacker than a cook stove just blacked." Moncure Conway, an upper-
class Harvard-educated Virginian, remarked that Charles was a nearly
white slave "of a remarkable beauty according to the European type."
Enslaved women with similar phenotypes, labeled "fancy," commanded
higher prices on the auction block than their dark-skinned sisters.[30]

Harriet Beecher Stowe noted variations in African Americans' skin
tones and linked favorable or unfavorable traits to the color of her characters in *Uncle Tom's Cabin*. The novel is peopled with intelligent mulattoes
of dazzling beauty or fine features. Stowe is unkind to unmixed characters with "kinky-hair" and broad features. Although *Uncle Tom's Cabin* is
a novel, the author worked diligently to create believable scenarios.[31]

White artists, illustrators, songwriters, and photographers exhibited
cultural incongruities and exaggerations when comparing blacks with
whites. Frederick Douglass, the slave-born editor and abolitionist, railed
about such representations in photographs, a new medium of interest

for him. He was critical of naturalists, ethnographers, and phrenologists when he complained, "The European face is drawn with the most scrupulous regard to excellence—in harmony with the highest ideals of beauty.... The negro is pictured with features distorted. Lips exaggerated—Forehead low and depressed—and the whole countenence made to harmonize with the popular idea of negro ignorance, degradation and imbecility." Presentations of this kind perpetuated the idea that "beautiful" subjects represented "civilized" whites, and "ugly" ones represented "uncivilized" blacks.[32]

"The Yellow Rose of Texas" touts the beauty of a woman of color, but she is not "black" in skin tone. The popular ballad associates the heroic twenty-two-year-old Emily West, also known erroneously as Emily Morgan, with the April 1836 Battle of San Jacinto during the Texas Revolution in which it gained independence from Mexico. West's role in the revolution remains entangled in folklore on one hand and history on the other. Following the Battle of the Alamo, the Mexican general Santa Anna met West and permitted her to join his entourage. There, she gathered and passed information about the general's army and battle plans to General Sam Houston. He capitalized on the data, defeated the Mexican army, and captured Santa Anna. A British diarist, William Bollaert, traveling in Texas, interviewed West and attributed the Mexican defeat to the "influence of a Mulatto Girl . . . who was closeted in the tent with General Santa Anna." Emily West's role in the revolution is acknowledged in the ballad published in 1858. The author of the lyrics, possibly an African American, known by the initials J. K., sang:

> There's a yellow rose in Texas
> That I am going to see
> No other darky knows her
> No one only me
> She cryed so when I left her
> It like to broke my heart
> And if I ever find her
> We nevermore will part.

The chorus touts her beauty:

> She's the sweetest rose of color
> This darky ever knew
> Her eyes are bright as diamonds
> They sparkle like the dew

You may talk about dearest May
And sing of Rosa Lee
But the yellow rose of Texas
Beats the belles of Tennessee.

Even Clementine of the more modern version of the song was a distant competitor.[33]

What black women thought about their beauty and its meaning varied. Harriet Jacobs could not speak for all black women, but her observations are important. "If God has bestowed beauty" on an enslaved woman, she cautioned, "it will prove her greatest curse. That which commands admiration in the white woman only hastens the degradation of the female slave." Stated or implied intentions to sell females as "fancy girls," harlots, in Washington, D.C., New Orleans, or Charleston are in keeping with Jacobs's observation.[34]

According to one slave trader, he could easily sell the biracial Emily Edmondson, "an extra, handsome, fancy piece," in New Orleans. The "beauty," he said, was like "a picture—a doll" of regular blood rather than one of the "thick-lipped, bullet-headed, cotton-picking niggers." He expected to fetch as much as five thousand dollars for her. Similarly, a Washington trader saw Mary and Emily Edmondson as "healthy girls" with "peculiar attractions of form, of feature, and of completion, which southern connoisseurs in sensualism so highly prize." He believed they would bring thousands of dollars on the New Orleans slave market in 1847. In both instances, phenotypical features subjected the young women to the lascivious whims of white men.[35]

Jacobs did not define what she considered beautiful but intimates that certain features, such as those described by the traders, attracted unwanted attention. If Jacobs were correct, it is reasonable to think enslaved women downplayed their beauty for the same reasons. This attitude was not confined to enslaved women.[36]

Comments from two northern free-born women offer insight regarding their ideas about beauty and the perceptions of others. A March 30, 1862, letter from Addie Brown to her friend Rebecca Primus contains remarks about Charity Jackson, a resident in the New York boardinghouse where Brown worked:

Aunt Chat [sat] along side of me fixing her teeth in her mouth you will say to your self what teeth She has a set. Those *stumps* she had they all out I dont think she look well with them [dentures] for they are one sided the Dentist will have to file her gums I wish you could see her she went out yesterday to spend the P.M. the friends told her they add to her beauty Dear Rebecca with out joking Aunt C think she is pretty she says every body has told [her] now since she has got her teeth she excel those are in the house.

Brown disagreed and was amused because "she look so funy." It was no laughing matter for Jackson, who, according to Brown, "was looking in the *glass* [mirror] for a half hour at herself." Perhaps Jackson's friends were complimentary of the improvement over the "stumps," and she interpreted it differently. In either case, the dentures added to her self-esteem.[37]

Charlotte Forten was not as self-absorbed as Jackson and shied away from compliments about her physical features. During an August 1862 visit with the poet John Greenleaf Whittier and his sister, Forten joined them in looking at images of white women. Forten said one woman's face was "faultless in outline and [the] coloring—exquisitely beautiful." She described another's face as "most gentle and yet most spirited, beautiful, noble, and lighted up by the soul within." Elizabeth Whittier showed the picture of an Italian woman and said Forten bore a striking resemblance. Forten disagreed.[38]

Perhaps Forten was uncomfortable with the comparison and felt obliged to demur. She reiterated, "I utterly failed to see it: *I* thought the Italian girl very pretty, and I know myself to be the very opposite." The self-effacing Forten downplayed her own looks and appeared to hold a high regard for European beauty. If Forten or Jackson themselves aspired to European standards, however, they did not leave clear accounts of such wishes in their own hand.[39]

By contrast, Martin H. Freeman addressed the matter in a 1859 essay for the *Anglo-African Magazine*, "The Educational Wants of the Free Colored People." Freeman's impressionistic and anecdotal account devotes attention to how children shaped perceptions of themselves and developed self-respect. According to the author, children were taught both directly and indirectly by parents and others that they were beautiful in proportion to the features that conformed to the Anglo-Saxon standard. As a result, Freeman explained, "Kinky hair must be subjected to a straightening process . . . Thick lips are puckered up, and drawn in until the mouth no longer resembles the opening designed by nature . . . beautiful black and brown faces by the application of rouge and lily white are made to assume unnatural tints."[40]

Freeman admits that "all this is very foolish," but the behaviors and cosmetics were "natural" responses to powerful societal pressures eroding self-esteem. The author was careful not to cast blame on those who were ashamed of their phenotypes but to offer suggestions for more positive perceptions by cultivating antislavery sentiments. He suggested linking "colorphobia" to slaveholding as a way to eradicate all "envy [of] the oppressor or desire of any of his ways." The author's observations provide a useful context for understanding the tensions many blacks endured along with a way to counter ethnocentrism and elevate their own self-esteem.[41]

As a way of thwarting negative perceptions and building self-esteem, a great number of free black women concerned themselves with values and acceptable standards of behavior. A letter from Second Lieutenant John H. Crowder to his mother Martha Ann Crowder Stars, during the Civil War, suggests that the desire for respectability went across geographical and class boundaries. The epistle contains a complaint from the sixteen-year-old officer about a soldier's behavior toward Mrs. Marsh, a "married lady" who had befriended and treated him "like a son." The soldier, wrote Crowder, took "from his pantaloons his privates and shook them at her." After the vulgar display, Mrs. Marsh complained to Captain Alcide Lewis, who did nothing. Appalled at what Crowder believed was Lewis's dereliction of duty, he arrested the soldier and had him punished.[42]

Crowder assured his mother that he would never condone such offensive behavior and deemed Captain Lewis among "the most pucillanamous [sic] dirty Low life men" he had ever seen. They seemed to think, wrote Crowder, "that there is not a woman that they cannot sleep with." Crowder's letter is a reflection of his mother's parenting skills and commentary on their relationship. Although he had assumed the manly responsibilities of a commissioned officer, he still adhered to the fundamentals of appropriate behavior learned in early childhood. He responded to the insult as if it had been his own mother." "I remmember your first lesson," he wrote, "that was to respect all females." As if seeking her approval, he added, "I do respect all." Mrs. Marsh's kindness to him and offer to have his mother stay in her home should she visit him had merited his respect. Besides, he wrote, "She is a lady."[43]

Crowder's chivalrous actions were not representative of all military men. He behaved differently from his comrade who seemed to believe Marsh was a camp-following prostitute and deserved no better treatment. Crowder, like many blacks, was concerned about a moral code of behavior or the appearance of one.

A review of published and unpublished correspondence from free blacks offers insight about their manners. For example, Marie Sophie Charlotte Bingaman and Felix Cazanave decided to get married at St. Louis

Cathedral in New Orleans on April 30, 1860. They issued no invitations, yet the mother of the bride notified friends of the upcoming event and promised to send "a piece of wedding cake." The explanation, "As we will have but a family wedding," would satisfy the curiosity of would-be gossip mongers better than a simple announcement afterward.[44]

An October 26, 1852, letter from Lavinia Miller McCary of New Orleans contained news of Annie Amie's hasty marriage. "You must not mention it," wrote McCary to her aunt in Natchez, Mississippi, but Amie is "four months gone in the family way." Amie's mother learned of her condition and "had her married" without informing the young woman's grandmother or other family members. According to McCary, Mr. Bruistee, whose relationship to the bride is unknown, was "so mad that he cried." It is not clear if Bruistee's disappointment was due to the bride's pregnancy, hasty marriage, or because her spouse had a trade but would not work. The newlyweds "had not one chair brought" and would be dependent on the groom's mother for support. They legalized their relationship, nevertheless, and brought respectability to themselves and saved the child from the stigma of illegitimacy.[45]

An 1860 letter discussing a "shot gun" wedding reveals the moral attitudes of several free black Charlestonians. The groom, a twenty-one-year-old widower, received pressure to remarry from his deceased wife's mother. Although he had not adhered to a proper period of bereavement, she believed his "honor" was at stake. The widower, James "Rixy" Gordon, had convinced the eighteen-year-old Christina Leman that he would "marry if first [he] indulged." When the trusting manatua maker became pregnant, Gordon distanced himself. Leman's friends refused to accept his excuses and said, "Marry or Die."[46]

The situation was out of the bride and groom's hands. Community mores took precedence. The free man James M. Johnson looked askance at the couple's behavior and quipped:

> Why the Knot should not have an immediate tie,
> he was made to verify what he meant for a lie
> & will learn him next time to Marry & then try.

Leman's actions did not escape commentary:

> Poor foolish Girl, all she did was to cry.
> But perhaps she will have a Baby Bye & Bye,
> & if he don't feed it, she may blame her Hurry.

Johnson condemned both parties for engaging in premarital sex.[47]

The examples above come from Charleston and New Orleans, cities known for sizable free populations with educated blacks of means. The Cazanave-Bingaman announcement signifies church affiliation, social status, and valued friendships along with resources for wedding favors. These examples are representative of the newlyweds' station and class. No doubt impoverished couples married with less fanfare because they could not afford church weddings and receptions. The urgency of the Gordon-Leman wedding precluded planning.

Under optimum conditions, some couples enjoyed a courtship and remembered it as a special time in their lives. Unlike the imagined letters of white critics, warm exchanges between H. Amelia Loguen from Lewis Douglass, son of Anna Murray and Frederick Douglass, offer some insight about these relationships. This is not to suggest that the Loguen-Douglass correspondence was representative of everyone, but it depicts the essence of their affection. Douglass asked his beloved, "Can any one give the reason why one person loves another to the exclusion of every one else?" As if mystified, Douglass wrote:

> I know many ladies, who are amiable kind, talented and refined, all that a man could wish, and yet I cannot love them or do not love them as I love you, and they may be like you, but to me they are different, now who can tell wherein is the difference. It cannot be antipathy on my part for they are all I could desire, reasonably, thus I am led to think that love is an unreasonable passion, that persons who love each other do so through the exercise of some other power than reason. For the life of me I cannot tell the reason that I love you. I may give a reason but it is impossible to give one that would not apply to many girls. So I say reason or no reason, some undefinable force attracts me to you, and I have no means of resisting it and would not if I had.

Douglass's inability to explain or understand why he loved Loguen did not prevent the couple from marrying after the Civil War.[48]

Older black women and men sometimes counseled couples as they considered marriage. James M. Johnson offered advice to his brother-in-law, Henry Ellison, whose twenty-eight-year-old wife, Mary Elizabeth Bonneau, had died September 15, 1852. Johnson was confident in recommending the "Ladies on Amherst St." whom he considered as "models." He urged Ellison to

> Seek to find out whether the disposition & character of the object is adapted to your own before concentrating your affections. And whatever regard a man's taste may prompt him to entertain for beauty, form, &c. in seeking a bosom companion for Life, let him see to it that

Figure 2.2. "The Lub Letter." Library Company
of Philadelphia, Philadelphia, Pennsylvania.

his predilections does not bias him to sacrifice the substance to the
shadow. For what else is beauty & form & where is the substance if not
assimilated to a kind & gentle disposition & a loving Heart. And where
is this to be found but in the Christian Ladies.

The suggestions appear unnecessary. Ellison had not rushed into marriage in the 1840s when he chose a woman seven years his junior. Nor had
he been quick to remarry once widowed. Johnson's advice is in keeping
with his general philosophy about the shortcomings of substituting a
"shadow" for "substance."[49]

The poet Frances Ellen Watkins, known as Frances Ellen Watkins
Harper after her 1860 marriage to Fenton Harper, published "Advice to

the Girls" in *Poems on Miscellaneous Subjects* (1854), which encouraged women to avoid flashy outward shows by men "that please your fancy so." The poet urged "the girls" to seek a partner who was free of pretense and endowed with common sense, if lacking a gifted mind. Watkins's "The Two Offers," a short story, appeared in 1859 and contained further words of wisdom to women considering marriage.[50]

Advice and good wishes flowed freely from family and friends. Prior to the Christmas Eve 1846 wedding of Philadelphian Mary Anne Dickerson and Baltimorean John A. Jones in the prestigious St. Thomas African Episcopal Church, a friend, identified only as A. M. C., proffered:

Peace be around thee; wherever thou rove'st
May life be, for thee, one summer's day,
And all that thou wishest, and all that thou lov'st,
Come smiling around thy sunny way!

A. M. C. was realistic enough to know their lives would be "half in shade, and half in sun," but she was positive when writing:

If sorrow w're this calm should break,
May e'en thy tears pass off so lightly,
Like spring showers, they'll only make
The smiles that follow shine more brightly.

May Time who sheds his blight o'er all,
And daily dooms some joy to death,
O'er thee let year so gently fall,
They shall not crush flower beneath!

Finally, A. M. C. hoped that the "side the sun's on, Be all that e'er shall meet thy [face]."[51]

Once married, the "perfect wife," according to *Freedom's Journal*, was a sensible and hardworking woman who relished cleanliness. She was to pay careful attention to details to assure the smooth operation of her household. The autobiographical writings of the free black woman Rebecca Jackson serve as an exemplary model for insight about routine activities within an African American home in the nineteenth century. Jackson and her husband had no children of their own, but she was an experienced homemaker and caregiver for her nieces and nephews after their mother died.[52]

The large family made considerable demands on her time and energy. Jackson's domestic responsibilities included keeping everyone "neat and clean" and seeing "that the house was in good order." Besides, she wrote, "I sewed all day" for the family and "took in sewing" as a source of income. The pious woman was close to the hearth in keeping with the domestic ideal of the cult of true womanhood. She did fit the model of womanhood seen in short stories and homilies published in many of the newspapers of the day. Closer observation reveals that Jackson's domestic responsibilities were far from satisfying. Dedication to the family left little time for self-actualization.[53]

Frederick Douglass, a supporter of women's rights, was among the few men who did not adhere strictly to circumscribing women with the cult of true womanhood. As an editor, Douglass quoted from white papers, as did the *Colored American*, but he was more catholic in his selections. In the October 30, 1851, *Frederick Douglass' Paper*, the editor explained, "We ask no rights, we advocate no rights for ourselves, which we would not ask and advocate for woman. Whatever may be said as to the division of duties and avocations, the rights of man and the rights of woman are one and inseparable, and stand on the same indestructible basis . . . Whatever is necessary to protect him, is necessary to protect her." Douglass's argument for gender equity was unequivocal.[54]

The Liberator, an antislavery newspaper edited by William Lloyd Garrison, like Douglass's paper did not limit women's sphere. Garrison's paper published an 1837 observation that was at odds with the ideology of the cult. The writer agreed that married persons are of one flesh, but "certainly not in any such sense as to destroy the personal identity of each, nor ensure perfect harmony of opinion on all subjects."[55]

However, harmony was more likely to prevail in households where women were submissive. Messages about the expected behavior of women appeared in abundance. For example, Martina Dickerson's album contains a veiled suggestion. In 1846, Sarah Mapps, Dickerson's teacher, painted a bunch of fuchsias and explained:

> All the species of Fuchsia droop their heads toward the ground in such a manner that their inner beauties can only be discerned when somewhat above the eye of the spectator.
>
> In a meaner flower this might not attract attention, but most of the fuchsias are eminently beautiful, both in form and color; and *this modest bending of the head* is the more remarked from the singular and peculiar beauty of the parts . . . which they would thus seem anxious to conceal.

A lesson existed in the metaphor. The flowers were lovely without thrusting themselves forward, and they were even more exquisite because of their retiring nature, "Beautifully and significantly typifying modesty,"

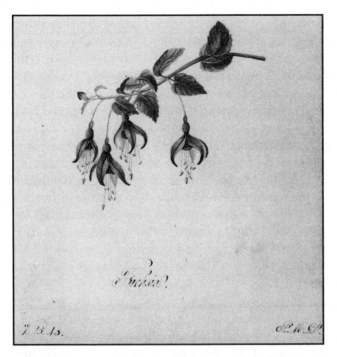

Figure 2.3. "Fuchsia," watercolor by Sarah Mapps Douglass.
Library Company of Philadelphia, Philadelphia, Pennsylvania.

as the teacher added. Perhaps the afterthought was to emphasize the splendor of tractability.[56]

Ironically, when the forty-nine-year-old Sarah Mapps married the Reverend William Douglass in 1855, the notion of subordination presented a conflict. She believed a woman was to be submissive to her husband, and "he shall rule over thee." But she did not exude pleasure in complying with the ideal. "Humiliating as it is," she wrote, "I am willing God's . . . word should stand." What were her options as a minister's wife?[57]

Zilpha Elaw, a Pennsylvania-born religious leader and free woman, accepted the idea that women were subordinates by nature. "Pride, consequential haughtiness, and independent arrogance in females, are the worst vices of humanity," Elaw wrote, "and are denounced in the Scriptures as insuring the severest retribution of God." Until women married, Elaw thought they should be guided and governed by their fathers. The "boastful speeches" of young women against their fathers or husbands were "both indecent and impious—conveying a wanton disrespect to the regulations of Scripture." "Fancied independence," Elaw wrote, had no foundation in the Bible or in nature.[58]

Women were not oblivious to gender conventions and did not ignore those that oppressed them. Readers of "Miscellaneous" in the June 9, 1837, *Liberator* faced the question, "By what principle of justice does the law wrest from a woman, the moment she is married, all the patrimony of her fathers and all her own hard earned wages, and place them at the entire disposal of her husband?" Women were subjected to dependency after marriage, but it does not mean that they accepted it cheerfully.[59]

The available evidence across geographical regions shows that free women were not all in agreement with accepting subservient positions and yielding completely to the wishes of men. The relationship Victoire Brustie, a woman in the Lower South, shared with her husband, Gabriel, is illustrative. He wrote to a mutual friend in 1858 asking for assistance in encouraging his "long lost wife" to return home. She had left him in New Orleans for an extended visit to Adams County, Mississippi. When pressed to return, she made excuses. After six weeks, he pled with her to return home.[60]

Perhaps he missed her, but he was also concerned that a piece of property was subject to seizure. The lot, he explained, was "in her name" and "she alone [could] arrange this business with that man," a creditor or tax collector. This, added Brustie, was "no time to neglect buissiness." He could not force her to return, however. "As my wife will have her own way," said the distraught husband, "I must adhere to all that she wants." Peace and harmony could prevail, but discord was also possible.[61]

Certainly discord was present in an unusual case before a New York court in 1808 when Doctor William Little was charged with the assault and battery of his wife, Jane Little, described as a "black lady." William Little pled not guilty while portraying himself as an affectionate husband. His April 29, 1808, letter revealed a different side of their dispute: "Jane—You know that I can prove by Mr. H— who took or pulled you off of me when you was a beating me as hard as you could on my breast; and I kept my bed all the next day. I was so hurt that I was obliged to bleed myself. T— T— held you one night for some time (you were so crazy mad) from beating me." He swore that she abused him but confessed his devotion.[62]

Little did not mention what had provoked his wife. One Captain B. owed him money, and Little suspected that his friend preferred to see him in jail rather than pay his honest debts. If Little was jailed, accounts would be settled. It seems that when Captain B. told Mrs. Little her husband planned to sell her property to "make a hundred dollars" and to go to Genesee, New York, the news precipitated a fight.[63]

Of importance here, Jane Little had property that she did not consider his possession once they had married. Little, unlike Brustie, did not avoid a conflict by leaving town. In each case, questions about property ownership were integral to the turmoil between the couples. The women refused to play a submissive role.[64]

A moderated dispute between an Upper South couple, George and Nancy Ruffin, is of interest. The idea of George W. Ruffin, a Virginia barber, controlling the purse strings rankled his wife, Nancy Lewis Ruffin. She had moved from Richmond to Boston so their eight children would have better educational opportunities. Maintaining two households was expensive, and the lack of money forced her to complain. In an undated letter, Ruffin wrote: "I don't like to ask you for money... but I am oblige to do so for I am so much in need of it." "My Dear Husband," she explained in 1858, "it is very disagrable to me to have to go to first one person and then to another to borrow money to pay when it is due." Obviously a proud woman, she added, "I would rather take my children and go to the poor house... perhaps it may be thrown in my face." She resented having to borrow money for coal and wood to get through the winter, and the water rent was due soon.[65]

At no time during their correspondence did Ruffin, a woman with considerable entrepreneurial knowledge, blame her husband of more than twenty-five years for their predicament. She was "very much disappointed," yet she did not accuse him of negligence. Instead she suggested, "I think you had better try and sell that house of mine." When money was not forthcoming, Ruffin wrote again: "I think I shall haft to take a few boarders." As a final solution, she suggested that he sell their property and move to Boston. Such a move would reduce expenses and reunite the family. Besides, she said, "I sleep cold." She missed him.[66]

Nancy Ruffin offered solutions to their dilemma, but she deferred to her husband. Rather than saying, "I *will* take in a few boarders," she explained, "I think I shall haft to take a few boarders." Her approach reflects progression before making a decision and leaves room for his input. The same is true of her statement, "I reckon we had better try and get rid of the place and trye and get a cheaper place." Under ideal circumstances, Ruffin may have considered conventions, but the circumstances were menacing. She wrote, "I think you had better try and sell that house of *mine* for the longer it stands the less *you* will get for it, in fact you had better sell all *your* property *you* have there."[67]

The ambiguities in Ruffin's letter are intriguing. The first reference to a house leaves no doubt about who owns the property. It is Nancy Ruffin's;

however, it is not clear if "the less *you* will get for it" refers to the collective you or to George Ruffin specifically. The suggestion to "sell all *your* property *you* have" indicates that he alone controlled that real estate. Nancy Ruffin then shifts to "*we.*" In this case, it appears that she refers to family property. Perhaps it was the family's home before she and the children relocated to Boston.[68]

Ambiguities aside, Ruffin understood property values and cost reductions. In the November 18, 1859, letter she explained, "You know the longer we keep the house the more we will haft to pay for it. The interest keeps runing up." This is a reasonable argument used to convince George Ruffin of the futility of not selling. One month later, her tone suggests exasperation when she demanded, "For the Lord's sake do try and sell that property. it is of no use to wate [sic] for a grate price."[69]

Each of the women above cast gender conventions aside and handled family matters in her own way, when necessary. Within their households, the couples were of "one flesh," but "not in any such sense as to destroy their personal identity of each, nor ensure perfect harmony of opinion on all subjects," as *The Liberator* article had put it.[70]

The data about Brustie, Ruffin, and Little holding real property in the Lower South, Upper South, and North after marriage are limited examples suggesting the need for further study to determine if their situations were anomalous. Victoria Bynum's examination of antebellum property ownership in several North Carolina counties indicates that married women retaining property as Brustie, Ruffin, and Little did was not entirely unusual. Changes in antebellum laws resulting in more flexibility when granting divorces made it possible for women to enjoy greater rights to their own property.[71]

A study of Petersburg, Virginia, between 1784 and 1860, offers different conclusions regarding free black women property owners. They outnumbered free black men and headed a majority of the free black households in Petersburg. On the surface, it appears that they preferred holding their own property to relinquishing it to a spouse.[72]

While it is possible that the women refrained from marriage to retain property, there are several other possible explanations for the occurrence. It is likely that some women, given the imbalance in the gender ratio among free blacks, shared marital unions with enslaved men. Such marriages were not legally recognized, and census takers as arms of the law were unlikely to record enslaved men as heads of households. Moreover, slaves, male or female, considered as chattel property, could not own real property legally. Finally, the relative state of poverty among free blacks may have rendered them too poor to marry legally or buy enslaved spouses. Therefore, in the cases of marriages between free women and unfree men, it is reasonable for public records to list "unmarried," propertied, free black women as heads of their own households.[73]

Perhaps a better indicator of how black females defined their womanhood, adhered to gender conventions, and associated with others is to view their roles as mothers interacting with their children. Economic deprivations forced many black women to work outside their homes, thus interfering with domestic responsibilities. To say they were not following the cult of true womanhood ignores the fact that their absences were not always within their control. In addition, they faced situations when time with their children made little difference in whether they lived or died: regardless of color and status, mothers were often helpless in fighting the diseases that killed their children in large numbers.[74]

The writings of Mary Anne Dickerson Jones reflect both the optimism and tragedy of daily life. After three years of marriage, she gave birth to John A. Jones Jr., born "Saturday night 10 minutes to 11–0'clock," November 20, 1847. Her second child, William Dickerson Jones, was born January 19, 1850. The mother connected the children firmly to their families through the selection of names following a pattern that was not uncommon among enslaved blacks, who named the first son for his father. The Jones family also linked their progeny to the maternal side of the family by making Dickerson a middle name.[75]

On January 28, 1851, one week after celebrating his first birthday, William Dickerson Jones died. The sorrowful mother eulogized:

> To my dear Willie
> Slumber, sweet infant,
> Thy spirit is free,
> The portals of Heaven
> Are open to thee.

"The hopes of fond parents," she wrote, "lie buried" in the grave. The lamentation continued, "For the pride of their hearts / Is cold in the tomb." Mary Anne Dickerson Jones's first-born son died August 20, 1852, three months prior to his fifth birthday.[76]

Jones's grief is similar to another mother, Tryphenia Blanche Holder Fox, who mused:

> For spirits round the Eternal Throne
> How vain the tears we shed!
> They are the living, they alone
> Whom thus we call the dead.

It mattered not that one mother lived in the North and the other in the Lower South, that one was black and the other was white, or that one child was male and the other was female. These mothers were very much a part of a national occurrence; nearly 40 percent of the deaths in the nineteenth century were to children five years of age and younger. The piercing loss of a child knew no racial, class, geographical, or gender boundaries.[77]

The WPA narratives are replete with accounts describing loving mother-child relationships in the slave community, defying claims that the women loved the white children whom they cared for more than their own offspring. The autobiographical writings of freedpersons, including William Wells Brown, Frederick Douglass, and Lucy Delany, praise their mothers for unfailing attention to their well-being. Differences in availability of resources make it impossible to cite sources about free blacks comparable to the WPA narratives. The absence of records does not mean an absence of incidences. The basic foundation of black motherhood was centered in the African tradition; therefore, black women, whether enslaved or emancipated, shared common concerns.[78]

Black women's interests in the welfare of their children helped to shape their conception of womanhood, which did not vary greatly from that of other women of their class and station. "The contempt we have been taught," wrote Alexander Hamilton, the Revolutionary War veteran, founding father, and first secretary of the treasury, "to entertain for blacks makes us fancy many things that are founded neither in reason nor in experience." Hamilton's comments may reflect a sensitivity about his own parentage. He was the illegitimate son of a woman described as "sexually wayward." Whether she was of African descent is open to question, but his birth in the British West Indies where the numbers of European men greatly outnumbered white women fuels the speculation.[79]

If black women were aware of Hamilton's remarks, they may have found consolation in knowing a man of his stature made such an astute observation. However, black women did not rely on whites as spokespersons or to shape their being. Black women developed their own concepts of womanhood based on their religion, love of families, and respect for themselves. Of equal importance, whether they were enslaved or emancipated, they passed their convictions on from one generation to another, and their quest for respectability did not change with the passing of time.

3

The Pursuit of Happiness

Work and Well-Being

I sincerely appeal to my colored brethren universally for patronage, hoping that they will not condemn this attempt of their sister to be erudite, but rally around me a faithful band of supporters and defenders.

Harriet Wilson

"How long shall the fair daughters of Africa be compelled to bury their minds and talents beneath a load of iron pots and kettles?" asked Maria W. Stewart. Was the drudgery of daily toil their sole lot in life? If not, what did the future hold for them? Free women held diverse jobs across regions of the United States and found a variety of means to confront adverse economic conditions. They succeeded in different degrees to free themselves of deprivations and develop a political consciousness.[1]

Free women lived in a gendered environment that assumed men, as primary breadwinners, headed households and that the women's place was at home. In an 1858 study of prosperous St. Louis blacks, Cyprian Clamorgan, the free-born offspring of a mulatto woman and white man, followed the patriarchal model and touted the accomplishments of the frugal entrepreneur William Johnson Sr. After a brief career in real estate, he sold property valued at $100,000. Clamorgan commented, "Not so bad a speculation for a colored man!" A single reference to Johnson's large family with "several accomplished and highly-educated daughters" suggests that he was or had been married. If Johnson's wife was key to his prosperity, Clamorgan ignored it.[2]

Clamorgan's profiles included a Mr. and Mrs. Cox, owners of an estate worth $150,000. Cox, a "good workman," who was "very attentive to business," had moved to St. Louis from Pennsylvania fifteen years earlier and entered a partnership with a man known only as Wilkinson. Clamorgan says nothing about Mrs. Cox as a helpmate. Instead, he says she was a "fine-looking woman" and "was wealthy previous to her marriage." How she acquired the fortune or if her resources figured importantly in her husband ending the partnership and founding a business of his own are not mentioned. Mrs. Cox is overshadowed by her husband; therefore, readers do not know if that arrangement was oppressive or liberating for her.[3]

The likes of Mrs. Johnson and Mrs. Cox were exceptions in most free black communities in that they were married to prosperous businessmen and probably did not work outside their homes. Many of their contemporaries headed households, and were desperately poor and worked long hours each week for meager wages. The general economic conditions of free blacks became worse after 1830 with increasing industrial development and competition from European immigrants. White racial animosity, especially among craftsmen who refused to train black apprentices, was significant in the economic decline. The results rippled to women and children who were dependent on the wages of men who aspired to be skilled craftsmen.[4]

Despite the varied economic conditions among free blacks, discussions about the women's labor before 1865 are skewed towards the slave experience. Frederick Douglass explained this phenomenon: "We hear much about the inadequate wages paid to women and the deficient representation of women in public life." He noted "the wrongs perpetrated against [women] in excluding [them] from the pursuit of the most lucrative branches of trade." But, he asked, "What are all those wrongs, compared with the stupendous and ghastly wrongs perpetrated on the defenseless slave woman?"[5]

Contrasting freedwomen's status in society with slave women's, Douglass wrote, "women suffer certain wrongs but the wrongs peculiar to women out of slavery great and terrible as they are, are endured as well by the slave woman, who has also to bear the ten thousand wrongs of slavery. It is hard to be underpaid for labor faithfully performed. It is harder still not to be paid at all . . . It is hard for the widow to receive the third part of the property of her deceased husband. It is harder still to be a chattel person." Few women, black or white, could sincerely deny that bondage was loathsome. Yet, when Douglass juxtaposed the conditions of enslaved women with emancipated women, he inadvertently marginalized free women's struggle for economic stability.[6]

Douglass's slant is understandable; however, it does not address the question of what the economic realities were for the majority of free black women before 1865. To be sure, differences in terms of emancipation in the North, Upper South, and Lower South had much to do with the true extent of the economic marginalization of free women. Manumissions by northern states in the late eighteenth and early nineteenth centuries freed blacks without distinctions and made no special provisions for their futures. Once freed, they eagerly sought jobs in a market dominated by whites, many of whom resented the competition. The majority of northern and Upper South freedpersons were less skilled, less educated, and darker in skin tone than their contemporaries in the Lower South where emancipations were often linked to special social and economic circumstances. A visible connection existed between many free Lower South women with sizable holdings in real and personal property and white relatives or benefactors. These women were exceptions.[7]

Most free black women made their way by dint of hard work. Much extant data about the work of free women focus on women alone. After Henrietta S. Duterte's husband died in 1858, she became known in her own right. With experience gained from working with him in the family's mortuary, she took over the Philadelphia business and became "the first practicing female mortician in the United States, if not in the world." Owning and managing the business for several decades set her apart from other women known for "laying out the dead." Otherwise it is unlikely that her name would have appeared in the R. G. Dun & Company report in the 1870s.[8]

The majority of free black working women received recognition for their efforts only from loved ones. When questioned about their occupations, women in Skunk Hollow, a small free black community in New Jersey, responded "at home," with no further specifics. The phrase was common among census takers when referring to women in nuclear families. Perhaps they were unemployed, but a relatively small number of free women lived in households with sufficient incomes to allow them to concentrate solely on their families. Less fortunate women combined their housekeeping responsibilities with child care, sewing, or laundering clothes for others. In both cases, families benefited from the women's "at home" status.[9]

The general poverty of the masses forced an untold number of black women, married and single, to work outside their homes. Their labor was essential to their standard of living and that of their loved ones. They were far from the lazy improvident characters many whites claimed them to be. Philadelphia's 1838 *Register of Trades of the Colored People* listed 643 persons in fifty-six different occupations including hairdressers, nurses, and hucksters. Most women were in the needle trade as quilters, plain sewers, dressmakers, tailoresses, or seamstresses.[10]

A study of the Upper South city of Petersburg, Virginia, shows that free black women were gainfully employed medical caregivers such as cuppers, leachers, nurses, and midwives. In the 1820s, some women worked in the tobacco industry. The licensed occupations of 324 free black women in the border city of St. Louis, Missouri, in the 1840s and 1850s included nurses, mantua makers, and seamstresses.[11]

Further south in Savannah, the home of Georgia's greatest concentration of free persons, the 1823 *Register of Free Colored Persons* listed twenty different occupations for 107 women. Approximately one-half of Savannah's free women worked independently as vendors, cooks, and nurses. By 1860 nearly 50 percent (fifty-six) of the women in the Lower South city were divided into two occupations, laundresses and seamstresses.[12]

The self-supporting New Englander Addie Brown worked as a laundress and seamstress in addition to a variety of other jobs. At one point as a gainfully employed worker, she labored in a dye factory and as a teamster. Driving teams of draft animals required crossing gender boundaries, but Brown's economic welfare was more important than social constraints.[13]

A small number of black women engaged in gender-neutral occupations as peddlers, investment bankers, and merchants. Mary Ellen Pleasant capitalized on the California gold rush in the 1850s by teaming up with acquaintances and businessmen Fred Langford and William West. Pleasant explained, "They put out my money at ten percent interest and I did an exchange business, sending down gold and having it exchanged for silver. Gold was then at a high premium. I had many bank books. I would deposit silver and draw out gold from friends in the banks where there was a good deal of silver. Most of this business was done through Wells Fargo." Pleasant, an exceptional woman, invested the profits in other enterprises. Entrepreneurs among persons of African descent were not unusual. Black women were highly visible in sales activities in colonial as well as in antebellum marketplaces of North America. Their presence in Charleston, New Orleans, Mobile, and Pensacola could not be overlooked, and the women left lasting impressions as peddlers in Philadelphia and New York.[14]

The majority of women worked at feminized or traditional women's jobs that were not time bound. They sewed, spun thread, laundered clothes, delivered babies, provided childcare, and nursed the sick. They also converted their homes into boardinghouses where they cooked and cleaned for paying residents. Their tasks varied little across time and place because of the uniformity in skills required for preparing food, laundering bedding, and serving the needs of the young, elderly, or mentally and physically challenged. The local conditions, such as collecting water from a pump in the town square or drawing it from wells and rivers, made differences in the amount of work performed without altering the skills required for scrubbing clothes clean or ironing them to perfection.[15]

Domestic work was available to black women including the well-known Phillis Wheatley, Elizabeth Freeman, Maria W. Stewart, Nancy Prince, Fannie Jackson Coppin, Frances Ellen Watkins, Amanda Berry Smith, Zilpha Elaw, and Jarena Lee along with less-well-known women. The work was accessible because of the refusal of many white Americans who linked paid domestic work to chores for slaves and considered it degrading. From these white Americans' viewpoint, "slaving like a nigger" in someone else's home was suitable only for immigrants and blacks. This racist assumption prevailed to the extent that many whites had no compunction about seeking domestic service from any black woman. When asked if she went "ahouse cleaning," Sarah Mapps Douglass was astonished. Her intellect and polished manners meant nothing to white women who saw black women only as potential housekeepers.[16]

In actuality, free black women did not have a monopoly in domestic service throughout antebellum America. Irish women submitted 59 percent of the applications for domestic jobs offered through New York's Society for the Encouragement of Faithful Domestic Servants in 1825. Only 21 percent of the applications came from "women of color." By 1855 nearly 75 percent of New York's domestics were Irish, a reflection of the influx of immigrants during the intervening years. Black women held only 3 percent of the domestic jobs in 1855. New York was not unusual with a larger number of European-born women in domestic service than American-born women, black and white.[17]

The competition for southern domestic jobs differed from that in the industrial North. Rather than white immigrants competing against free black women, the challenge came from enslaved women. This was a special problem for black women heading households because their options

Table 3.1
Population in Selected Cities, 1850

	Free Blacks		Whites	
	Women	Men	Women	Men
NORTH				
Albany, NY	470	390	25,716	24,187
Boston, MA	1,080	919	70,027	64,855
Chicago, IL	142	181	13,521	16,119
Cincinnati, OH	1,675	1,562	52,892	59,306
Cleveland, OH	120	104	8,311	8,499
Detroit, MI	279	308	9,876	10,556
Hartford, CN	250	193	3,643	4,043
Indianapolis, IN	211	194	3,643	4,043
Milwaukee, WI	41	57	9,530	10,433
New York, NY	7,717	6,098	253,724	248,008
Philadelphia, PA	11,326	8,435	201,045	187,956
Pittsburgh, PA	1,052	907	22,036	22,606

	Free and Enslaved Blacks		Whites	
	Women	Men	Women	Men
UPPER SOUTH				
Baltimore, MD	14,610	10,832	69,793	70,873
Slaves	**1,299**	**947**		
Louisville, KY	840	698	16,756	19,468
Slaves	**3,022**	**2,410**		
Memphis, TN	75	51	2,776	3,579
Slaves	**1,266**	**1,094**		
Norfolk, VA	592	364	4,879	4,196
Slaves	**2,618**	**1,677**		
Petersburg, VA	1,439	1,177	3,488	5,177
Slaves	**2,353**	**2,376**		
Richmond, VA	1,294	1,075	7,491	7,783
Slaves	**4,620**	**5,307**		
St. Louis, MO	656	742	31,439	42,367
Slaves	**1,390**	**1,266**		
Washington, DC	4,760	3,398	15,204	14,526
Slaves	**1,380**	**733**		
Wilmington, NC	367	285	1,786	1,795
Slaves				

	Free and Enslaved Blacks		Whites	
	Women	Men	Women	Men
LOWER SOUTH				
Charleston, SC	2,086	1,355	9,774	10,238
Slaves	**10,901**	**8,631**		
Little Rock, AR	16	5	795	826
Slaves	**295**	**230**		
Mobile, AL	429	286	5,975	7,022
Slaves	**3,591**	**3,212**		
Natchez, MS	113	100	1,367	1,343
Slaves	**825**	**686**		
New Orleans, LA	6,196	4,104	44,431	59,312
Slaves	**11,595**	**8,012**		
Savannah, GA	422	264	3,986	4,409
Slaves	**3,282**	**2,949**		

Source: Source: J. B. B. DeBow, *Statistical View of the United States, being a Compendium of the Seventh Census* (Washington, DC: A. O. P. Nicholson, 1854), 396–99.

were limited, and the available jobs paid poorly. This situation was even more of a problem in cities with large numbers of free black women, especially where enslaved women were prominent in market activities and hired their own time. No doubt competition among black women was keen in nine of Virginia's largest cities where women made up 56 to 65 percent of the free black population in 1860.[18]

Domestic work in private families in the North, Upper South, and Lower South involved a multiplicity of chores for the comfort and convenience of employers. Most servants worked in homes without running water, indoor plumbing, gas or electric lights, and central heat; the widespread availability of modern conveniences occurred after 1865.[19]

Well-to-do homeowners often hired staffs rather than lone servants. After Harriet Jacobs fled from slavery in 1842, she secured a position in the New York home of Imogen and Nathaniel Parker Willis. The family employed a laundress and other servants. Jacobs's sole responsibility was caring for the Willises' child, and she accompanied Nathaniel Willis to England in 1845 where she served as the child's nurse for ten months. Similarly, in the 1840s, the free-born Eliza Potter sailed to France with a family in the diplomatic corps to work solely as the caregiver for a child.[20]

Few free black women left firsthand accounts of domestic work; therefore, it is virtually impossible to know about the interactions between free-born and freed black women domestics and the persons, black and white, who hired them. In developing an argument on the dialectics of labor power, the political scientist Gayle T. Tate writes that labor activities were intertwined with the forces that defined "slave women's oppression as well as the transforming vehicles of survival and resistance." Tate's argument may serve as the basis for inquiry into the relationship between the work of free black women, racial discrimination in the workplace, and resistance to circumscribing labor forces. Aggrieved workers, without regard for color, gender, or status, are likely to resist oppressive conditions. Tate acknowledges that a "culture of resistance" existed in the slave community, and it follows that black women would not abandon it once emancipated since they often encountered oppression in the workplace, albeit from a different "master."[21]

Letters written between 1859 and 1867 by Addie Brown reflect outstanding efforts to survive in addition to her will to resist oppressive forces in the workplace. Brown's missives indicate that her economic conditions remained consistently poor throughout her life. Yet being near destitution did not snuff out this self-supporting woman's determination and wit. When a Mrs. Lewis Freeman of Providence, Rhode Island, contacted Brown about work in the mid-1860s, Brown told a friend, "She will not hold out any in ducement to me dont wish to have me do any scrubing or washing but take an interst in her affars, and also do some sewing."[22]

Ideally, an incentive for Brown was an invitation to forgo all drudgery and to participate in leisure reading, develop an interest in charitable work, and show enthusiasm for social activities. With regard to her reference to "do some sewing," Brown knew well-to-do women did not turn themselves into human sewing machines. Instead, they hired seamstresses to cut, baste, and sew in their own homes or that of the employer. Once basic tasks were completed, some employers finished the garments and had time for ornamental sewing. Brown understood the business and knew seamstresses in employers' homes received better treatment than domestics.[23]

Theoretically, as a free woman, Brown was at liberty to select jobs that best suited her purposes. She also had the option of quitting if the working conditions were oppressive. However, her color and limited skills precluded her ability to fully exercise her options and select positions based upon the best "in ducement."

Instead, the laundry or "washing," an arduous task, awaited Brown, and it was the bane of many domestic servants' existence. When Mary Ellen Pleasant negotiated wages as a cook near the California gold fields in the 1850s, she insisted that "she should do no washing, not even dishwashing." The writings of the Massachusetts-born Nancy Prince reveal the tedious nature of laundering clothes for a family of seven. Two family members were ill and probably generated more laundry than usual. Prince, who was a teenager at the time, described her weekly routine: "Sabbath evening I had to prepare for the wash; soap the clothes and put them into the steamer, set the kettle of water to boiling...At two o'clock, on the morning of Monday, the bell was rung for me to get up; but, that was not all, they said I was too slow, and the washing was not done well; I had to leave the tub to tend the door and wait on the family, and was not spoken kind to, at that." Only three months on the job took a toll on her health. Prince left her place of employment, but it is unclear if she quit or was fired.[24]

In either case, Addie Brown could sympathize with Prince, for she understood the demands of domestic work, especially laundering clothes. In 1861, she lived in a boardinghouse owned by black New Yorkers and worked as a servant and caregiver for their nine children. Ordinarily, the family hired a laundress for half a day, which was not enough time to finish the task. In March 1862, Brown and the laundress worked in an open room that "had no fire there and no carpet on the floor." Brown developed a cold and linked her illness to the drudgery that was sickening, figuratively and literally. After visiting a friend, Brown wrote, "She looks just the same up to [her] eyes in washing." Brown added, "I hope I never have to take in washing for my livlyhood."[25]

"To take in washing" for whites was a common occupation among black women across geographical boundaries. An 1847 survey conducted by the Society of Friends in Philadelphia reported that 1,970 black women out of 4,249 were washerwomen. The majority of free black women in Baltimore between 1817 and 1860 worked as laundresses. Between 1841 and 1859, 232 out of 324 women received licenses from the St. Louis, Missouri, county court to ply their trade as laundresses. The 1850 and 1860 U.S. Censuses for Duval County, Florida, including Jacksonville; and Leon County, including Tallahassee, listed washing as the dominant occupation of free black women.[26]

Regardless of where the women laundered clothes or the methods used, the scrubbing, lifting, wringing, and hanging garments out to dry tested the mettle of the best washerwomen. Once clothes dried, the women folded or ironed them and delivered the garments to owners. The labor-intensive task consumed the better part of two days. Aside from washing clothes, laundresses needed time to make soap and starch in addition to hauling water and gathering wood to heat it.[27]

On the mitigating side of the taxing chore, some enterprising washerwomen ran profitable operations and carved out degrees of autonomy. Self-employed laundresses could limit the number of customers and

Table 3.2
Occupations of Free Black Women in Baltimore, 1817–1860

	Laundress	Total no. of Women
1817–1818	48	62
1822–1823	194	231
1831	227	289
1840–1841	392	526
1849–1850	273	372
1860	329	456

Source: Compiled from Barbara Elizabeth Wallace, " 'Fair Daughters of Africa': African American Women in Baltimore, 1790–1860" (PhD diss., University of California, Los Angeles, 2001), 115–21.

Table 3.3
Occupations of Free Black Women in Philadelphia, 1838

Confectioners	1
Dress-Makers	81
Dress-Makers/Tailoresses	14
Hair-Workers	4
Millers/Dress-Makers	24
Tailoresses	18
Weavers	1

Source: Compiled from the *Register of Trades of the Colored People in the City of Philadelphia and Districts* (Philadelphia: Merrihew and Gunn, 1838).

Table 3.4
Occupations of Free Black Women in Philadelphia, 1847

Washerwomen	1970
Needlewomen	486
(Dressmakers	(216)
(Seamstresses	(231)
(Tailoresses	(19)
(Milliners	(19)
Cooks	173
Occupied at home	290
*Occupied at day's work	786
*Living in families	156
Various	72
Trades	213
Raggers and boners	103

Source: *A Statistical Inquiry into the Condition of the People of Colour of the City and Districts of Philadelphia* (Philadelphia: Kite & Walton, 1849), 18.

Table 3.5
Occupations of Free Black Women Licensed by St. Louis County Court,
1841–1859

Chambermaids	30
Cooks	3
Dressmakers	1
Housekeepers	5
House Servants	5
Mantua Makers	3
Nurses	5
Seamstresses	3
Servants	14
Waiters	5
Washers	232

Source: "List of Free Negroes, Licensed by the County Court of St. Louis County," Missouri Historical Society, St. Louis, Missouri.

control the amounts of their work. If they worked in their own homes, the women could earn money while juggling their own childcare or household responsibilities. They lost that autonomy in working in customers' homes where they had no time for personal matters and were subjected to another's authority.[28]

A washerwoman in Plaquemines Parish, Louisiana, worked in her employer's home between 1861 and 1865 earning 50 cents a day by completing the weekly laundry for two adults and children. The employer claimed the woman arrived early, finished "the washing one day & the ironing the next." At this rate she could earn $2.50 to $3.00 per week, if she had a job each day and charged other customers the same rate.[29]

These close interactions with whites probably required blacks to assume "a humble pose." Many learned early on to pay deference to whites publicly while privately maintaining self-respect. This act fit into the culture of resistance as did the much-discussed "mask." The mask was a protective strategy for disguising personal convictions, the psyche, facial expressions, and body language, and it was a significant factor in maintaining associations with whites whose patronage was critical to black economic survival. Certainly, free blacks were at liberty to decide if they would or would not assume the humble pose.[30]

Many women supported themselves through the needle trade. Without readily accessible and affordable manufactured clothes, the needs for ordinary and extraordinary wearing apparel for children and adults, living or dead, were filled by hand sewing. A black woman in Philadelphia

Figure 3.1. "The Lady Patroness of Alblacks." Library
Company of Philadelphia, Philadelphia, Pennsylvania.

listed herself as a "shroud maker" in a 1838 survey conducted by the
Pennsylvania Abolition Society. Dressmakers also served patrons, especially readers of ladies' magazines, who were familiar with popular trends
or maintained separate wardrobes for special occasions. Additionally,
"properly" dressed women covered their heads, and the skills of milliners and mantua makers were necessary to complete a wardrobe.[31]

African Americans' interests in their own clothes attracted the attention
of white detractors who labeled their fondness for clothes as "extrava-
gant gratification." Graphic racist caricatures drawn by Edward Clay in

the 1820s aimed barbs at Philadelphia's black elite and served as the subject of the "Life in Philadelphia" series. Even when they could not afford the luxury, beautiful or lavish clothes camouflaged the actual economic status of wearers and cloaked them in finery that garnered a place in society, however illusionary, that would not be achieved otherwise. This is analogous to the "negation of pretend" concept wherein individuals transport themselves from real-life situations by imagining or pretending to live under conditions contrasting with reality. Beyond reflecting economic and social positions, clothes indicated individuality and creativity. Skilled dressmakers, regardless of color, found a niche supplying garments that did more than clothe the body.[32]

Of the black dressmakers before 1865, only the highly skilled Virginia-born Elizabeth Keckley's autobiographical writings containing extensive discussion about the sewing business have been published. Once freed, she tried to support herself by offering sewing classes in Baltimore. When that enterprise failed, she moved to Washington, D.C., and earned $2.50 per day as a dressmaker. Initially too impoverished to buy a license permitting her to work longer than ten days at a time, Keckley eventually became one of the most-sought-after dressmakers in the city.[33]

Keckley's account of an 1861 interaction with a demanding client, Margaret McLean, wife of Colonel Eugene McLean, whom Keckley called "Mrs. Gen. McClean" illustrates the dressmaker's finesse in customer relations. McLean arrived at Keckley's abode with fabric in hand and insisted that she "commence work on it right away." Keckley refused, saying she had more work on hand than she could complete. McLean continued to demand that she accept the job; Keckley refused to assume the "humble pose." This was not the expected behavior of a black woman, even a free one. Keckley relented only after McLean promised to introduce her to potential clients, "ladies of the White House." That, writes Keckley, was the best inducement "that could have been offered."[34]

Keckley, unlike Brown, was in an excellent position to negotiate an agreement that resulted in mutual satisfaction. She eventually counted Mary Todd Lincoln, wife of Abraham Lincoln; Varina Davis, wife of Jefferson Davis; and Adèle Cutts, wife of Stephen A. Douglas, as customers. To complete the orders, Keckley hired other dressmakers and soon earned enough to satisfy debts incurred for purchasing her freedom and that of her son.[35]

Accomplished dressmaking required different skills from those used for sewing bare necessities. Descriptions of fine clothes by the well-traveled Eliza Potter add to an understanding of why high-fashion dress-

THE SARAGOSSA.

[From the establishment of G. Brodie, 51 Canal Street, New York   Drawn by L. T. Voight, from actual articles of costume.]

This beautiful novelty is constructed of two colors of silk—a light hue, and black taffeta; purple is much esteemed for the lighter tint. This is ornamented with exquisite designs of passementerie. The character of the garment requires no elucidation beyond the engraving.
33*   389

Figure 3.2. "The Saragossa." From *Godey's Lady's Book*.

making could be lucrative. She rhapsodized about a "white silk dress, with over-dress of elegant Swiss, flounced; each flounce fluted and edged with costly lace." Even more elegant was the

gold colored silk, of unusual brilliance, the skirt was plain and exceedingly full, with a train of half a yard, but sufficiently short in front to expose an exquisitely formed foot, encased in a silk gaiter, the precise shade of the dress; white point lace with buff cape pleatings formed the trimming for the drooping angel sleeves... confined at the shoulder by a silk cord and tassel, displaying an elegant point lace undersleeve corresponding with the trimming of the neck, which was al la

Figure 3.3. "La Coiffure Francaise." From *Godey's Lady's Book.*

Pompadour, and long tassels which drooped gracefully on the skirt from the waist and confined with white and scarlet ostrich feathers.

Richly woven fabrics in beautiful hues are not alone in making fashionable garments. Creativity combined with fitting and sewing skills are indispensable. The minute details in the trimmings, fluted flounces, and pleats required extra skill and hours of labor.[36]

Addie Brown was not a haute couture dressmaker, yet she knew the demands of sewing and explained, "I am not feeling well . . . have been lying down all the Morn. for the past three or four days I have the most excruciateing pain in my back I have been out sewing for two weeks I guess siting so steady is the cause of my pain . . . I was sewing for Miss Mary Goodwin . . . and I expect to go tomorrow and friday and satuday and the rest of the days to Mrs Saunders. I dont think I could stand going out everday." The backbreaking work was not an inducement for Brown or any other seamstress. If Brown hired herself out, she, unlike enslaved women, could determine when and how long she worked. Of course, her economic situation figured importantly in any decisions she made.[37]

Perhaps Potter also experienced the backbreaking demands of sewing and preferred looking at beautiful dresses more than creating them. She shifted occupations and became a hairdresser after gaining new skills in France. "Combing" hair for the well-to-do was more profitable than sewing and allowed the independent-thinking woman a greater degree of autonomy and mobility. Potter, an independent woman without qualms about traveling, followed customers to posh resorts in Saratoga, New York, and Newport, Rhode Island, where she earned as much as $200 in one summer season.[38]

By 1860, after more than fifteen years in the beauty trade, the twice-married Potter moved to Cincinnati, Ohio, where she owned a dwelling worth $2,000 at 6 Home Street. As head of her household and owner of personal property valued at $400, the mother of two mulatto children maintained high standards and was ever vigilant about her profession. She had taught the art of dressing hair in London and operated a school of beauty culture in Cincinnati. She may have earned additional income from students boarding in her home while studying her techniques. Potter's skill and business acumen earned her a place among the black nouveau riches in antebellum Cincinnati.[39]

Other women operated beauty salons and performed related services. A survey of occupations among free blacks in antebellum Philadelphia listed several women as hairworkers or wigmakers. Virginia Vashon Proctor operated a shop where she made wigs above a barber shop owned by her husband. Cecelia Remond Babcock and her sisters Maritcha Remond and Caroline Remond Putnam were proprietors of the Ladies Hair Work Salon where they manufactured wigs and produced a medicated tonic to retard hair loss. Their fashionable and lucrative business was the largest in Massachusetts.[40]

Marie Laveau, daughter of a well-known voodoo queen also named Marie Laveau and resident of antebellum New Orleans, supported herself as a hairdresser. The "gay," "bright and brilliant" social life of the Crescent City, as described by Eliza Potter who resided in New Orleans for a brief period, required skilled professionals to "comb" for special occasions. Laveau's biographer, Martha Ward, also asserts that the demand for hairdressers was high in New Orleans, and free women of color "had a lock on the profession." Laveau, like Potter, served fashionable clients in the privacy of their own homes or the hotel rooms of sojourners in the city.[41]

Combined with the personal beauty care that Laveau provided, she, a reputed voodoo practitioner, dispensed spiritual advice and induced magical trances in addition to driving husbands away from or enticing them to remain with their spouses. In the 1930s, Works Progress Administration informants claimed that she used the knowledge of voodoo to ease her clients' anxieties about intimate concerns while arranging their hair beautifully. Eliza Potter's narrative supports the suggestion that some well-to-do white women divulged intimate details of their personal lives to the hairdressers.[42]

Most free black women could not afford the services of a professional

Figure 3.4. Esclaves nègres, de différentes nations.
Library of Congress, Washington, D.C.

hairdresser although they were interested in beautifying themselves. Such an absence of patronage meant some black hairdressers catered primarily to whites. This dimension of the work was even more complex in the South where they competed with enslaved women serving persons who owned or hired them.

A relatively small number of free women, hairdressers and dressmakers included, operated successful businesses before 1865. More often than not, their businesses were located in urban areas and catered to customers of different colors and classes. Of course specialized skills and services probably drew clients with highly discriminating tastes or interests. Other black entrepreneurs included Harriet Lee, operator of an oyster and refreshment house in Columbia, Pennsylvania; Adelia Dickerson, a Philadelphian, who ran a bar in the Walnut Street Theatre; and Aletha Tanner, who sold vegetables in a Washington, D.C., market near the White House. No doubt the location was influential in Thomas Jefferson's patronage. Molly Horniblow's livelihood depended on her skills as a baker, perfected while enslaved in North Carolina. Horniblow had "a grand big oven . . . that baked bread and nice things for the town," wrote her granddaughter Harriet Jacobs. Susan Jackson of Savannah, Georgia, operated a bakery in the city's business district that was successful enough for her to purchase a building appraised at $10,000.[43]

Some free women whose livelihood depended upon food services worked alone while others were assisted by persons they hired or owned. Sally Seymour bought one slave in the early 1800s and another in 1814 to assist in her Charleston catering enterprise. At the time of her death in 1824, Seymour owned four slaves. One of her contemporaries and competitors, Camillia Johnson, owned five slaves who worked in her food service. Ann Deas, also of Charleston, earned a reputation for high-quality food services and hotel accommodations. Deas, unlike Seymour and Johnson, trained slaves in culinary skills and then sold them to work elsewhere.[44]

Whether the women received assistance or worked alone, food services could be lucrative businesses. Mary Ellen Pleasant's reputation for her culinary skills catapulted her into a position of selling her services to gold miners for $500 per month at a California auction in the 1850s. She could command an extraordinary salary due to the limited number of cooks and the high demand. Pleasant was successful enough at lending money and cooking to diversify and channel her earnings into laundries and a boardinghouse.[45]

An estimated 5 percent of the free black women operated boardinghouses between New Haven and New Orleans. Among them was the freedwoman Chloe Spear, who lived in Boston and counted seamen and laborers among her residents. It was not unusual for a private individual to take in lodgers. Newcomers in cities, without resources to rent or buy a place of their own, found boarding a convenient stopgap. Heads of households wanting supplementary income were ready matches for potential boarders, and it benefited both parties. The woman of the house could supplement the family's income further by laundering clothes for tenants.[46]

In other situations, women operated lodging establishments designed especially for that purpose. There were nearly one hundred such facilities in New Orleans operated by free black women in 1860. In Nashville, Sarah Estelle maintained a boardinghouse at 89 North Cherry Street and advertised in the *Nashville Business Directory*. Her ad stands out among other notices because of its specificity. Readers knew at a glance that Sarah Estelle was "*Colored*" and kept a "fashionable boarding house one door north of [the] theatre" on Cherry Street. Interested parties also learned that Estelle was capable of providing "Ice Creams, Refreshments, &c." Additionally, said the advertisement, Estelle "Furnishes and Superintends Suppers, and Fashionable Parties." Hotels and boardinghouses such as the one run by Sarah Estelle were not as common in rural areas as in urban centers.[47]

Whenever women in the North, Upper South, or Lower South pro-vided services related to housekeeping, catering, hairstyling, sewing, or lodging, the skills required were uniform and may be compared from region to region. This was not true of the free women involved in pro-ducing and marketing cash crops across regions. Women were involved in the production of rice, cotton, sugar cane, or tobacco, and each is pecu-liar to specific regions of the South. For example, rice was cultivated pri-marily in coastal South Carolina, and sugar cane grew in southern Louisiana. The methods of cultivation varied for each crop, and each required different soils, climates, and growing seasons. These variations make combining cash crops or comparing growers from one region to another problematic. Comparisons within specific agricultural regions and crops are possible, to be sure.[48]

Beyond general statements about agricultural work, there has been no sustained study focusing on free black women working alone or along-side slaves on farms and plantations owned by blacks. In all probability, persons owning agricultural land made few, if any, distinctions among their laborers according to gender. The needs of persons hiring or own-ing workers prevailed over gender conventions. The legendary "Ar'n't I a Woman?" speech attributed to Sojourner Truth conveys a message about the intensity of labor involved in plowing, planting, or gathering crops, and it touts one woman's ability to work "like a man." Male and female agricultural laborers shared a mean equality. Both were exploited whether they suckled tobacco, picked cotton, winnowed rice, or cut sugar cane.[49]

In 1840, the freedman William Ellison cultivated 330 acres of prime land with eleven of the thirty slaves he owned. Among Ellison's hands were five women between twenty-four and fifty-four years of age. Ordinarily, mature women gathered 200 pounds of cotton a day, and the most agile among them could pick over 300 pounds per day. Although Matilda Elli-son, William's wife, left no historical records, she must have been familiar with cotton cultivation and had opinions about it from her own enslave-ment and as "lady of the house" at Wisdom Hall, the Ellison plantation. Cotton production was a major source of William Ellison's income, and he increased the number of 400-pound bales from 35 to 100 between 1849 and 1861. Enslaved women figured prominently in that effort.[50]

Enslaved women were also essential to the agricultural success of the free-born Margaret Mitchell Harris, a Georgetown, South Carolina, rice planter. Harris inherited twenty-one males and females from her father, a free mulatto, in 1842, and she received sixteen more from her mother's estate in 1844. The legacy combined with her own personal property cata-pulted Harris into the planter class. She owned forty-four persons worth

$25,300 in 1860. With her own labor force and nearly 1,000 acres of land, Harris produced 150 bushels of sweet potatoes and 100 bushels of corn in 1849 in addition to a cash crop, rice.[51]

When compared to other planters in the vicinity, Harris is exceptional. She harvested 240,000 pounds of rice in 1849 with twenty-two slaves, eleven of whom were women, of her own and several others owned by her brother. Planters with more slaves and land in nearby All Saints Parish produced more rice, but the yields per hand were less. Why Harris's laborers produced more rice per hand than those of other planters raises questions. Did they identify with Harris, internalize her interests, and work more efficiently to assure her success? Could they have worked more diligently out of fear? Whatever the case, Harris sold the rice for $7,632. Based on the capital investment in land and the estimated costs of maintaining her workers, Harris's return on her investment was 18.43 percent. Unlike her parents, Harris did not bequeath her slaves to others. She sold them at an 1860 auction and invested in stocks and bonds.[52]

There were a few other black women among the most prosperous slaveholding sugarcane growers in antebellum Louisiana. Included in that number were the widowed Madam Cyprien Ricaud and Octave Reggio. Records show that the Ricaud and the Reggio households had assets valued at $221,500 and $160,000 respectively. In 1860, the greater portion of August and Octave Reggios' assets was personal property. The same is probably true of the Ricauds who owned 152 slaves.[53]

There are more questions than answers about the nature of the relationship between black slaveholding women and the women they owned for pecuniary reasons. It is unlikely that these planters or wives of planters worked alongside, shared friendships, or mitigated the working conditions of the persons they owned. The paucity of manuscripts left by black slaveholding women makes it nearly impossible to know their thoughts about persons as property. Correspondence between two women in 1857 provides a glimmer of insight into the world of two slaveholding women. In a July 11, 1857, letter to her aunt, Emma Miller Hoggartt wrote, "Now for me to tell you about a woman that jeff bought today. She seems to be a woman very willing. Says she can make homemade bread, buscuits, pies and do everythin thats wanting about the house and if she suits I will be just fixed wich I hope she will." Tryphena Blanche Holder Fox wrote to her mother about her intent to buy a domestic servant. She explained, "She came & worked two days, so we could see what she was capable of doing, and I find her a good washer & ironer and pastry cook & able to cook plain, every day meals ... How much trouble she will give me, I dont know, but I think I can get along with her, passable well any how."

It did not matter that the first letter was written by a black woman and the second by a white one. The slaveholding women shared similar expectations and interests. Owning slaves reflected material well-being and boosted owners' egos.[54]

Planters or entrepreneurs, black or white, would do nothing to jeopardize their economic success. They were subjected to cyclical fiscal pressures associated with national and international fluctuations. If free blacks weathered economic crises, overcame racist laws, and general hostilities to succeed, they worked diligently to secure their holdings. They bequeathed property to family members and selected spouses from inside a narrow circle of friends and relatives. The intricacies of such arrangements are evident among the descendants of Marie Thérèze Coincoin and Claude Metoyer. Their efforts resulted in the ownership of an estimated 15,000 acres of land in Louisiana and 436 males and females by 1860. The Metoyers were the largest black slaveowning family in the United States.[55]

Betsy Sompayrac, a free woman of color also in Natchitoches, Louisiana, like the Metoyers, had few resources when compared to the Metoyers, but her will reveals much about her plans to secure her children's economic future. The document is informative about the relationship between a slaveowner and the folk she owned. Sompayrac, the mother of four, dictated her will January 15, 1845. Concerned about her debts, the welfare of her three young children, and her inevitable demise, Sompayrac parceled out five slaves, a woman and four children, to her own offspring. Daniel fell heir to the "boy Alexander," an eight-year-old child. The four-month-old infant James along with the five-year-old Solomon would be Stephen's property. The "little negro girl named Elizabeth" and a woman, Jane, were set aside for Sarah Ann Sompayrac.[56]

Essential differences in the legacies go beyond Sompayrac's sons receiving males and her daughter receiving females. Encumbrances prevented Stephen and Sarah from enjoying their inheritances permanently. Solomon would become Stephen's property, but he would be freed at thirty years of age in consideration of his position. He was Sompayrac's godson. Similarly, the thirty-five-year-old Jane would become Sarah's property only after the liquidation of Sompayrac's debts. Rather than selling her real and personal property for that purpose, Sompayrac, who had sold an enslaved mulatto woman in 1837, decided to rent her home and hire Jane out. The proceeds were to pay off her debts. Afterward, Sarah could take possession of Jane but not of any children she might have. Despite its limitations, Sarah's legacy had great potential since she had clear title to a two-year-old girl and her progeny.[57]

Sompayrac willed Jane's issue to her son, Benjamin, who was away at the time, if he ever returned to Natchitoches. Wills like Sompayrac's served as the basis for prosperity in pre-emancipation days; however, the abolition of slavery eradicated white and black slaveowners' fortunes in chattel.[58]

Another will that provides fertile ground for examining issues regarding relationships between free black and enslaved women is that of Anna Madgigine Jai Kingsley, an African-born slaveowner in Florida, which provided for the disposal of three females and one male between nine and seventeen years of age upon her death. There were commonalities among enslaved and slaveowning black women based on their African background and the color and gender oppression that they encountered, but the shared characteristics did not erase class distinctions, legal status, and economic interests. Historian Ira Berlin argues that in the Lower South, many free blacks of means wanted little part of slaves except as property. While this observation may reflect the positions of Sompayrac and Kingsley, other free women, many of whom were slave-born, maintained associations with enslaved loved ones and sometimes assisted them in gaining freedom.[59]

Slave ownership was a business venture, albeit a reprehensible one, in which neither a majority of blacks nor whites engaged. Of the 59,466 free blacks in 1790, only 195 owned slaves. Nearly 19 percent of black owners were in Charleston, South Carolina. By 1830, the free population in the United States had increased to 233,524, and 3,775 black women and men owned 12,760 slaves. At that time, 450 blacks in Charleston owned 2,412 slaves.[60]

While there are many examples of successful free blacks—slaveowners and non-slaveowners among them—they represent a small percentage of the overall free black population. The majority of free blacks struggled mightily for their daily bread and did not escape the pernicious effects of racist customs and laws that affected their economic well-being. The scholar Gayle T. Tate argues cogently that the race-based discriminatory economic conditions black women encountered, individually and collectively, were among the catalysts that fostered their political consciousness.[61]

Discriminatory practices were readily evident following the War of 1812 when white women comprised a majority of the estimated 100,000 industrial workers in the United States, and many labored in textile factories and shoe factories. A significant number of women worked on specific parts of a product at home and received wages according to the quantity, or pieces, completed. Pieceworkers, some of whom had gained skills in the needle trade, earned wages binding or stitching shoe uppers in the factories such as those of Lynn, Massachusetts. Black women were conspicuously absent from industrial employment as pieceworkers. The failure to hire them may be attributed to racial animosity and the presence of immigrants who often accepted lower wages. An exception was Anna Murray Douglass who probably received work because of her anti-slavery connections.[62]

In addition to regional customs, local and state statutes interfered with black economic choices through prohibitive legislation. Officials in Sparta, Georgia, passed an ordinance in 1827 prohibiting free persons from keeping "a house of public or private entertainment," vending "any goods, wares, or merchandise," and carrying "on any kind of traffic for the purpose of gain." The 1831 Washington, D.C., Corporate Council enacted a statute requiring a license to operate specific businesses; however, free blacks could only purchase licenses to "drive carts, drays, hackney-carriages, or wagons." And lawmakers in Richmond, Virginia, passed an ordinance in April 1853 proclaiming that "no negro shall keep a cook-shop within said city, under the penalty of stripes, at the discretion of the mayor." Protests generally brought little or no relief as evidenced by *Mayo v. James* (1855), when a Virginia court said, "Cook-shops kept by free negroes, being in effect . . . taverns of the lowest description, and liable to become sources of infinite disorder and corruption among the black population, slave as well as free, the propriety of regulating or wholly interdicting them in the city of Richmond, must be apparent to all." Laws in Maryland and Georgia subjected blacks to similar rulings.[63]

Beyond the circumscriptions of independent black business owners, other statutes interfered with their general freedom to earn a livelihood, especially in the South. White citizens submitted countless petitions to their legislatures regarding black competition. Some petitioners asked that blacks be required to purchase licenses to operate businesses or that they pay prohibitive taxes. Clearly, the objectives were to reduce, if not eliminate, black competition.[64]

The passage and enforcement of pejorative legislation served to kindle political consciousness and spark resistance. After the 1831 Nat Turner rebellion, many of the slave states passed laws prohibiting free persons from teaching enslaved or free blacks. Violators suffered penalties of fines or incarceration. Only four states enforced the laws consistently; however, the threatening atmosphere associated with imparting literacy to slaves was pervasive and had widespread results. Many schools run by blacks ceased to exist, thereby displacing teachers. The prohibitions against educating blacks interfered with the teachers economically and impeded the intellectual development of their people. Certainly, some teachers resisted for reasons more significant than the incomes earned from their students and continued to operate schools surreptitiously.[65]

Northern blacks did not have the same kinds of legal disabilities, but they faced obstacles nonetheless. Because of the segregation and racial discrimination in public schools, they sometimes opened private schools. Ultimately, the general poverty of students made collecting tuition difficult and interfered with the teachers' abilities to earn a living.

When adverse economic conditions or hostile racial climates prevented free persons from working in traditional ways, they sought alternatives. When faced with threatening economic circumstances, Massachusetts-born Nancy Prince mulled over her options before she wrote, "Not wishing to throw myself on [friends], I take this method to help myself." The method was to offer public lectures and publish an account of her travel experiences in Russia and Jamaica. The objective was "not a vain desire to appear before the public," she wrote, "but, by the sale, I hope to obtain the means to supply my necessities." *A Black Woman's Odyssey* (1850) merited a second edition in 1856.[66]

Harriet Wilson also tried to extricate herself from poverty by writing a book after venturing into the beauty trade with a formula that restored grey hair to its natural color. The business was apparently successful, but poor health interfered with her ability to pursue it. As a last resort, the bedridden Wilson attempted the "experiment" of writing about racism in the North through the eyes of her protagonist, Frado, a free black servant who experienced abusive treatment at the hands of white employers. Wilson appealed to her "colored brethren universally for patronage" while hoping they would not condemn her attempt to be erudite. She begged them to purchase *"Our Nig": or Sketches from the Life of a Free Black, in a Two-Story White House, North. Showing That Slavery's Shadows Fall Even There.*[67]

Neither Wilson nor Prince received as much attention from their publications as Sojourner Truth's *Narrative*. Truth, who never learned to read or write, employed marketing and distribution techniques that advanced her cause as an author. Truth solicited an endorsement from the highly successful writer Harriet Beecher Stowe and sold photographs of herself in addition to copies of her autobiography following public lectures, including the 1851 women's rights convention in Akron, Ohio. Purchasers were often more interested in Truth as a personality than in her text. Truth's sales techniques did much to support her and to make her story known to future generations.[68]

Eliza Potter enjoyed the brisk sales of her gossipy *A Hairdresser's Experience*. She had assumed the position of confidante for customers who talked freely about any subject, including extramarital affairs, in her presence. Their disclosures became fodder for her 1859 "tell-all," a commentary on America society. It does not appear that Potter's primary interest was economic, and she used initials or dashes to conceal the customers' identities. That prevented the book from interfering with her hairdressing business or suffering economic sanctions, and she made money from its sales.[69]

Unlike Potter, a large number of free black women lacked financial security, and poverty forced them to change their habits or seek alternatives. Addie Brown's economic condition was consistently desperate, and when a friend advised her to keep her spirits up, Brown responded, "I have no money and I stand to live out to service long at a time that [is] all I can aspire [to] in this place. I must and shall do somthing in the spring if I have to leave Hartford." Brown, an unmarried, marginally educated woman without specific skills, knew the economic limitations engulfing her.[70]

Poverty figured in the decision of some women who turned to illegal or socially unacceptable means, including prostitution, to support themselves. It is impossible to determine the extent to which black women in antebellum Philadelphia engaged in the business from the City Register of Prostitutes. It did not designate the color of the "fallen women." Places of birth such as Baltimore, Detroit, or Washington, D.C., give no hints of color or ethnicity; however, Ireland, Germany, or England are better indicators. Regardless of a woman's place of birth, color, or marital status, when asked the reason for commencing "this kind of life," prostitution, they answered: "fell into bad company." No one said she became a prostitute for economic reasons.[71]

The antebellum court records of three central-piedmont North Carolina counties rarely included arrests of black women for prostitution. The greater number of prostitutes were poor white women. Historian Victoria Bynum posits that "white men's sexual access to slave women no doubt lessened the market for black prostitutes." Rather than participating in the trade, free blacks in the area waged a vigorous campaign against the illicit activity, thereby reducing the traffic.[72]

New York City's police records between 1790 and 1810 reveal the presence of prostitutes and brothels operated by black women. Nine women were counted as prostitutes in 1855 but, the extent to which harlotry, which was not a statutory offense, flourished in New York City and the number of free black women actually involved is unknown because of the nature of the business. Participants became part of the statistical records only when they ran afoul of other laws, such as vagrancy and keeping a disorderly house, under which prostitution fell as a statutory offense. Those avoiding arrest went uncounted.[73]

Harlotry was not illegal in antebellum St. Louis either, yet under a vagrancy law police arrested women believed to sell sexual favors. The broad and poorly defined statute was a favorite tool of police, for it covered a multitude of "indiscretions." "Fallen women," practically any women who did not conform to acceptable standards of behavior, were "disgraces to their sex," and police arrested them. The greater problem for officials was not prostitution but maintaining segregation. When blacks and whites intermingled in the bawdy houses of assignation, they interfered with the ambitions of public officials. Unless the women involved were arrested for vagrancy, they went unnoticed. "Prostitution alone," said one attorney, "does not constitute vagrancy."[74]

According to the dockets in Pennsylvania between 1790 and 1835 and the city of Philadelphia between 1838 and 1866, the greater incidence of criminal behavior among women, black and white, was larceny not prostitution. Similar statistics indicate that theft was the major offense among female prisoners in pre–Civil War Washington, D.C. No distinctions existed in what black and white women stole, and there were no great variations according to the color of the inmates. The stark difference was the longer prison terms for black women than for their white cohorts.[75]

Black women were more likely to be arrested than native-born white women. Furthermore, it was not unusual for blacks to receive harsher sentences and fewer pardons than whites. Baltimore's eighth ward penitentiary serves as an illustrative example. The punishments that black women received kept them away from their families and off the job market for longer periods than was true of equally guilty whites. This was especially true of the criminal justice system in Maryland when the legislature decided in 1836 that free blacks guilty of second serious offenses could be sold into term slavery with the length of time specified in lieu of incarceration. An 1858 act extended the harsh punishment to petty larceny involving as little as five dollars. A guilty verdict could result in five years of bondage. In other cases, failures to pay lawful debts and taxes could also result in sales to the highest bidder and the subsequent loss of freedom.[76]

Ironically, although a deterrent to crime for many was the fear of being incarcerated or enslaved, on rare occasions women indentured them-

Table 3.6
Prison Population in Eighth Ward, Baltimore, Maryland, by Color, Sex, and Length of Sentences, 1860

Inmates	Number of Inmates	Total Length of Sentences	Average Length of Sentence
White Women	9	15.5	1 yrs 8 mos
White Men	308	847.5	2 yrs 9 mos
Black Women	13	53.0	4 yrs 1 mo
Black Men	96	424.0	4 yrs 5 mos

Source: Ralph Clayton, *Slavery, Slaveholding, and the Free Black Population of Antebellum Baltimore* (Bowie, MD: Heritage, 1993), 53.

selves for five years or longer. Still others entered slavery voluntarily. Ordinarily, adults bound their children out when they could not afford to care for them properly or wanted their offspring to gain specific skills through apprenticeships. It was unusual for adults with children to indenture themselves along with their children. The petitions of indentures do not always state specific reasons for these choices, but poverty seems to be the primary cause. Life was extraordinarily difficult for many poor black female heads of households with dependent children, and the indentures assured basic necessities and helped them avoid further devastating economic challenges.[77]

Even more rare than the adult indentures were petitions for enslavement. In 1859, a sixteen-year-old mulatto, Lucy Andrews, mother of a four-month-old infant in South Carolina, believed she could not support herself from earnings during brief spates of work; therefore, she asked the legislature to pass an act authorizing her enslavement. Two years later Andrews again asked to be enslaved. The 1861 petition said bondage provided the "benefit of a master, protector & friend." The Committee on Colored Population recommended accommodating her and reported the same to the House of Representatives. Similar petitions came from Sally Scott, a twenty-two-year-old North Carolinian and mother of an eleven-month-old child. North Carolinian Eliza Hassell, aged twenty-five, and Kissiah Trueblood, a twenty-three-year-old Mississippian, also asked their state legislators to pass acts for their enslavement. Certainly, enslavement was not an option that very many impoverished free women exercised.[78]

Most sought other alternatives, but economic deprivation literally sent some women to the poorhouse as was the case of Ann Brown, a twenty-two-year-old Delaware-born woman, who entered the Philadelphia Alms House, March 9, 1846. She gave birth to a son, Issac, and said his father was at sea. The author Harriet Wilson also spent some time in the poorhouse, but her circumstances differed in that Wilson was married while Brown was unmarried. They, like other women admitted to alms houses, had few alternatives.[79]

A cursory review of records of women admitted to the Philadelphia Alms House Hospital shows that the greater number of deaths were among black women, many of whom were desperately poor. This is also a reflection of their general health conditions when admitted. For example, Hannah Burton was too "sick to give any acct. of herself" when taken in January 15, 1846, and died four days later. The forty-year-old widowed Maria Albert, who suffered from dropsy, died the day of admission.[80]

Peggy Scott of St. James's Goose Creek, Berkeley County, South Carolina, "was a poor woman—had no husband or friends to take care of her" and never made it to the poorhouse. She died suddenly on April 12, 1857. John Packer, owner of the plantation where Scott lived and worked, petitioned the court to recover costs "for his time trouble and expense" related to her death and burial. Scott was a woman without links to the free black community through benevolent organizations, significant aspects of the black community's infrastructure.[81]

The history of black women's societies, which were much more than charitable organizations, begins in the eighteenth century. Antebellum Philadelphia was the home of more than one hundred such organizations, and approximately fifty benevolent societies existed in New York City at the time. Members of the organizations, which were quite diverse in scope, serving social, political, and economic functions, contributed modest sums to keep members afloat in times of need, especially illnesses and deaths. The high morbidity and mortality rates took great tolls on the organizations' meager treasuries.[82]

In 1822, members of the Daughters of Africa Society in Philadelphia received $1.50 per week in sick benefits. Two years later, a committee suggested that "sick members ought to receive one dollar fifty cents a week for too weeks." A similar measure in 1827 restricted benefits to widows. The organization paid ten dollars upon the death of a spouse one time, regardless of the number of marriages and subsequent deaths of spouses. Given the high mortality rate among African American children, it is understandable that the society made loans repayable in three months for defraying the cost of funerals rather than assume portions of the expense. The club's assets were too limited to do otherwise.[83]

A noticeable void exists in the published scholarship about black women's benevolent organizations in the Lower South, thereby making comparisons with those in the North and Upper South impossible. While it is known that black benevolent societies in New Orleans may have been organized as early as the eighteenth century, it is not known if they were open to women. If women founded separate societies, their records are not readily available.[84]

There is also a dearth of information about Charleston, the home of more than one organization for black men. The Friendly Moralist Society, founded in 1838, offers insight about black benevolence in Charleston toward women. It did not overlook the widows of its deceased members. Ordinarily the men met monthly, but they held a special meeting on January 17, 1842, to discuss the case of the widowed Mrs. Gordon and her family. The men agreed to give her ten dollars, a generous gift considering she had no claim on the organization, whose members received $1.50 per week in cases of their own illness.[85]

The organization's action reflected both respect for a deceased member and recognition of his widow's financial distress, but it could not offer unlimited support. The same committee that awarded Mrs. Gordon ten dollars met September 18, 1846, and decided that Edward Cotton's widow should be "taken on the County immediately." If she received public assistance, the society could close out its activities by the end of the quarter. The committee also discussed the tuition of a deceased member's children and recommended that the youngsters "be placed in some other school." In short, limited resources determined how much assistance the society could give to people who paid no dues.[86]

The minutes from a special meeting in June 1847 reveal the organization's continued willingness to assist widows, especially if they were not in financial distress. One widow, unlike many of her poverty-stricken contemporaries, belonged to the "monied interest of the Society." In this case, assistance did not involve any financial outlay. As a result, one member urged the others to use "all of their abilities . . . in making the safest and most profitable investments of her funds."[87]

In addition to the charitable concerns of the benevolent societies, they were stabilizing influences in times of sickness or death, and the organizations served as fora for discussing matters of importance to the black community. Group-centered economic oppression forced members of organizations to focus on self-help and community improvement. Uplifting and assuring the economic survival of blacks individually and as a race were paramount.

When reviewing the labor force activities of free black women, it is clear that the economic well-being of many free women was precarious, while others enjoyed a more stable status. It is also evident that some of the daughters of Africa used their talents and financial acumen exceedingly well to free themselves from economic insecurity. Whenever possible, they tried to prevent their offspring and other blacks from succumbing beneath a "load of heavy iron pots and kettles."[88]

4

"Knowledge is power"

Educational and Cultural Achievements

We that are free are expected to be the means of bringing them out of Slavery & how can we do it, unless we have proper educational advantages? We must get the knowledge, & use it well.

Matilda A. Jones

"O, ye daughters of Africa, awake! Awake! Arise!" wrote Maria W. Stewart, who believed the salvation of black Americans could be attained best through education. "No longer sleep nor slumber, but distinguish yourselves. Show forth to the world that ye are endowed with noble and exalted faculties." Railing against burying talents under mean servile labor, she called for assiduous intellectual development. In her opinion, death was preferable to drudgery because "continual hard labor deadens the energies of the soul, and benumbs the faculties of the mind." In the same vein, "uncultivated soil" yields "thorns and thistles." Stewart was adamant about breaking the chains of ignorance shackling the mind in ways analogous to the iron fetters used to restrain enslaved women and men. Education freed the mind, fostered the ability to recognize societal ills, and made it possible to envision the creation of a better world.[1]

Ordinarily, the manner in which free people learned to read and write receives little attention when compared with the extraordinary efforts of enslaved women and men to gain literacy. Discrimination and limited access to schools across geographical regions made it especially difficult for many free women to acquire literacy. Nevertheless, they found ways to succeed, used literacy to earn a living, and made creative use of their knowledge. Once some women acquired an education, they moved beyond individual aspirations towards a social and political consciousness in the interest of empowering their people. Having accepted the challenging responsibility of serving the race, they often involved themselves in liberating their sisters and brothers in bondage.[2]

Maria W. Stewart knew that many whites believed Africans were "an inferior race of beings." Jane A. Crouch, a free-born Virginian, was also aware of the myth and learned early on that "this was a one Sided world," with domination "on the white Side." As a result, "I tried to be the exception," Crouch explained, "and get as near that [white] side as possible as far as *information* [was] concerned." Perhaps Stewart, Crouch, and other well-read Americans were familiar with Thomas Jefferson's ideas about persons of African descent as published in his *Notes on the State of Virginia* in 1787.[3]

"Comparing them by their faculties of memory, reason, and imagination, it appears to me," wrote Jefferson, "that in memory they are equal to the whites; in reason much inferior." He thought blacks were "dull, tasteless, and anomalous." Jefferson argued that it would be "right to make great allowances for the differences of condition, of education, of conversation, of the sphere in which they move." Yet the Virginia aristocrat claimed he never encountered a black who "had uttered a thought above the level of plain narration" or had painted or written anything worthy of the "dignity of criticism." Americans less learned than Jefferson accepted these ideas that resurfaced with regularity.[4]

Added to assertions of innate inferiority were claims of high rates of insanity among free blacks, according to the 1840 Census of the United States, and notions that women were less intelligent than men. Sojourner Truth, an illiterate woman, appeared to accept the idea about women's limited intellectual capacity when she said, "If a woman have a pint and man a quart, why cant she have her little pint full?" Truth only asked that women receive their due. "You need not be afraid to give us our rights for fear we will take too much," she told men in the audience at the May 1851 Women's Rights Convention in Akron, Ohio. "We can't take more than our pint 'll hold," added Truth with a twinge of sarcasm.[5]

Decades earlier, Maria W. Stewart had suggested that blacks lift themselves up through education. Education was more than mere literacy. It defied racist stereotypes while embracing an orientation toward achievement and social responsibility. It also expanded employment opportunities and commanded respectability. "Knowledge is power," said Stewart repeatedly. Moreover, she placed the responsibility for acquiring this power and creating children's thirst for knowledge on women. Stewart, a childless widow, knew many blacks had few resources for high schools or academies, but she believed they should give their children the "first rudiments of useful knowledge." She proposed hiring private instructors to teach the "higher branches."[6]

Stewart's dream of creating a powerful educated populace was possible through the combined efforts of women pooling their earnings, or uniting in raising money to build high schools. Ultimately, her objective was to develop generations of girls and boys whose knowledge would surpass their parents'. Stewart believed women had a special role in this endeavor. In her 1831 tract, "Religion and the Pure Principles of Morality, the Sure Foundation on Which We Must Build," she asked, "What examples have ye set before the rising generation?" and "What foundation have ye laid for generations yet unborn?"[7]

Stewart's argument is analogous to the "Republican Mother" concept. Following the American Revolution, the idea gained public acceptance and reverberated among many white women who believed their patriotic duty was to prepare their sons for citizenship. Women did not vote but were capable of molding the electorate's moral character. This political socialization process involved interest and participation in civic affairs beyond family needs to benefit the nation. Stewart envisioned black women as teachers of the race and nurturers, "racial mothers," who socialized children to be good citizens who in turn would elevate their people. Ultimately, they and the society would benefit.[8]

Although free black men were generally denied the right to participate in electoral politics, Stewart believed preparation to serve her people was important. Uplifting blacks through education was a burning ambition for many free women since it was more immediately at hand than the ballot. Besides, education would serve a useful purpose until slavery and ignorance disappeared. "I am of a strong opinion that the day on which we unite, heart and soul, and turn our attention to knowledge and improvement," wrote Stewart, "will be the day the hissing and reproach among the nations of the earth against us will cease."[9]

If education was to be the panacea for respectability and racial uplift, effective teachers were essential. But how would free black women, especially in the South, meet the challenge? Access to education was uneven but available in some areas, such as Baltimore, Maryland. The ambitions of several black women, including Mary Elizabeth Lange, Marie Magdaleine Balas, and Marie Rosine Boegue, who longed to dedicate their lives to God and teaching their people, coincided with ideals of the French Sulpician priest Jacques Marie Hector Joubert. The women sought a more permanent school arrangement than his Sunday classes. James Whitfield, archbishop of Baltimore, sanctioned the plans that resulted in establishing the Sisters of Providence on June 5, 1829. The order received papal recognition October 2, 1831, and the Oblate Sisters of Providence made significant contributions to the education of black children. That these aspirations developed in Baltimore is not surprising. The city, dubbed the "Rome of the United States," was the home of the Carmelites, the Visitation Sisters of Georgetown, and the Sisters of Charity of St. Joseph, established between 1790 and 1809.[10]

The mission of the Oblate Sisters included the religious instruction of black children, especially girls. Since their aim was to proselytize through education, the Sisters established the School for Colored Girls at 5 St. Mary's Court, which evolved into St. Frances Academy. The theologian Thaddeus J. Posey noted the contributions of Sister Mary Langue, the first elected superior, when he described her "steady, persevering commitment not only to educate those who were considered unteachable, but to nurture in them the self confidence essential for them to become productive citizens."[11]

The Sisters offered a basic curriculum along with religion, French, and "Rule of Conduct for Young Ladies." The nuns, who served as role models for the girls, encouraged the study of fine arts and introduced music into their curriculum. The Sisters also met the educational needs of many black women by conducting a night school as well as offering vocational and career training. Ultimately, the influence of the Oblate Sisters had a long-term impact on blacks in Baltimore and elsewhere.[12]

Educational opportunities became more remote for free blacks in several of the southern states following the 1829 incendiary publication of the *Appeal, in Four Articles,* written by the free-born David Walker. It outlines the wretchedness of blacks as a result of bondage, ignorance, religion, and colonization. Walker intended to reach enslaved blacks and encourage them to seize their freedom regardless of its cost in blood. Death, he wrote, was better than slavery. "Kill," he intoned, "or be killed." The militant antislavery publication frightened whites who feared the slaves would indeed follow Walker's advice. Whites denounced the work, and the editor of a Boston newspaper said it was "one of the most wicked and inflammatory productions that ever issued from the press." Whites tried to halt the pamphlet's distribution and considered it the insurrectionary railings of a free literate man.[13]

The *Appeal* represented a divide in the abolition movement between moral suasion and militancy. Two years after its appearance, *The Liberator*, an influential abolitionist newspaper published by William Lloyd Garrison, made its debut. In the hands of literate slaves, according to proslavery whites, the *Appeal* or *The Liberator* could be a catalyst for rebellion. Whites who feared the potentially lethal nature of literacy also believed the Bible in the hands of literate slaves could be incendiary. To further exacerbate their anxieties, in 1831 the literate enslaved preacher Nat Turner led the most deadly rebellion against bondage to date in the United States. Many whites believed Turner's religion and literacy were incentives for the uprising.

As a result, some southern states passed legislation prohibiting the instruction of blacks regardless of their status. In 1831, the Virginia Assembly enacted a law that forbade all gatherings of blacks at schools, churches, or other places for the purpose of instruction "under whatsoever pretext." The penalty for violating the law was up to twenty lashes for free blacks. White offenders could be fined as much as fifty dollars and receive two months in prison. The expansiveness of antebellum laws against black literacy has been overstated. Only four states were consistent in their prohibitions. This is not to minimize white anxiety, however, over black literacy or deliberate interference with blacks' chances to learn to read and write.[14]

Notwithstanding the greater number of legal prohibitions and slaveholders' anxieties about literacy for slaves, free blacks in the South were never completely without access to education following the Turner rebellion. Clandestine schools began operation. Additionally, the Sisters of the Holy Family, founded by the free-born Henriette Delille in 1842, played a role in educating blacks in New Orleans. In keeping their vow to give "charitable assistance to the poor and unfortunate of their race, bond and free," the Sisters have opened nearly fifty schools since 1842 and enjoyed successes comparable to the Oblate Sisters.[15]

Besides the institutions established by churches, individual blacks conducted schools both clandestinely and openly across the South before the Civil War. The teachers, often free women, introduced enslaved and free children to the basic rudiments of education and bolstered their self-esteem. Moreover, letters written in the 1850s and 1860s as an English class assignment by boys at *Société Catholique pour l'instruction des orphelins dans l'indigence* in New Orleans provide a cornucopia of data about the teachers' instructions and students' comprehension of historical and political occurrences. A study of the letters by the historian Mary Niall Mitchell argues that the assignment educated the children to the possibilities of establishing themselves as prospering citizens in places far away from New Orleans. Knowledge of black migration from the United States after the passage of the Compromise of 1850 and its more stringent fugitive slave clause made Haiti and Mexico the children's destinations of choice.[16]

Unfortunately, only the boys' compositions have survived; however, it is reasonable to believe that schoolgirls had similar assignments. To be sure, they were as aware of the effects of the Compromise of 1850 as they were of New Orleans being a port of debarkation for African Americans fleeing from the law's perniciousness.

In 1835, Susan Paul, a free-born teacher in antebellum Boston, memorialized the nearly seven-year-old James Jackson, one of her pupils who died October 30, 1833, in a didactic publication, *Memoir of James Jackson*. Paul touted Jackson's moral consciousness and humanitarian qualities while encouraging young readers to imitate his admirable behavior.[17]

In eulogizing the child, Paul recounted a lesson wherein she introduced the subject of slavery and emphasized its abusive nature by telling the boys and girls that, while they were in school, enslaved children were working "very hard." Enslaved children, she told her students, had neither opportunities to attend school and study their letters nor did they learn of Jesus Christ. In short, they were not liberated physically or mentally. Considering their deprived status, Paul encouraged her pupils to pray for their enslaved contemporaries. Paul's lesson served several purposes. It made the schoolchildren or readers aware, or reinforced their awareness, of the contrast between their lives and those of enslaved children, encouraged sympathy toward the less fortunate, and nudged the schoolchildren to appreciate their own educational opportunities more fully. Finally, Paul's lesson blends her notions about the efficacy of literacy with civil religion or moral duty and the possibility of social progress.[18]

Perhaps Mary Peake, a free black woman and resident of Hampton, Virginia, shared Susan Paul's ideology as she "attached prime importance to the training of the rising generation." Peake and her husband lived a short distance from the town's main thoroughfare, Queen Street, and diagonally across a lane from a fashionable academy for whites. She ignored prohibitions and began teaching enslaved and free children in the 1840s. Local authorities must have noticed the comings and goings of pupils but did not interfere. During the Civil War, Peake's health deteriorated as her enrollment increased to more than fifty pupils during the day and over twenty students at night. Between "terrible paroxysms of coughing," she continued instructions, selflessly "giving her strength to help her people." An American Missionary Association (AMA) official, Lewis C. Lockwood, commented, "It was beautiful, though sad, to see her... when too sick to sit, lying on her bed, surrounded by her scholars, teaching them to read." When admonished by William Coan of the AMA to dismiss her pupils, Peake refused and helped her people until she died. She believed it was her responsibility to provide an education "for eternity as well as for [the present] time."[19]

A fellow teacher in Alexandria, Jane A. Crouch was less zealous. The sixth of eleven children born in 1835 to a free mother and enslaved father who eventually purchased himself, Crouch entered school when only six years old and learned to read, write, and "cipher to some extent." Once she opened a school, unlike Peake, Crouch "took care not to take in any slave children." Her "will was good to do so," but she feared arrest and decided not to "run the risk." As a child she had attended a school operated by Sylvia M. Rogers, "a colored lady... considered to be an excellent teacher," which local police forced to close. Although Crouch choose "the ounce of prevention rather than the pound of cure," she made some progress towards uplifting the race. Curiously, Crouch was less hesitant about defying the law by maintaining a school of forty free pupils than by including some enslaved children. Nevertheless, Crouch combated the "one-sidedness" of American society, and as a lifelong student she was ever conscientious of self-improvement for all.[20]

While Stewart was vocal about the social responsibility of black women to their race, Crouch never specifically articulated a commitment when drafting what she called "a rough Sketch" of her life. However, it is implied in her own case and stated clearly in comments about her daughter. The veteran teacher insisted that her thirteen-year-old child receive a quality education. "I have her under a master, and am trying to give [her] a thorough course of training," wrote Crouch, "so that her usefulness may be a blessing to her race."[21]

In the South where schools were unavailable or local enforcement measures thwarted ambitions, blacks sought alternatives. For example, Nancy Ruffin moved from Richmond, Virginia, to Boston where her children attended school. Michigan's public and private schools dating back to 1842 beckoned to others. Meta Pelham's family migrated from Petersburg, Virginia, to Detroit where she became the first black woman to graduate from Central High School. And Fannie Richards, Pelham's contemporary from Fredricksburg, Virginia, became the first black woman teacher in the Detroit school system.[22]

The existence of educational opportunities for blacks in the North were uneven at best. In 1827 *Freedom's Journal* conducted a survey covering seven locations from Portland, Maine, where the black population numbered 900, to Philadelphia, where the black population was 15,000, and found that the number of schools and teachers remained pitifully small. Two towns included in the survey had no facilities for blacks. In other instances, racial discrimination dissuaded some blacks from attending the available schools. Persons unwilling to endure racism established private schools or moved to more hospitable locations. But paying tuition or relocating was prohibitive for most free blacks.[23]

Public schools were available to blacks in Philadelphia, but attendance was low. No doubt some children stayed home to care for others younger than themselves, to assist parents, or to work elsewhere for the family's support. Still other children were apprenticed and received the basic rudiments of education in the homes of persons who bound them. Finally, some children simply did not have the necessary clothing to attend school. The mutual aid societies organized by black women rendered assistance to orphaned children, but the general poverty of the organizations limited their benevolence. The deserving poor were frequently seen as social outcasts, and this probably contributed to the high rate of absenteeism in schools.[24]

Theodore Hershberg studied free- and slave-born blacks in Philadelphia, based in part on an 1838 Pennsylvania Abolition Society report, the 1847 census of 11,600 households in the city, and the 1850 U.S. Population and Manufacturing census. He found that only 25 percent of the free-born children were in school. The number of former slaves in the sample had slightly fewer children than their free-born contemporaries, but the percentage of their children attending school was "considerably greater" than those from the free-born households.[25]

Having been denied access to education, former slaves probably had fewer objections to poor, segregated facilities and limited curricular offerings than did free persons with viable alternatives. It is also conceivable that freedpersons considered conditions in the North better than those generally available to free persons in the South and were more inclined to accept them. It is not unusual for migrant and immigrant populations to measure progress vertically when comparing their old and new situations. The horizontal gauge of progress gives a better comparison with contemporaries surrounding migrants or immigrants in the new environment.

People with options refused to accept racial discrimination. Frederick Douglass's daughter Rosetta attended Seward Seminary because

Rochester's public schools were closed to blacks until 1857. Bostonian George Putnam withdrew his children from a segregated public school and relocated them. Wealthy Philadelphia sailmaker James Forten objected to segregated schools in the city; therefore, his granddaughter Charlotte received private tutoring and attended school in Salem, Massachusetts, between 1853 and 1856. In Salem, she boarded with Amy Matilda and Charles Lenox Remond. Remond, a well-known abolitionist and brother of Sarah Parker Remond, could empathize with Forten since his parents, John and Nancy Remond, had moved from Salem to Newport, Rhode Island, in the mid-1830s so their children "might not suffer from the discriminatory practices found in the high schools of Salem."[26]

While Forten was in Salem, the conditions in Pennsylvania hardly changed. In 1856 her cousin Hattie Purvis reported that she tutored her younger siblings at home because "there was no school [in Bayberry, Pennsylvania] . . . for them except a *Public School*," where they sat by themselves "because their faces are not as white as the rest of the scholars." It made her "blood boil" to think of it. When Purvis's own private tutoring ended, she entered a New Jersey boarding school run by Theodore D. Weld, his wife Angelina, and sister-in-law Sarah Grimké. At Eagleswood, Purvis mingled with the children and grandchildren of white abolitionists. Although boarding away from home was not an ideal situation, she established a meaningful friendship with peers, including Ellen Wright, who eventually married William Lloyd Garrison.[27]

Sending children to private schools or relocating them was not the only option black parents exercised. In situations where blatant discrimination existed, blacks sometimes boycotted the school to force change, or they demanded a role in policy making. Blacks were unrelenting in their efforts to desegregate Boston's public schools. According to William Cooper Nell, a black activist in the city, "It was the community's women who had really been the unwavering backbone of the struggle." They had kept the flame alive while weaving "bright visions for the future."[28]

Benjamin Roberts sued the city of Boston in 1849 on behalf of Sarah, his five-year-old daughter, who walked past five white elementary schools before reaching the overcrowded and badly deteriorated Smith Grammar School for blacks. Roberts based the suit on an 1845 statute saying children excluded unlawfully from the city's schools were eligible for relief. The well-known Charles Sumner along with Robert Morris, the first African American lawyer to try a case before a jury, represented the plaintiff in *Roberts v. City of Boston* (1849) before the Supreme Judicial Court of Massachusetts headed by Chief Justice Lemuel Shaw. Sumner argued that Sarah Roberts was disadvantaged by attending a separate school, and that white children were also harmed by segregation. "Their hearts, while yet tender with childhood, are necessarily hardened by this conduct," said Sumner, and "their subsequent lives, perhaps, bear enduring testimony to this legalized uncharitableness."[29]

Justice Shaw, a former member of the Boston School Committee, disagreed and maintained that segregation was for the good of both black and white children. In his opinion, the School Committee, which supported "separate but equal," was solely responsible for the operation of the city's schools. Roberts did not win, but it was not for the lack of support from the community's women and men or the legal team.[30]

The negative decision precipitated a massive petition and publicity campaign to seek relief from the legislature. The Roberts case received widespread attention, and that helped to sustain interest over the next few years. Black women and men believed equal access to educational opportunities was the key to freedom. The state legislature heard the plea of its black citizens and ended segregation in Boston's public schools in 1855. In assessing the struggle initiated on behalf of his daughter, Benjamin Roberts, a printer by profession, wrote, "Who among us can refrain from giving vent to his feelings in the highest exultation over these remarkable events? But amid all this we have important duties to perform. We must be true to each other. We must encourage each other. We must devote our energies, if we mean [to achieve] success, to the acquirement of *education*, which is power." In all probability acceptance of the adage "Knowledge is power," and that it could be used to uplift black females and males of all ages, helped to sustain the black Bostonians as they dismantled segregation in the city's schools.[31]

Not all northern schools practiced racial discrimination; however, access to integrated schools did not mean that the atmosphere was conducive to learning. Black students faced open biases and covert slights. Sarah Remond remarked that nothing her parents had taught her prepared her for the scorn and contempt of a hostile world. The adolescent Charlotte Forten remained amazed that African Americans were not misanthropes after enduring such trials. She concluded:

> Surely we have everything to make us hate mankind. I have met girls in the schoolroom [who] have been thoroughly kind and cordial to me—perhaps the next day met them in the street—they feared to recognize me; these I can but regard now with scorn and contempt, once I liked them, believing them incapable of such measures. Others give the most distant recognition possible. I, of course, acknowledge no such recognitions, and they soon cease entirely.[32]

Forten treated callous classmates with indifference while Maritcha Lyons, another a sixteen-year-old schoolgirl, addressed insults in a more proactive manner. Lyons, whose family had relocated from New York, described herself as the "observed of all observers" in her Providence, Rhode Island, school. No doubt white students were aware of the appeal by Lyons's mother to the governor for her daughter's admission, which in itself drew attention. Lyons tolerated affronts, and by the time she reached her senior year, "The iron had entered my soul," she admitted. She never forgot that she "had to sue for a privilege which any but a colored girl could have without asking."[33]

Laboring under the intense "observations" of teachers and peers exacted courage and careful attention to interpersonal relations. "Most of the classmates were more or less friendly," remembered Lyons; however, "if any girl tried to put 'on airs,'" she found a way to make her own academic achievements the topic of conversation because she "never had less than the highest marks." Lyons defied pernicious labels and flaunted her scholastic superiority. She met rudeness with a braggadocio that her classmates may have regarded as offensive. She may not have considered herself to be "putting on airs" since her achievements were genuine. However, it is difficult to believe the one-upsmanship created goodwill among her peers.[34]

Charlotte Forten responded to racism by appearing to ignore her peers' crass behavior. She labeled their rudeness as "trifles" when compared to the "great, public wrongs" that blacks, especially slaves, endured. "But," she wrote, "to those who experience them, these apparent trifles are more wearing and discouraging." Beyond creating unnecessary stress, students encountering such conditions daily recognized the "volumes of deceit and heartlessness" in others, which taught them, according to Forten, "a lesson of suspicion and distrust."[35]

"Suspicion and distrust" in response to "deceit and heartlessness" neither destroyed barriers between black and white classmates, nor did it foster the kind of camaraderie that is legendary among schoolgirls. Color and class boundaries prevented blacks from enjoying friendships with whites comparable to those that many nineteenth-century white women cherished from their school days. Given the circumstances, success in school was a remarkable feat for black women.[36]

Barriers to their success were everywhere, and discrimination was not confined to public schools or schoolgirls. Amanda Berry Smith's experience as a thirteen-year-old among her white contemporaries in a Shrewsbury, Pennsylvania, Sabbath school reflects the extent to which racism existed. The social custom of not allowing blacks to recite before whites interfered with her return to work in a timely fashion. Smith resorted to an ingenious plan:

> I thought I [would] change my seat in the class, maybe that [would] help me, and sat in the first end of the pew, as the leader would always commence on the first end and go down. When I sat in the first end, then he would commence at the lower end and come up and leave me last. Then I sat between two, thinking he would lead the two above me and then lead me in turn, but he would lead the two and then jump across me and lead all the others and lead me last.

Her frustration was understandable. She decided to forgo the lessons and ended her formal education.[37]

Unlike Smith, the black females who attended Prudence Crandall's school in Canterbury, Connecticut, did not face hostility from their classmates or teacher. Crandall, who had a well-established reputation as an educator, admitted the seventeen-year-old Sarah Harris to her school in 1832. When white parents protested by withdrawing their daughters, Crandall filled their places with African Americans. Had she opened a "college for the spread of contagious diseases," wrote a journalist, the community would not have been more agitated. One insult after another ranged from local merchants refusing to sell Crandall necessary supplies to unknown persons polluting her well with manure. Crandall was arrested for violating the hastily passed 1833 "Black Law" prohibiting the founding of schools for blacks. The town's hostility eventually forced the Quaker woman to give up her idea of educating blacks.[38]

Racial discrimination and physical intimidation did not force free blacks to abandon their desire to free themselves and their people from ignorance. Nor did their educational quest languish. When confronted with these obstacles, they turned to private tutors, sent their children to school elsewhere, or migrated to cities with accessible schools.[39]

Otherwise, they fought for a voice in policy-making decisions in schools established by whites or founded their own institutions. The experiences of Sarah Mapps Douglass, a Philadelphia teacher dedicated to the educational uplift of her race, are illustrative. The privately educated woman began her professional career in 1820 when she was only a little older than many of her pupils. Maturity beyond her years and dedication to helping her people won the confidence of the Philadelphia Female Anti-Slavery Society (PFASS), and the organization gave Douglass financial support for her school. Such a situation set the stage for a power relationship between the white-dominated board, whose dollars helped maintain the facility, and the black instructional staff.[40]

Blacks appreciated schools founded by organizations such as the PFASS, but they were not above demanding a voice in policy matters and teacher selection. One of the earliest records of black intervention on behalf of their children was in a New York Manumission Society's African Free School staffing decision. In 1832 blacks kept their children home after learning one teacher, Charles C. Andrews, had "decided colonization views," favoring the resettlement of free and freed blacks outside the United States. When blacks urged the trustees to dismiss Andrews, he resigned.[41]

Afterward, community leaders pressured the trustees to hire a black replacement, and the society agreed. As the enrollment increased, additional schools opened primarily with black teachers. The next step was to influence curricular decisions. This proved less successful since the private organization transferred its schools to the Public School Society, which made radical changes without considering input from the black leaders. In the reorganization, the "African Free Schools" became known as "Colored Schools." This was less devastating than reducing all schools, except one, to primary or elementary institutions. However, black mothers and fathers responded to the change by withdrawing their children and enrolling them elsewhere.[42]

Benjamin S. Hughes, a teacher dismissed in 1836 by the Public School Society trustees, founded his own academy for "Colored Children of Both Sexes" in the undercroft of St. Philip's Church. Among his pupils were the children of social activist Thomas L. Jennings, whose daughter Elizabeth witnessed New York's "school wars" from two vantage points. Her siblings were caught up in the struggle for control in the 1830s, and she became a teacher before the "great school wars" ended. In the 1850s, Jennings worked as interim principal of School No. 1 operated by New York's Society for the Promotion of Education among Colored Children. As a result, she had a greater understanding of the black community's sustained determination to address the educational needs of its own children.[43]

Sarah Douglass's relationship with the PFASS never escalated to a full-blown struggle with the founding organization as did the one between black New Yorkers and the school societies, yet her concerns about meeting the needs of black children were similar. And the PFASS's interference with Douglass's operation of the school became insufferable. The board "reprimanded" her for permitting children to make up work missed due to illnesses or inclement weather. Also, the board refused to pay an assistant whom Douglass chose. These actions were easily construed as meddling and patronizing behavior by the board.[44]

The PFASS board created uncertainty on the part of parents who believed extenuating circumstances deserved consideration. To ignore what parents considered reasonable made the board appear callous. Such a situation assured the loss of the support, confidence, and perhaps respect of parents who were not privy to the decision-making process. To further exacerbate the problem, the society threatened to relocate the school unless the owner of the building lowered the rent. The combined irritants prompted Douglass's 1840 decision to ask the PFASS to waive its oversight. The society yielded and freed her to run the school without intense scrutiny by people whose views about the needs of black children differed from her own.[45]

By 1853 Douglass was still teaching, but her circumstances differed. She was now in charge of the Girls' Department at Philadelphia's Institute for Colored Youth, a classical high school founded in 1837 by the Society of Friends. Never content with the traditional curriculum, the stellar teacher enrolled in medical classes at the Ladies Institute of Pennsylvania Medical University between 1855 and 1858 in order to introduce new subjects, including physiology, into the Institute for Colored Youth's offerings. A more progressive curriculum meant greater possibilities for its students and the advancement of African Americans.[46]

Following her graduation from Oberlin College in 1865, Fanny Jackson accepted what she deemed "the delightful task of teaching my own people." In the autobiographical *Reminiscences of School Life, and Hints on Teaching,* she recounted an anecdote about John C. Calhoun, who once said that if he could find an African American who could conjugate a Greek verb, he would willingly discard his ideas about the inferiority of blacks. The stellar teacher noted that many students at the Institute for Colored Youth were "mastering Caesar, Virgil, Cicero, Horace and Xenophon's Anabasis." To prepare the students for such studies, New Testament Greek was a vital part of the curriculum.[47]

Based on an 1862 program of study completed by H. Amelia Loguen, daughter of J. M. Loguen, the African Methodist Episcopal Zion bishop of Syracuse, New York, her classes were rigorous and would challenge the notion of black inferiority. Loguen wrote:

Spring has brought with it as usual, the ever dreaded, yearly school examinations, *dreaded* because they are so *very tedious.* Monday I thought of nothing but Chloride of Sodium, Nitrate of Silver detection of arsenic, uses of Zinc etc etc; Tuesday, Parlez-vous francais? Comment-vous appelez-vouz? and Je me porte tres bien, yesterday oh! terrible thought Plane Trigonometry; do you wonder then that last night I dreamed of being in France? After... trying to show that Chemistry is one of the most useful and interesting studies imaginable and lastly I was alone in some queer place trying to accertain the height of a "fort on a distant hill inaccessable on account of an intervening swamp." O! how refreshing on awaking this morning to know that all *such* is for a time past and that vacation is close at hand.

Despite lapses in her letter, Loguen was challenged academically and could use her knowledge to assist in uplifting her people.[48]

Before the Civil War, educational opportunities such as those received by Loguen were limited but readily available at Myrtilla Miner's normal school. In 1851 Miner, a white New Yorker dedicated to the mental and moral uplift of African Americans, founded the school for black women in Washington, D.C., a city with more than 10,000 free blacks. The curriculum included scientific studies, horticulture, and literary subjects. A fine art collection of paintings and engravings along with large library holdings, museum visits, and lectures by well-known people enhanced the students' education.[49]

Along with the steady prodding of students to improve themselves was condescension from Miner, whose patronizing remarks about the need for "bathing all over every day" and indifference to the hospitality offered by poor blacks were offensive. As a result, one student confessed, "I do not like or respect Miss M." Some students dropped out, but the majority stayed. Their objective, to "get the knowledge, & use it well," overshadowed their abhorrence of Miner's insults.[50]

Unlike Miner's Teachers College, which eventually became the University of the District of Columbia Teachers College, Oberlin Collegiate Institute, founded in February 1834 near Elyria, Ohio, was not established for African Americans. However, the historian Carter G. Woodson said Oberlin "did so much for the education of Negroes before the Civil War that it was often spoken of as an institution for the education of the people of color." The college's reputation as an abolitionist stronghold, its commitment to equal access to education, and an excellent curriculum attracted white as well as black students. By 1865, Oberlin had enrolled nearly one hundred black women and men, 2 to 5 percent of the student population.[51]

The black community near the college consisted of residents who had migrated to Ohio in the interest of their children's education. Rebecca Harris and her husband relocated in the 1850s in order for their four

Figure 4.1. Class of 1855, Oberlin College.
Oberlin College Archives, Oberlin, Ohio.

children to attend the college. The parents had worked at a seminary in Michigan that refused to admit their children because of color. Their daughter Blanche graduated from Oberlin in 1860 and began teaching. Their son Thomas graduated several years later and became a physician.[52]

Oberlin offered both preparatory and college courses. Students in the College Department completed admission requirements, including Greek and Latin, in public and private schools, or in the college's preparatory department. The bachelor of arts program was considerably smaller than the preparatory department with an enrollment of 855 in 1860. Many students in the preparatory department never entered the college division. Perhaps they believed their educations were sufficient and left Oberlin, or they enrolled elsewhere.[53]

Among Oberlin's preparatory students was Sarah Kinson, also known as Margru, one of four children on board the Spanish slaver *Amistad* when Joseph Cinqué led a July 1839 mutiny. Following the survivors' 1841 Supreme Court victory, they returned to Africa. Margru and the other children did not reunite with their families; instead, they remained at Kaw Mendi near Freetown, Liberia, with Congregationalist missionaries. One of the missionaries, a Reverend Raymond, concluded that Margru was a "born teacher" and decided to send her to his alma mater for formal training.[54]

While at Oberlin, Margru studied English composition, philosophy, algebra, history of Rome, and physiology. Her ambition was to become a missionary teacher and work in Africa. As a result, she gravitated toward courses that would make her "qualified to do good in the world." Her goals and acceptance of a social responsibility were not unlike that of her African American contemporaries at Oberlin and elsewhere.[55]

Most Oberlin women, without regard for color, enrolled in the two-year "Ladies' Course," which, unlike the college department, did not require Latin, Greek, or higher mathematics. In 1850, Lucy Stanton from Cleveland, Ohio, was the program's first black woman to graduate. Over the next decade, ten of the sixteen African American graduates were women in the Ladies' Course. Rosetta Douglass, the daughter of Anna and Frederick Douglass, attended Oberlin but is not listed among its graduates. Douglass, like other students who do not appear to have graduated, may have continued her education elsewhere.[56]

One of the college's most distinguished graduates is Fanny Jackson, also known as Fanny Jackson-Coppin following her marriage to Levi Jenkins Coppin in 1881. She had demonstrated an eagerness to learn once freed from slavery in the 1840s as a six-year-old child. At fourteen years of age, the self-supporting Jackson entered a working agreement with George H. Calvert whereby she received private lessons several days a week. This preparation, along with limited attendance in the public schools of Rhode Island, enabled her to pass an 1859 entrance examination at the State Normal School in Bristol.[57]

Jackson entered Oberlin in 1860 for further study and to fulfill her life-long ambition of uplifting her race through education. She, like Maria W. Stewart, often said "Knowledge is power." Jackson explained the standards of excellence she held for herself when she wrote, "I never rose to recite in my classes at Oberlin but I felt that I had the honor of the whole African race on my shoulders. I felt that, should I fail, it would be ascribed to the fact that I was colored."[58]

Jackson's remarks emanate from her knowledge of prejudices such as those espoused by Thomas Jefferson in his *Notes*. Charlotte Forten never entertained the idea that blacks were naturally inferior but worried that limited access to opportunities would prevent them from eradicating inequities. The weight of the whole race's honor on Jackson's shoulders was a great burden for a person to bear, and her comments speak volumes about the meaning of being black in a prejudiced society.[59]

Ordinarily racism was not a problem at Oberlin, but "Wildfire," better known as Mary Edmonia Lewis, the daughter of a Chippewa Indian woman and an African American man, faced unusual hostilities from the local community following a still unexplained incident involving the mysterious illnesses of several students. Lewis was accused of poisoning them. John Mercer Langston, a black alumnus, defended her and won an acquittal. By that time Lewis had completed the preparatory requirements and entered the liberal arts program, but the school refused to allow her to graduate in 1862.[60]

Later, Edmonia Lewis earned an international reputation as the first major sculptress of African American heritage. Her bust of Colonel Robert Gould Shaw received accolades from Harriet Hosmer, a neoclassical sculptor, who praised the finely crafted work. Lewis financed a trip to Europe for further study through the sale of plaster copies and other pieces. Over time she shifted from sculpting white abolitionists to creating pieces representing African Americans. Lewis's *The Freed Woman and Child* portrays the subject kneeling in prayer after learning of the emancipation of her and the child in her arms. The artist said the inspiration for the piece came from her desire to recognize her African American heritage.[61]

Lewis's unfortunate story highlights the experiences of a student whose culture differed from that of the majority. Racial prejudice forced students of color to endure insults unlike their white peers. Despite adversity, the idea of getting knowledge and using it well remained paramount.

Sarah Mapps Douglass penned a pithy reminder in a student's album to reenforce the idea of a social responsibility to blacks. She wrote, "Thou hast youth, health, talents! So use these precious gifts that when the Great Householder calls for an account of thou stewardship thou mayest return him his own with usury." Thoughts of accountability at the bar of God probably dissuaded her students from misusing talents or ignoring social responsibilities to others.[62]

The idea of social responsibility to the race is further highlighted by a look at Sarah Jane Woodson, born in Chillicothe, Ohio, in 1825, who came of age in a devoutly religious home where she was exposed to ideas about self-help, black nationalism, and duty to her people. Woodson and her family had participated in organizing their own Methodist church when faced with discrimination shortly after arriving in Ohio in 1821. Several years later, her older brother Lewis founded an African Education and Benefit Society for children who were denied admission to the public schools in Chillicothe. Before long, Sarah's family and other free blacks established their own community complete with a school and church in Jackson County, Ohio.[63]

Considering her background, it is not surprising that Sarah Woodson would receive a formal education and use it in the interests of her people. In fact, Lewis by this time was a trustee at Wilberforce University, a Meth-

Figure 4.2. *Urania*, by Mary Edmonia Lewis.
Oberlin College Archives, Oberlin, Ohio.

odist institution in Xenia, Ohio, named in honor of the British abolitionist, wrote, "Advantages are opening for educational purposes among
us, but we must prepare our minds to avail ourselves to these advantages; and if we cannot adorn our children's bodies with costly attire, let
us provide to adorn their minds with that jewel that will elevate, ennoble,
and rescue the bodies of our long injured race from the shackles of bondage, and their minds from the trammels of ignorance and vice." Sarah
sought to meet his challenge as a teacher in several black communities
in Ohio between 1856 and 1866 before accepting the positions of "Pre-
ceptress of English and Latin" and "Lady Principal and Matron" at Wilberforce University. As a member of the faculty, Woodson was integral to
the preparation of students.[64]

When the students' formal education ended, work for their people as
teachers began. It was one of the few professional occupations open to

women, and "the community's stress on education led most educated black women to become educators," writes scholar Gayle T. Tate in her study of black women's political activism in antebellum America. Among the well-known teachers was Elizabeth Jennings, who after years of study and work, completed requirements for certification at New York's Colored Normal School by 1859. Frederick Douglass touted her as "the most learned of our female teachers in the city of New York." Jennings's interest was not in winning accolades but in expanding the minds of her pupils.[65]

Jennings had many like-minded colleagues. Fannie Jackson graduated from Oberlin in 1865 and accepted a position at Philadelphia's Institute for Colored Youth. An 1862 Oberlin alumna, Mary Jane Patterson, the first African American woman to receive the B.A. degree from a recognized college, was Jackson's assistant at the institute, which eventually became Cheyney University of Pennsylvania. By 1870, Patterson had become principal of the first high school for blacks in Washington, D.C. Her sisters, Chanie and Emeline, also Oberlin alumnae, worked as teachers in Washington.[66]

Charlotte Forten, a contemporary of Jackson and Jennings, graduated from the Salem Normal School in 1856 and accepted a teaching position in Massachusetts, but recurring health problems interrupted her career. Nevertheless, she heeded the 1863 call to teach in South Carolina. She worked with many formerly enslaved children whose excitement for "letters" created a challenge unlike any she had faced. Forten stood in bold relief from her students because of class differences.[67]

Similarly, a gulf existed between Emma Brown, a teacher who attended Miner's normal school and Oberlin College, and her students. On October 7, 1858, Brown expressed disappointment in a group of young women. "I tried," she wrote, "but all say that they have their living to work for and...have no time to spare." Begging the women to sacrifice time in exchange for more education did not sway them. The dismayed Brown continued:

> I spoke of the advantages to be derived from a knowledge of Astronomy and of the delight of wandering in thought [through] the sky, among myriads of stars, but all to no purpose. They replied that it would be of no use to them...I spoke of Algebra, but they said it was useless for *women* to study Algebra. I spoke of the pleasure of studying Botany, but they had no time for plants and flowers. I told them how much they needed a more thorough knowledge of literature, but their time was too precious. There is no hope of educating the girls who are grown. The only hope is in the younger portion whose minds are free.

Disillusionments such as those articulated by Brown were frequent but rarely enough to dissuade dedicated teachers permanently.[68]

Besides employing literacy as the basis of their livelihood, some black women used their education creatively and accomplished a respectable record of publications. "Philosophically, their achievements in writing," notes literary scholar Nellie Y. McKay, "are further proof that for black women as well as men, there was a close relationship between *freedom* and *literacy* in the minds of eighteenth-century and nineteenth-century Afro-Americans."[69]

Literacy figured importantly in Phillis Wheatley's vision of freedom. Her *Poems on Various Subjects, Religious and Moral* (1773) was at the forefront of the black literary tradition, and revolutionary luminaries including George Washington, Benjamin Franklin, and Thomas Jefferson were aware of her poetry. Jefferson mentions Wheatley in *Notes on the State of Virginia* and evaluates her talent: "Religion indeed has produced a Phyllis Whately [*sic*]; but it could not produce a poet." In his opinion, "The compositions published under her name are below the dignity of criticism. The heroes of the Dunciad are to her, as Hercules to the author of that poem." Jefferson's disdain for her work is obvious in his reference to Alexander Pope's "Dunciad," a parody of Virgil's *Aeneid*. The poem, Pope's personal war against "duncery," rails about the corruption of literary standards and misuse of the verbal art.[70]

By contrast, Charlotte Forten believed Wheatley "was a wonderfully gifted woman" and said, "many of her poems are very beautiful." Forten, an avid reader, completed scores of books annually. Included among those titles are Hawthorne's *Scarlet Letter*, Macaulay's *History of England*, and Stowe's *Uncle Tom's Cabin*. From that background, Forten believed Wheatley's "character and genius" provided "striking proof of the falseness of the assertion made by some that hers is an inferior race."[71]

As an aspiring writer, Forten hoped to use her talent in the interests of her people. She vowed that if the muse blessed her, the "first offering [w]ould be on the shrine of Liberty." Regardless of the quality of a black writer's creativity, most whites, including Jefferson, were not likely to give it a fair assessment because of their notions about racial inferiority. Black writers, especially women, received the greatest encouragement from members of their own literary societies such as the Afric American Female Intelligence Society in Boston, the Female Literary Association in Philadelphia, and the Female Literary Society of New York.[72]

Members of these organizations—which were integral aspects of the black community's infrastructure and training ground for developing leadership skills—included a cross-section of the population, but many were middle class with the leisure and wherewithal to attend meetings and pay modest membership dues. Ordinarily, the clubs and societies were gender specific. Exceptions were Boston's Adelphic Union Library Association and Philadelphia's Gilbert Lyceum. Among the eleven founding members of the Gilbert Lyceum were Sarah Mapps Douglass and her mother.[73]

The organizations functioned as fora, friendly social spaces, where members read and discussed current publications. They used a portion of the dues to add reading materials to the collections. The interest in developing their intellectual acumen was ever present. "You have minds—enrich them," wrote one member of Philadelphia's Female Literary Association. She also urged, "You have talents—only cultivate them."[74]

In 1840 Rebecca Peterson copied "On A Lady's Writing" into Martina Dickerson's album. She linked gender conventions to talent and urged the young woman to hone her skills:

> Her even lines her steady temper show,
> Neat as her dress, and polished as her brow;
> Strong as her judgement, easy is her air;
> Correct though free, and regular though fair;
> And the same graces o'er her pen preside,
> That form her manners, and her footsteps guide.

The advice leaves little room for inattention to details that could attract unfair criticism, especially from whites.[75]

Before presenting their creative work to the public, society members provided anonymous critiques of the aspiring authors' work. This was an essential step in developing thoughtful literature. In all probability, the exercises were beneficial since members' prose and poetry sometimes appeared in "friendly publications."[76]

In addition to promoting creative writers, the interests of the organizations were diverse, and they served as platforms for politicizing members about local and national events that affected blacks individually and collectively. Unmistakable links exist between their tradition of self-help, the organizations in the black community, and the formation of organized antislavery activities. For example, the Pan-Afric Female Intelligence Society, Boston, Massachusetts, involved itself in dramatic readings as well as abolitionist debates.[77]

Furthermore, members of the various organizations in the Northeast were certain to read Frederick Douglass's *North Star*, and they contributed pieces to *The Liberator*. The papers were possible venues for the women's antislavery musings.

Publication opportunities for black women in the Lower South to make their views heard were more limited than in the Upper South and North. Additionally, whites imposed laws to curtail liberties leading to scholarly and creative productivity following the Nat Turner rebellion. No doubt some black women recorded their musings privately as in the case of Mississippian Catharine Johnson, the daughter of a prosperous Natchez barber, whose violent death at the hands of a white neighbor in 1851 made an indelible impression upon her. "Suffice it to say it fills my soul with a bitterness that will remain forever. I cannot *forget* & I cannot *forgive*," she wrote. Johnson's May 10, 1864, diary entry is indicative of her ruminations:

> It has been a gloomy day for May. The rain has been falling all day. It has been hailing also. And to night the wind is wild and whistling through the tree grove more like dreary autumn than bright sunny May. Hark, how the rain falls sadly on the housetop and the wind howls.... To me it sounds like the Cries of sorrow. Yet I love the sound for at present it becomes well my feelings which are like the day, gloomy and sad.[78]

The young woman admitted never expressing a serious thought to anyone and attributed her penchant for dissembling to a "strange affliction." Her writings are introspective, and she appears to lack self-confidence. She was of the opinion that her acquaintances saw her as "light and frivolous, incapable of understanding or entertaining serious thoughts." The young woman acknowledged that such opinions were not without foundation since she only showed "one side" of her character to friends. She wished for the strength to change her behavior, but she wrote, "I am morally a coward." Johnson never disclosed what she considered as a "serious subject" nor why she called herself a moral coward. As a result, her hopes and dreams along with her beliefs about slavery, abolition, and the Civil War remain unknown.[79]

The writings of Frances E. W. Harper, the most prolific of the black women writers in the nineteenth century, represent a different segment of the free black population from this diarist. The productivity of Harper, Maria W. Stewart, Mary Ann Shadd, Sojourner Truth, and Harriet Jacobs is testimony to their tenacity in facing the obstacles to publishing their work. Beyond a recognition of the nexus in their thoughts between literacy and freedom, the women used their knowledge to identify and address social problems.

Harper's poems convey her interest in contemporary issues, including temperance, one of the largest nineteenth-century reform movements.

Her poem "The Drunkard's Child" appeared in *Poems on Miscellaneous Subjects* (1854), a slim volume that sold more than 10,000 copies. The pro-temperance work suggests a link between the consumption of alcohol and the neglect of loved ones. The poem portrays a drunk father who was literally pulled away from a den of vice "to see his first-born die." The chilling scene contrasts the child's innocence with the father's dissipation.[80]

Many free blacks living in the North supported the temperance movement not because they were inclined to drunkenness, but because they believed the movement encouraged moral uplift. Free blacks also believed the consumption of alcohol in a social context was more harmful to African Americans than to others. As a result, blacks tried to avoid both the financial costs and negative images associated with alcohol consumption. The absence of drunkards would rob proslavery apologists of an argument claiming that African Americans were incapable of making good decisions about their own welfare.[81]

Harper combined her temperance stance with commentary on respectability and women's independence in "The Two Offers." Her short story, the first published by a black woman in the United States, appeared in an 1859 issue of the *Anglo-African*, a magazine designed to educate, encourage, and represent African Americans. According to the author, the short story allows readers to see that the protagonist learned "one of life's most precious lessons: that true happiness consists not so much in the fruition of our wishes as in the regulation of desires and the full development and right culture of our whole nature."[82]

Harper's "Advice to the Girls" and "The Two Offers" show that choices based on superficial reasons or material motives may result in disappointment. Harper's romantic fiction is much like that published by other nineteenth-century writers such as Lydia Maria Child and Harriet Beecher Stowe. In fact, Harper's characters are sometimes without racial designation. The social and historical construction of race may cause readers to assume the characters are black.[83]

A selected number of black women used the print media to attack the institution of slavery. The "Ladies' Department," a column in *The Liberator*, welcomed their sketches, poems, and commentaries in keeping with the paper's stand against slavery. The paper once carried a story naming two "capital errors" of great detriment to the abolitionist cause. "The first," said the writer, was "a proneness on the part of the advocates of immediate and universal emancipation to ignore the influence of women in the promotion of the cause." The author's gendered analysis of the abolitionist movement was timely. Of equal importance was the second major error. There was "a similar disposition on the part of females," the writer charged, "to undervalue their own power, or through a misconception of duty to excuse themselves from engaging in the enterprise."[84]

Frances E. W. Harper, best known of the black women abolitionist writers, was not self-effacing. She contributed her literary talent willingly. Her poem "Eliza Harris," based on the fugitive mother in *Uncle Tom's Cabin* who runs away with her child to prevent him from being sold, appeared in *The Liberator* and other nationally distributed papers. The mother-child theme is prevalent in Harper's writings and reveals much about the author, an orphan at three years old.[85]

The separation of mothers and children by death was akin to the separation of mothers and children by slavery in the minds of Harper and others who opposed bondage. Harper's "The Slave Mother" comments on the act:

> They tear him from her circling arms,
>   Her last and fond embrace.
> Oh! never more may her sad eyes
>   Gaze on his mournful face.[86]

In addition to the poetry, the narratives of former slaves were popular and used widely by abolitionists. Firsthand accounts of bondage are distinctly American but not entirely limited to the United States. The narratives generally begin with an author's birth and tell of cruelties in bondage before ending with an escape to freedom. Some autobiographies were hastily written and seriously flawed, while others made significant literary contributions. The most independent, imaginative, talented, and rebellious slave-born women and men wrote the most penetrating narratives.[87]

Black women published fewer of these accounts than men because of gender disparities in literacy and ability to attract publishers. Moreover, women were less likely than men to run away to the North where they could receive publication assistance. Harriet Jacobs is an exception in that she was literate, fled to the North, and published *Incidents in the Life of a Slave Girl* (1861) before slavery ended.[88]

Her aim was to make northern women aware that two million black women were still in bondage and politicize this knowledge, that no woman was free as long as slavery existed. Jacobs began with a moving preface declaring that her narrative was no exaggeration of the "wrongs inflicted by Slavery." She argued that her descriptions fell "far short of the facts" and that while slavery was terrible for men, it was far worse for women.[89]

Although published under a pseudonym, Jacobs soon became known as the author of *Incidents in the Life of a Slave Girl* among abolitionists in the New York Antislavery office. Lydia M. Child, who made modest editorial changes in the manuscript and wrote the preface, convinced a small group of New York abolitionists to purchase Jacobs's book for distribution by antislavery agents at one dollar per copy. Both the *National Anti-Slavery Standard* and the *Weekly Anglo-African* reviewed *Incidents in the Life of a Slave Girl,* but its publication coincided with the onset of the Civil War; therefore, its initial impact fell short of the writer's expectations.[90]

Mary Ann Shadd used *The Provincial Freeman,* a paper published in Canada, to comment about American society and sensitize readers to the antislavery cause in the 1850s. Blacks in the United States and Canada read the paper for its coverage of temperance, education, politics, international relations, family life, social events, and abolition. The well-known Samuel Ringgold Ward was considered its editor, but Shadd, the business manager, was an integral force behind the paper's existence. Ward was often away on the lecture circuit; therefore, much of the work fell to Shadd, who is recognized as the first black woman newspaper editor.[91]

At the outset, Shadd used her initials to hide her identity because of the opposition to women working at "men's jobs." In an 1856 editorial, "Canada," Frederick Douglass asserted that she was capable of the job regardless of her gender. He wrote:

> This lady, with very little assistance from others has sustained *The Provincial Freeman* for more than two years. She has had to contend with lukewarmness, false friends, open enemies, ignorance and small pecuniary means. The tone of her paper has been at times harsh and complaining and whatever may be thought or felt of this we are bound to bear testimony to the unceasing industry, the unconquerable zeal and commendable ability which she has shown. We do not know her equal among the colored ladies of the United States.

As a newspaper editor, Douglass knew of the difficulties in getting the paper out and the value of public support.[92]

By nineteenth-century standards, Shadd's style was ill-suited for a woman. She tended to favor language laden with political meaning such as "wormwood," "moral pest," and "petty despot." Strident tones and biting criticism aside, the paper offered a glimpse of life in Canada. Moreover, it was a vital communications link between African Americans in Canada and those in the United States.[93]

Ultimately, free black women gained literacy in a variety of ways and liberated themselves from ignorance. Furthermore, some women used their educations as the basis for their economic well-being and moved beyond individual aspirations to develop a social consciousness with the assistance of multifaceted organizations for the benefit of the black community. This was a challenging responsibility, but many willingly adopted the adage "knowledge is power" and believed it was incumbent upon them to "get the knowledge, & use it well." Many believed societal ills that affected blacks negatively could be resolved by uplifting the race through education. Others believed the problems could be solved through religion.[94]

5

"Whom do you serve, God or man?"

Spiritualists and Reformers

May all who are of the household of faith stand fast in the *liberty* wherewith Christ has made them *free.*

Zilpha Elaw

"Lord! send by whom thou wilt send, only send not by me; for thou
knowest that I am ignorant; how can I be a mouth for God?" asked Zilpha
Elaw. Describing herself as "a poor coloured female," she added, "Thou
knowest we have many things to endure which others have not." What
did she, a widow with a child, suffer that was different from the ordeals of
others? Were the "many things" of which she spoke based on her gender,
color, class, or vocation? Without articulating it, Elaw knew that preaching women placed themselves on a trajectory in opposition to accepted
social and religious conventions.[1]

The autobiographies of several nineteenth-century black women chronicle their fights for liberty within traditional religious structures. Some
narratives suggest that the authors were most concerned about freeing
their souls and solidifying personal relationships with their god. Their
ideologies lifted them above worldly matters and led them to help others

toward a salvation beyond anything influenced by mere mortals. But mere mortals were responsible for withholding religious teachings from millions of enslaved women and men. This chapter answers questions about how and why the spiritualists fought for their religious freedom within the sexist or racist environments of their churches.[2]

Extraordinary religious experiences freed the women from a previously "socially constructed self" and worldly oppressions to make way for a new "spiritually constructed self" once converted. As they received calls, through extraordinary visions, to preach, most of the spiritual autobiographers appropriated biblical scriptures for authorization. Perhaps they pondered the miracle of the immaculate conception and saw direct linkages between God and Mary as illustrative. In her legendary "Ar'n't I a Woman?" speech, Sojourner Truth asked, "Whar did your Christ come from?" Jesus' birth from a virgin, she said, was "from God and a woman. Man had nothing to do with him." Similarly, man had nothing to do with God calling "morally superior women" to preach. In heeding their call, women faced patriarchal ideas and struggled for acceptance in a profession ordinarily closed to them. To succeed, the women redefined gender roles based on biblical scripture and societal customs.[3]

The women's religious experiences were links to their feminism and interests in social reform, another dimension wherein they exercised their freedom and liberty. William L. Andrews, editor of spiritual narratives written by Zilpha Elaw, Julia A. J. Foote, and Jarena Lee, concluded that a careful study of these and other spiritual autobiographies will illuminate "their historical significance to the evolution of American feminism."[4]

It is well known that many black women, without church affiliations and geographical boundaries, used religion to ease suffering, explain mysteries, and ward off adversities. What is less well known from institutional records and the writings of ordained clerics is how the women experienced a personal relationship with their God. The autobiographical writings of Elizabeth (1766–?), Maria W. Stewart (1803–1879), Jarena Lee (1783–?), Zilpha Elaw (1790–?), Julia A. J. Foote (1823–1900), Rebecca Cox Jackson (1795–1871), and Sojourner Truth (1799–1883) are central to this study. On the one hand, the narratives contain valuable discussions about the authors' efforts to liberate themselves from confining ideologies, overwhelming paternalism, or suffocating racism. On the other hand, two matters interfere with a balanced view of the authors' experiences over time. First, the authors tend to ignore chronology and change over time. Second, the narratives are skewed toward the northern experience. Only one author in this group, Elizabeth, was a southern-born freedwoman. Nevertheless, these published accounts illuminate the authors' own religiosity and that of other women who supported them as they preached the gospel or practiced their religions.[5]

Christianity was not widely embraced by blacks in colonial America because its presentation was from the dominant white male's viewpoint. Some slaveowners believed Africans were not intellectually capable of conversion, while others refrained from encouraging religiosity because they lacked a clear understanding of the relationship between conversion and emancipation.[6]

Seventeenth- and eighteenth-century slaveholders did not undertake systematic efforts to proselytize bondservants, and slaves found little attraction in a religion practiced by people who treated them badly by segregating and prohibiting them from full participation in the church's organization. However, when introduced to Christianity, blacks often syncretized it with African traditional religions since Christianity, especially as practiced by evangelicals, was compatible. Spirit possession and initiation, highly significant events for West Africans, were not unknown in evangelical churches.[7]

The spread of Christianity among blacks coincided with protestant revivalism in the eighteenth century when followers experienced personal encounters with their God. These religious episodes often manifested themselves in emotional outbursts during conversions. George Whitefield, a well-known Methodist evangelist, and Gilbert Tennent, a Presbyterian minister in New Jersey, commented about seeing blacks in their congregations during the First Great Awakening in the 1730s and 1740s. This emotionally charged multidenominational revival movement appealed to women and men regardless of color and class. Following a religious revival in the 1730s, the Congregationalist Jonathan Edwards reported that some of the "Negroes . . . appear to have been truly born again in the late remarkable season."[8]

Scores of blacks visited George Whitefield in 1740 to express appreciation "for what God had done to their souls" due to his preaching. Phillis Wheatley eulogized the great evangelist in 1770. Her poem "On the Death of Rev. Mr. George Whitefield" touts his sermons that caused "ev'ry bosom [to glow] with devotion." She lamented the loss of the "music of [his] tongue," which did "inflame the heart, and captivate the mind" of the "num'rous throng." The poet likened Whitefield's mourners to orphans grieving for "their more than father."[9]

Blacks, emancipated and enslaved, females and males, were among the "num'rous throngs" when followers of various denominations gathered at revivals and camp meetings. The emotionalism associated with the Great Awakening was similar to the religious behavior of many blacks. As a result, their interests in Christianity intensified, and large numbers of blacks converted during the religious movement. In 1786, Methodist membership totaled 18,791. Of that number, 1,890 or 10 percent were black. Their membership increased until it reached 12,215, or nearly 25 percent of the total. During the Second Great Awakening (from the turn of the nineteenth century to the 1830s), black women and men continued to gravitate toward the Methodist church because of its mass appeal and initial reputation as an antislavery institution.[10]

It is difficult to estimate the number of black Baptists because of differences in record keeping. However, the number of Baptist converts rivaled that reported by the Methodists. Religious revivals were largely responsible for attracting blacks to both Methodist and Baptist camp meetings. Among the earliest churches established by southern blacks was the Silver Bluff, South Carolina, Baptist church founded in the 1770s. It became the nucleus of the First African Baptist Church in Augusta, Georgia, founded in 1793.[11]

There was little interference with southern black churches and religious meetings until after the 1831 insurrection led by Nat Turner, an enslaved literate preacher in Virginia. Whites feared that gatherings of blacks for religious purposes fomented rebellion. After the Turner revolt, some southern states prohibited blacks from conducting religious services without at least one white person present. Black congregations resented the monitoring and sometimes resorted to secret services. By the mid-nineteenth century, religious societies succeeded in pressuring states to relax these prohibitions, but it was not until after emancipation that black churches fully regained their autonomy.[12]

The first independent African American church in the North predates Augusta's African Baptist Church. The founding of Philadelphia's Bethel African Methodist Episcopal Church, established in 1787, resulted in part from the prejudicial treatment of blacks at St. George Methodist Church. Although they had suffered racism, Bethel's male founders and early supporters were not catholic enough, ideologically, to welcome women on equal terms as they tried to establish themselves as spiritual leaders. Richard Allen, one of Bethel's founders and its first minister, claimed that women preaching before the congregation was "contrary to the discipline of the Methodist church."[13]

Women experienced sexism based on literal interpretations of selected scriptures and faced class biases in social conventions prescribed by the

"cult of true womanhood." Both circumscribed women's religious freedom and equality. In all probability, many women were in agreement
with two of the cult's attributes, purity and piety, but the remaining tenets,
submissiveness and domesticity, were potential barriers for religious aspirations. This was especially true if women sublimated calls to preach
to their husbands' wishes, or if women ignored the calls to fulfill domestic and child-rearing responsibilities. The women spiritualists were determined to liberate themselves through religious perseverance, and they
resisted sexist practices.[14]

In 1831 Maria W. Stewart, author of *Meditations from the Pen of Mrs.
Maria W. Stewart* and the first woman to address women and men publicly, used the Bible to authorize her actions. She claimed "spiritual inter-
rogation" enabled her to engage in political sermonizing. She, like other
women seeking to redefine their roles, was familiar with the apostle
Paul's admonitions for women to remain silent and defer to men in religious matters. "Did St. Paul but know of our wrongs and deprivations?"
asked Stewart. "I presume he would make no objection to our pleading
in public for our rights," she posited. Any attempt to keep women solely
in traditional roles filled Stewart with "holy indignation" and made her
a "warrior" for social justice. As a public speaker, Stewart admitted that
she "felt ashamed" stepping out of the place society defined. Without
yielding to a foreboding presence, Stewart wrote, "A *something* . . . within
my breast [said] 'press forward, I will be with thee.' And my heart made
this reply, 'Lord, if thou wilt be with me, then I will speak for thee as
long as I live.'" In Stewart's view, religion and social justice were intertwined, and she could not devote herself to one cause without a commitment to the other.[15]

Agency and independence gained through studying Christian doctrine and active participation in women's groups combined with their religious faith helped many women to emancipate themselves from society's
oppressive gender conventions. With liberation came self-assurance and
empowerment for challenging time-bound male authority. "What if I am
a woman," asked the deeply religious Stewart in 1833, "is not the God of
ancient times the God of these modern days?" She invoked the names of
Deborah and Esther, biblical women of great leadership abilities. They
were role models for Stewart who described herself as a passive instrument in God's hands. She asked questions about women's roles in public
and private spheres, but Jarena Lee went further and pursued the funda-
mental issue of female autonomy in the church.[16]

Before cultivating a feminist consciousness, the women underwent a conversion, beginning with distressing incidents causing feelings of depression or sinfulness. The belief that a supreme being could remove the "melancholia religiosa" motivated likely aspirants to search for deliverance. After this intense interlude, their spiritual journey began. During an emotional low point, as in "the lonesome valley" of Negro spirituals, the seeker recognizes her sinfulness and helplessness. Prayer, meditation, and fasting follow. Powerful experiences with auditories or visions, sometimes both, induce a trance-like condition. Sojourner Truth recalled, "God revealed himself . . . with all the suddenness of a flash of lightning, showing her, 'in the twinkling of an eye, that he was *all over'* — that he pervaded the universe–'and that there was no place where God was not.'" During the episode, she lost consciousness. After such deeply spiritual and emotional interludes, Truth and others told of a sense of assured salvation followed by an unfurled peace.[17]

Zilpha Elaw's description of her 1817 conversion is also illustrative. It occurred after a display of blasphemy primarily to entertain friends. The irreverent act resulted in an "exceedingly sinful" feeling. Elaw refrained from swearing and imagined "God looking down and frowning." The repentant teenager disengaged herself from her "frolicsome companions" and spent time praying before the disappearance of an ominous cloud weighing heavily on her spirit. The most arresting time prior to her conversion was the vision of a smiling Christ with open arms assuring her that her prayers were accepted. "From that happy hour," Elaw wrote, "my soul was set at *glorious liberty.*" Conversion removed the threat of damnation and empowered believers to face worldly challenges, such as sexism and racism, fearlessly as if clothed in divine protection.[18]

Conversion, the extraordinary liberating experience regarding a supreme being, occurred in public and private settings and during revivals or camp meetings. This remarkable phenomenon may be compared to Paul's conversion on the road to Damascus. After conversion, true believers longed for sanctification, or purification of themselves from sin. The key to understanding sanctification is knowing that the spirit dwells within the soul. In other words, God occupied a place within the body, and this presence caused the women to hear, feel, and see the spirit.[19]

Zilpha Elaw entered a state of sanctification or Christian perfection at an 1817 camp meeting beginning with an overpowering presence of God that pushed her into a trance. Her "spirit seemed to ascend up into the clear circle of the sun's disc . . . in the glorious effulgence of [God's] rays." Elaw awakened and declared that her "heart and soul were rendered completely spotless." The metamorphosis from the old socially constructed self to a new spiritually constructed one made Elaw "God's instrument." In fact, the spirit compelled her to encourage others to seek that same saving grace.[20]

Once delivered from sin, Jarena Lee and Julia A. J. Foote were anxious to serve God. They believed it was their duty to proselytize and bring others to conversion and sanctification, freedom from intentional sin. Rather than permitting the women to fulfill their aspirations as their male contemporaries did, however, organized churches relegated women to the role of itinerant ministers or to work exclusively in Sunday schools, church auxiliaries, and missionary societies. Also, women became exhorters, a subordinate position to ministers. On occasions they preached, but a licensed minister selected the text. Such arrangements limited women's freedom and were unsatisfactory to them.[21]

The social encumbrances made leading others toward conversion and sanctification, if it meant preaching, virtually impossible; yet the women scoured the Bible for passages to justify their callings. Elaw favored Isaiah 61:1, which affirmed, "The Spirit of the Lord God *is* on me; because the Lord hath anointed me to preach good tidings unto the meek; he hath sent me to bind up the brokenhearted, to proclaim liberty to the captives, and the opening of the prison to *them* that are bound." The freedwoman Elizabeth selected a verse from Galatians: "There is neither Jew nor Greek, there is neither bond nor free, there is neither male nor female, for ye are one in Christ Jesus."[22]

Jarena Lee also sought legitimation for her call to preach and began her 1836 narrative, *The Life and Religious Experience of Jarena Lee,* with the headnote, "And it shall come to pass...that I will pour out my Spirit upon all flesh; and your sons, and your *daughters* shall prophesy." Like Lee, the New Yorker Julia Foote looked to the Book of Joel for vindication: "It is expressly stated that women were among those who continued in prayer and supplication, waiting for the fulfillment of the promise. Women and men are classed together, and if the power to preach the Gospel is short-lived and spasmodic in the case of women, it must be *equally* so in that of men; and if women have lost the gift of prophecy, so have men." She interpreted Joel 2:28 and 2:29 to assert women's rights to a place in the pulpit.[23]

Obviously, a conflict existed between the defined place of women in the church and larger society on one hand and their inner convictions of harmony and acceptance of God's will on the other hand. The women were obliged to answer the question "Whom do you serve, God or man?" Elaw wrote, "May all who are of the household of faith stand fast in the *liberty* wherewith Christ has made them free." Maintaining their special relationship with the Supreme Being was more important than following accepted customs. As a result, these women were indeed sisters in the spirit when challenging ecclesiastical and social conventions.[24]

Each of the spiritual autobiographers overcame repressive church dogma in her own way and as family circumstances permitted. In the search for religious fulfillment, the slave-born Isabella Van Wagenen left her partner and children, except the youngest, changed her name to Sojourner Truth, and followed a new calling. Truth's religious background was a mixture of African American culture, Calvinist Dutch Reformed Church, and Armenian Methodist. She claimed to have heard the voice of God tell her to go out on her own as a free woman in 1826.[25]

Elizabeth, Truth's slave-born contemporary, received freedom from her Presbyterian owner based on religious grounds. Her autobiography does not mention a family or domestic responsibilities that encouraged or discouraged her religiosity.[26]

Julia Foote, a childless woman, prayed with her husband, George, but an "indescribable something" existed between them. She prayed for his sanctification but saw his face with a "dark shadow ever-present." It never disappeared but was less visible once he went to sea for six months. There was disaffection between the couple, yet George Foote arranged for her to "draw half of his wages." She agreed reluctantly, perhaps because of her desire for economic and physical independence.[27]

Julie Foote was free of all domestic responsibilities and could take her ministry from Boston to Pittsburgh and then to Cincinnati. While on her mission, she learned of her husband's death several months earlier. She returned to Boston and observed a brief period of mourning before resuming her work.[28]

By contrast, Jarena Lee, a married woman with two children, sublimated her 1807 call to preach in the interest of her husband's ministerial career. During this time, she suffered a debilitating illness that was probably as much physical as it was psychological. In either case, she literally lingered between life and death. "There was but one thing which bound me to the earth," wrote Lee, "and that was, I had not as yet preached the gospel to the fallen sons and daughters of Adam's race, to the satisfaction of my mind." In time she recovered, but it was Reverend Lee's death that actually freed her to preach.[29]

Zilpha Elaw's and Rebecca Jackson's marital circumstances were more complicated. Elaw quickly realized that she had "surrendered" herself to a husband in an 1810 union where she was "unequally yoked." This prompted her to write, "In general your lot would be better if a millstone were hung about your necks, and you were drowned in the depths of the sea, than that you should disobey the law of Jesus [Matthew 18:6], and plunge yourselves into all the sorrows, sins, and anomalies involved in a matrimonial alliance with an unbeliever." Elaw complained of "continually endur[ing] such sore trials" from her husband who was "extremely hostile" on occasions and demanded that she refrain from preaching. She ignored him, entered the ministry, and continued to adhere faithfully to her "commission."[30]

Elaw maneuvered around her husband's objections and encountered fewer obstacles than the itinerant preacher Rebecca Cox Jackson, whose husband was extremely threatening. According to Jackson, he "sought my life day and night." To further exacerbate the strain on their marriage after sanctification, she decided to refrain from intimacy with him. She believed sexual gratification was sinful. Without the ability to foresee her husband's intentions, she was certain that he would have killed her.[31]

Unlike her spiritual sisters whose husbands never accepted their ministry, Samuel Jackson eventually recognized his wife as a "woman of God" and could not ignore the powerful and prophetic religious aura surrounding her. He encouraged her to "go forth and do the will of God." Rebecca Jackson chronicled his plea for forgiveness without recording her response to his change of heart. Surprisingly, Samuel and Rebecca Jackson did not put their differences aside and strengthen their marriage through religion. Instead, she received the January 31, 1836, "command" to tell her husband she would devote her "heart, soul, mind, and strength" to "the Lord and Him only."[32]

Rebecca Jackson left her husband and recorded the event as "My Release from Bondage" in her autobiography. Of greater interest than equating her marriage to slavery is Jackson's rejection of traditional gender roles in the name of religion at a time when her husband accepted her mission and vowed to stop interfering. She had no faith in his promises and yielded to her God, source of the command to end their marriage. Obeying the command freed Rebecca and rendered the previously wicked Samuel powerless. In short, it liberated her and fettered him. Rebecca Jackson's situation is unique when compared to her cohorts, whose husbands rejected their calls to preach and died without making amends.[33]

The spiritualists found support in women-centered "praying bands." Scholar Jean McMahon Humez describes the women's organizations as "relatively intimate, highly participatory, democratic religious gatherings in the familiar world of women friends" that fostered religious actualization. The bands gathered weekly in homes and prayed for sanctification. Once believers reached that stage, they experienced a personal freedom from gender conventions that buffeted them from abuses rooted in sexism and racism. In such nurturing environments, the women honed their talents and skills.[34]

Jarena Lee associated herself with a praying band, a group of women who provided social space for women with a common interest, in Philadelphia and missed it sorely when she moved six miles away to Snow Hill in 1811. None "but those who have been in sweet fellowship with such [a group] as really love God, and have together drank bliss and happiness from the same fountain can tell how dear such company is," she wrote. The relocation ended her spiritual companionship with women who were either converted and in a state of holiness or were striving for religious purity. "How hard" it was, Lee reminded readers, "to part from them." "This was a great trial," and Lee never experienced camaraderie as she had enjoyed among the women in Philadelphia.[35]

With or without support from the prayer groups, religious women remained hesitant about heeding the call to preach. Of the Methodist autobiographers, Elaw was the most reticent. The exceptionally convincing word that she was to preach came from her dying sister, Hannah, who had seen a vision of Jesus, replete with a company of angels, relaying the message that Zilpha "must preach the gospel." She still doubted that God had chosen "so poor and ignorant a creature" as herself. No amount of prodding could change Elaw's mind; therefore, God moved her through other means. At length, she accepted the idea and proclaimed the gospel. Surprisingly, objections came from her erstwhile "loving and happy band" of women. Rather than offering support, the group was critical. It saw faults and imperfections in a woman whose opinion had carried much weight previously.[36]

Neither Elaw nor her contemporary spiritualists were likely to allow prayer bands or organized churches to thwart their calls to preach. When church leaders told Elizabeth, who began preaching in 1808 at age forty-two, that "there was nothing in Scripture that would sanction such exercises," she went to the Bible for reassurance. Opening the book randomly and seeing the passage "Gird up thy loins now like a man, and answer thou me. Obey God rather than man" was encouraging. After trying to dissuade her from the hierarchical point of view, the elders pointed to the difficulties of travel for a woman. When Elizabeth ignored their advice, they charged her with "impudency."[37]

Jarena Lee faced obstacles from church officials after receiving the 1811 auditory command "Go preach the Gospel." Lee summoned the courage to tell Richard Allen that she believed it her duty to prophesy. He was not supportive and maintained that the Methodist church "did not call for women preachers." Lee admitted that the fire, enthusiasm, and holy energy burning in her soul "began to be smothered," and she questioned the rationale for denying women access to the pulpit. Why would anyone consider it "impossible, heterodox, or improper for a woman to preach," she asked. "If a man may preach," because the Savior died for him, "why not the woman? seeing he died for her also." Lee did not believe God favored "man exclusively." She asked, "Is he not a whole Savior, instead of a half one?" Refusing women the right to preach "would seem," wrote Lee, to indicate that the Supreme Being was less encompassing than she had believed.[38]

Without mentioning the promise of the spirit in God's message, "Your sons and daughters will prophesy," according to the prophet Joel, Lee interpreted it as referring to Mary, the mother of Jesus. "Did not Mary, a woman," asked Lee, "preach the gospel?" She retorted, "Some will say, that Mary did not expound the Scripture, therefore, she did not preach, in the proper sense of the term." Aware of criticism from detractors, Lee concluded, "the term *preach*, in those primitive times, did not mean exactly what it is now *made* to mean."[39]

Lee emphasized lexicology and implied that changes in word meanings were "manufactured" by the powers that be: men. As if the point were not lucid enough, Lee argued that to preach was "a great deal more simple then, than it is now." If that were not the case, she added, "the unlearned fishermen could not have preached the gospel at all, as they had no learning." To mention the men's ignorance suggests that she was sensitive about distinctions in opportunities based on gender and class. It also implies that if unlettered men could preach so could uneducated women. Lee believed God had called her, and she was willing "to labour according to what [she] . . . received, in his vineyard."[40]

The boldness with which she discusses her call to preach and Allen's rebuff, along with her inquiries about the bishop's interpretations, would not win sanction from Allen or any other church leaders. Rather than currying favor, Lee challenged them when she asked, "May he not, did he not, and can he not inspire a female to preach the simple story of the birth, life, death and resurrection of our lord, and accompany it too, with power to the sinner's heart."[41]

Jarena Lee holds the distinction of being the first woman known to petition the African Methodist Episcopal church for the right to preach. The literary scholar Joanne Braxton posited:

> Lee's inner voice is important, especially in the context of a sexist, slaveholding antebellum culture, in that it is essentially self-authorizing, defying secular laws, and, ultimately, the settled ways of white [and

black] patriarchy; for Jarena Lee, black, female, and thus denied a public voice, the promise of a divine gift of words and friends had a powerful effect. Ultimately, Lee's inner voice sets up a tension between her inner self and external religious authority... to carve out an identity and a voice for herself.[42]

Lee would not allow men to silence her or use her voice.

She was far from silent with her labor in the vineyard of the Lord, and it caused her to travel more than 2,000 miles in 1827 and 1832–1833. Two years later, she reported having delivered 692 sermons. In the course of her preaching, without church sanction, Lee converted many souls.[43]

She and Foote noted that when men interpreted the Bible, specific words and nuances changed according to the subject's gender. In the case of the biblical Phebe and Tychicus, she was a "servant of the church" whereas he was the "minister." Needless to say, the women's interpretations differed. Female spiritualists were more inclined to see equality, especially between Priscilla and Aquila, her husband, when the Bible commended women to the church at Cenchrea, saying, "Greet Priscilla and Aquila my helpers in Christ Jesus." The inseparable husband-wife team appear as a unified whole in the Bible; one is never mentioned without the other. In a similar vein, Foote was convinced that the women mentioned by the Apostle Paul as laboring with him did more than pour tea or serve food.[44]

With respect to Paul's edicts, Gerda Lerner, author of *The Creation of Feminist Consciousness*, writes, "Modern biblical scholarship has reached near-consensus in the judgment that most of the comments pertaining to women attributed to Paul were not in fact written or spoken by Paul but were the product of post-apostolic writers who ascribed the texts to him for greater authority."[45]

Among the black women spiritual autobiographers who questioned the writings attributed to Paul were Julia Foote and Jarena Lee. Foote understood gender conventions but had few domestic responsibilities since her husband was often away and they were childless. This is not to suggest that she would not have combined domesticity and religious callings, if necessary. In fact, one of her spiritual contemporaries, Rebecca Cox Jackson, balanced the two. She and her husband lived with her widowed brother, Joseph Cox, a pastor at Bethel A. M. E. Church. She assumed gendered responsibilities within his home and often worked until 2:00 or 3:00 a. m. The long hours did not interfere with her rising at dawn to "wait on the Lord."[46]

Domestic responsibilities were not substitutes for religious duties. Foote deconstructed the Apostle Paul's injunction, "Help those women who labor with me in the Gospel," to mean they did more than domestic work. Rather than using Paul's writings to confine women to a private sphere, Foote believed they had other roles based on Paul's instructions about how women and men should appear at public gatherings to prophesy or pray. Foote believed that both women and men could prophesy, yet in a self-serving way she ignored Paul's edict, "Christ is the head of every man, and the man is the head of woman," found in the same chapter of First Corinthians.[47]

Julia A. J. Foote addressed the matter of women and men as instruments of God forthrightly in an 1851 sermon employing Micah 4:13, "Arise and thresh, O daughter of Zion," as the basis of "A Threshing Sermon." In contextualizing the sermon she delivered in Detroit, Foote noted how in 710 B.C. animals with iron horns and brass hoofs were used in the separation of corn from loose sheaves. By way of analogy, Foote suggested that the scripture was applicable to "preachers of the word" and referred subtly to Joel 2:28–29, verses authorizing men and women to prophesy. The faithful would receive "supernatural aid"—iron horns and brass hoofs—from God to ferret sinfulness out of their own lives and that of others. Once the ministers flailed with the Gospel, they could be satisfied that the work of the Devil would be "beat in pieces" or eradicated and Christ would live in the purified soul without temptations from the Devil. As Foote interpreted the Bible, there were no differences in the duties of religious men and women.[48]

The intelligent but illiterate Sojourner Truth was also well-versed in the scriptures. People, preferably children, read and reread passages to her until she gained the desired mastery. Truth's use of the Book of Esther epitomizes her understanding of how women and ethnic groups fell prey to patriarchy and prejudice. She pushed the discussion far beyond the recognized place of women in organized churches. With a larger worldview, Truth employed the Book of Esther as a reference in her examination of women's subordinate positions and used the Jews as symbolic representations for enslaved blacks.[49]

Esther, a woman of recognized beauty, was born in Persia where her family was in captivity. She came to the attention of King Ahasuerus following the deposing of Queen Vashti. Vashti, a woman described as "fair to look on," fell from favor when she refused to comply with the king's command to present herself so that he and his guests, a group of besotted men, might enjoy her beauty. This occurred during the king's lavish week-long celebration in Shushan while displaying his power and wealth. The king reigned over 127 provinces stretching from India to Ethiopia. Queen Vashti's behavior embarrassed him, and he angrily dismissed her.[50]

The queen's disobedience, according to the seven princes who advised Ahasuerus, was more than a personal affront to him "but also to all the princes, and to all the people . . . in all the provinces." Knowledge of the queen's actions would become known "unto all women, so that they shall despise their husbands." If not dealt with properly and promptly, Vashti's defiance would lay the groundwork for "too much contempt and wrath" from women who were expected to honor and obey their husbands.[51]

Queen Vashti's objection was more complex than simple disobedience. She refused to abandon her self-respect and modesty. Perhaps she wished to avoid humiliation among a group of drunken men. Ordinarily, concubines, not the queen, would have gone into the banquet hall while the king and his guests indulged in rare wines. Queen Vashti's reaction was within the customs of the Persian tradition to refuse his command.[52]

A lengthy 1871 poem "Vashti" written by Frances E. W. Harper argues that the queen preferred to take the crown from her head, "tread it 'neath" her feet, and die rather than appear before a group of inebriated men. Harper notes the importance of patriarchy to the king and his men while showing the dethroned queen as "strong in her earnest womanhood":

[Queen Vashti] left the palace of the King,
Proud of her spotless name—
A woman who could bend to grief,
But would not bow to shame.

Such a stance was admirable according to the ideology of the cult of true womanhood.[53]

Sojourner Truth did not deconstruct Queen Vashti's behavior as did the poet, but Truth must have asked whether the queen should have obeyed a man whose "heart was merry with wine" after seven days of festivities. Zilpha Elaw's comments about a woman's obedience to her husband are instructive in this regard. "The wife," Elaw believed, was "destined to be the help-meet of her husband; but if he be a worldly man, she cannot, she dare not be either his instrument or abettor in worldly lusts and sinful pursuits." Both Truth and Elaw lived in the nineteenth century while Queen Vashti came of age around 500 B.C. Regardless of the epoch, it seemed wrong for thinking women to obey misguided men.[54]

In some ways, the spiritual autobiographers underwent an antinomian crisis by defying accepted gender conventions. Their rebellion against the norm was as much about differences in theological beliefs as it was about power and freedom of conscience. Their revolt was a necessary step in their own liberation from binding doctrine and dominating men. If women freed themselves from the accepted religious structure and decided to serve God, they sought endorsement for their ministries by organized churches.

Julia Foote and Rebecca Jackson encountered more difficulties than the other autobiographers. Foote charged that Bostonian Jehial C. Beman "instigated" barriers by refusing to grant permission for her use of a hall. When a proposed intercession by several church women proved ineffective, Foote's supporters arranged for her to preach in a private home. Beman objected and appointed a committee to censure them with threats of excommunication. Foote remained steadfast and affirmed that her "business was with the Lord." She promised to preach wherever she found an open door, a welcoming social space. After several futile committee visits, Foote agreed to hear the pastor and his delegation. She considered herself a church member in good standing until she actually did "something worthy of dismembership." When questioned about her willingness to obey church rules, Foote emphasized that she would not follow regulations prohibiting her from carrying out God's bidding. "I fear God," Foote said, "more than man."[55]

The church cast Foote out for violating "the rules of the discipline by preaching." Responses to questions about her dismissal varied. The minister claimed she insisted on speaking from the pulpit and charged that she scheduled a meeting that conflicted with his own. Foote said he was disingenuous. In her opinion, the minister told a "falsehood" to "cover up" his "deception [and] unrighteous course." In a letter to the conference, she asserted that no one could "truthfully" bring charges against her moral or religious character.[56]

In a bold move, Foote asked for an impartial hearing and a written assessment of findings. To comply would permit her to challenge church administrators, who happened to be men. This perceptive woman asked, "Why should they notice? It was only the grievance of a woman, and there was no justice meted out to women in those days." Even ministers, she wrote, "did not feel that women had any rights which they were bound to respect." Man's opinion weighed nothing with Foote. Empowerment came from heaven, and "my reward," she added, "was with the Most High."[57]

In the final chapters of her autobiography, Foote begged women to refrain from allowing the wishes of men to interfere with the will of God, thereby "using the gifts you have for the good of others." Foote further implored women not to be "kept in bondage by those who say, 'We suffer not a woman to teach.'" She acknowledged the Apostle Paul's words but said the persons who used them to prohibit women from preaching were "not rightly applying them."[58]

Foote's choice of the word "bondage" is arresting. She viewed the denial of a woman's freedom to preach the gospel as analogous to the denial of a person's liberty. When couched in this way, it is understandable that Foote, like enslaved women or men, would struggle to remove the fetters from her religious freedom. Elaw was as astute as Foote in extolling scriptures focusing on women and their place in the church, but her tone was less strident. "In the ordinary course of Church arrangement and order the Apostle Paul laid it down as a rule, that females should not speak in the church, not be suffered to teach," Elaw noted, "but the Scriptures made it evident that this rule was not intended to limit the extraordinary directions of the Holy Ghost, in reference to female Evangelists, or oracular sisters." The rule, said Elaw, was not to be "rigidly observed in particular circumstances." Her interpretation allowed for the exceptional woman, and Elaw foresaw the consequences of ignoring special cases. "Brethren certainly err, who fetter all and every ecclesiastical circumstance, and even the extraordinary inspirations of the Holy spirit" if they adhered strictly to Paul's writings or assumed that men "extensively possessed the gift of utterance."[59]

Rebecca Jackson was an exceptional person etching out a place for herself among religious women and men. In order to put God's plan into action, she initiated weekly meetings of cohorts to provide a supportive atmosphere for her husband, Samuel Jackson, and two women. They sought conversion but were too self-conscious to testify in the larger church body. As the size of the group increased, Morris Brown, Richard Allen's successor as bishop of the African Methodist Episcopal Church, charged, albeit falsely, that Jackson was intent on "chopping up the churches" and had exhibited improper behavior for a woman. Brown's declaration was tantamount to saying Jackson was teaching and leading men, contrary to church policy.[60]

She responded to his charges by asking for a formal trial conducted by Methodist and Presbyterian representatives along with three or four mothers of the churches. Since she did not belong to an organized church, Jackson requested the trial in her home. The clergymen ignored her, yet she claimed a moral victory. In her view, the ordeal was God's way of testing her faith. It did not occur to her that the trial did not come to fruition because she was not a church member and therefore not technically subject to the authority of any organized church.[61]

Following what she termed a dreadful "persecution" for living what she preached, Jackson gravitated toward the United Society of Believers in Christ's Second Appearing, commonly called Shakers, in 1842. They believed the millennium had already occurred with the second appearance of Christ in the person of the British-born Ann Lee, head of the Shakers in America. Jackson concluded that Shakers were the "true people of God" because their religious beliefs, including celibacy, ecstaticism, and revelations, were in agreement with her own ideals. The Shakers, headquartered in Watervliet, New York, provided the spiritual community Jackson sought. Moreover, its gendered theology eliminated the sexist barriers Jackson had encountered elsewhere.[62]

The Shakers' four-in-one godhead, the Father and Son alongside the Holy Mother Wisdom and Daughter in Deity, coequal partners, provided the balance Jackson wanted as a woman leader in a religious community. Knowing that equality existed among the godheads gave her the confidence needed to value her source of wisdom as a woman. Jackson no longer visualized spiritual authority as solely male. Besides, more than one vision of a Shaker woman served as an inspiring role model. In a dream, Jackson saw herself lagging behind but striding to reach the symbolic woman and eventually to keep pace with her as they trod along together.[63]

The Shaker faith was attractive to Jackson because it ended conflicts regarding women preachers in organized religions. But she became disillusioned because the Shakers, she wrote, "seemed to be gathering to themselves, in praying for themselves and not for the world, which lay in midnight darkness, [she] wondered how the world was to be saved, if Shakers were the only people of God on the earth, and they seemed to be busy in their own concerns, which were mostly temporal." This disturbed Jackson who wanted the Shakers' theology to be accessible to the larger community.[64]

It troubled her to know that blacks outside the Shakers' communities would not hear their message. Jackson's inner voice urged her to initiate missionary work among her own people. That would serve a spiritual need and possibly expand the number of converts, yet the idea precipitated a conflict in the Shaker hierarchy. The church disapproved of exposing Believers to worldly corruption and values at odds with their own.[65]

The conflict for Jackson was between primacy based on her inner voice and the external authority of Shaker Eldress Paulina Bates. Jackson refused to "submit to anything outward that was contrary to the inward." Her inner voice, like Jarena Lee's, was self-authorizing and defiant. The lack of a satisfactory explanation regarding the eldress's refusal to establish a mission among blacks disillusioned her. Jackson left Watervliet in 1851 but remained a firm believer in the Shaker doctrine.[66]

She returned to Watervliet in 1857 following a disturbing dream in which she saw herself going there primarily to seek authority from Eldress Paulina to extend her religious work. The visionary interpreted the dream in which African Americans were being discriminated against by the Shakers as her charge to convert blacks to the Shaker theology. Jackson also believed the dream predicted the favorable outcome of an imminent meeting with the eldress. Jackson made immediate plans to return to Watervliet, and the meeting with Paulina Bates mirrored her dream.[67]

Jackson was not the only nineteenth-century black woman spiritual to perceive or experience race-based differences among fellow congregationalists. For example, after 1817 and without ordination, Jarena Lee preached to mixed audiences at camp meetings; however, protocol determined that the ministers carry out specific responsibilities based on color. Prior to entering the ministry, Lee experienced discomfort in Joseph Philmore's predominately white congregation in Philadelphia. After several months of attending Philmore's church, "It appeared that there was a wall between me and the communion with that people," Lee observed. She had the impression of a foreboding presence that seemed to say, "This is not the people for you." The "wall" between black and white worshipers convinced her to find a more satisfying congregational home.[68]

Lee united with Bethel African Methodist Episcopal Church. In all probability, the sermons of Bethel's pastor Richard Allen were as important as the fellowship with those associated with Bethel. Bethel's congregation had grown from 108 members in 1794, the year of its founding, to 211 in 1799. Over the next five years, the membership increased to 457, and by 1813, the church had 1,272 members. The church's growth was a reflection of the increasing free black population in Philadelphia and its importance in the free black community. No doubt Lee was more at ease with a growing black congregation that shared her cultural values. Moreover, the church was an integral part of the black community and extended itself to all.[69]

Sojourner Truth sought an accepting church after becoming dissatisfied with New York City's John Street Church where blacks met in separate classes. She left the predominately white church and united with Zion African Church.[70]

Elaw did not write about racial discrimination among fellow religious adherents; however, her awareness of ethnocentricism is evident when she wrote, "The Pride of white skin is a bauble of great value with many in some parts of the United States, who readily sacrifice their intelligence to their prejudices, and possess more knowledge than wisdom." Elaw limited her indictment while recognizing that color was inconsequential in Christ. She found support for her convictions in Acts 17:26, which asserts God "hath made of one blood all nations of women."[71]

Jackson did not resort to the Bible for consolation. Instead, she acted firmly against what she perceived as racism among the Shakers, specifically their denial of a mission to blacks. Eventually she was able to persuade church elders to endorse that goal. In an October 2, 1858, meeting with Eldress Paulina Bates, Jackson was told, "You may go to your people and do them all the good you can. Now you can go in the gift of God, and in the gift of the Ministry and Elders. Now you are endowed with power and authority. Now the Lord hath sent you. You have waited for the Lord, and you go under a blessing." Paulina Bates agreed to bless and accept Jackson's converts and promised to "withhold no good thing," material or emotional support, from Jackson or her people.[72]

It is significant that Jackson's religious odyssey culminated with an endorsement and support from a woman. She had found sustenance and friendships in the praying bands in the early stages of her career and shared a special relationship in her declining years with Rebecca Perot, a coreligionist and companion. The close bond between the two Rebeccas raises questions about the nature of their personal association. Same-sex friendships among middle-class white women in the nineteenth century were "casually accepted by American society," according to historian Carroll Smith-Rosenberg. However, in the introduction to Jackson's *Gifts of Power*, editor Jean McMahon Humez writes, "Perhaps, had she [Rebecca Jackson] been born in the modern age, she would have been an open lesbian."[73]

Credence for such an idea may be located in the research findings of James S. Tinney, who reported, according to Humez, an "often-vocalized belief among male preachers [was] that the Pentecostal women preachers were closeted lesbians." Humez admits that Jackson's writings contain almost nothing that would support or refute the theory that intimacy existed between Jackson and her dedicated disciple, steadfast companion, and successor. Without factual evidence to undergird the assumption that the women were lesbians, it is incongruent to suggest that Rebecca Jackson, or other celibate religious women such as the Catholic nuns, engaged in homoerotic relationships.[74]

On February 15, 1850, Rebecca Jackson noted that it was her fifty-fifth birthday and that she had been in "the service of God," and in "obedience to [the] call to the Gospel" for nineteen years. For thirteen of those years, she wrote, "*I have dedicated my soul and body to the Lord in a virgin life.*"

Once sanctified, Jackson's spirituality overshadowed carnality. If she saw sinfulness in intimacy among heterosexuals, and in her own case as a married woman, she probably viewed intimacy between partners of the same sex as sinful also.[75]

For Jackson, embracing celibacy and controlling her sexuality were unmistakable signs of independence that threatened male ministers. Freedom as defined by Jackson alienated people who believed she enjoyed too much autonomy. As a result, disaffected ministers and other detractors might stoop to slandering any women who challenged them for positions of authority, the ear of church members, or a place in the pulpit. The friendship between Jackson and Perot probably thrived because they shared common experiences of sexism and racism hurled at black preaching women. Nevertheless, Jackson was successful in founding a Shaker community among blacks that fulfilled her mission and survived her death by forty years.[76]

Jackson's success is unrivaled by other spiritualists who continued trying to convince their churches to accept women preachers. Nearly a decade after Allen discouraged Lee from preaching, he agreed that she had indeed been called and defended her against the objections of other male preachers. Allen allowed Lee to assist him at services and permitted her to preach on occasion. Allen's successor, Daniel Payne, refused to continue even that limited practice. Neither Lee nor her spiritual sisters saw the destruction of all barriers against women preachers in the Methodist church. The greatest contribution of the women preachers was in initiating the fight for acceptance in the organized church. In the meantime, the women traveled to camp meetings and revivals where they were able to preach.[77]

Unlike the Protestant women who challenged gender-related barriers to proselytizing, women of the Catholic faith seemed to accept their church's hierarchical structure, which determined that clerical positions, whether priests or popes, were to be filled by men. Conventional wisdom suggested that white men, not black, received holy orders. Concomitantly, the Catholic Church in the United States and elsewhere had long recognized and endorsed the religious work of women as teachers, caregivers, and missionaries. The Ursulines, an order founded in the sixteenth century, were the first to dedicate themselves to teaching. Conventional wisdom suggested that white women took religious vows.[78]

So it is not surprising that when Henriette Delille, Juliette Gaudin, and Josephine Charles, free women of color in antebellum New Orleans, expressed their desires to dedicate their lives to God and live in a convent, white Catholics rebuffed them. In choosing a vocation ordinarily closed to them, the black Catholic women, no doubt influenced by the Ursulines, defied the prevailing expectations and social conventions of their time and place. Delille, described as "uncommonly beautiful, educated, and refined" in a study of the Sisters of the Holy Family, refused to enter into a *placage* arrangement, that neither the church nor the state sanctioned, as did her mother, Marie Josefe Diaz, and sister, Cecile Bonille. The decision to dedicate her life to God was the same for Delille's cofounders and other women who joined the Sisters of the Holy Family. As was true of Shaker eldress Rebecca Jackson, the Catholic sisters' decision to embrace celibacy and control their sexuality were unmistakable signs of independence.[79]

Furthermore, their steadfast determination to fulfill their ideals is an indication of their mettle and belief in their religious missions. It was incongruent to think these pious black Catholic women could not dedicate their lives to God when they had regular interactions with white nuns in New Orleans. Although it was without the sanction of the Catholic church, Delille organized the Congregation of the Sisters of Presentation of the Blessed Virgin Mary in 1836. Within a decade, the Catholic church recognized the African American order, renamed the Sisters of the Holy Family, and recorded its official founding date as 1842. The recognition came only after years of persistence by the black Catholic women who insisted upon honoring their commitments to dedicate themselves to charitable, educational, and religious work among their people whether free or enslaved.[80]

Unlike the Protestant spiritualists who fought for a leadership position usually occupied by black men in organized churches, the Sisters of the Holy Family fought for acceptance in a hierarchal structure controlled by whites. The Catholic women achieved measures of success, albeit within a segregated structure. They convinced their archbishop and priest that their order should not be cloistered to better serve the needs of their people. The sisters catechized free and enslaved blacks to fulfill ecclesiastical law, whereas the white religious teachers had been less enthusiastic in fulfilling that duty.[81]

While all of the spiritualists discussed herein continued work within the religious realm, Sojourner Truth's ministry was more expansive. The eminent historian Gerda Lerner noted, "Sojourner Truth stands virtually alone among black women in the 19th century in staunchly combining the defense of her race with the defense of her sex."[82]

Although Truth was unique in that regard, she was very much like her spiritual contemporaries in other ways. She also found liberation in the Supreme Being, but, unlike the other women who scoured the Bible for passages that freed them to preach within an organized church, Truth did not seek biblical authorization or acceptance from others regarding her ministry. Moreover, she moved to another level in using the Bible to throw off the patriarchal subjugation of women in areas unrelated to the ministry and to speak openly for women's rights and the abolition of slavery.[83]

After adopting a new persona June 1, 1843, Truth vowed to go where the spirit sent her. At this juncture she was not likely to bow to the influence of anyone except that of her God. As a free woman, physically and spiritually, she dedicated her new life entirely to exhorting listeners to "embrace Jesus, and refrain from sin." She traveled on foot from New York to western Massachusetts where she preached to crowds wherever she found them. At other times, Truth organized gatherings of her own.[84]

With the onset of winter in 1843, Truth decided to take up residence at the Northampton Association for Education and Industry, a utopian community in Massachusetts. A group of religious men including George W. Benson, a Connecticut lawyer and brother-in-law of William Lloyd Garrison, founded the association dedicated to antislavery issues. In addition to offering refuge from the New England winter, the association fostered the development of Truth's antislavery feminism. Certainly, this set Truth apart from other black women preachers who remained linked to churches.[85]

Because of her stay in Northampton, Truth's network of acquaintances and friends soon included abolitionists and feminists of public acclaim. None of Truth's spiritual contemporaries had a comparable array of acquaintances. Truth knew William Lloyd Garrison, Frederick Douglass, and Lucretia Mott along with Amy and Issac Post. After her stay in Northampton, Truth's name began appearing sporadically in newspapers as an antislavery lecturer. In 1851, she agreed to join the antislavery and women's rights circuit with stops in Massachusetts, western New York, and Ohio.[86]

While in Salem, Ohio, Truth lived with friends, Emily and Marcus Robinson. Robinson, a former student at Lane Theological Seminary in Cincinnati, was president of the Western Anti-Slavery Society, and editor of Salem's *Anti-Slavery Bugle*. Truth learned of the May 28, 1851, Ohio women's rights convention in Akron from Robinson. The subject interested her. She had spoken at the 1850 women's rights conference in Worcester, Massachusetts.[87]

Truth's comments at the 1851 convention catapulted her into historical prominence and continue to capture the imagination. Convention secretary Marius Robinson recorded and printed her remarks in the June 21, 1851, *Bugle* while the more familiar and highly embellished "Ar'n't I a woman?" version, written by Frances Dana Gage, appeared April 23, 1863. Gage's account must be considered alongside the rationale for publishing it twelve years after the event.[88]

Gage had taken exception to Harriet Beecher Stowe's imaginative essay, "The Libyan Sibyl," about Truth in the April 1863 *Atlantic*. Stowe's stark commercialization rankled Gage, and she responded with her own stylized portrayal of Truth. In attempting to offer a more accurate account, writes Truth's biographer, Nell Irwin Painter, Gage "invented" the "Ar'n't I a woman?" speech. Painter's textual analysis of accounts by Gage and Robinson shows that Gage's interpretation turned Truth's remarks into a "spectacular performance."[89]

To be sure, the more creative speech emphasizes the intersection of the abolitionist and women's rights movements of which Truth was a part. The repetitive use of the phrase "Ar'n't I a Woman?" punctuates the speech enumerating wrongs against blacks and women. But of more significance than the accuracy in reporting comments or rhetorical devices is the itinerant preacher's true recognition of color and gender discrimination and her boldness in attacking both. Truth presented a definite challenge, writes scholar Jacquelyne Grant, to "white women for their racism and white men for both their racism and sexism."[90]

Neither racism nor sexism stopped Truth from speaking for women's rights and against slavery. Her speeches highlight the controversial issue of rights for African Americans and women, timely topics on the reform agendas. Of the black women spiritual autobiographers discussed herein, Truth stands alone in combining her spirituality with abolitionism and women's rights. Others limited their comments to obstacles women faced in the ministry. This is understandable in terms of their original ambitions, individual circumstances, and interactions with others.[91]

Truth's contemporaries could not ignore slavery, and several referred to bondage in biblical times. Elaw wrote:

> Oh, the abominations of slavery! though Philemon be the proprietor, and Onesimus the slave, yet every case of slavery, however lenient its inflictions and mitigated its atrocities, indicates an oppressor, the oppressed, and the oppression. Slavery in every case, save those of parental government, criminal punishment, or the self-protecting detention of justifiable war, if such can happen, involves a wrong, the deepest in wickedness of any included within the range of the second table.

Obviously, she was passionate about the subject, but there is nothing to suggest that she incorporated antislavery protests in sermons when preaching in antebellum Maryland and Virginia. In fact, she writes about her paralyzing fear of being kidnapped and her adherence to "prudent advice" while in the South.[92]

What then is the place or value of black women spiritualists in the struggle for freedom and human rights? Elaw's primary concern was liberating the soul from sin, a kind of emancipation that she exalted above physical freedom. This brand of liberty provided psychological and emotional relief, thus making it possible for women and men to endure trials until freed from chattel slavery. If Elaw or her contemporaries preached openly about the evils of slavery in the South, they jeopardized their personal liberty. Although this could be devastating, it does not appear that the religious women would suffer the loss of freedom of faith in the powers of an almighty God. After all, spiritual freedom was of more importance to them than physical liberation.[93]

The Oblate Sisters of Providence and Sisters of the Holy Family appear to have been of the same accord. The Catholic church subscribed to the philosophy that there was no difference among people in God's eyes. Yet Catholic clergy and religious women, including Bishop John Carroll and the Ursulines, owned slaves. Moreover, Henriette Delille, known as the "servant of slaves," owned a woman whom she had inherited from her sister. What the black nuns thought privately about slavery, the church's stance, or the abolition of slavery remains unknown. Furthermore, there is no evidence in the studies of the Sisters of the Holy Family to suggest that they advocated the abolition of slavery. The Oblate Sisters, writes Diane Batts Morrow, "neither expressed abolitionist sentiments nor engaged in antislavery activities."[94]

Of the nineteenth-century black women spiritualists, only Truth and Stewart spoke clearly in public against slavery and in favor of expanding women's roles outside the home. Rather than ask why the other women were not more outspoken as women's rights advocates or abolitionists, it is more instructive to ask why they waged the fights they chose or to inquire about the burdens and responsibilities of choosing one struggle versus another.

Sojourner Truth, unlike her free-born sisters in the spirit, had firsthand knowledge of bondage and had seen her offspring sold away. No doubt this was a catalyst for her speaking out against slavery. This is not to say the women needed personal experiences to empathize with enslaved contemporaries. Rather, it is to underscore the fact that Truth associated with nationally known reformers and had more opportunities to speak on the subject. Her acceptance of God's omnipotence made her confident enough to expand her mission to blacks, enslaved and emancipated, females and males.

Truth's knowledge of the biblical Esther's selfless petition to King Ahasuerus asking him to rescind his decree ordering the slaughter of Jews throughout his kingdom must have bolstered her own courage. Esther risked her own life by appearing before the king without being summoned. She was more alarmed about the fate of her people than any concern for herself. Ahasuerus heard Esther's plea and granted the Jews the right to defend themselves and the authority to "cause to perish, all the power of the people and province what would assault them." Success on the battlefield turned the Jews' sorrow into joy.[95]

Sojourner Truth did not advocate bloodletting, but she could not abide the continued inequities blacks suffered. "You may hiss as much as you like," Truth told her audience, but "it is comin'." Truth, like Esther, had the interests of her people at heart. "We *will* have our rights; see if we don't," she said. To fulfill her role in this effort, Truth moved outside circles confined by religion. Her association with abolitionists at Northampton was not strictly within a religious setting but because of her religious beliefs. Her women's rights interests also reflect the intersection of Truth's own race and gender within an environment ready to fight for both the destruction of slavery and the institution of women's rights.[96]

After undergoing a riveting 1827 sanctification experience, Sojourner Truth exclaimed, "Oh, God, I did not know you were so big." Her perception of God's omnipotence leaves no doubt as to whom she would serve and how she defined her social responsibility to her people. The expansiveness of that realization made it possible for Truth to render service in the fight to win equal rights for women and free enslaved women and men from bondage.[97]

6

"Female sympathy in the cause
of freedom and humanity"

Activists and Abolitionists

Our greatest need is not gold or silver, but true men and true women. We
need men and women whose hearts are the homes of a high and lofty
enthusiasm, and a noble devotion to the cause of *emancipation*.

Frances Ellen Watkins

In 1832 Maria W. Stewart posited that the condition of free blacks, "with
few exceptions," was "but little better" than that of enslaved women
and men. She admitted the possibility of being "very erroneous" due to
variations according to region, class, and gender.[1]

Similarly, the British actress Frances Kemble noted that they were "free
from the chain, the whip, the enforced task and unpaid toil of slavery,"
but they were "also degraded, rejected, the offscum and the offscouring
of the very dregs of society."[2]

Both women were astute observers, but neither tells how free blacks
ameliorated the oppressiveness. In fact, free black women had multiple
strategies for responding to encroachments upon their liberty. Their
common African heritage, linkages to slavery, and concerns about uplifting their people served as a basis for solidarity in their two-pronged
struggle against discrimination and slavery. In the interest of mutual progress, many acted spontaneously while others joined formal organizations.[3]

The actual number of free black women involved in any or all facets of abolitionist activities across geographical regions is likely to be forever unknown, particularly that work requiring spontaneous or surreptitious action to assist enslaved women and men to freedom. The October 20, 1848, issue of *The North Star* included a story, "Convention of Colored People," from the Lynn *Pioneer* about the Negro Convention in Cleveland that adopted an "Address to the Colored People of the United States" in which the speaker urged African Americans to "take an active interest in the cause of Abolitionism." The address questioned "if a fifth part of the free colored people are Abolitionists" but suggested "as many as nine-tenths of the slaves are such."[4]

On the surface, the address paints a comparatively dim picture of abolitionist activities on the part of free blacks whose population reached 386,293 in 1840 and increased to 434,495 by 1850. The estimated 20 percent black abolitionists would be more meaningful if readers knew whether the statements were based upon actual data: for example, was the reference to the total number of free black adults across all regions of the United States or only to black adult males in the North? Knowing if the estimate included only persons who actually joined formal organizations is as significant as revealing if the count also considered persons who acted spontaneously or covertly. Of the 213,991 free black southerners in 1840, many woman and men were dedicated to the abolition of slavery, such as the North Carolinian Molly Horniblow and her contemporary Thomas Cole in South Carolina, but they did not join formal organizations, which were never as widespread in the South as in the North. To be sure, the estimated 90 percent of enslaved women and men believed to be abolitionists were not members of formal organizations. Ultimately, more information is needed to determine the extent to which free blacks were abolitionists.[5]

Whatever the number of black activists, fetters to their freedom were present in private acts, state statutes, and federal laws. Social customs further exacerbated conditions, and racial bigotry was boundless whether it involved a worship service, marketplace, or public conveyance in the North or Upper or Lower South. The range of hostilities prompted the free-born Sarah Remond to write, "Our home discipline did not—could not, fit us for the scorn and contempt which met us on every hand when faced with the world, a world which hated all who were identified with the enslaved race."[6]

Prejudices within the Society of Friends, or Quakers, rendered Sarah Mapps Douglass mute until 1838 when she recounted painful memories of attending Philadelphia's Arch Street meeting. "Even when a child my soul was made sad," wrote the thirty-two-year-old Douglass, when recalling how she and her mother sat alone and heard fellow worshipers say, "This bench is for the people of color." As a dissenting adult, she withdrew from the meetings while her mother remained and frequently "had a whole long bench to herself." Dedication to Quaker principles made a deeper impression on the pious, older woman than the behavior of the congregation. Perhaps she saw herself as subverting racism by reinterpreting it as something positive in having her own seat.[7]

Segregated churches were common in the North and South, and they were cause for blacks to question the efficacy of remaining in churches where they did not receive full acceptance. In 1832, "Zelmire" addressed the subject forthrightly in an antislavery paper. She asked why blacks humbled themselves by occupying color-defined seats. Zelmire, probably a pseudonym, asserted that whites would not bow to such indignities. "And why," she wrote, "should we submit to such distinction, any more than the whites?" Accepting segregation, in her opinion, was acknowledging inferiority. It was better to join black churches than submit to the insults.[8]

Leaving white churches could be traumatic since severing relationships meant finding and adjusting to a new congregation. It required courage to make such a protest; however, to remain in the church and confront racial bigotry were also courageous acts. One of the earliest examples of such dissent is that of blacks separating from Philadelphia's predominately white St. George Church in 1794 and founding Bethel African Methodist Episcopal Church.[9]

Outside the churchgoing population, discrimination on public conveyances affected a greater cross-section of blacks. Neither class nor gender saved them from racial prejudices. Susan Paul, a well-known Boston teacher, felt the sting of prejudice when she traveled to New York by steamboat in 1841. Although described as "the most respected black woman in Boston," she was not welcome in the ladies' car. As a result, she spent the night on the deck where exposure to inclement weather either caused a respiratory illness or exacerbated an existing condition.[10]

Paul's conflict involved interstate transportation whereas the New Yorker Elizabeth Jennings experienced degrading treatment from a local transit employee. On Sunday, July 16, 1854, a Third Avenue Railway conductor ejected the twenty-four-year-old teacher from a horse-drawn carrier. He dragged Jennings, a church organist, across the platform and prompted the abolitionist William Lloyd Garrison to label his behavior "vulgar and shameful in the extreme." Jennings, a community activist, initiated a class-action suit. Chester A. Arthur, who would become president of the United States in 1881, was a partner in the Erastus Culver firm, known for its sympathy to the abolitionist cause. He argued the February 1855 case before the Brooklyn Circuit Court and won. Frederick Douglass heralded the *Elizabeth Jennings v. Third Avenue Railway Company* decision as ground breaking. Both the *Anti-Slavery Standard* and the *New York Daily Tribune*, popular newspapers, reported the details. In all probability, readers were encouraged and believed the case would end discrimination. Sadly, officials failed to uphold the decision.[11]

Black challenges to segregation in public places continued. Examples of protests are plentiful due to the expansiveness of racism and the resolve of aggrieved persons. Sarah Remond experienced discrimination after purchasing a ticket for *Don Pasquale,* an 1853 opera featuring Madame Henriette Sontag at Boston's Howard Atheneum. The management objected to Remond and her friends sitting in the "Family Circle" section. When they refused a refund or gallery seats, a policeman attempted to remove them and injured her shoulder. Remond hired an attorney, filed a civil suit, and won the case. The settlement did not cover legal expenses, but she reveled in the court recognizing the violation of her civil rights.[12]

While legal action did not eradicate discrimination in public places, it did serve notice that Remond, Jennings, and others were not content with segregation. Their protests focused on a small facet of a much larger problem, such as the practice of blacks entertaining white-only audiences. For example, an 1853 concert to an audience of whites in New York's Metropolitan Hall featuring the freedwoman Elizabeth Greenfield prompted Frederick Douglass to pen the biting words: "We marvel that Miss Greenfield can allow herself to be treated with such palpable disrespect." It was an insult to her and her people. It created a moral and economic quandary for the entertainers. On one hand, if they refused to work under such conditions, the policy threatened their livelihood. On the other hand, acceptance made them appear more concerned about finances than fair treatment of all patrons. Greenfield apologized with a benefit concert for orphaned and aged blacks.[13]

Like Greenfield, the itinerant preacher Julia A. J. Foote faced a dilemma when white Methodists in Ohio asked her to preach but "did not want the colored people to attend the meeting." Foote's economic circumstances were precarious, but she was a religious woman dedicated to spreading the gospel. She believed a higher power would assure that basic necessities were within her reach just as the lilies of the fields thrived without work or care. Foote rejected the invitation. Her refusal to yield to blatant racism served as a criticism of the Methodists and their narrow view of Christian fellowship.[14]

Charlotte Forten had long pondered why blacks were not misanthropes as a result of such treatment. An especially unsettling 1857 experience forced her to question black attitudes toward mankind. Having attended school in Massachusetts, she contrasted Salem's hospitable atmosphere with Philadelphia's hostile environment. "Oh, how terribly I felt!" she wrote, after being refused service at two ice cream parlors in the "City of Brotherly Love." The twenty-year-old "could say but few words," yet wrote, "It is dreadful! dreadful!" "I cannot stay in such a place." She had encountered less racism in New England and longed to return.[15]

Without regard for geographical locations, free blacks were not insulated from color-based assaults upon their person or psyche. The mere presence of free blacks often raised the color prejudices of whites ready to petition legislatures to regulate them more rigorously. Many southern whites said free blacks exerted negative influences on those who were not free and caused restiveness among them; therefore, free persons were not above reproach or chastisement. All too often white citizens and lawmakers lumped blacks together, free and enslaved, when passing laws and punishing offenders.[16]

Local and state lawmakers imposed heavy burdens on free blacks through statutes circumscribing their rights to political participation, religious expression, geographical mobility, and economic access along with their rights to assemble, testify against whites, and bear arms. Under particularly arresting circumstances, free blacks could lose their independence. An 1811 law in New Kent, Delaware, permitted the sheriff to sell free blacks convicted of felonies.[17]

Harsh legal circumscriptions abounded. Missouri, a slaveholding border state, required registration and bond of free black residents. Ohio, Iowa, Michigan, and Indiana demanded that free blacks post bond "with good and sufficient security" of $500 upon entry into the state. Blacks failing to comply in Iowa and Indiana could be hired out for six months. Illinois required free blacks to register and in 1830 prohibited them from establishing residency without security and bond. By 1841, blacks migrating into Illinois and remaining ten days without meeting the requirements were deemed guilty of a misdemeanor and fined fifty dollars. Failure to pay fines subjected them to arrest and sale at public auctions. When sold, they owed labor to "owners" for a specified period of time. Afterward, the convict was to leave the state within ten days or be subject to prosecution.[18]

Free blacks registered disaffections for the laws in varied ways. Of interest is a petition in response to the 1811 Delaware statute permitting the sheriff to sell free blacks found guilty of crimes. The petitioners called attention to the U.S. Constitution's admonitions against excessive fines and cruel punishments. It would be virtually impossible to reunite with loved ones after two to seven years of imposed bondage at a distance or in another state. That, said the petitioners, was cruel punishment indeed.[19]

Both free women and men submitted petitions to state legislatures, but they expressed dissatisfactions differently. Having enjoyed the right to vote in selected states before 1840, men signed and circulated petitions protesting draconian laws or asking for repeals. Their protests were in the realm of changing or shaping legislation. Men often situated arguments in constitutional rights or war experiences. On occasion, they referred to themselves as "free mail sitisons," veterans, or men of color. By contrast, petitions by women were frequently humble supplications for permission to remain in a state or appeals to manumit a loved one. Without the "earned" rights of men, the women's language was less direct and more self-effacing, yet both men and women refused to placidly accept the laws as written.[20]

Petitions to southern legislatures between 1778 and 1864 reveal the complex nature of relationships among whites, free blacks, and slaves. One facet of those relationships is evident in the petitions submitted in opposition to laws or as requests for special dispensations. Relationships changed over time in keeping with changes to local, state, and national social, economic, and political circumstances.

Consider the controversy regarding the expansion of slavery when Missouri applied for statehood in 1819–1820. After the Missouri Compromise (1820), a lull in the slavery debate ensued, but the more vociferous abolitionists' attacks on slavery caused intensification, especially after the appearance of the *Appeal* (1829) by David Walker, a North Carolina–born militant abolitionist, and William Lloyd Garrison's *The Liberator,* a radical antislavery newspaper. Nat Turner's 1831 rebellion heightened anxieties, and proslavery advocates honed their arguments in response. Thomas Roderick Dew, author of *Review of the Debate in the Virginia Legislature* (1832), opened the new era by claiming slavery was a "positive good."[21]

Despite the general hostilities towards free blacks, there was still space in which they gave meaning to their liberty and freed themselves from harsh laws. A representative example is that of Elvira Jones, a freedwoman in Richmond, Virginia, who had purchased herself and two children. She was building a new life, but the law required that they migrate from the state. Relocation was prohibitive financially and would separate the Jones family from its community. Opposing the move, she petitioned lawmakers in 1823, saying: "Tis with anxious and trembling for[e]bodings then that your Petitioner presents herself before the Legislature to supplicate of their liberality and clemency, permission to herself and children to live and die in the Land of their nativity." By hard work and "great frugality," she owned a home and "small pecuniary resources." More importantly, she objected to separation from "endearments of kindred."[22]

A summary of Virginia's changing stance toward manumissions explains why Jones was threatened with removal and sought relief. The 1782 legislature had enacted a law permitting owners to free slaves at will and allowed them to remain in the state. In 1806, a new statute required freed persons to migrate within six months. Petitions to be excepted from the statute swamped the legislature and forced lawmakers to enforce the law or enslave miscreants. A decade later, the legislature allowed former slaves to remain in the state if freedom resulted from exceptional merit. What action constituted "meritorious service" was vague and open to interpretation. Consequently, even mundane deeds could win approval. Floods of petitions to remain caused state legislators to authorize county courts to decide the fate of freed persons on an individual basis. Alas, an 1852 law required all manumitted persons to migrate.[23]

Virginia was not unique in adopting prohibitive legislation changing the statutes or passing acts to grant individual relief. Among the states with similar statutes were Delaware, Mississippi, Georgia, North Carolina, and Tennessee. As a result, blacks petitioned legislatures for reprieves. The Mississippian Ann Caldwell asked for an exemption from removal in 1859, and Amelia Saulsbury, a nonresident free black in Delaware, requested permission in 1859 to reside in the state with "all privileges" and "rights" as "possessed and enjoyed by resident free negroes and mulattoes." The sixty-eight-year-old Sookey asked for special permission in 1856 to spend the balance of her days in North Carolina, the place of her nativity.[24]

Relief from draconian laws depended on the local, state, and national climate. Chances were better in placid times rather than those associated with economic downturns, increases in the free black population, and slave rebellions or rumor thereof. Turbulent times were certain to bring a spate of hate-filled laws designed to regulate blacks stringently and punish offenders, real or imaginary, more severely with fines and incarcerations.

Table 6.1
Slaves Manumitted According to the Seventh Census, 1850

States	Slaves	Manumissions	One out of	Per Cent
Upper South				
Delaware	2,290	277	8	12.0960
Kentucky	210,981	152	1,388	.0720
Maryland	90,368	493	183	.5455
Missouri	87,422	50	1,748	.0571
N. Carolina	288,548	2	144,274	.0006
Tennessee	239,459	45	5,321	.0187
Virginia	472,528	218	2,167	.0461
Lower South				
Alabama	342,844	16	21,427	.0046
Arkansas	47,100	1	27,100	.0021
Florida	39,310	22	1,786	.0559
Georgia	381,682	19	20,088	.0049
Louisiana	244,809	159	1,539	.0649
Mississippi	309,878	6	51,646	.0019
S. Carolina	384,984	2	192,492	.0005
Texas	58,161	5	11,632	.0085
	3,200,364	1,467	2,181	.0458

Sources: Jos. C. G. Kennedy, *Preliminary Report on the Eighth Census* (Washington, DC: Government Printing Office, 1862), 137.

Public flogging was a common form of chastisement meted out to blacks and whites in colonial America. Over time, society viewed whipping as barbaric for whites but continued to deem it suitable for blacks, enslaved and free. Eliza Gallie's brush with the law in 1853 shows the attitude toward whippings in southern society. Alexander Stevens accused the free woman of stealing vegetables, and the mayor of Petersburg, Virginia, heard the case. Gallie hired several lawyers who resorted to the social construction of race for her defense. They claimed she had white ancestors and should not be tried as a black person. The court found her guilty and sentenced her to thirty-nine lashes. After review, the court reduced the sentence to "twenty lashes on her bare back at the public whipping post."[25]

No doubt fewer stripes reflected a consideration of her status, but the humiliation of being stripped and beaten in public must have been devastating. This was a reminder of the continued existence of slavery and racist notions about blacks who were viewed as chattel regardless of their legal standing.[26]

Table 6.2
Slaves Manumitted According to the Eighth Census, 1860

States	Slaves	Manumitted	One out of	Per cent
Upper South				
Delaware	1,798	12	149	.6674
Kentucky	225,483	176	1,281	.0780
Maryland	87,189	1,017	85	1.1664
Missouri	114,931	89	1,291	.0774
North Carolina	331,059	258	1,283	.0079
Tennessee	275,719	174	1,584	.0630
Virginia	490,865	277	1,771	.0564
Washington, DC	3,185	8	398	.2514
Lower South				
Alabama	35,080	101	4,310	.0231
Arkansas	111,115	41	2,711	.0369
Florida	61,745	17	3,632	.0275
Georgia	462,198	160	4,360	.0229
Louisiana	331,726	517	641	.1558
Mississippi	436,631	182	2,399	.0416
South Carolina	402,406	12	33,533	.0029
Texas	182,566	31	5,889	.0169
	3,953,696	3,072	1,278	.0763

Source: Jos. C. G. Kennedy, *Preliminary Report of the Eighth Census, 1868* (Washington, DC: Government Printing Office, 1962), 137.

By the 1850s, corporal punishment, with few exceptions, was reserved for blacks. An unusual case in antebellum Kentucky indicates the extent to which corporal punishment for white adults had become "prohibitive." Stripes laid upon a convicted white thief in the 1850s raised the ire of a Kentucky jury, which made restitution of six hundred dollars to the injured party. The antebellum Chatham County, Georgia, Superior Court was clear in the distinction made in corporal punishment according to color. Whites who committed misdemeanors usually paid fines whereas blacks guilty of misdemeanors were whipped.[27]

No geographical region had a monopoly on vile legislation directed toward blacks. Alabama and Georgia provide many examples, and laws were unusually stringent in South Carolina where an annual capitation tax, a fee required of each individual, worked hardships on many free persons. The penalty for ignoring the 1792 law was enslavement. In 1794, thirty-four free black women and men petitioned the legislature for repeal of the law. In the masculine voice, they called themselves free

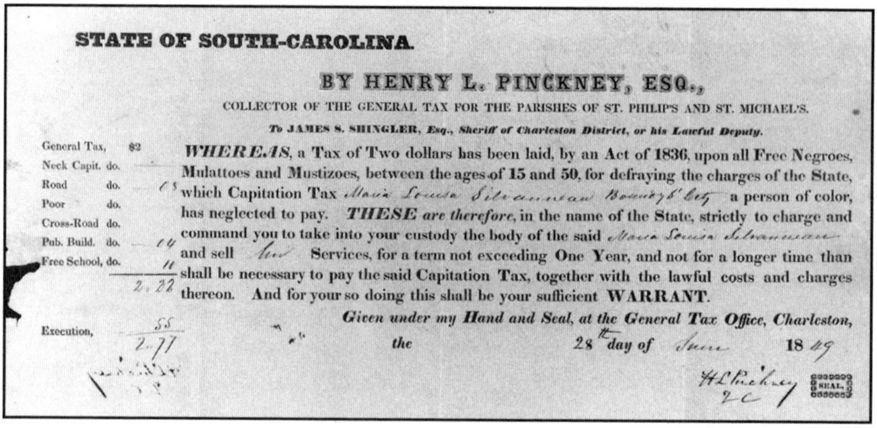

Figure 6.1. Warrant for the arrest of Maria Louisa Silvanneau. Special Collections, College of Charleston, Charleston, South Carolina.

citizens and paid deference by indicating their willingness to support the government. The petitioners worried about the fate of large families without means to pay the taxes, especially "women scarcly able to support themselves." Harsh laws in South Carolina demanded that newly freed persons migrate, and in 1822, lawmakers passed a bill prohibiting free persons from entering the state. The penalty for violating the law was enslavement.[28]

One must ask how effective were such legislative acts and the corresponding protests. "Laws alone," writes historian Ira Berlin, "could not control the free Negroes." To be sure, legislation was threatening but never strictly enforced nor was it drastic enough to snuff out all black aspirations. Enforcement required vigilance, and black persistence often overwhelmed white diligence. Some blacks evaded and ignored laws with impunity. Printed forms regarding violators of the May 26, 1845, resident license requirements in St. Louis suggest that officials handled more than a few cases and produced forms en masse to expedite matters. Furthermore, whites were never unified philosophically in stripping free persons of all rights any more than they were a cohesive unit in holding all blacks in bondage. As a result, proscriptive statutes were occasionally modified or fell into disuse.[29]

The failure to enforce statutes did not mean free persons were unencumbered by the laws or free to enjoy the same privileges as whites. Instead, blacks defined the essence of their liberty by working within the system, securing white associates for protection, or evading the laws without calling attention to themselves. This could be a precarious state of being, but it was not slavery. The discomfort was in never knowing when or if whites would enforce laws and take black liberty away. Freedom of this sort could be illusory, but even the essence of liberty was more desirable than enslavement.

A petition submitted to the Texas legislature points to the laxity in enforcement and one woman's will to protect her freedom. Once Texas gained independence from Mexico in 1836, the constitution prohibited the 150 free blacks in the republic from maintaining residency without congressional approval. In 1837, the legislature removed the residency stipulation and passed a joint resolution granting free blacks permission to remain. Persons migrating to Texas or those receiving freedom after 1837 were vulnerable to legislation requiring removal.[30]

The forty-two-year-old Mary Madison, "an honest, sober and industrious woman" had lived in Galveston for more than ten years and fell into the latter category. In 1851, she submitted a humble but defiant petition to the legislature. The request shows how she shaped and protected her freedom in violation of the law. The white community's perception of Madison as a woman who "conducted herself with the strictest propriety" probably bolstered her determination. In fact, a Galveston County official had served notice to free blacks, including Madison, to migrate in 1840. "But in view of her good conduct, her excellent behavior and general usefulness," he had allowed her to stay until she applied to the legislature for permanent residency.[31]

Madison, a caregiver, aided many white Galvestonians, who had "experienced her kindness . . . attention and watchfulness, when such qualities [were] really needed." Her "general usefulness" and stellar conduct convinced one supporter to say she was a "good and orderly citizen." Others proclaimed that Madison was "a valuable citizen." She had forged a relationship with whites based on her personal behavior and professional demeanor. She used these characteristics to defy the law and to encourage ninety-four women and men to sign her petition. They resented the idea of forcing Madison to migrate "at her period of life to seek a home in another land and among strangers."[32]

The memorial was void of any protests about Texas not extending privileges and immunities to free persons comparable to those in other states following annexation to the Union in 1845. Madison's friends agreed that she was a "valuable citizen" but appeared more concerned about the loss of an accomplished caregiver than about the violations of her civil rights. If the state denied her request, Madison faced the loss of her occupation, family, and friends after eleven years of evading the law.[33]

Separation was one of the harshest aspects of slavery, and it follows that the gravity of parting from loved ones, living or dead, was no less significant for free blacks, many of whom were slave-born and had family or friends remaining in bondage. If discriminatory laws forced free blacks to relocate, the possibility of ever returning to the places and people holding special meaning for them was remote, especially when some slaveholding states forbade free blacks from entering upon penalty of enslavement.[34]

Restrictions on travel and residence were not the only threats to the liberty of free blacks. David Ruggles, founder of a predominately black vigilance committee in New York City, reminded free blacks of their vulnerability to kidnapping and enslavement in 1836. "Self-defense," he said, "is the first law of nature." Free men and women, especially in New York and Philadelphia, were cautious about kidnappings because of the brisk sale of slaves in Baltimore and Richmond. Washington, D.C., was also an active slave-trading venue until a provision in the Compromise of 1850 prohibited it.[35]

"Manstealing," the physical abduction of persons with the intent to enslave, was of longstanding importance to free blacks who could be "mistaken" for slaves. In slaveholding states, it was commonly believed that all blacks were enslaved; consequently, free blacks were subjected to kidnapping and enslavement. The cessation of the overseas slave trade in 1808 made many free persons more anxious about their liberty. In non-slaveholding states, it was commonly assumed that all blacks were free; therefore, slaveowners were adamant about stopping flights to the North where runaway slaves hoped to blend in with the free population, thereby emancipating themselves. Owners were vigilant about retrieving such fugitives, and free persons were sometimes arrested and enslaved in the South.[36]

Article IV, Section 2 of the U.S. Constitution provided for the extradition of fugitives from labor, but its execution was vague. The Fugitive Slave Act of 1793 clarified the procedure, saying slaveowners could seize runaways, present them to any federal or state court along with proof of identity, and receive authorization for their return. Clearly, this was advantageous to slaveholding states in the event of conflicts over the status of fugitives. The 1793 law also prevented northern states from exercising absolute power over their citizens' personal and civil rights.[37]

The 1793 statute did not deter would-be kidnappers. As a result, several northern states passed protective laws. An 1826 Pennsylvania statute required jury trials and testimony from alleged fugitives. The law also imposed strict requirements on claimants and prohibited lower courts from taking jurisdiction of cases according to the federal law. On the surface, it appears that the Pennsylvania law conflicted with the federal statute. The Supreme Court decided the constitutionality of the state law in *Prigg v. Pennsylvania* (1842), which involved Margaret Morgan, a "virtually free" woman who lived in Maryland until 1832 when she and her family moved to Pennsylvania.[38]

In 1837, Edward Prigg, an attorney for Morgan's owner, seized the fugitive and her children—one of whom was born in Pennsylvania. A local justice of the peace refused Prigg's request for a certificate to remove Morgan, claiming the state's 1826 statute had higher "evidentiary requirements than the federal law." The state law prohibited a magistrate from taking cognizance of such cases according to the 1793 statute. Without action from the Pennsylvania courts, Prigg returned the Morgans to Maryland. Two weeks later, officials arrested and charged him with kidnapping under the Pennsylvania law.[39]

The Supreme Court acknowledged the founding fathers' intent to grant citizens all rights and titles to their chattel should they escape, but the Constitution made no provisions for reclaiming fugitives. States could not be compelled to enforce the statute, said Justice Joseph Story, who implied that it could be an unconstitutional exercise to insist that states execute the duties of the federal government when the Constitution was silent on the matter. "Each State is at liberty," declared Story, "to prescribe just such regulations as suit its own policy, local convenience, and local feelings." Procedures might differ from state to state. The Court, Story affirmed, would not interfere with state police power. The decision upheld the 1793 act without requiring the states to enforce it.[40]

Prigg, a landmark case considered the most famous fugitive slave case up to that time, did not satisfy proslavery or antislavery advocates. As a result, between 1843 and 1848, northern states, including New York, Massachusetts, Vermont, Connecticut, New Hampshire, Pennsylvania, and Rhode Island, passed personal liberty laws wherein jury trials were common. The laws forbade state assistance in the return of runaways and prohibited the use of state facilities to detain them. New York and Vermont appointed lawyers for defendants, if needed. The scholar Joseph Nogee termed the acts the "first real Personal Liberty laws" designed to assist free blacks and alleged fugitives.[41]

Aside from personal liberty laws, there were organizations and private individuals dedicated to guaranteeing the liberty of free persons. Those who were vigilant about their own liberty and that of others responded to threatening situations and advertised warnings such as a July 1834 broadside urging New Yorkers to "LOOK OUT FOR KIDNAP-PERS": a Raleigh, North Carolina, slave hunter, Dr. Rufus Haywood, was in their midst.[42]

Haywood's mission was identical to that of his fellow North Carolinian Dr. James Norcom, who made three trips to New York between 1835 and 1837 in search of Harriet Jacobs. She manipulated him into thinking she had fled to the North while she remained hidden for nearly seven years in the attic of her grandmother, Mollie Horniblow. When it became too dangerous to stay there, Jacobs fled to the North where friends, including members of the Anti-Slavery Society, assisted in the continued struggle to maintain her liberty.[43]

Neither Haywood nor Norcom's search generated the kind of attention that Matthew Turner created when he sought the return of Eliza Small and Polly Ann Bates, travelers to Boston in 1836 aboard the brig *Chickasaw*. Turner acted as an agent for John B. Morris, a wealthy Maryland slaveholder, who claimed the women were fugitives. *The Liberator* reported that they were free and had proof of their status. Nevertheless, Turner treated the women as runaways and asked Captain Henry Eldridge to detain them until he received a warrant for their arrest.[44]

Once local residents learned of the women's detention, they milled about the wharf. A local black man secured a writ of habeas corpus directing Eldridge to release the women. Afterward, hundreds of spectators, including five women from the Boston Female Anti-Slavery Society, attended a hearing. They were jubilant when the chief justice said the "fugitives" were "discharged from all further detention."[45]

What happened next, according to a witness, was one of the "grossest outrages of public justice." Turner indicated that he would pursue the "fugitives," which alarmed their supporters, including free black women. In the midst of confusion, the judge tried to block the door while the mob seized and throttled a court officer. One newspaper reported that "a colored woman of great size who scrubbed floors for a living...threw her arms around the neck of one officer immobilizing him." The crowd spirited Small and Bates out of the court and into a carriage. The court never arrested anyone for inciting the "Abolition Riot."[46]

The 1836 riot set a precedent for direct action following passage of the more stringent Fugitive Slave Act in 1850. This law authorized commissioners to issue arrest warrants for suspected fugitives and certificates for their return to bondage. The fate of an accused person depended on the claimant's description, not prima facie evidence. Since cases were not subject to jury trials and the accused could not testify, the possibilities of kidnapping with the intent to enslave escalated. As slaveowners and slave catchers hunted for fugitives, real or imagined, abolitionists became more determined to save any accused persons from perpetual bondage.[47]

The offensiveness of the 1850 act and the increased responses mark a dramatic shift in the attention given to the retrieval of runaways and the increased possibilities of free persons losing their liberty. In 1851 black Bostonians rushed the court and freed Frederick "Shadrach" Wilkins, a Virginia-born fugitive. Bostonians also attempted to thwart the law by helping Georgia-born fugitive Thomas Sims in 1851 and Virginia-born runaway Anthony Burns in 1854.[48]

The Burns case prompted Charlotte Forten to muse: "[I] did not intend to write this evening [May 25, 1854], but have just heard of something that is worth recording;—something which must ever rouse in the mind of every true friend of liberty and humanity, feelings of the deepest indignation and sorrow. Another fugitive from bondage has been arrested . . . like a criminal."[49]

The Burns case was the most publicized of all responses to the Fugitive Slave Act of 1850. Hordes of people rushed to the courthouse where Burns was under arrest, and a group of men, mostly black, used a battering ram to smash the door. After a brief fray in which one deputy was killed, the men retreated. Following a second assault through a basement door, the city police and two artillery companies responded to restore order and arrest protesters. "All this is done to prevent a man," Forten wailed, "whom God has created in his own image, from regaining that freedom with which, he, in common with every human being, is endowed."[50]

One could argue these events occurred in Boston because of its reputation as one of America's most liberal cities with a long history of civil protests. Boston, the hub of antislavery activities and reform, ended segregation on public carriers in the 1840s and in its public schools in 1855. It was also home of *The Liberator*, whose editor was one of America's best-known abolitionists. The city never had more than a 3 percent black population before the Civil War, but it was sufficient to lend support to the abolitionist cause. The city was distinctive, but impassioned crowds rescuing fugitives were very much the same regardless of the location.[51]

The behavior of more than 200 people in Troy, New York, April 27, 1860, at a federal commissioner's office as authorities were making plans to send the fugitive Charles Nalle back to Virginia, differed from the Bostonians only in that Harriet Tubman, a woman who had freed herself, was the "mastermind of the event," according to a Tubman biographer, Sarah H. Bradford. The *Troy Arena* described the scene as a "theater of war," with over twenty rounds of shots fired during the melee. Amid the chaos, Tubman broke through the crowd, tore Charles Nalle away from a court officer, placed her sunbonnet on his head, and held on to him until they reached safety. She emerged as the heroine; however, other women and men assisted her.[52]

Not all rescue attempts were successful, yet the efforts of black women cannot be underestimated. Women made up a larger percentage of the free black urban populations and maintained informal communications networks regarding concerns of interest to the community, according to scholar Gayle T. Tate. They were also diligent about assisting runaways who fled to cities to blend in with the larger population. Since many women took in laundry and worked at home, they were more readily available to thwart slave catchers. This is illustrated by an 1847 incident involving a group of women led by the prominent Bostonian Nancy Prince. They successfully thwarted a slave catcher seen at a Smith Court home. According to one report, the men were away at work, but "there were those around that showed themselves equal to the occasion." With a dramatic flair, the report said, before the kidnapper realized his position, Prince and several black women dragged him to the door and threw him outside. The commotion attracted a crowd of women and children who pelted him with missiles at Prince's direction and chased him away.[53]

The women's intent was to protect any person from a lifetime of bondage. Whether they achieved that end was more important than the means. After all, said an 1834 broadside warning New Yorkers about kidnappers, "OPPOSITION TO TYRANTS" was "OBEDIENCE TO GOD." Fulfilling their Christian duty required strong moral convictions and action when needed. The *Colored American* looked askance at the women who "so degraded themselves" in an 1837 attempt to stave off kidnappers. In fact, the *Colored American* cast aspersions and begged their husbands "to keep them at home and find some better occupation for them." However, to fulfill their duty to themselves and others against the loss of liberty was more important to these women than perceptions of what constituted proper behavior for women and negative remarks.[54]

It is unlikely that Eliza Ann Parker or her husband, William, thought of gender conventions on September 11, 1851, when the shouts of armed white men awakened them. Edward Gorsuch, a Baltimore, Maryland, slaveowner, along with his son, nephew, cousin, and two neighbors, had come to Christiana, Pennsylvania, to retrieve four runaways whom they believed the Parkers were sheltering. The Parkers were known for assisting runaways and offering their home as a gathering place for blacks organized for mutual protection against slave catchers.[55]

Gorsuch was within his rights to pursue the men, who fled Maryland during the 1849–1850 winter. Although Henry S. Kline, a deputy U.S. marshal, had warrants for their arrest, the slave-born William Parker and his wife refused to yield the fugitives. As it became clear that they were in danger, Eliza Parker summoned help by sounding an alarm. Kline ordered his men to shoot whomever was responsible, and two men fired at Eliza. This precipitated the confrontation known as the Christiana Riot.[56]

To quell the tumult, federal officials dispatched fifty marines to Lancaster County. By the time they arrived, the upheaval had ended, and Gorsuch was dead. William Parker feared arrest for obstructing justice and murder. Consequently, he and two other rioters fled to Rochester, New York, where Frederick Douglass provided them with food and shelter. He described them as "heroic defenders of the rights of man against mansthieves and murderers." Eliza Parker joined her husband in Canada where they escaped punishment. Neither Eliza nor William Parker considered their roles in the riot a "crime" or a violation of natural law.[57]

The publicity surrounding the riot and the Anthony Burns case provided both pro- and antislavery factions with fodder for their propaganda mills. Abolitionists gained converts by keeping the fugitive's cause before the public. Active participation in Boston, Troy, or Christiana riots emboldened the spirit and made the women and men more willing to fight for change regardless of the proslavery advocates' resolve.

Challenges from individual proslavery advocates or state and local laws never deterred the female and male agents of the "Underground Railroad," an intricate network of people who assisted fugitives with food, clothing, and shelter on their way north. The free-born Tennessean Mary Richardson Jones along with a group of black women known as the "Big Four" helped runaways passing through Chicago, but the identities of many of their contemporaries are unknown due to the secret nature of the illegal rescue operation.[58]

By contrast, the exploits on behalf of fugitives by Harriet Tubman, a well-known conductor on the Underground Railroad, are legendary. She is credited with fifteen trips into the South to rescue more than 200 enslaved men, women, and children. Her successes were due to clever disguises, unwavering courage, and the lack of tolerance for fugitives who changed their minds about running away. To avoid detection because of crying babies or faltering fugitives, Tubman gave paregoric to the former and threatened the latter with a pistol, saying, "Dead men tell no tales." After passage of the 1850 fugitive slave law, Tubman guided many runaways to Canada beyond the vile law.[59]

An untold number of unheralded women and men assisted slaves in gaining their liberty. Without fanfare or membership in organizations, they helped to destroy slavery at every opportunity as did the well-traveled Eliza Potter. The highly opinionated woman described herself as the "humble means of unloosing the shackles of one upright and manly soul." She told an enslaved man whom she met in Louisville all she knew about Canada including specific travel directions. Officials arrested and tried her as an accessory. Potter was indignant but never denied complicity in "directing his footsteps to a new world." She recognized "no crime in what [she] had done—[and] meant none."[60]

People of Potter's ilk caused proslavery advocates to complain vehemently about free blacks encouraging enslaved women and men to run away or foment other forms of rebellion. The notion that free persons were lazy, improvident evil-doers was the catalyst for legislation in the 1850s to expel them from the slaveholding states. If free persons refused to migrate, they were subject to enslavement. George Fitzhugh, a southern proslavery apologist, said, "Humanity, self-interest, [and] consistency, all require that we should enslave the free negro." But was it legal to take away their liberty and make them slaves for life?[61]

Readers of the *Arkansas State Gazette and Democrat* saw an increase in discussion about legislation to remove free persons. The tone was more strident in the 1850s with the increased agitation for the expulsion of free blacks. When the paper did not publish commentary on its own, it included articles from other sources such as a June 19, 1858, editorial in the *Fort Smith Times and Democrat* asserting that western Arkansas was "overrun" with "troublesome" free blacks, called a "pest and a Nuisance." The editor asked slaveowners to stop enslaved women and men from behaving as free persons by "running at lodge" and hiring their own time.[62]

In July 1858, the *Arkansas State Gazette* published a circular, "To the People of Arkansas," from a twelve-member committee claiming to represent the citizens of Little Rock and Pulaski County. The protest, a litany of complaints against the "evil among us," free blacks, said they "instinctively take the side of those under government [of slaveowners and] console with them when they complain, harbor them when they escape, tell them they are entitled to be free, and encourage them in insubordination and to pilfer and defraud if not to commit offense more serious, and do acts more dangerous still." The committee complained about slaveowners' inabilities to make their chattel submissive and loyal based on the conviction that "servitude to a higher race" was the slave's "natural condition." The committee believed free blacks were responsible for slaves' recalcitrance and sought to eject free persons from the state.[63]

The public sentiments against free blacks persuaded Arkansas legislators to pass a November 1859 bill expelling them. The law affected 294 free black females of all ages who had until January 1, 1860, to migrate or bind themselves to white "masters." Otherwise, sheriffs could arrest and sell free persons to the highest bidder. Persons without the means to relocate were subject to a sheriff's hiring for one year to earn moving expenses. Ultimately, the legislation took its toll. Only seventy-two free black women remained in the state in 1860.[64]

Frances E. W. Harper lent her support to twelve migrants from Arkansas, including Elizabeth T. West, Agnes West, Rachel Love, Polly Taylor, Caroline Parker, Jane Thompson, and Nelly Grinton, by writing "The Appeal to Christians Throughout the World." The publication encapsulates the violations of their civil rights. Even the loss of a tenuous freedom was devastating for a people who claimed their only "fault, in a land of Bibles and Churches, of baptisms and prayers" was the blood of "an outcast race; a race oppressed by power and proscribed by prejudice; a race cradled in wrong and nurtured in oppression." The move separated them from loved ones. Harper asked all influential persons to raise their voices in protest against this injustice.[65]

Ironically, as the masses of free blacks were leaving Arkansas to avoid slavery, a small number of blacks in Arkansas and elsewhere sought to enslave themselves. By the onset of the Civil War, nine states had passed legislation legitimizing the enslavement of free persons. Why would anyone discard freedom? It is likely that those seeking enslavement were actually arranging for white "guardians" to protect their liberty surreptitiously, prevent migration, or avoid capitation tax. On January 31, 1859, the free-born Lizzie Jones filed a petition in South Carolina requesting enslavement. According to the document, she was of clear mind and acted voluntarily, but it did not cite reasons for her actions. The same is true of enslavement petitions submitted between 1858 and 1860 by the Virginians Judy Cullin, Lavinia Napper, Mary Elizabeth, Fanny Williams, Margarett Price, and Mary Browne. The majority of free persons did not abandon their liberty, despite its tenuous nature and the oppressive laws. In 1860, of the 30,321 women and 27,721 men in Virginia's free black population, only twenty-nine of them petitioned the legislature with requests for enslavement.[66]

Once they relinquished their free status, it was nearly impossible to recover it. In spite of the constraints for blacks in antebellum society, however, there was no comparison between the quality of a fettered life and a free one. The free-born Polly Crocket understood this because she had been kidnapped as a child and come of age in bondage. Crocket's daughter, Lucy Delaney, published the autobiographical *From the Darkness Cometh the Light* (1891), which illuminates their quest to regain and maintain freedom. Delaney remembered that her mother "never spared an opportunity" to tell her children to seek liberty "whenever the chance offered." No scheme was "too wild" for consideration.[67]

Lucy Delaney's narrative stands alone as a detailed account of a kidnapping and the successful quest for freedom by several black women across two generations. Only the narrative of the free-born New Yorker Solomon Northup compares with Delaney's in terms of a comprehensive chronicle of his bondage in Louisiana. During Solomon's absence, his wife, Anne Hampton Northup, and their children, Elizabeth, Margaret, and Alonzo, held him in "constant remembrance." They learned of the kidnapping in 1841 and heard nothing more for over a decade. On November 19, 1852, Anne Northup submitted a memorial to New York's governor asking for an intercession on her husband's behalf. The state had passed an 1840 act to protect free citizens from kidnapping and enslavement. Her petition was central to reunification of the Northup family.[68]

The enslavement of Crocket and Northup ultimately failed, but that result was atypical by comparison with most kidnapped and falsely enslaved persons. For example, the fate of Rebecca Cronch or Crouch, a woman emancipated in Alabama by James B. Rowley, exemplifies the difficulties freedpersons encountered if re-enslaved. In 1838, Cronch moved to Ohio, and Rowley placed a certificate of her freedom on file in Mobile, Alabama, and forwarded necessary legal papers to her. Cronch traveled to Vicksburg, Mississippi, in 1840. By that time, Rowley was an innkeeper in the city with mounting debts. Hereafter, the details of Crouch's case are confusing. She was arrested as Rowley's property and held in jail. As late as 1845, Crouch's case remained in litigation, and the results are unknown.[69]

Kidnappings received far more attention than free persons who lost their freedom for failure to pay capitation tax or to migrate within the prescribed time, and those who enslaved themselves because of dire poverty. The dreadful conditions that fostered such infringements upon their rights as free persons made their lives little better than those of persons in bondage. The North Carolina attorney William D. Valentine observed that free blacks were indicted on presentments for emigrating into North Carolina in 1852. If convicted, they were obliged to pay court costs and forced to leave the state. Valentine was sensitive to the tenuous nature of their freedom and wrote, "In what a miserable condition these poor free persons of color are . . . Where will they go? They must go some where. What can be done for them? Something must be done."[70]

Valentine was probably familiar with the American Colonization Society (ACS), formed in 1816 for the repatriation of free or freed blacks and their descendants to Africa. The ACS founders assumed free blacks could not blend into mainstream American society; therefore, the quality of their lives would be better elsewhere. The ACS believed Liberia was the best alternative. Others in favor of colonization, including white slave-owners, believed the presence of free blacks created restiveness among enslaved ones and caused them to seek their own freedom. To remove free persons would eliminate a potential source for rebelliousness.[71]

Repatriation was virtually impossible for most free persons because of distance and cost. Besides, they considered the United States their home. In the two centuries since the initial arrival of Africans, they had helped build the nation economically by the sweat of their brow and politically through service in the Revolutionary War and the War of 1812. Many resented the idea of colonization as a deliberate attempt to separate them from their enslaved kindred.[72]

White sentiments about blacks leaving the United States probably intensified in relationship to the increased hostility toward them in the first half of the nineteenth century. Examples of racial conflicts are numerous. Cincinnati was the site of tumult in 1829 and 1841. Riots occurred in Providence in 1831, and New York City was the scene of chaos in 1834. Washington, D.C., and Boston witnessed turmoil in 1835 and 1843, respectively. There were riots in Philadelphia in 1829, 1834, 1835, and 1841. Rebecca Cox Jackson's biographer suggests that the spiritualist's dreams of violence against persons were related to the times in which she lived. The racial climate became even more oppressive after the adoption of the Compromise of 1850. Many free blacks did not feel safe from slavery's punitive arm as long as the Constitution protected "the peculiar institution."[73]

If free blacks chose to remove themselves beyond the United States' racist laws, Liberia was not their only alternative. In spring 1857, thirty-five free blacks departed from Pensacola, Florida, for Tampico, Mexico, aboard the *Pinta*. As the ship sailed, a woman tossed a rock overboard and said bitterly she would return when it floated up to the surface. Several months later, the schooner *William* carried other free women and men to Tampico. The outflow continued. In June 1859, *Douglass' Monthly* estimated that more than 2,000 of Louisiana's free blacks had migrated to Haiti, an independent black nation.[74]

Letters written for an English class assignment in the 1850s and 1860s by adolescent boys attending the *Ecole catholique pour l'instruction des orphelins dan l'indigence* in New Orleans provide a cornucopia of data about their grasp of historical occurrences. Moreover, the letters are significant as a reflection of their teachers', free persons of color, understanding of the possibilities of living in hospitable environments where blacks could prosper as farmers, merchants, or entrepreneurs in Haiti or Mexico. Knowledge of black migration from New Orleans, a port of debarkation, after the passage of the Compromise of 1850 and its more stringent fugitive slave clause made Haiti and Mexico destinations of choice. The teachers at the *Ecole catholique* encouraged their pupils to imagine living and working there.[75]

The greater number of disaffected African Americans migrated to Canada, the northernmost stop on the Underground Railroad. Mary Ann Shadd and her family were among them. Blacks could learn much about Canada, an accessible refuge, from Shadd's *A Plea for Emigration: or Notes of Canada West* (1852). The forty-four-page pamphlet described the climate, soil, churches, and schools in support of emigration. Perhaps Shadd's father, Abraham Doros Shadd, an agent for *The Liberator* and member of the American Anti-Slavery Society's board, had influenced her thoughts and actions. She is recognized as the first African American woman to develop and use a database of primary sources for propaganda purposes.[76]

Whether free blacks migrated to Liberia, Mexico, Haiti, or Canada, the disengagement from loved ones could be consuming. Matilda Skipwith, a former slave who lived in Liberia, missed her family and friends sorely. "Nothing could afford me more pleasure," she wrote in 1851, "than to visit again the scenes of childhood & look on those faces which were once familiar to me." Her longing for loved ones in a distant land was no different from that of many other emigrants.[77]

The majority of free black women remained in the United States where they adapted survival skills to insulate themselves or fight prejudices openly. Samuel Cornish, editor of *Freedom's Journal*, a New York publication between 1827 and 1829, once encouraged blacks to "attend to business by mail or go by foot" to avoid discrimination on public conveyances. Similarly, Sarah Forten, daughter of the prosperous Philadelphia abolitionist James Forten, reported that her family avoided contact with racially biased whites. Consequently, "We feel it but in a slight degree compared with many others," she explained, adding, "We are not much dependant upon the tender mercies of our enemies—always having resources within ourselves to which we can apply." The Fortens' secure economic and social status provided a sanctuary. The masses of blacks were not as fortunate.[78]

Forten admitted that her family avoided public places unless "quite sure that admission is free to all" to avoid "mortifications which might otherwise ensue." Isolating oneself was less painful, but it only delayed the inevitable since racist practices did not simply disappear. Forten claims her isolation was akin to having her mind "too long wrapt in selfish darkness." This is perplexing considering her family opened its home to abolitionists over two generations. Perhaps Forten was too young to understand the circumstances initially, but with maturity she developed a social consciousness and credited the abolition cause with arousing her from apathy and indifference. She rankled at discrimination and saw blacks as innocent victims of racism. "Many were preferred before me," she wrote, "who by education—birth—or worldly circumstances were no better than myself—their sole claim to notice depending on the superior advantage of being White."[79]

The middle-class Sarah Mapps Douglass also admitted that a self-imposed isolation was a coping mechanism. She "formed a little world" of her own and "cared not to move beyond its precincts." Once the Pennsylvania legislature debated an 1832 bill requiring free blacks to carry passes, it shattered her security. She saw the tyrannical "iron hand" lurking over her peaceful home. As a result, "I started up, and with one mighty effort threw from me the lethargy which had covered me as a mantle for years," wrote Douglass. "The cause of the slave became my own."[80]

Frances E. W. Harper believed the welfare of blacks demanded the aid of every "helping hand" in taking up "the cause" of social responsibility. This was essential in freeing blacks from ignorance and bondage. "Helping hands" belonged to black and white women and men who attacked slavery through the press, from the pulpit, and on the lecture platform. Others helped through private and sometimes secret methods. Historian Waldo E. Martin Jr. posited that blacks became abolitionists out of necessity and whites became abolitionists out of choice. Motivations for action and methods used varied according to backgrounds and worldviews. Accepting a social responsibility and becoming an abolitionist was not an unexpected choice for Mary Ann Shadd, whose family was steeped in the cause. Frances E. W. Harper's uncle, William J. Watkins Sr., a respected mathematician and abolitionist, influenced her mode of thinking. Susan Paul could link her activism to her family, notably her father, uncles, and brothers. Segregation and "unchristian" treatment in a predominately white Baptist church had forced Thomas Paul Sr. and twenty followers to found the First African Baptist Church of Boston in 1805. The church, known as the Independence Baptist and the Abolition Church, hosted William Lloyd Garrison's January 6, 1832, organizational meeting for the New England Anti-Slavery Society.[81]

In *Black Bostonians,* a study of social reform among African Americans in antebellum Boston, James Horton and Lois Horton argue that a pattern of family activism existed across generations in the city. Comparable situations existed in antebellum Philadelphia, Wilmington, and Salem. Beyond the Revolutionary War experience, a strong social consciousness along with educational and financial successes made it possible for the Shadd, Remond, Douglass, Forten, and other families to recognize the need for reform. Furthermore, they responded. Without knowledge, money, and time, the transference of philosophies would have been more difficult. Persons overburdened with earning a living had less time to devote to causes outside their immediate families.[82]

The Forten women stand in sharp contrast to many other women. Their activities included assisting runaways, organizing bazaars and fairs, or publishing and speaking for the abolitionist cause. A major project of the Philadelphia Female Anti-Slavery Society (PFASS), founded in 1833, was an extensive petition campaign. Between 1835 and 1838, Sarah Forten helped write and circulate petitions appealing to the U.S. Congress to abolish the slave trade in Washington, D.C. The organization also led an active protest against the annexation of Texas.[83]

Antislavery women used the petition especially after Congress passed an 1836 gag rule permitting the tabling of abolitionists' petitions without discussion. In 1838 when speaking at the Second Anti-Slavery Convention of American Women, Angelina Grimké, the South Carolina–born daughter of a prominent white slaveholder, urged antislavery women to continue their protests since they did not have the right to vote. Some women were reluctant to sign petitions because they viewed it as engaging in political activities, but others believed using antislavery petitions was a moral issue. Women in the PFAAS agreed and conducted a campaign.[84]

Black and white women also boycotted produce grown by enslaved laborers and won support from abolitionists, notably Quakers, whose influence was greatest in Pennsylvania. Although the *North Star,* an abolitionist newspaper edited by Frederick Douglass, was located in Rochester, New York, it carried comparatively lengthy advertisements on a regular basis from a "Free Produce Store" located at the "Northwest corner Fifth and Cherry-sts., Philadelphia." The ad assured interested consumers that the store's "whole stock [was] exclusively Free Labor Goods" and that "much pain [was] taken by the Managers of the Free Produce Association, to assist the Subscriber to enlarge the assortment from time to time." The costs, said the advertisement, were either reduced or "cheap." Among the items for sale were "Curtain Calico, Superior fine Chintz Umbrellas, Oil cloths,...Linens, warranted free from cotton," and "Refined Loaf, Crushed, and Pulverized Sugar."[85]

No doubt consumers were familiar with the backbreaking labor required in the cultivation of cotton or sugar and knew that both were staple cash crops in the slaveholding South. *The Liberator* encouraged its readers to consider the intricacies of sugar production by asking if they would "indulge their palates with a blood-bought sweetness—a luxury of which it may be truly said, when we consider all the wickedness and the misery which its culture has produced,—that the awful price is immortal souls!" The poem "Negro's Forget Me Not" emphasized the suffering associated with sugarcane, "The fruit of so much grief and pain." Its cultivation was more arduous than cotton. With this in mind, the author continues,

> No, dear Lady, none for me!
> Though squeamish some may think it,
> West Indian Sugar spoils my tea,
> I cannot, dare not, drink it.

Sugar, a nonessential food, could be deleted from diets. But for those without willpower, the paper warned, "If you dare to do it, after what you have just read, take another spoonful of sugar to your cup of tea, and it is a hundred to one if there is not a tear of anguish and horror blended along with it."[86]

Frances E. W. Harper spoke in favor of free produce and boycotted garments made from slave-grown cotton. "It does seem to strike at one of the principal roots of the matter," she commented to her friend William Still, the well-known Underground Railroad conductor. She was grateful for her ability to pay more for a free-labor dress, albeit somewhat more coarse and less comfortable. But Harper gained emotional satisfaction from knowing no blood, tears, or broken hearts went into the making of her garments.[87]

Advocates of free products raised the consciousness of consumers; however, the extent to which boycotts were successful is difficult to measure. The origin and conditions under which some items, especially cotton, were produced, made it impossible to determine the extent and effectiveness of the boycotts.[88]

It was easier to see the success of the abolitionists' annual fairs and bazaars, fund-raisers to heighten consciousness about slavery. The organizers prohibited goods produced with slave labor. Among the popular items were handkerchiefs, samplers, and tokens. Chinaware and needle crafts often included the symbol of a person in chains crying, "Am I not a Woman and Sister," "Am I not a man and a brother," or "Remember the Slave." The widely used images evoked sympathy for oppressed slaves in the hands of unchecked power.[89]

A greater number of Americans were sensitized to the conditions of enslaved women and men through the popular media and public speakers. Gender conventions prohibited women from active participation in some facets of American social and political life, yet the urgency of eliminating bondage was too demanding for men to systematically deny women a platform on the abolitionist lecture circuit.[90]

In September 1832, Maria W. Stewart, the first American woman to address a public audience of women and men, spoke out against slavery and colonization. She crossed gender boundaries in the interest of freedom and equality. "Resistance to oppression was," for Stewart, "the highest form of obedience to God." She asked, "Who shall go forward and take off the reproach that is cast on the people of color? Shall it be a woman?" Stewart was willing to sacrifice her life for the freedom and equality for her people. This bold public stance placed her well beyond the boundaries society set for women.[91]

As a childless widow, familial obligations or patriarchal conventions at home did not limit her. In a February 27, 1833, address delivered at Boston's African Masonic Hall, Stewart questioned the manner of black leadership and asked, "Is it blindness of mind, or stupidity of soul, or the want of education that has caused our men who are 60 or 70 years of age, never to let their voices be heard, nor their hand be raised in behalf of their color? Or has it been for the fear of offending the whites?" Stewart challenged men to "throw off . . . fearfulness, and come forth in the name of the Lord" to make themselves "useful and active members in society."[92]

Stewart had stepped out of her designated place, not only in speaking publicly to a mixed audience but in criticizing men. Her actions violated gender conventions requiring deference to men and the African tradition of paying homage to elders. She berated men and questioned their masculinity in an open forum. Her stinging prod was similar to the salvo delivered by David Walker, a radical abolitionist, whose publication the *Appeal* (1829) also criticized black men.[93]

The differences in the two self-styled abolitionists were most visible in the receptions of written and spoken words. Walker's pamphlet did not move readers to immediate action whereas some men listening to Stewart disrupted the meeting, pelted her with vegetables, and denounced her criticism. Their "hissing" and contempt tested Stewart's mettle, causing her to decide to leave Boston by the year's end. In saying farewell, she defended her right to speak in public. "What if I am a woman," she asked. She admitted making herself "contemptible in the eyes of many," but it was in the interest of a greater cause. She had set a precedent for women to lend their voices to that cause.[94]

Following the passage of the Fugitive Slave Act in 1850, the national debate on slavery intensified. Concomitantly, the gender conventions against women speaking to a mixed audience eroded, and they joined the abolitionist circuit. Among the best-known black women lecturers are Sarah Parker Remond, Sojourner Truth, Frances E. W. Harper, Mary Ann Shadd, and Ellen Craft.

As a lecturer, Craft recounted her bold escape from slavery, which began in late December 1848. She disguised herself in a fine new suit of men's clothing and traveled from Georgia to Philadelphia with her enslaved dark-skinned husband. He posed as her valet, and she assumed the persona of a slaveowner journeying into the North with a faithful servant. They stayed in hotels but remained above suspicion despite their inabilities to sign the registers. The illiterate woman succeeded in the charade by casting herself as a physically challenged planter with a rheumatic complaint that prevented her from writing. No one expected the servant to be literate.[95]

Hers was a fascinating story because as an enslaved white-skinned woman she manipulated received wisdom to her advantage and convincingly portrayed herself as a white man of means. It was commonly assumed that whites could and did travel freely. It was not unusual for whites of means to spend the night in hotels along with their servants. Finally, men were more likely than women to travel alone and without interference. Craft's success made her a likely abolitionist lecturer, but her role was limited. Passage of the more stringent fugitive slave act in 1850 caused both Ellen and her husband to flee the country.

Free-born black women spoke on the abolitionist platform but could not present the horrors of slavery as did persons who had actually endured bondage. Even so, they made a lasting impression on listeners. After hearing the nationally known Frances E. W. Harper, Mary Ann Shadd, also known as Mary Ann Shadd Cary after marrying Thomas F. Cary in 1856, wrote to her husband saying "white & colored people here are just crazy with excitement about her. She is the greatest female speaker ever." Shadd Cary did not believe her speaking abilities were comparable to Watkins, yet she made a worthy contribution to the abolitionist cause.[96]

A number of free black women contributed to the abolitionist cause by supporting John Brown's 1859 raid at Harpers Ferry, Virginia. Black abolitionists learned of his intentions as early as 1858. Brown received financial contributions from Mary Ellen Pleasant, a southern-born black woman who wanted the epitaph "She was a Friend of John Brown's" on her grave marker. Pleasant, who lived in Canada in 1858 and was a member of the Chatham Vigilance Committee, was among thirty-four blacks who met Brown when he explained his venture. The zealot invited Harriet Tubman to join him, and she willingly agreed but did not participate in the raid because of miscommunications and illness. Brown's ill-fated plot ending with his arrest and trial.[97]

Frances E. W. Harper addressed Brown as "Dear Friend" in a November 1859 letter to him as he awaited execution and expressed gratitude for extending his hands "to the crushed and blighted of [her] race." His actions, she wrote, had "rocked the bloody Bastile." She anticipated that "great good may arise to the cause of freedom" from his "sad fate." After the failure of Brown's raid, many proponents of freedom were as intent as ever in securing liberty for themselves and the enslaved persons.[98]

The 1850s had been one of the most politically charged periods in antebellum America in which the subject of slavery moved from the margins to the center of national political debates. The Republican party formed in the 1850s with stopping the expansion of slavery as a tenet of its political ideology. In the 1860 election, Republican Abraham Lincoln received only 40 percent of the popular votes but won the presidential election by a large margin in the electoral college. This victory came in spite of the South's threats to secede from the Union if the Republicans won the election.

When Lincoln arrived in Washington for his March 4, 1861, inauguration, efforts at preventing secession had failed. Lincoln proceeded cautiously with his inaugural address, which was intended to assure the southern states remaining in the Union that there was no reasonable cause for anxiety. He did not consider the Union broken and promised no bloodshed unless forced to respond in such a manner. In closing the well-crafted address, he said, "We are not enemies, but friends. We must not be enemies." Contrary to Lincoln's wishes, the strained bond between the North and South had made them enemies. It was simply a matter of days before the onset of the Civil War.[99]

Frances E. W. Harper corresponded with William Still and asked, "Well, what think you of the war?" She shared her own fascination with General John C. Fremont's August 30, 1861, proclamation placing Missouri under martial law and promising to execute guerrillas captured within Union lines. The proclamation ordered the confiscation of property and freeing of slaves belonging to Confederate sympathizers. "I hope the boldness of his stand will inspire others," she wrote, "to look the real cause of the war in the face and inspire the government with uncompromising earnestness to remove the festering curse."[100]

Harper was confident about how the war would end. She saw it as "God's controversy with the nation; His arising to plead by fire and blood the cause of His poor and needy people." She believed an intricate bond existed between herself and her people who remained enslaved. In making that connection, Harper attempted to paraphrase a question John C. Breckinridge asked Charles Sumner. "If I rightly remember," wrote Harper, the question was "What is the fate of a few negroes to me or mine?" She understood that "a few negroes" and others were "bound up in one great bundle of humanity," and their "fates seem linked together." Their destinies were intertwined, and their rights were interwoven. Distinctions between enslaved and emancipated women were often blurred in terms of color, gender prescriptions, and economic conditions. Harper believed neither she nor any other black women and men could ever be truly free until they were all free. Would this ever come to fruition? What would make freedom a reality? A generation earlier Maria W. Stewart had asked, "Who shall go forward and take off the reproach that is cast on the people of color? Shall it be a woman?" It was now time to respond.[101]

7

The Civil War and Emancipation

Freedom for All

Some... freedwomen had exaggerated ideas of freedom. To them it was a beautiful vision, a land of sunshine, rest, and glorious promise... it was but natural that many of them should bitterly feel their disappointment.

Elizabeth Keckley

The Civil War marked changes in the lives of free and unfree women of African descent throughout the United States. The mere appearance of Union soldiers in slaveholding areas created tumultuous conditions. Amid the chaos of war, many enslaved women and men viewed the soldiers as liberators and emancipated themselves by fleeing to Union lines, while others took advantage of the fluidity and left owners in search of loved ones from whom they had been separated. In the midst of war, the slaves probably thought little about the black soldiers' families at home or the black women and men, including the recruiters among them, who had encouraged the men to join the U.S. Army and fight for freedom.[1] This chapter focuses on the role black women played in abolishing slavery and shaping freedom for themselves and others. It also looks at the interactions among black women following the Civil War to determine the extent to which their African heritage pulled them together or the degree to which education and class standing pushed them apart.

At the outset of war, President Abraham Lincoln made it clear that the abolition of slavery was not the government's objective. Saving the Union was paramount. Since this was "a white man's war" and not expected to last long, the government did not make an effort to recruit black men: the U.S. Army did not welcome them whereas the U.S. Navy accepted them. Despite the government's uneven policy, in spring 1862 General David Hunter solicited the services of black men through the creation of the 1st South Carolina Volunteer Regiment. The president, who remained sensitive to public opinion and believed Hunter's action was premature, did not support him. As a result, the regiment disbanded nearly as quickly as it originated.[2]

Eventually the need for additional manpower made the army's refusal to enlist blacks appear foolhardy. In July 1862, Congress enacted a militia act permitting black men to enter the U.S. Army and the War Department created the Bureau of Colored Troops to facilitate recruitment. Among the best-known black units were the 54th Massachusetts Regiment and 1st South Carolina Volunteers along with the 1st and 3rd Regiments of the (Louisiana) Native Guards. Ordinarily, whites commanded black units, but black officers commanded the *Corps d'Afrique,* a regiment organized from the 1st and 3rd Regiments of the Native Guards.[3]

White objections to blacks in the military had begun dissipating in 1862 when Lincoln drafted the Emancipation Proclamation, effective January 1, 1863, freeing enslaved women and men in rebellious regions and allowing able-bodied blacks to garrison Union forts and man vessels. Lincoln's intent was to undermine slavery without offending southern Unionists. As a result, the proclamation had no impact in many areas under Union control. According to the 1860 census, 225,483 enslaved women and men lived in Kentucky and 114,931 in Missouri. Maryland had considerably fewer, 87,189, unfree souls, and Delaware had the smallest number, 1,798, of all slaveholding states in 1860. When combined with the number of slaves in cities, counties, and parishes also under Union control, the numbers escalate. For example, the proclamation exempted thirteen Louisiana parishes containing 86,492 slaves, and western Tennessee had an enslaved population of 250,000. Ultimately, more than 750,000 blacks were beyond the reaches of the Emancipation Proclamation.[4]

Lincoln's edict did not liberate anyone, but it kindled the hope of freedom. News of the Emancipation Proclamation brought jubilation to many enslaved women and men. Others tempered celebrations with religious songs and prayers of thanksgiving as they anticipated the future. The comments of an enslaved woman who learned of the proclamation in

1863 is instructive. She remembered, "We done heared dat Lincum gonna turn de niggers freed. Ole missus say dey warn't nothin' to it. Den a yankee soldier tole someone in Williamsburg dat marse Lincum done signed de mancipation . . . ev'ybody commence gitin' ready to leave. Didn't care nothin' 'bout Missus . . . An' all dat night de niggers danced an' sang." The excitement was infectious. The slave-born Susie Baker King Taylor heralded January 1, 1863, as a memorable day, and Charlotte Forten, who relocated to St. Helena Island, South Carolina, in 1862 to teach under the auspices of the Port Royal Relief Association, declared January 1, 1863, "the most glorious day [the] nation has yet seen." Forten attended a formal exercise at Camp Saxton where Colonel Thomas Wentworth Higginson introduced Dr. William H. Brisbane, a South Carolina slaveholder turned abolitionist. He read the proclamation to a crowd of blacks whose faces beamed with anticipation. "It all seemed, and seems still," Forten wrote, "like a brilliant dream."[5]

Whether they celebrated joyfully or reverently, it was impossible to prepare adequately for the challenges awaiting them. In March 1863, Congress enacted a draft to fill manpower needs. In heavily Democratic areas of the North, the draft precipitated furious opposition and riots when potential draftees, especially German and Irish, believed the government inducted them disproportionately when compared to African Americans. The whites demanded that blacks also share the fighting and dying. Anxieties over the imminent danger and racial prejudices surfaced in "Sambo's Right to be Kilt," a song written by Charles Graham Halpine. The lyrics were popular among the Irish, who sang:

Some tell us 'tis a burnin' shame
To make the naygers fight;
An' that the thrade of bein' kilt
Belongs but to the white;
But as for me, on my soul!
So liberal are we here,
I'll let Sambo be murthered instead of myself
On every day in the year.
On every day in the year, boys,
And in every hour of the day;
The right to be kilt I'll divide wid him,
An' divil a word I'll say.[6]

Beyond sharing the "right to be kilt," some whites were anxious about the potentially leveling effects of the perceptions of black men. Many northern working-class whites feared that emancipation would cause southern blacks to migrate northward. The possibility heightened fears of job competition and miscegenation. Democratic newspapers exacerbated these concerns in anti-draft editorials.[7]

Anti-black and anti-draft protests led to riots in New Jersey, Indiana, Ohio, Wisconsin, and Illinois, but the most chaotic of all occurred in New York City in July 1863. Perceptions of criminality, immorality, and miscegenation in the city caused intensely hostile feelings against black New Yorkers. As early as the 1830s, many white New Yorkers linked radical abolitionists to discussions about amalgamation, which were not confined to sexual intimacy between women and men of different colors. Abolitionists expanded the meaning of politics by depending on moral suasion in addition to questioning universal manhood suffrage and the Constitution as the best example of democracy and equality. Although white abolitionists were not strong advocates of interracial marriages, they blurred color lines when encouraging blacks to speak as political equals on antislavery platforms. This threatened the established economic, social, and political order in New York and continued to upset some whites who misinterpreted the abolitionists' intentions.[8]

New York City represented contested terrain, politically, economically, and socially. It was against this background of social upheaval that anti-black and anti-draft New Yorkers rioted, burned a draft office, damaged the homes of well-known Republicans and abolitionists, and destroyed an orphanage for black children. As a fifteen-year-old schoolgirl, Maritcha Lyons remembered the mob's July 13, 1863, attack on her family's Brooklyn home: "father advanced into the dooway and fired point blank into the crowd" and stopped the would-be-attackers temporarily. The next day, the mob entered the Lyons home. "This sent father over the back fence while mother took refuge on the premises of a neighbor," Lyons wrote. Eventually, the family fled to Salem, Massachusetts. The Lyonses escaped with their lives while the rioter destroyed the family's business.[9]

Violence against the Lyonses paled in comparison with the brutality in the home of a black woman in childbed. Once the "horde of ruffins" was inside the new mother's home, an eyewitness known only as Mrs. Statts recalled that they "dismantled the interior and destroyed furniture before setting a fire. Some . . . broke through the front door with pick axes, and came rushing into the room where this poor woman lay, and commenced to pull the clothes off from her . . . In a little while I saw the innocent babe, of three days old, come crashing down into the yards; some of the rioters had dashed it out of the back window, killing it instantly." Statts had sought refuge in the home but met a disastrous fate. Rioters flooded the basement where she and her child hid. Statts knew the mob directed more of its violence at black males and tried to protect the boy. "Two ruffians seized him," she said, "while a third, armed with a crow-bar, deliberately struck him a heavy blow over the head." He died two days later.[10]

During the riots, mobs lynched more than a dozen blacks by hanging, drowning, or beating them to death. The crowds seemed intent on reducing male victims to less than men by cutting off their fingers and toes or genitalia. Nancy Robinson said the atrocities inflicted on her husband were "so indecent, they [were] unfit for publication." Rowdy whites, including teenaged boys, mutilated corpses. In their twisted logic of emasculating black males, they saw themselves as more than ordinary men. Such grisly acts reflected the perpetrators' objections to the notion that black men might receive equal recognition as worthy participants in the Civil War.[11]

Sadly, this mode of thinking touched the family of First Sgt. Robert J. Simmons of the 54th Massachusetts. Simmons had distinguished himself during the assault on Fort Wagner and sustained a serious injury. He had gone into the July 18, 1863, battle not knowing rioters had terrorized his mother and sister three days earlier. During the attack, the New York mob had clubbed and stoned Simmons's seven-year-old nephew to death. The Simmons women, like other free black women amid the riots, suffered as their husbands, fathers, brothers, sons, and lovers fell prey to bloodthirsty whites. The child's mother and grandmother had little time to grieve before learning that Robert, who answered the call to arms and fought to abolish slavery, had died in Charleston after the amputation of his arm.[12]

The riots and violence against blacks speak volumes about the hostile environments in which they lived. No doubt many free women hoped for better conditions for themselves and their enslaved counterparts. As a result, they were supportive of the 20,000 to 30,000 black sailors and 186,000 black soldiers who fought in the Civil War. Black men made up nearly 10 percent of the U.S. Army and served in 166 regiments seeing action in over 250 skirmishes. At least one-half of the U.S. Colored Troops came from the seceding states.[13]

Black women encouraged their men on the battlefront and contributed to the effort as recruiters. The Boston-born free woman Josephine St. Pierre Ruffin had moved to England to escape racism but returned to the United States once the Civil War began and worked to enlist black men in Massachusetts as did Harriet Jacobs. In December 1863 when Martin Delany sought to enroll blacks in the 29th Regiment of Connecticut Volunteers,

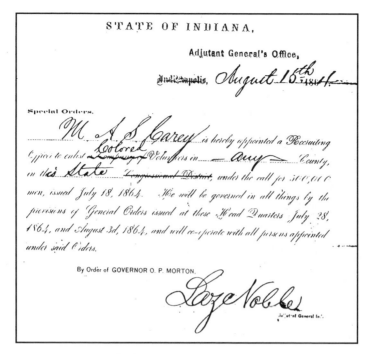

Figure 7.1. Mary Ann Shadd Cary's authorization as an army recruiter.
Mary Ann Shadd Cary Papers, Howard University, Washington, D.C.

he invited Mary Ann Shadd Cary to join him. She agreed and by the end
of the war had enrolled black soldiers from Connecticut, Massachusetts,
and Indiana. The slave-born novelist William Wells Brown praised her
"skill, tact and order." In his opinion, the men she enlisted were "always
considered the best lot." Cary's work prompted Brown to declare, "It
takes a woman to pick out a good man."[14]

Other free-born and newly freed women rendered a variety of services
to the overall military operation, especially after President Lincoln signed
the First Confiscation Act on August 6, 1861, and the Second Confiscation
Act on July 17, 1862. The first act allowed commanders to seize enslaved
women and men working directly for the Confederate States of America
(CSA) and make them "contraband of war" under international law. The
second act freed persons belonging to Confederates, and the U.S. Army
put the able-bodied women to work as laundresses or cooks while the
men labored as teamsters, stevedores, and carpenters. Both women and
men raised cotton and foodstuffs for government sales. The U.S. quarter-
master paid women four dollars per month while men received twice as
much from the proceeds.[15]

Figure 7.2. Civil War Camp, 1862. Library of Congress, Washington, D.C.

A sharp contrast existed between what happened to enslaved women fleeing to Union lines and those who remained on plantations and farms. As black men joined the U.S. Army, the women in the Upper and Lower South were especially vulnerable to mistreatment at the hands of slaveowners. Conditions became especially harsh for black women in Kentucky when more than 50 percent of the enslaved men between fifteen and forty-four years old joined the U.S. Army between April 1864 and April 1865. Once men deployed, owners evicted the soldiers' families or demolished cabins occupied by women and children. Similarly, slaveholders in Louisiana abused women and children solely because of their connections to soldiers.[16]

These women faced crises in gender unlike any they had known previously. Without their partners, they relied on other women whose conditions mirrored their own. A December 30, 1863, letter from a Mexico, Missouri, woman to her husband is illustrative. "They abuse me because you went," she wrote. The dire situation forced her to refuse his plea to encourage acquaintances to join the U.S. Army. "I see too much trouble to try to get any more into trouble too," she explained. In her own way, she protected them.[17]

Throughout the slave era, many women shared a common bond, and ties often grew stronger as they faced the wartime turmoil together. While the solidarity among women may have been comforting, they remained vulnerable to hostile whites. As black men joined the U.S. Army, women fled to military posts to be near loved ones, seek protection, or simply because they had no other alternatives. General Benjamin Butler was sensitive to their privations and did not object to their presence at Fortress Monroe in Virginia. Butler believed it was "manifestly wrong to take husbands and fathers while leaving wives and children to be mistreated."[18]

Speed Smith Fry, commander at Camp Nelson in Kentucky, handled what he called the "Nigger Woman Question" differently. In late 1864, 400 black women and children were expelled from Camp Nelson. They had gravitated to Union lines to be near loved ones only to suffer separations similar to those enslaved families had encountered. Without places to stay, support from their men, or shelter from the frigid weather, the women and children were reduced to vagrancy and begging.[19]

Furthermore, the government's racially biased pay scale exacerbated the economic conditions of many black women who depended on their service members' salary. The July 17, 1862, Enlistment Act entitled privates to $13.00 per month along with a $3.50 clothing allowance. After June 4, 1863, the government paid blacks $7.00 per month and $3.00 for clothing. This decision wreaked financial and emotional havoc on many free and newly freed black families who equated unequal pay with the perception that black soldiers were less worthy than white ones.[20]

The pension request initiated by Martha Ann Stars, mother of John H. Crowder, a second lieutenant in Company K, 1st Louisiana Native Guard, illustrates the anxiety created by the government's racist method of disbursing salaries. Crowder had a family history of economic depravation. His father, Jacob, "went off with the United States Army to Mexico" and never returned. Without his financial support, John began working at an early age. By the time he was eight years old, he worked as a cabin boy on a Mississippi River steamboat and earned $5 per month. In 1862, he worked as a porter in a jewelry store and earned $25 per month. As a dutiful son, he gave his entire salary to his mother. Crowder's letters tell nothing about why he joined the U.S. Army. But the decision provided an opportunity to fight for his people's freedom and guaranteed a salary.[21]

The Crowder-Stars correspondence reveals both a son's devotion to a mother and the anxiety created when the U.S. Army failed to pay in a timely fashion or changed its pay rate for black soldiers. In February 1863, Crowder mentioned "waiting dayly for the paymaster." The young officer responded to a rumor that the federal government was "not going to pay the colored soldiers" with the firm retort, "They are bound to pay us." Once compensated, he promised his mother to travel from Camp Houston to New Orleans on horseback to deliver the money to her.[22]

By May 4, 1863, he had received only five months' pay for eight months of active duty. The men in the 33rd U.S. Colored Infantry and the Louisiana Native Guard, Crowder's unit, received the standard pay in early 1863. Afterward, the government instituted its pay differential. This did not affect Crowder's case since he died May 27, 1863, when the 1st Louisiana Native Guard attacked the Confederates at Port Hudson, the first major battle in which a black regiment engaged. Crowder's death was an emotional and financial loss to his mother.[23]

The discriminatory pay policy affected black dependents of the 54th Massachusetts Regiment and South Carolina Volunteers sorely when the soldiers preferred, as a matter of principle, to fight without pay rather than accept further racial bigotry. Adhering to their principles created emotional turmoil and financial distress for many blacks. One soldier observed, "The Horible Suferings of our deer Sufering familys at a Distant Home its Most more than our *manhood* Can beare." No doubt others shared his sentiments. The tension was severe between what was necessary for the men to validate their masculinity via their earning power in a patriarchal society and its cost to their wives, mothers, sisters, and other loved ones. The men must have asked themselves about the importance of refusing unfair pay and the financial and emotional crisis it created.[24]

Ultimately, the crisis related to gender constructions that evolved as men left to fight and women transcended prescribed roles. While males were proving their masculinity on the battlefield, women assumed new responsibilities at home and in the workplace. Some southern white women found it extremely difficult to run agricultural units and manage slaves in the absence of their fathers, husbands, and sons. Texan Lizzy Neblett complained bitterly about the woes of "trying to do a man's business" when her husband, Will, enlisted in the Confederate Army. Her plight was not very different from that of other white slaveholding women. But the crisis in gender differed greatly from that of free-born and newly freed black women who assumed added responsibilities and suffered the indignation of discrimination in their service members' pay.[25]

Many black men believed that the government's betrayal robbed them of their masculinity and interfered with their patriarchal duty to support their families. The men were conflicted over fulfilling obligations to a government that failed to honor its commitment. If they refused to serve, punishment was swift and could be lethal. The vast majority of men executed for mutiny were black: one example was William Walker, a sergeant assigned to the 21st U.S. Colored Infantry. He concluded that his enlistment was null and void since the U.S. Army did not pay him the same as white soldiers. The U.S. Army disagreed and charged him with mutiny. The governor of Massachusetts, John Andrews, noted, "The Government which found no law to pay him except as a nondescript and a contraband found law enough to shoot him as a soldier." Andrews's observation points to the contradictions in a war that promised freedom for blacks on one hand but oppressed them on the other hand. Walker's loved ones grappled with this reality as they experienced the crisis.[26]

The discriminatory pay policy continued until mid-1864 when Congress authorized equal salaries and retroactive compensation. On the surface, it appeared that the government intended to rectify its initial callousness. In actuality, only the men who were free as of April 19, 1861, received equal and retroactive pay for 1862 and 1863. After a series of protests and other measures to help former slaves prove their legal status, they received equal compensation.[27]

In the meantime, military dependents suffered financial hardships. Many worked as cooks and laundresses or operated makeshift restaurants or bakeries and sold food to soldiers. The presence of black women near Union lines irritated some commanders who misinterpreted their intentions. "White officers," writes Ira Berlin, "villified the soldiers' wives as 'whores' and 'bitches.'" Colonel F. W. Lister addressed a letter to Brigadier General W. D. Whipple, saying, "Large herds of colored prostitutes flocked to Brideport from both ends of the line. But the guard regulations not suiting them, the greater proportion soon left for 'fresh fields & pastures new.'" Lister's aspersions portrayed the women's actions as animalistic behavior.[28]

All too often, women near military posts were labeled "camp followers," prostitutes plying their trade. Such malicious statements were readily accepted due to the influence of the mythical and oversexualized Jezebel. It is fallacious to assume that all black women in the vicinity of a military camp engaged in illicit sex. Nevertheless, the aspersions persisted as the women struggled to support themselves and give meaning to their freedom.

To alleviate the suffering of the families of black soldiers, benevolent societies and charitable organizations offered help. Much of the relief in the South came from generous northern whites; however, benevolent blacks also rendered assistance. The Israel Bethel Church in Washington,

D.C., formed the Union Relief Association while Philadelphia's Bethel Church organized a Contraband Committee. Blacks formed other organizations including the Freedmen's Friend Society in Brooklyn, New York; the African Civilization Society in New York City; and the Contraband Aid Association in Cincinnati, Ohio.[29]

Elizabeth Keckley was among the first to organize help for the newly freed women and men. She had been touched directly by the Civil War when her only child left Wilberforce University and enlisted in the U.S. Army. That he, as a freedman, had a special interest in seeing the war end slavery is understandable. Knowing that he enlisted as a white man calling himself George W. D. Kirkland raises questions about his rationale. Perhaps the young man, like his mother, had asked, "Why should not the Anglo-Saxon [blood] triumph—why should it be weighed down with the rich blood" of their African ancestors. In all probability, he enlisted as a white man because blacks were denied enrollment at the time. The social and historical construction of race allowed the mixed-race man to manipulate the slippery concept to his advantage. As a white man, he could fight for the freedom of blacks. Ultimately, his skin color was inconsequential; he died at Wilson's Creek in 1861.[30]

Despite her loss, Elizabeth Keckley was attentive to the needs of the thousands of black refugees in Washington, D.C. After noticing an August 1862 festival organized for the benefit of sick and wounded white soldiers, Keckley asked herself, "If the white people can give festivals to raise funds for the relief of suffering soldiers... should not the well-to-do colored people... work for the benefit of the suffering blacks?" She carried her idea to local congregations, and they immediately formed a society with forty active members.[31]

Keckley was president of the organization known as the Freedmen and Soldiers' Relief Association of Washington. Its members pledged themselves to "ameliorating the condition of that class of suffering people, who by existing circumstances, have been released from the tyranny of the oppressor, and cast in our midst in a state of utter destitution." With contributions from blacks and whites across the United States, the organization distributed over $1,600 in aid within a two-year period. Benefit balls, fairs, and other public programs were also ways of raising money to relieve the suffering of former slaves. Aside from financial contributions, there were material gifts. Black Bostonians alone contributed more than eighty large boxes of useful items, including clothing, for the freedwomen and men. These efforts moved the organization closer to its goal of helping the newly freed "towards a higher plane of civilization."[32]

As southern black women on the home front coped with the disruptions of war, many were not entirely distanced from the actual fighting. Susie King Taylor remembered "'loyal women,' as well as men, in those days who did not fear shell or shot." In fact, Taylor viewed herself as essential to the 33rd U.S. Colored Troops in South Carolina in a variety of capacities. Each man carried 150 rounds of ammunition. She packed the haversacks and cartridge boxes as the 1st South Carolina Volunteers prepared to attack Fort Gregg. In her autobiography, Taylor wrote about cleaning and reloading guns and claimed she "learned to handle a musket very well." She could "shoot straight and often hit the target." Of the relationship with men in "her" regiment, Taylor added, "The officers and comrades of my regiment [stood] ready to render me assistance whenever required." She saw herself as belonging to the regiment and enjoyed its camaraderie.[33]

Colonel Higgingson, commander of the 33rd South Carolina Volunteers, noted that Taylor was "very exceptional" in his introduction to her book, *Reminiscences of My Life with the 33d United States Colored Troops Late 1st S. C. Volunteers,* and praised her ability to read and write. Literacy, he believed, was most unusual among "colored laundresses." Rather than addressing Taylor's assessment of her own military usefulness, he wrote, "Actual military life is rarely described by a woman, and this is especially true of a woman whose place was in the ranks, as the wife of a soldier and herself a regimental laundress." This was a moot point since women, regardless of color, had no official duties in the military such as those described by Taylor. Under the circumstances, it is understandable why his account was "from a wholly different point of view." Additionally, Higginson wrote, "I did not see the book until the sheets were in print, and have left it wholly untouched, except as to a few errors in proper names." Differences in interpretations raise questions about the role of women in the Civil War and the recognition thereof.[34]

Harriet Tubman's work as a Union scout and spy is easier to assess in terms of specific military contributions. Under the command of Colonel James Montgomery, Tubman received accolades for her role in the spring 1863 Combahee River raid. She dictated a letter to friends in Boston and boasted, "You have, without doubt, seen a full account of the expedition . . . Don't you think we colored people are entitled to some credit for that exploit, under the lead of the brave Colonel Montgomery? We weakened the rebels somewhat on the Combahee river by taking and bringing away *seven hundred and fifty-six head* of their most valuable livestock, known up in your region as 'contrabands.'" She was especially pleased that some of the able-bodied men among them "joined the colored regiments."[35]

In the meantime, a small number of newly freed women served as cooks and nurses in U.S. Navy facilities and aboard ships. A forty-five-year-old woman listed as a "first-class boy" worked in a North Carolina hospital. Harriet Ruth and Harriet Little were aboard the *U.S.S. Black Hawk* and *U.S.S. Hartford*, respectively. Eight black women were on the muster rolls of the *U.S.S. Red Rover*, a hospital ship in the Mississippi Squadron commissioned December 2, 1862. The historian Lisa Y. King notes, "Sallie Bohannon and Nancy Buel served onboard the *U.S.S. Red Rover* until November 25 and October 26, 1863 respectively, while Lucinda Jenkins, a 26 year-old picked up on the Yazoo River served briefly from January first through the thirteenth of the following year... Ellen Campbell... rated as a 'nurse'... [served] until her discharge in March of 1864. Similarly, Betsey Young... was employed in the hospital for a least a full year from December, 1863 to January, 1865." Margaret Jackson and Ann Stokes were also aboard the *U.S.S. Red Rover* along with their husbands. The Navy called them contraband and put the women to work as nurses and laundresses. Their duties as nurses made them an important part of the Union's July 1863 victory over the CSA stronghold at Vicksburg.[36]

As the war continued, families and friends at home received news about their loved ones on the battlefield. The free-born Catharine Johnson, a resident of Natchez, Mississippi, wrote:

> To day we received papers stating that another large Battle has been fought in which the 5 s had been literally cut to pieces. God grant that the life of one who has been dear to us may be spared—just two short months and 17 days since he was with us full of life and hope, now he is far away engaged in cruel and bloody struggle the issue of which no morteil can tell and to night who knows but that he mae be among the fated ones that fell Eleven days ago—I can not bear to think it so. Alas when we part from our friends and breath the simple word good by how little know we what may transpire ere we feel the friendly clasp of their hand again your times when we part as we are thinking only for a few weeks long every month and years intervene we meet again, and sometimes the dark—forever in cruelties above that parting scene But that such may not be the present case I can only hope.

Johnson was anxious about William Gardner, a friend who had joined the 5th Regiment of the Confederate Army.[37]

The preponderance of black Civil War veterans aligned themselves with the United States rather than the Confederate States of America. However, aside from the enslaved body servants accompanying owners to the battlefields and the blacks impressed by the CSA, there were African American volunteers. Some reasoned that loyalty to the Confederacy would lead to white gratitude resulting in an improved status for themselves. Certainly African Americans who owned slaves for pecuniary reasons would not join in the fighting to abolish slavery. In the interest of protecting their property and way of life, they sided with the Confederacy.[38]

An outstanding example of the behavior exhibited by black Confederates is that of the William Ellison family. Ellison's biographers summarized the family's record of support for the CSA, which was better than that of most planters. Michael P. Johnson and James L. Roark write that the Ellisons "more than fulfilled every obligation the government imposed. As soon as the call went out, they quit growing cotton and began producing food crops. They supplied their neighbors and the rebel armies with provisions. They hired out their skilled slaves...paid all their taxes...and invested their profits in government notes." That the Ellisons were loyal to the CSA could not be doubted. Beyond their model behavior as Confederate citizens, one family member served in the 1st South Carolina Artillery.[39]

In many ways, the Ellisons' loyalty to the CSA was not unlike that demonstrated by other free blacks who supported the USA. Their concerns about the outcome of the war and fate of loved ones were significant regardless of the side they chose.

The northern-born H. Amelia Loguen, daughter of the Underground Railroad agent and African Methodist Episcopal Zion bishop J. W. Loguen, also worried about her beloved when he went into battle. A July 20, 1863, letter from Lewis Douglass, son of Anna Murray and Frederick Douglass, relieved some of her anxieties. Douglass, who fought along with the 54th Massachusetts at Fort Wagner, said he had escaped "unhurt from amidst that perfect hail of shot and shell." The unit, he added,

> has established its reputation as a fighting regiment not a man flinched, though it was a trying time. Men fell all around me. A shell would explode and clear a space of twenty feet, our men would close up again, but it was no use we had to retreat, which was a very hazardous undertaking. How I got out of that fight alive I cannot tell, but I am here... I must bid you farewell should I be killed. Remember if I die I die in a good cause. I wish we had a hundred thousand colored troops we would put an end to this war.

Douglass included brief details about several missing, wounded, or hospitalized mutual friends. The horrors of war did not discourage him, and he explained his commitment to the war to Loguen. "Should I fall in the next fight killed or wounded," he wrote, "I hope to fall with my face to the foe."[40]

Charlotte Forten also received news on July 20, 1863, about the 54th Massachusetts Regiment at Fort Wagner and commented about its impact: "For nearly two weeks we have waited, oh how anxiously for news of our regt. which went, we know to Morris Is.[land] to take part in the attack on Charleston. To-night comes news oh, so sad, so heart sickening. It is too terrible, too terrible to write. We can only hope it may not all be true. That our noble, beautiful Colonel [Robert Gould Shaw] is killed, and the regt. cut to pieces! I cannot, cannot believe it. And yet I know it may be so. But oh, I am stunned, sick at heart. I can scarcely write." The news was heartbreaking, yet she reveled in knowing "the 54th put in advance; fought bravely, desperately." The men entered the fort but were driven back. Despite their defeat, Forten wrote, "Thank Heaven! they fought bravely!"[41]

Loguen shared Forten's pride in the soldiers' bravery. The men had defied the stereotype that they were incapable of fighting admirably. Their record would stand on its own and show whites their mettle, if allowed the opportunity. Unfortunately, many blacks at Fort Wagner and elsewhere proved themselves "men" and worthy soldiers by dying in battle. Nearly 250 blacks were counted among the 1,515 Union fatalities at Fort Wagner.[42]

As injured soldiers left the battlefields, Charlotte Forten volunteered her services. While waiting for the doctor to finish dressing their wounds, she busied herself. "It was with a full heart that I sewed up bullet holes and bayonets cuts," she wrote and added, "Sometimes I found a jacket that told a sad tale—so torn to pieces that it was far past mending."[43]

Harriet Tubman and Susie King Taylor also served as nurses and recounted details about their work among wounded soldiers. Tubman was concerned but not too disturbed about the unsanitary conditions in the hospital where she started work "early eb'ry mornin'." She "thrash[ed] away de flies" and began "to bathe der wounds." Seeing the water turn "as red as clar blood" sent her for clean water to go on "to de nex' ones [wounded soldier]." Taylor steeled herself against "the most sickening sights, such as men with their limbs blown off and mangled by the deadly shells." She cared for injured soldiers "without a shudder" and hurriedly assisted in "alleviating their pain . . . bind[ing] up their wounds, and press[ing] the cool water to their parched lips."[44]

The voices of most black nurses among Union soldiers were unrecorded, and they faced discrimination. Many white nurses refused to recognize black women as medical caregivers who shared similar responsibilities although the surgeon general's Order No. 23, issued July 16, 1864, permitted the "employment of persons of African descent, male or female, as cooks or nurses" in all U.S. general hospitals. Without specificity regarding gender, the order said, "When so employed they will receive ten dollars per month and one ration." They were to be paid by the nearest medical disbursing officer in a manner like that used for paying "men of the Hospital Corps." Order No. 23 permitted blacks to render medical service and proffered a degree of equality in the method of payment, yet whites did not consider them as colleagues. This had long-lasting effects, especially when black women applied for pensions.[45]

Order No. 23 notwithstanding, job classifications and salaries, based on color and class, discriminated against black hospital workers who did more than prepare meals, scrub floors, and launder bedding. For example, the newly freed Tennessean Rachael Anderson followed orders to "assist in handling the sick" as a nurse in Knoxville's Asylum General Hospital, but she received the wages of a cook. Emily Parsons, a white nurse, testified that she had trained black women to perform nursing responsibilities at Benton Barracks, Missouri. Amy Morris Bradley, another white nurse, asserted that she worked with black women when directing relief services at a convalescent camp near Washington, D.C., in 1862 and 1863. Black women were among the more than 15,000 working-class laborers performing a variety of tasks at Union hospitals in Baltimore, Louisville, Nashville, and other cities.[46]

Regardless of the care provided by dedicated nurses, war injuries and diseases snuffed out the lives of many black soldiers. By the end of the war, the number of dead exceeded 38,000. The losses to families and loved ones were immense. Even more costly to the emotional well-being of loved ones were the deaths that could not be classified as war casualties but were related to racial hostilities and arbitrary violence such as the April 12, 1864, occurrence at Fort Pillow, Tennessee.[47]

Following more than eight hours of intense fighting, Union soldiers surrendered to Major General Nathan Bedford Forrest. After the surrender, however, the bloodletting continued. Among the accounts of "uncivilized" warfare at Fort Pillow were reports of Confederates shooting or burning black soldiers alive. The heinous behavior apparently influenced some Confederate officials and historians to deny or gloss over what had actually happened. More recently, scholars John Cimprich and Robert Mainfort Jr. examined military records and concluded, "Black troops suffered a casualty rate nearly double that of their white counterparts (64 percent compared to 31–34 percent)." The quantitative and documentary data demonstrate unequivocally that a massacre of blacks occurred at Fort Pillow.[48]

Despite the discrimination against and humiliation of African Americans during the Civil War era, they eventually received an immeasurable reward. By the end of 1865, nearly four million women, men, and children were freed as a result of the wartime acts, abolition of slavery in Maryland, Missouri, Washington, D.C., and the U.S. territories. Finally, the Thirteenth Amendment, ratified by Congress in December 1865, freed all persons remaining enslaved.[49]

Freedom was a priceless possession. Newly freed women must have wondered about its meaning as they emerged from bondage. How they responded to and gave meaning to their liberty varied across regions. The Virginia-born Booker T. Washington wrote, "Finally the war closed, and the day of freedom came. It was a momentous and eventful day." He remembered his mother's reaction after they heard a stranger, whom he assumed was a government agent, make "a little speech and then read a rather long paper." Although a child at the time, Washington linked this occasion to being awakened by his mother's fervent prayers for freedom. It was as if her supplications had been answered. "My mother who was standing by my side...leaned over and kissed her children while tears of joy ran down her cheeks," Washington added. The meaning of freedom was not as poignant for the child as for the mother who had endured bondage and was repulsed at the thought of perpetual servitude for her offspring.[50]

The response of Washington's mother was mild when compared to those of Peggy, a South Carolinian. Her former owner, Charles Manigault, noted that Peggy "seizes as *Her part* of the *spoils* my wife's large & handsome Mahogany Bedstead & Mattrass & arranged it in her own Negro House *on which she slept* for some time." Manigault imagined that Peggy had *"Sweet Dreams of freedom."* When the former owner attempted to retrieve the appropriated goods, Peggy took a firm stand, "placing her arms akimbo," and promised to stop the "unlawful proceedings" by reporting them to the provost marshal. With newfound agency and determination Peggy redefined the ownership of property and appropriated what she determined was rightfully hers.[51]

Peggy, who now owned herself, challenged the authority that had once loomed large in her life. Freedom bolstered her courage. She was free from threats or actual sales but not completely out of Manigault's reach for corporal punishment. However, if he thrashed her, Peggy, no doubt, would complain to the authorities.

The postwar experiences of the biracial "quasi-slaves" Imogene and Adaline Johnson, daughters of Richard M. Johnson; and Amanda America Dickson, the offspring of David Dickson, differed. They had lived as free persons and enjoyed amicable relationships with white relatives, inherited property, and married white men. There is nothing to indicate that the emancipation made significant impacts on their lives.[52]

The Thirteenth Amendment rendered the arrangements made between the freedman William Ellison and William McCreight regarding Maria Ann Ellison's liberty unnecessary. McCreight held title to Maria Ann due to South Carolina's prohibition against the emancipation of slaves. The Ellison-McCreight agreement was similar to one devised in 1833 between Sally Thomas and Ephraim H. Foster regarding her son James. Neither McCreight nor Foster had any interest in actually enslaving the children. Mutual respect governed these complex black-white relationships, yet it was liberating to know that McCreight and Foster no longer figured importantly in the enjoyment of freedom for Maria Ann or James.[53]

Emancipation was more meaningful for the South Carolinian Nancy Weston, who understood the very tenuous nature of "technical arrangements," such as that between Ellison and McCreight, regarding the virtual freedom she and her sons enjoyed for a limited time. They were now legally free. Without threats to their liberty, Weston and other freedwomen could now protect the integrity of their families legally. This perhaps was one of the greatest privileges of freedom for black women.

Emancipated women were also free to earn a living, worship in churches of their choice, travel at will, and gain an education as free black women had done prior to the Civil War. With the freedom of all blacks after 1865, it is appropriate to ask whether women who had enjoyed liberty for some time separated themselves from their newly freed sisters, or if the women's interests benefited all. In actuality, many free-born women had maintained long and enduring interest in the freedom of women and men in bondage. As a result, many had helped fugitives, supported abolitionism, and assisted with the former slaves' transition from slavery to freedom.[54]

With freedom at hand, black women across classes and regions attempted to make that liberty meaningful. Few, if any, sources present the thoughts and actions of free and newly freed women in this undertaking. The best, albeit limited, sources are manuscripts left by teachers in the postwar South. In his autobiography, *Up from Slavery*, Washington describes the intense desire for literacy among blacks and says it was a time when a whole race was trying to go to school. The vast amount of literature on the subject generally highlights the work of northern white missionaries who busied themselves lifting the veil of ignorance from masses of blacks hungry for knowledge.[55]

Many teachers were white New Englanders, but black women with varied backgrounds also worked as teachers among freedpersons. The free-born Olivia Davidson, who had attended the black-owned Albany Enterprise Academy in Ohio, was among the teachers. Prior to her 1882 marriage to Booker T. Washington, Davidson taught in Hernando, Mississippi, and Memphis, Tennessee. Her dedication was no less than that of the Oberlin-educated Blanche Harris who taught in Mississippi, North Carolina, and Kentucky under the auspices of the American Missionary Association.[56]

The most detailed accounts of a teacher's work are in journals kept by Charlotte Forten while employed in South Carolina between 1862 and 1864. The journals offer a rare glimpse of the times and tell much about her relationship with freedwomen in her adopted community. While aboard the steamer *United States,* Forten wrote, "One long-cherished wish of my heart was fulfilled at last. I was southward bound, on the mission which I have long felt called." It was her sincere desire to teach and do all she could for her people. After seeing the schoolchildren, she prayed, "May God preserve to you all the blessings of freedom, and may you be in every possible way fitted to enjoy them." Committed to serving them, she wrote, "My heart goes out to you. I shall be glad to do all that I can to help you."[57]

As a northern-educated woman, Forten was often mystified about cultural differences between herself and those she sought to help. At other times, Forten was condescending when writing about the schoolchildren, especially their religious dance while singing, or "ring shout." The children's "'shouts' are very strange," explained Forten, "in truth, almost indescribable." Yet she managed to describe the event: they formed a circle, moved "around in a kind of shuffling dance, singing all the time" while clapping their hands and rocking to and fro. The "little children, not more than three or four years old," amazed her as they entered "into the performance with all their might." Prince, "the principal shouter," was most striking, and she noted that his "performances were most amusing specimens of Ethiopian gymnastics."[58]

Forten's references to the children as "crude little specimens" and her penchant for words such as "strange," "wild," and "creature" when writing about them place her outside their Lower South cultural traditions and more firmly in her own New England customs. Forten mentioned a December 1862 visit from Mr. Pillsbury, a local minister and his family. "They seem good, kindly people though not very cultivated," wrote

Forten. Her evaluation is strikingly similar to that penned by Tryphena Fox following a June 1860 visit from a Louisiana plantation manager and his family. "They are good-hearted people," she wrote, "but not very intelligent or refined."[59]

Both comments reflect the gaze of educated women, and it did not matter that one was black and the other was white. The differences between their northern background and class standing are jarring when compared to those they observed. Both Forten and Fox enjoyed or aspired to middle- or upper-class standing. Both appeared ill at ease with poor, unlettered folk, or they did not always understand the situations others faced.

Rebecca Primus is another example of this phenomenon. She maintained a long-standing social relationship with Addie Brown, who was often impoverished, yet Primus seemed to misunderstand Brown's actual situation. Responding to a letter written by Primus, Brown retorted anxiously, "You say don't allow myself to indulge in glumy forebodings... How can I help it? I can't get any work." Certainly, this is only a small glimpse of their relationship, yet it appears to be a plea for Primus's understanding of her disparate situation.[60]

Primus worked as a teacher in Talbot County, Maryland, Frederick Douglass's birthplace, after the Civil War, and her comments about life there also reflect class differences. The superior air is hard to ignore in an April 20, 1867, letter when Primus noted that "the ladies [were] coming out in their spring costumes and at a distance they look tolerably well but I know not how they'll bear closer inspection." Following a church service several weeks later, the teacher again saw "a number of the blacks attired in their new spring hats, bonnets & dresses." "Some," she continued, "in the latest styles I judge, & oh! such looks some presented!" Readers would not miss her point when she wrote, "Some of these people do make themselves appear so much more ridiculous than they really are."[61]

Forten was no less acerbic when writing about weddings, "a very common occurrence" in the vicinity. She commented that the brides' dresses were "unique" and speculated that one in particular was a former owner's cast-off because of its shabby condition. "The lace sleeves, and other trimmings were in a rather decayed state," Forten observed, "and the white cotton gloves were well ventilated." Forten was amused at the bride's headdresses "of tattered flowers and ribbons." In her estimation, they were "very ridiculous." Only one member of a wedding party "had the slightest claim to good looks," Forten noted, "and she was a demure little thing with a neat, plain silk dress on." The distance between Forten's ideas about good taste and those in the wedding parties was immense. While Forten thought the "bridal costumes" were "very unique and comical," the "principal actors," she believed, were "fortunately quite unconscious of it." They looked "so proud and happy." The teacher's word choices—"actors," "costumes," and "comical"—reveal cynicism and arrogance. The writing emphasizes the gulf between a privileged, northern-born, free woman, and poor, southern freedwomen defining their liberty.[62]

Both Primus and Forten were critical of the freedwomen's penchant for stylish clothes. The teachers seemed oblivious to possible reasons for the extraordinary interests in fashion. While in bondage, the women had few if any chances to wear clothing, no matter how becoming, of their own choice. They received two simply cut calico or homespun dresses when owners distributed summer and winter clothes. The freedwoman Harriet Jacobs hated homespun garments because they were badges of slavery. Some distinctions existed between the clothing of field hands and that of domestic servants, who were likely to receive discards from owners. In either case, slaves often wore apparel that had nothing to do with their own creativity or self-esteem.[63]

Once freed, black women put distance between themselves and clothes reminiscent of bondage, and the results were not in keeping with Primus's or Forten's tastes. What the teachers thought of the styles remained personal opinions enveloped in private epistles. Their writings were not for public consumption, yet it is obvious that distinctions existed between the free-born women and newly freed women based on background, education, and class.[64]

Could these women, whose families had enjoyed many years of freedom, establish lasting friendships with recently freed women? If one ignores infelicitous remarks, Forten appears delighted to see women and men enjoying the privileges freedom offered, including legal marriages. Forten and other teachers were often solicitous. They visited the sick, mourned the dead, and shared the joys of dreams fulfilled. On occasion, Forten reminded herself, "It was for no selfish motive that I came here." She pledged that her work would fill her "whole existence to the exclusion of all vain longings."[65]

In their dedication to helping freedpersons, teachers were sometimes responsible for the organization and construction of schools to fulfill their dreams despite the cramped spaces and inadequate supplies. Hettie E. Sabattie, a free-born Georgian, held classes in 1868–1869 with "a great many children" in a Darien, South Carolina, church. They had no books initially. In early January 1869, Captain J. Murray Hoag, assistant superintendent of education for the Freedmen's Bureau in Georgia, forwarded thirty primers and readers along with fifteen spellers and fifteen second readers. This was far from adequate for 125 pupils. Sabattie continued her work despite shortages. Limited supplies and texts were better than none at all.[66]

The correspondence from Sabattie, a middle-class woman from a small slaveholding family, is limited in volume and addressed to a government official, unlike Forten's private journals or Primus's personal letters to her family. As a result, Sabattie's letters are formal and contain nothing that would reveal her intimate thoughts about the many children who attended her school. In fact, she decided to close the school temporarily because it was too "Dificult . . . to controle the children." The difficulty was with the 125 children rather than a cultural or behavioral disjuncture. She willingly reopened the school once another teacher joined her.[67]

Sabattie, like Rebecca Primus and Charlotte Forten, had their students' best interests at heart. Notwithstanding Primus's petty remarks about freedwomen and men, she attended to constructing a school for their children. Throughout each stage of building, Primus played an integral role, beginning with negotiations for the land. Afterward, she busied herself with the actual details of erecting the structure. When a local ex-slaveholder donated two trees for sills, she thought of the gift in terms of saving the cost of transporting lumber from afar. Involvement in this kind of work earned special praise for her and served as the basis for an amicable relationship with local black women. A common cause united them and could have long-term consequences since Primus taught their children. Although local people admired teachers and worked fervently to hire and retain them, class differences often prevented them from creating bonds besides those associated with parent-teacher relationships.[68]

Whites made no distinction between educated, free, black women and their unlettered, freed sisters. In an April 7, 1866, letter to her family, Rebecca Primus recounted the story of a colleague, a Miss Anderson, who was "stoned by white children, & repeatedly subjected to insults from white men." Several men jostled her on the sidewalk and injured her shoulder. Primus did not encounter such treatment but heard about enough incidents to convince her that whites were "very mean" in Maryland. She was saddened to learn that white children took books from black girls and boys in addition to treating the black youngsters poorly.[69]

Abusive white behavior reminded black women that they remained vulnerable to aggression. The women experienced a sense of solidarity in the matter and rejoiced when Miss Anderson *"prosecuted* a fellow for pushing *her* off the walk." She lost in the lower court but "carried the suit up and beat him" on an appeal. The black women in Anderson's community probably tempered public responses to her victory because they knew many local whites were not likely to accept the verdict peacefully. Neither would they receive Anderson, or any other black woman, as a social equal.[70]

Violence against black women regardless of background was not uncommon in the post–Civil War South. In fact, the abuse probably worsened as gangs of rowdy white men raped black women with impunity. Rhoda Ann Childs of Griffin, Georgia, complained to the Freedmen's Bureau that several men seized and beat her by "bucking" her across a log. Afterward, they threw her on the ground with one man standing on her breast, "while two others took hold of [her] feet and stretched [her] limbs as far apart as they could." One man "applied the strap to [her] private parts until fatigued into stopping." Before they released her, she testified, one man "ran his pistol into me" and threatened to pull the trigger. Another man on crutches "ravished" her. The men believed this was just treatment for a woman whose husband had joined the Union army.[71]

Hostilities against black women during the 1866 Memphis race riot underscores the hatred some whites felt toward emancipated blacks. The riot lasted three days and left scores of blacks dead and wounded. Among the casualties were several women who testified before a U.S. congressional committee that they had been raped by white men. Although the congressmen asked questions about whether the women were dressed and if they tried to resist the offenders, the women provided enough information about the brutality to dispel any myth about tempting the men into sexual intimacy.[72]

In these cases as in others, the assailants did not stop with raping black women but further brutalized them with whippings, burning pubic hair from their bodies, and "cutting [them] in the private parts." Such violent attacks were against individuals who were powerless in defending their nation, race, and themselves under such conditions. Rape, as an instrument of terror, often accompanies war. As an incidental atrocity without regard for time, race, or religion, the victors use rape to destroy national pride and to solidify conquest in the wider world or locally.[73]

As violence against blacks became more widespread at the hand of organized disaffected white groups, Frances E. W. Harper incorporated it into the historical context of her 1869 serialized novel, *Minnie's Sacrifice,* which appeared in the *Christian Recorder,* a journal published by the African Methodist Episcopal Church. Harper situates the fictitious characters within the realistic environment of Reconstruction. The author's protagonists are northern-educated teachers in the post–Civil War South

Figure 7.3. Memphis Riot, 1866, Library of Congress, Washington, D.C.

amid racial violence and hostility. Harper wrote, "The spirit of the lost cause revived, murders multiplied. The Ku Klux [Klan] spread terror and death around...Men advocating equal rights did so at the peril of their lives, for violence and murder were rampant in the land."[74]

Threats to their physical and emotional well-being remained ever present, yet free and recently freed women struggled to remain optimistic about their futures. Some believed migration from the South was the solution, while others saw possibilities in the public arena. A study of black women in Richmond, Virginia, following the Civil War argues that the absence of the franchise did not prevent them from active participation in the political arena. They attended meetings, listened to debates, and "took the day off from work and went to the polls." As a part of their political worldview, black women believed freedom "would accrue to each of them individually only when it was acquired by all of them collectively." Therefore, it was in their best interests to follow debates and encourage their menfolk to vote the "right" way for the benefit of the African American community. This behavior was not unique to Virginians.[75]

Harper's poem "Deliverance," published in *Sketches of Southern Life* (1872), lends credence to the belief in collectivity and how black women used their influence. The narrator, Aunt Chloe, says:

Day after day did Milly Green
Just follow after Joe,
And told him if he voted wrong
To take his rags and go.

Black women used other methods of intimidation according to the slave-born Robert Smalls, a South Carolina ex-slave who fought in the U.S. Navy during the Civil War and became a politician during Reconstruction. He claimed women, with clubs in hand, accompanied men to the polls to persuade them to vote against the Democrats.[76]

Rebecca Primus followed the debate and passage of the 1866 Civil Rights Act. It "is excellent I think, only I hope the *col[ore]d* people will not take the advantage of the privileges it prescribes," she declared. Primus was anxious about the hostile post–Civil War climate in which virulently racist whites looked for any excuse to mistreat recently freed women and men. The teacher observed, "I hope there will be justice, impartial justice, given to the colored people one of these days."[77]

To be sure, many black women were bitterly disappointed with freedom, according to Elizabeth Keckley, because they held "exaggerated ideas of liberty." The women believed freedom would be "a land of sun-shine, [and] rest," which was a fallacious image. Yet when facing reality, freedwomen did not merely wait until "given" impartial justice. Nor would they be willing to entertain the notion that the true *essence of liberty* could be more imaginary than real. Their interest was in doing whatever was necessary to make freedom "a beautiful vision" and fulfill its "glorious promise" of liberty, equality, and autonomy to all.[78]

Notes

Abbreviations

ACMS	Adams County Courthouse, Natchez, Mississippi
ARC	Amistad Research Center, Tulane University, New Orleans, Louisiana
CAPPA	City Archives of Philadelphia, Philadelphia, Pennsylvania
CHS	Connecticut Historical Society, Hartford, Connecticut
GDAH	Georgia Department of Archives and History, Atlanta, Georgia
HNO	Historic New Orleans Collection, New Orleans, Louisiana
HUA	Hampton University Archives, Hampton, Virginia
LCP	Library Company of Philadelphia, Philadelphia, Pennsylvania
LSU	Louisiana and Lower Mississippi Collection, Louisiana State University, Baton Rouge, Louisiana
MDAH	Mississippi Department of Archives and History, Jackson, Mississippi
MHS	Missouri Historical Society, St. Louis, Missouri
NA	National Archives, Washington, D.C.
PCNLA	Parish Clerk, Natchitoches, Louisiana
SCDAH	South Carolina Department of Archives and History, Columbia, South Carolina
SPCC	College of Charleston, Special Collection, Charleston, South Carolina
UT	Center for American History, University of Texas, Austin
VSL	Virginia State Library, Richmond, Virginia

Introduction

1. See Fannie Jackson-Coppin, Reminiscences of School Life, and Hints on Teaching; Zilpha Elaw, "Memoirs of the Life, Religious Experience, Ministerial Travels and Labors of Mrs. Zilpha Elaw"; "A Faithful Report of the Trial of Doctor William Little, on an indictment for an assault and battery, committed upon the body of his lawful wife, Mrs. Jane Little, A Black Lady," in Paul Finkelman, ed., *Free Blacks, Slaves, and Slaveowners in Civil and Criminal Courts: The Pamphlet Literature*, series 4, 1:103–11; Julia A. J. Foote, "A Brand Plucked from the Fire: An Autobiographical Sketch by Mrs. Julia A. J. Foote"; Brenda Stevenson, ed., *The Journals of Charlotte Forten Grimké*, 1; Frances E. Watkins [Harper], *Poems on*

197

Miscellaneous Subjects; Rebecca Jackson, *Gifts of Power: The Writings of Rebecca Jackson, Black Visionary, Shaker Eldress;* Harriet Jacobs, *Incidents in the Life of a Slave Girl: Written by Herself;* Michael P. Johnson and James L. Roark, eds., *No Chariot Let Down: Charleston's Free People of Color on the Eve of the Civil War;* Elizabeth Keckley, *Behind the Scenes; or Thirty Years a Slave, and Four Years in the White House;* Jarena Lee, "The Life and Religious Experience of Jarena Lee"; Gerda Lerner, ed., *Black Women in White America: A Documentary History;* Eliza Potter, *A Hairdresser's Experiences in the High Life;* Nancy Prince, *A Black Woman's Odyssey Through Russia and Jamaica;* Amanda Berry Smith, *An Autobiography: The Story of the Lord's Dealings with Mrs Amanda Smith . . . ;* Marilyn Richardson, ed., *Maria W. Stewart, America's First Black Woman Political Writer: Essays and Speeches;* Dorothy Sterling, ed., *We Are Your Sisters: Black Women in the Nineteenth Century;* Sojourner Truth, *Narrative of Sojourner Truth: A Bondswoman of Olden Time . . . ;* John C. Shields, ed., *The Collected Works of Phillis Wheatley: The Schomburg Library of Nineteenth-Century Black Women Writers;* Harriet Wilson, *Our Nig; or, Sketches from the Life of a Free Black in a Two-Story White House, North. Showing that Slavery's Shadows Fall Even There.*

2. See Ira Berlin, *Slaves Without Masters: The Free Negro in the Antebellum South,* for a comprehensive study of legislation designed to control free persons. Especially useful are Berlin's findings regarding the will of free persons to resist and their success in evading the laws.

3. Deborah Gray White, *Ar'n't I a Woman? Female Slaves in the Plantation South,* 23.

4. Susan M. Socolow, "Economic Roles of the Free Women of Color of Cap Francasi."

5. See Arlene J. Diaz, " 'Ciudadanas' and 'Padres de Familia': Gender Conflicts in the Early Venezuelan Republic," American Bar Foundation Working Paper #9412, Department of History, University of Minnesota.

1. *"Full Liberty to go and live with whom & Where She may Chuse": Founts of Freedom*

1. Phillis Wheatley to the Rev. Samson Occom, February 11, 1774, in Roger Bruns, ed., *Am I Not a Man and a Brother: The Antislavery Crusade of Revolutionary America, 1688–1788,* 306. Note the similarities in Wheatley's observations and those of George Tucker, a colonist, who wrote, "The love of freedom, sir, is an inborn sentiment, which the God of nature has planted deep in the heart: long may it be kept under by the arbitrary institutions of society; but, at the first favourable moment, it springs forth, and flourishes with a vigour that defies all check" (quoted in Ira Berlin, *Slaves Without Masters: The Free Negro in the Antebellum South,* 15). See Lillian Ashcraft-Eason, "Freedom among African Women Servants and Slaves in the Seventeenth-Century British Colonies," 62–79.

2. Herbert S. Klein, "African Women in the Atlantic Slave Trade," 73.

3. T. H. Breen and Stephen Innes, *"Myne Owne Ground": Race and Freedom on Virginia's Eastern Shore, 1640–1676,* 6, 8, 10, 12, 114; Kathleen M. Brown, *Good Wives, Nasty Wenches, and Anxious Patriarchs: Gender, Race, and Power in Colonial Virginia,* 107–9.

4. Edmund S. Morgan, *American Slavery—American Freedom: The Ordeal of Colonial Virginia*, 421.

5. Morgan, *American Slavery*, 111 n. 16, 336.

6. Morgan, *American Slavery*, 333; Joel Williamson, *New People: Miscegenation and Mulattoes in the United States*, 6–7; Thomas D. Morris, *Southern Slavery and the Law, 1619–1860*, 40–45; Joane Nagel, *Race, Ethnicity, and Sexuality: Intimate Intersections, Forbidden Frontiers*, 1.

7. Elizabeth Keckley, *Behind the Scenes or Thirty Years a Slave, and Four Years in the White House*, 47 (emphases added); Morgan, *American Slavery*, 333; Williamson, *New People*, 6–7; Morris, *Southern Slavery and the Law*, 40, 44–45; Michael P. Johnson and James L. Roark, *Black Masters: A Free Family of Color in the Old South*, 53–55. Jennifer Fleischner, *Mrs. Lincoln and Mrs. Keckly: The Remarkable Story of the Friendship Between a First Lady and a Former Slave*, 7, maintains that Elizabeth Keckly did not sign "Keckley" as often appears in previous publications.

8. A. Leon Higginbotham Jr., *In the Matter of Color: Race and the American Legal Process, The Colonial Period*, 40–47; Paul Finkelman, "Crimes of Love, Misdemeanors of Passion: The Regulation of Race and Sex in the Colonial South," 129–31; Williamson, *New People*, 8; Morris, *Southern Slavery and the Law*, 45. See Michael L. Nicholls, "Passing Through this Troublesome World: Free Blacks in the Early Southside," 50–70; Victoria E. Bynum, *Unruly Women: The Politics of Social and Sexual Control in the Old South*, 88–89.

9. Arthur Zilversmit, *The First Emancipation: The Abolition of Slavery in the North*, 93–96; Bruns, *Am I Not a Man and a Brother*, 452–56.

10. Zilversmit, *The First Emancipation*, 107–8.

11. Bruns, *Am I Not a Man and a Brother*, 104; L. H. Butterfield, Wendell D. Garrett, and Marjorie E. Sprague, eds., *Adams Family Correspondence*, vol. 1, December 1761–May 1776, 162; Charles Francis Adams, ed., *Familiar Letters of John Adams and His Wife Abigail Adams, During the Revolution. With a Memoir of Mrs. Adams*, 41–42; Bernard Bailyn, *The Ideological Origins of the American Revolution*, 239; Gary B. Nash, *Race and Revolution*, 7–9, 10. See Ian F. Haney Lopez, "The Social Construction of Race: Some Observations on Illusion, Fabrication, and Choice," 1–62; David Brion Davis, *The Problem of Slavery in Western Culture*, 13–21; Barbara J. Fields, "Slavery, Race and Ideology in the United States of America," 95–118; Tracy Fessenden, "The Sisters of the Holy Family and the Veil of Race," 199, for further discussion regarding the construction of race.

12. Phillis Wheatley, "To the Right Hon. William, Earl of Dartmouth, His Majesty's Principal Secretary of State for N. America," 156; John C. Shields, ed., *The Collected Works of Phillis Wheatley*, 73–74; R. Lynn Matson, "Phillis Wheatley—Soul Sister?" 222–30.

13. Gary B. Nash, *Forging Freedom: The Formation of Philadelphia's Black Community, 1720–1840*, 61–63.

14. Nell Irvin Painter, *Sojourner Truth: A Life, A Symbol*, 23; Joanne Pope Melish, *Disowning Slavery: Gradual Emancipation and "Race" in New England, 1780–1860*, 84–118; Robert William Fogel and Stanley L. Engerman, "Philanthropy at Bargain Prices: Notes on the Economics of Gradual Emancipation," 381; Ira Berlin, *Many Thousands Gone: The First Two Centuries of Slavery in North America*, 228, 234; Nash, *Race and Revolution*, 34; Gary B. Nash, *Red, White, and Black: The Peoples of Early North America*, 279–80.

15. Carolyn E. Fick, *The Making of Haiti: The Saint Domingue Revolution from Below*, 15; Ralph Korngold, *Citizen Toussaint*, 11; C. L. R. James, *The Black Jacobins: Toussaint L'Ouverture and the San Domingo Revolution*, ix; Vincent Bakpetu Thompson, *The Making of the African Diaspora in the Americas 1441–1900*, 304; H. P. Davis, *Black Democracy: The Story of Haiti*, 24.

16. Fick, *The Making of Haiti*, 76–77.

17. Ibid., 163–64.

18. Alfred N. Hunt, *Haiti's Influence on Antebellum America: Slumbering Volcano in the Caribbean*, 38, 40, 43, 45–47; Shane White, *Somewhat More Independent: The End of Slavery in New York City, 1770–1810*, 155; Orville Vernon Burton, "Anatomy of an Antebellum Rural Free Black Community: Social Structure and Social Interaction in Edgefield District, South Carolina, 1850–1860," 297; Johnson and Roark, *Black Masters*, 33; Bernard E. Powers Jr., *Black Charlestonians: A Social History, 1822–1885*, 28; Ira Berlin, "The Structure of the Free Negro Caste in the Antebellum United States," 310.

19. Robert H. Ferrell, *American Diplomacy: A History*, 67, 70, 102–3; Howard Jones, *The Course of American Diplomacy: From the Revolution to the Present*, 45–47.

20. Thomas N. Ingersoll, "Free Blacks in a Slave Society: New Orleans, 1718–1812," 192. For a discussion regarding the United States's attitude toward Haiti, see Tim Matthewson, "Jefferson and Haiti," 209–48.

21. See L. Virginia Gould, "Urban Slavery—Urban Freedom: The Manumission of Jacqueline Lemelle," 305; Lois Virginia Meacham Gould, "In Full Enjoyment of Their Liberty: The Free Women of Color in the Gulf Ports of New Orleans, Mobile, and Pensacola, 1769–1860," 86–89, 91; Kimberly S. Hanger, "'The Fortunes of Women in America': Spanish New Orleans's Free Women of African Descent and Their Relations with Slave Women," 158–60; Kimberly S. Hanger, "Patronage, Property and Persistence: The Emergence of a Free Black Elite in Spanish New Orleans," 46–48; Berlin, *Many Thousands Gone*, 213.

22. B. Finette Ball Lynch to Argus Ball, undated, Manus Papers #83542, Connecticut Historical Society, Hartford, Connecticut (hereafter cited as CHS).

23. Keckley, *Behind the Scenes*, 45–46, 55, 63; Mary Beth Corrigan, "'It's a Family Affair': Buying Freedom in the District of Columbia, 1850–1860," 178.

24. Gary B. Mills, *The Forgotten People: Cane River's Creoles of Color*, 39, 40, 41–42, 48. See Constance McLaughlin Green, *The Secret City: A History of Race Relations in the Nation's Capital*; Carter Woodson, *Free Negro Owners of Slaves in the United States in 1830: Together with Absentee Ownership of Slaves in the United States in 1830*; Susan M. Socolow, "Economic Roles of the Free Women of Color on Cap Francais," 289–90; Gould, "Urban Slavery—Urban Freedom," 309. For a discussion of self-purchases, emancipations, and slave ownerships by African Americans, see R. Halliburton Jr., "Free Black Owners of Slaves: A Reappraisal of the Woodson Thesis," 129–42.

25. Green, *The Secret City*, 16; Frances LaJune Johnson Powell, "A Study of the Structure of the Freed Black Family in Washington, DC, 1850–1880," 50; Corrigan, "'It's a Family Affair,'" 177–78. Tanner's name also appears as "Aletha."

26. Corrigan, "'It's a Family Affair,'" 179, 186 n. 13.

27. Manumission Document, March 11, 1839, Thomas Sewall Papers, Library of Congress, Washington, DC; William Cohen, "Thomas Jefferson and the Problem of Slavery," 519; Ulrich B. Phillips, *American Negro Slavery: A Survey of the*

Supply, Employment and Control of Negro Labor As Determined by the Plantation Regime, 426–27; Berlin, *Slaves Without Masters*, 21, 29–31; Sherrie S. McLeRoy and William R. McLeRoy, *Strangers in Their Midst: The Free Black Population of Amherst County, Virginia*, 21. See Loren Schweninger, ed., *The Microfilm Edition of Race, Slavery, and Free Blacks, Series 1, Petitions to Southern Legislatures, 1777–1867* (hereafter cited as *Microfilm Petitions*), twenty-three reels containing hundreds of petitions for emancipations often with reasons given.

28. See Daniel F. Littlefield Jr., ed., *The Life of Okah Tubbee*, ix, 132 n. 17. See also Isabel Vandervelde, *Other Free People in Early Barnwell District*, 48.

29. T. Stephen Whitman, *The Price of Freedom: Slavery and Manumission in Baltimore and Early National Maryland*, 95; Cynthia M. Kennedy, " 'Noctural Adventures in Mulatto Alley': Sex in Charleston, South Carolina," 37–56; Beverly Greene Bond, " 'The Extent of the Law': Free Women of Color in Antebellum Memphis, Tennessee," 11–13; Annette Gordon-Reed, *Thomas Jefferson and Sally Hemings: An American Controversy*, 164–65; Judith Kelleher Schafer, " 'Open and Notorious Concubinage': The Emancipation of Slave Mistresses by Will and the Supreme Court in Antebellum Louisiana," 165–82.

30. See Sarah Robinson's Will, August 6, 1835, Adams County Court House, Natchez, Mississippi (hereafter cited as ACMS); Esther Russell Will, 1821, Virginia, reel 18, in Schweninger, *Microfilm Edition;* Hanger, "Patronage, Property and Persistence," 46; Virginia Glenn Crane, "Two Women, White and Brown in the South Carolina Court of Equity, 1842–1845," 210; McLeRoy and McLeRoy, *Strangers in Their Midst*, 21.

The subject of intimacy between white women and black men is beyond the scope of this work. Several studies including Fay A. Yarbrough, "Power, Perception, and Interracial Sex: Former Slaves Recall a Multiracial South," 571–73; Bertram Wyatt-Brown, *Southern Honor: Ethics and Behavior in the Old South*, 315; Martha Hodes, *White Women, Black Men: Illicit Sex in the Nineteenth-Century South*, 11–14, 211–12; Brown, *Good Wives, Nasty Wenches, and Anxious Patriarchs*, 98, 104; White, *Somewhat More Independent*, 168–69, provide relevant references. Also T. O. Madden Jr. with Ann L. Miller, *We Were Always Free: The Maddens of Culpeper County, Virginia, a 200-Year Family History;* Silvio A. Bedini, *The Life of Benjamin Banneker*, 10–21; Bynum, *Unruly Women*, 97–98; provide further insight.

31. Stephen Whitman, "Diverse Good Causes: Manumission and the Transformation of Urban Slavery," 337, 340; Wyatt-Brown, *Southern Honor*, 315–16.

32. Seventh Census of the United States, 1850, 82, 83; Williamson, *New People*, 24–25.

33. Nathaniel E. Janney, November 22, 1843, Dexter Tiffany Papers (hereafter cited as Tiffany Papers), Missouri Historical Society, St. Louis, Missouri (hereafter cited as MHS); Adrienne D. Davis, "The Private Law of Race and Sex: An Antebellum Perspective," 238–41; Schafer, " 'Open and Notorious Concubinage,' " 165–82; Larry Koger, *Black Slaveowners: Free Black Slave Masters in South Carolina*, 49; Cohen, "Thomas Jefferson and the Problem of Slavery," 503–26; Robert Brent Toplin, "Between Black and White: Attitudes Toward Southern Mulattoes, 1830–1861," 193. See "Manumission of Judah," October 18, 1845, Tiffany Papers, MHS; "The Last Will and Testament," of Alexander Parker, Will Book, ACMS; "The Last Will and Testament of B. F. Conner," February 14, 1832, ACMS; Order Books, Jefferson County Kentucky, Kentucky Department of Archives and

History, Frankfort Kentucky; Barnwell County Judge of Probate Manumission Book, 1803–1845 (Typewritten transcription, Works Progress Administration Project 65–33–118, 1938), South Carolina Department of Archives and History (hereafter cited as SCDAH).

34. "Last Will and Testament," of William Barland, April 11, 1789, ACMS; April 22, 1803, Barnwell County Judge of Probate, SCDAH; Carl Lane and Rhoda Freeman, "John Dipper and the Experience of the Free Black Elite, 1816–1836," 491; Emancipation of Eliza Davis, May 18, 1844, Tiffany Papers, MHS; Becky Carlson, "'Manumitted and Forever Set Free': The Children of Charles Lee Younger and Elizabeth, a Woman of Color," 19, 22–23; Craddock Vaughn Will, 1851, Virginia, reel 22, Schweninger, *Microfilm Petition*.

35. Whitman, *The Price of Freedom*, 94; Whitman, "Diverse Good Causes," 338–39; Johnson and Roark, *Black Masters*, 33.

36. Corrigan, "'It's a Family Affair'," 175–76.

37. Bruns, *Am I Not a Man and a Brother*, 468.

38. Ibid., 468.

39. Helen Tunnicliff Catterall, ed., *Judicial Cases Concerning American Slavery and the Negro*, 1:138–39. See Michael L. Nicholls, "'The squint of freedom': African-American Freedom Suits in Post-Revolutionary Virginia," 47–62.

40. Catterall, *Judicial Cases*, 1:139.

41. *The Code of Virginia* second edition, 511; Catterall, *Judicial Cases*, 1:139 nn.

42. Catterall, *Judicial Cases*, 1:112; Lopez, "The Social Construction of Race," 1–2. See Walter Johnson, "The Slave Trader, the White Slave, and the Politics of Racial Determination in the 1850s," 13–38.

43. Paul Finkelman, *Dred Scott v. Sandford: A Brief History with Documents*, 1–2; Lea Vander Velde and Sandhya Subramanian, "Mrs. Dred Scott," 1073. See William E. Foley, "Slave Freedom Suits Before Dred Scott: The Case of Marie Jean Scypion's Descendants," 1–23.

44. Velde and Subramanian, "Mrs. Dred Scott," 1041, 1055, 1057, 1089, 1098–99.

45. Finkelman, *Dred Scott*, 10–19; Velde and Subramanian, "Mrs. Dred Scott," 1034–35, 1089.

46. Finkelman, *Dred Scott*, 31–32.

47. Ibid., 51.

48. Whitman, "Diverse Good Causes," 355; John Hope Franklin and Loren Schweninger, *Runaway Slaves: Rebels on the Plantation*, 282. For biographies of women who ran away, see Catherine Clinton, *Harriet Tubman: The Road to Freedom*; Jean M. Humez, *Harriet Tubman: The Life and the Life Stories*; Kate Clifford Larson, *Bound for the Promised Land: Harriet Tubman, Portrait of an American Hero*; Nell Irvin Painter, *Sojourner Truth: A Life, a Symbol*; and Jean M. Yellin, *Harriet Jacobs*.

49. Franklin and Schweninger, *Runaway Slaves*, 282; Richard Wade, *Slavery in the Cities: The South, 1820–1860*, 214–16; Barbara Jeanne Fields, *Slavery and Freedom on the Middle Ground: Maryland during the Nineteenth Century*, 52–53; Herbert G. Gutman, *The Black Family in Slavery and Freedom, 1750–1925*, 264; Michael P. Johnson, "Runaway Slaves and the Slave Communities in South Carolina, 1799 to 1830," 418; Judith Kelleher Schafer, "New Orleans Slavery in 1850 as Seen in Advertisements," 33–56.

50. Sterling, *We Are Your Sisters*, 45. It was not unusual for enslaved women and men to attempt to find buyers for themselves or their loved ones to avoid separation. See letters from two enslaved women facing potential sales who beg their spouses to find buyers for themselves in Mary Beth Norton and Ruth M. Alexander, eds., *Major Problems in American Women's History*, 144–45.

51. Richard J. Hinton, *John Brown and His Men: With Some Account of the Roads They Traveled to Reach Harper's Ferry*, 29–36; Sterling, *We Are Your Sisters*, 45.

52. Hinton, *John Brown and His Men*, 298.

53. Ibid., 313.

54. Sterling, *We Are Your Sisters*, 45.

55. Berlin, *Slaves Without Masters*, 90, 79–107; *Population of the United States in 1860*, ix.

56. Pauli Murray, *Proud Shoes: The Story of an American Family*, 49, 162. See Wilma King, "Within the Professional Household: Slave Children in the Antebellum South," 523–40; Kent Anderson Leslie, *Woman of Color, Daughter of Privilege: Amanda America Dickson*.

57. [John Jacobs], "A True Tale of Slavery," 86; Jacobs, *Incidents in the Life of a Slave Girl*, 262 n. 6; Marion B. Lucas, A History of Blacks in Kentucky, 1:114. See Halliburton, "Free Black Owners of Slaves," 129–42; Koger, *Black Slaveowners*, 80–86; David L. Lightner and Alexander M. Ragan, "Were African American Slaveholders Benevolent or Exploitative? A Quantitative Approach," 535–58; Suzanne Lebsock, "Free Black Women and the Question of Matriarchy: Petersburg, Virginia, 1784–1820," 279.

58. Johnson and Roark, *Black Masters*, 14–15, 101–6.

59. Loren Schweninger, *James T. Rapier and Reconstruction*, 2–4; Loren Schweninger, "A Slave Family in the Ante Bellum South," 31, 34–35. See John Hope Franklin, "Slaves Virtually Free in Ante-Bellum North Carolina," 284–310.

60. See documents #105, #107–112 related to kidnapping, Polly Case, Ohio Historical Society, Columbus, Ohio; Joseph Watson to James Rogers, February 24, 1827, General Reference #706, Negroes Kidnapped, Delaware Public Archives, Hall of Records, Dover, Delaware.

61. Emily Mason Certificate of Freedom, August 16, 1838, Tiffany Papers, MHS; Walter Johnson, *Soul by Soul: Life Inside the Antebellum Slave Market*, 139, 150, 155, 157.

Clerks recording the registration of free blacks in Staunton, and Augusta County, Virginia, used the following descriptors: "black," "high black," "light black," "pale black," "very black"; "bright"; "brown," "light brown," "dark brown"; "chocolate"; "colored"; "copper," "light copper," "dark copper"; "dark"; "light"; "mulatto," "bright mulatto," "dark mulatto," "high mulatto," "light mulatto," "very bright mulatto," "very dark mulatto"; "yellow," "bright yellow," and "dark yellow." See "Register of Free Negroes and Mulattoes in the Corporation of Staunton (Virginia)" and "Register of Free Blacks Augusta County, Virginia."

62. Register of Free Persons of Color, 1818, Camden County, Georgia, Georgia Department of Archives and History (hereafter cited as GDAH); Register of Free Persons of Color, Talliferro, Georgia, 1829–1861, GDAH; Register of Free Persons of Color, Chatham County, 1826–1835, Georgia, GDAH; Register of

Free Persons of Color, Columbia County, 1819–1836, GDAH; James Oliver Horton, *Free People of Color: Inside the African American Community*, 126–28.

63. Theodore Hershberg and Henry William, "Mulattoes and Blacks: Intragroup Color Differences and Social Stratification in Nineteenth-Century Philadelphia," 397; Charles H. Wesley, *Negro Labor in the United States*, 40; Kwando Mbiassi Kinshasa, "Free Blacks' Quest for National Identity: Debates in the African American Press on Assimilation and Emigration," 94.

64. Yarbrough, "Power, Perception, and Interracial Sex," 573–75; Horton, *Free People of Color*, 124–45.

65. Horton, *Free People of Color*, 125, 139–40; Johnson and Roark, *Black Masters*, 208–12; Toplin, "Between Black and White," 193–94; Powers, *Black Charlestonians*, 51–52; Berlin, *Slaves Without Masters*, 58. See George P. Rawick, ed., *The American Slave: A Composite Autobiography* and the two supplements, for a discussion of color by former slaves.

66. Williamson, *New People*, 16; Toplin, "Between Black and White," 188; Berlin, *Slaves Without Masters*, 57–58; Mia Bay, *The White Image in the Black Mind: African-American Ideas about White People, 1830–1925*, 78, 79–80; Fessenden, "The Sisters of the Holy Family," 198–20. For an expanded discussion of color and class among free blacks, see Berlin, "The Free People of Color of Louisiana and the Gulf Ports," in *Slaves Without Masters*, 108–32; Virginia R. Dominguez, *White by Definition: Social Classification in Creole Louisiana*.

67. Harriet Beecher Stowe, *Uncle Tom's Cabin; or, Life Among the Lowly*, 54, 69; Toplin, "Between Black and White," 192, 194. See David W. Levy, "Racial Stereotypes in Antislavery Fiction," 265–79.

68. Blassingame, *Black New Orleans*, 14, 17; Eliza Potter, *A Hairdresser's Experience in the High Life*, 190; Monique Guillory, "Under One Roof: The Sins and Sanctity of the New Orleans Quadroon Balls," 82–84; Mills, *The Forgotten People*, 79, 80–81, 90–92, 94–98; Sister Audrey Marie Detiege, *Henriette Delille, Free Woman of Color: Foundress of the Sisters of the Holy Family*, 8; John W. Blassingame, *Black New Orleans, 1860–1880*, 14; Loren Schweninger, "Prosperous Blacks in the South, 1790–1880," 35.

69. *The Code of Mississippi*, 514, 521; *The Revised Code of Mississippi*, 235; Horton, *Free People of Color*, 123; Powers, *Black Charleston*, 52; Litwack, *North of Slavery*, 182–83; Leonard P. Curry, *The Free Black in Urban America, 1800–1850: The Shadow of the Dream*, 81.

70. Berlin, "The Structure of the Free Negro Caste," 298, 308–9; Berlin, *Slaves Without Masters*, 269–71; Michael P. Johnson and James L. Roark, "Strategies of Survival: Free Negro Families and the Problem of Slavery," 89.

71. Berlin, *Many Thousands Gone*, 214; Whittington B. Johnson, *Black Savannah, 1788–1864*, 1–2, 4; Whittington B. Johnson, "A Black Teacher and Her School in Reconstruction Darien: The Correspondence of Hettie Sabattie and J. Murray Hoag, 1868–1869," 96; Tommy L. Bogger, *Free Blacks in Norfolk, Virginia, 1796–1860: The Darker Side of Freedom*; Powers, *Black Charlestonians*, 61; Lois Virginia Meacham Gould, "In Full Enjoyment of Their Liberty," 8, 56, 58, 72, 107–17; Lucas, *A History of Blacks in Kentucky*, 1:110; Kinshasa, "Free Blacks' Quest for National Identity," 94; Fessenden, "The Sisters of the Holy Family," 199. See Wilma King, "'Out of Bounds': Emancipated and Enslaved Women in Ante-

bellum America," 127–44; Loren Schweninger, "The Underside of Slavery: The Internal Economy, Self-Hire, and Quasi-Freedom in Virginia, 1780–1865," 1–22; Victoria E. Bynum, *Unruly Women: The Politics of Social and Sexual Control in the Old South*, 39–40; Kimberly S. Hanger, *Bounded Lives, Bounded Places: Free Black Society in Colonial New Orleans, 1769–1803*.

72. See Berlin, *Many Thousands Gone*, 321; Whitman, *The Price of Freedom*, 119–23.

73. See Hanger, *Bounded Lives*; King, "Out of Bounds."

74. Edwin Adams Davis and William Ransom Hogan, *The Barber of Natchez*, 54–68, 241. See William Ransom Hogan and Edwin Adam Davis, eds., *William Johnson's Natchez: The Ante-Bellum Diary of a Free Negro*.

75. Johnson and Roark, *Black Masters*, 131–33.

76. Ibid., 133–34. It was not unusual for enslaved women to appeal to slave-holding women as an attempt to mitigate their conditions. See Frances Anne Kemble, *Journal of a Residence on a Georgian Plantation in 1838–1839*, 214, 222; Lavina to Dear Missis, July 1849, Lawton Family Papers, University of South Carolina, Columbia, South Carolina.

77. Sterling, *We Are Your Sisters*, 103; *Population of the United States in 1860*, 2; Fields, *Slavery and Freedom on the Middle Ground*, 15, 30; Free papers, April 10, 1839, Enoch Tucker Papers, LC; Berlin, *Slaves Without Masters*, 102.

2. "This modest bending of the head": Gender Conventions, Expectations, and Misrepresentations

Title quote from Sarah Mapps Douglass to Mary Ann Dickerson, November 14, 1846, Album, Dickerson Family Papers, Library Company of Philadelphia, Philadelphia, Pennsylvania (hereafter cited as LCP).

1. Mary Ann Elizabeth Stevens Cogdell, Diary and Copy Book, 1805–1823, Box 1, Stevens-Cogdell/Sanders-Venning Collection, LCP; Phillip S. Lapsansky, "Afro-Americana: Family Values, in Black and White," *The Annual Report of the Library Company of Philadelphia*, 26–27.

2. See genealogical chart, Cogdell/Sanders Collection, LCP.

3. Nell Irvin Painter, "Sojourner Truth in Life and Memory: Writing the Biography of an American Exotic," 9; Hazel V. Carby, *Reconstructing Womanhood: The Emergence of the Afro-American Woman Novelist*, 33. See Deborah Gray White, *Ar'n't I a Woman? Female Slaves in the Plantation South*, 27–61; Barbara Bush, *Slave Women in Caribbean Society, 1650–1838*, 14–17. See also Patricia Morton, *Disfigured Images: The Historical Assault on African American Women*, chapter 2.

4. See Lois Virginia Meacham Gould, "In Full Enjoyment of Their Liberty: The Free Women of Color of the Gulf Ports of New Orleans, Mobile, and Pensacola, 1769–1860"; Barbara Elizabeth Wallace, "Fair Daughters of Africa: African American Women in Baltimore, 1790–1860"; Beverly Greene Bond, "'Till Fair Aurora Rise': African-American Women in Memphis, Tennessee, 1840–1915." See also Adele Logan Alexander, *Ambiguous Lives: Free Women of Color in Rural Georgia, 1789–1879*; Gayle T. Tate, *Unknown Tongues: Black Women's Political Activism in the Antebellum Era, 1830–1860*. Catherine Clinton, *The Plantation Mistress: Woman's World in the Old South*, 201–3; Morton, *Disfigured Images*, 9;

White, *Ar'n't I a Woman?* , 27–61; Cheryl Thurber, "The Development of the Mammy Image and Mythology," 87–108; Phil Patton, "Mammy, Her Life and Times," 78–87, for extensive discussions of free black women.

5. Marilyn Richardson, ed., *Maria W. Stewart, America's First Black Woman Political Writer: Essays and Speeches*, 48; R. J. Young, *Antebellum Black Activists: Race, Gender and Self*, 148. See Barbara Welter, "The True Cult of True Womanhood, 1820–1860," 151–74; Shirley J. Yee, *Black Women Abolitionists: A Study in Activism, 1828–1860*, 40–59; Nancy Cott, The Bonds of Womanhood: "Woman's Sphere" in New England, 1780–1835, 1–2, 8–9 197–99; Mary H. Blewett, *Men, Women, and Work: Class, Gender, and Protest in the New England Shoe Industry*, 14, 15, 18. See also Christine Stansell, *City of Women: Sex and Class in New York, 1789–1860;* Jeanne Boydston, *Home and Work: Housework, Wages, and the Ideology of Labor in the Early Republic.*

6. Carby, *Reconstructing Womanhood*, 20–24. See D. Harland Hagler, "The Ideal Woman in the Antebellum South: Lady or Farmwife?"

7. White, *Ar'n't I a Woman?* 31–34; Bush, *Slave Women in Caribbean Society*, 20–21. See Winthrop D. Jordan, *White over Black: American Attitudes Toward the Negro, 1550–1812, 33–40.*

8. Kathleen M. Brown, *Good Wives, Nasty Wenches, and Anxious Patriarchs: Gender, Race, and Power in Colonial Virginia*, 1–2, 9, 104, 115, 370.

9. Diane Miller Sommerville, "The Rape Myth in the Old South Reconsidered," 494 n. 34.

10. Helen Tunnicliff Catterall, ed., *Judicial Cases Concerning American Slavery and the Negro*, 2:193.

11. Eric Lott, *Love and Theft: Blackface Minstrelsy and American Working Class*, 120, 146.

12. See Harriet Jacobs, *Incidents in the Life of a Slave Girl Written by Herself,* ed. Jean Fagan Yellin, 27–29; George P. Rawick, ed., *The American Slave: A Composite Autobiography* and supplements; Maria Diedrich, "'My Love Is Black as Yours Is Fair': Premarital Love and Sexuality in the Antebellum Slave Narrative," 238–47.

13. Jacobs, *Incidents in the Life of a Slave Girl*, 27, 51.

14. Lavina to Dear Missis, July 1849, Lawton Family Papers, University of South Carolina, Columbia, South Carolina. Thanks to Stephanie McCurry for bringing this letter to my attention.

15. Ibid.

16. Ibid.

17. Ibid.

18. John Greenleaf Whittier, "To the Daughters of James Forten," Charlotte Forten Grimké Papers, Howard University, Washington, DC.

19. Nell Irvin Painter, *Sojourner Truth: A Life, a Symbol*, 45–46, 181–82, 185–99.

20. Dorothy Sterling, ed., *We Are Your Sisters: Black Women in the Nineteenth Century*, 220; Cott, *The Bonds of Womanhood*, 73–74. For thorough discussions related to the origins of differences in gender construction, see Gerda Lerner, *The Creation of Patriarchy;* and *The Creation of the Feminist Consciousness: From the Middle Ages to Eighteenth Seventy.*

21. James Oliver Horton, "Freedom's Yoke: Gender Conventions among Antebellum Free Blacks," 56. See Cott, *The Bonds of Womanhood*, 71–72.

22. Horton, "Freedom's Yoke," 56.

23. See Painter, *Sojourner Truth*, 164–78, for a discussion regarding the authenticity of the "Ar'n't I a Woman?" speech.

24. Judith Sealander, "The Antebellum Black Press Images of Women," 160, 164.

25. Eliza Potter, *A Hairdresser's Experience in the High Life*, 279–80. Thanks to Lois Virginia Gould for bringing this source to my attention.

26. See Order Book, Daughters of Africa, Historical Society of Pennsylvania, Philadelphia, Pennsylvania; Sterling, *We Are Your Sisters*, 105, 109.

27. Sterling, *We Are Your Sisters*, 107–9; Willi Coleman, "Architects of a Vision: Black Women and Their Antebellum Quest for Political and Social Equality," 25.

28. R. F. Peterson to Martina Dickerson, July 16, 1840, Album, LPC; I Timothy 2:9.

29. Gary B. Nash, *Forging Freedom: The Formation of Philadelphia's Black Community, 1720–1840*, 254–58; Nancy Reynolds Davidson, "E. W. Clay: American Political Caricaturist of the Jacksonian Era," 214–17. See Joanne Pope Melish, *Disowning Slavery: Gradual Emancipation and "Race" in New England, 1780–1860*, 165–66, 172–78.

30. Silas Everett Fales to Mary, February 18, 1863, Silas Everett Fales Papers, Southern Historical Collection, University of North Carolina, Chapel Hill, North Carolina; "The White Boys Outgrow Charles," in *A Documentary History of Slavery in North America*, ed. Willie Lee Rose, 408–9. See Edward E. Baptist, "'Cuffy,' 'Fancy Maids,' and 'One-Eyed Men': Rape, Commodification, and the Domestic Slave Trade in the United States," 1619–50; Walter Johnson, *Soul by Soul: Life Inside the Antebellum Slave Market*, 113–115, 138–39, for discussions regarding the sale of slaves and the significance of skin color.

31. Harriet Beecher Stowe, *Uncle Tom's Cabin; or, Life Among the Lowly*, ed. Ann Douglas, 54, 66–67, 107, 127, 351–52.

32. See Frederick Douglass, "The Negro as Man" [n.d.], Frederick Douglass Papers, Library of Congress, Washington, DC. Thanks to Donna M. Wells for bringing this citation to my attention. See Donna M. Wells, "Frederick Douglass and the Power of the Photograph: Annotated Bibliography," 6; Hugh Honour, *The Image of the Black in Western Art: From the American Revolution to World War I, Black Models and White Myths*, vol. 4.

33. Lee Paul, "The Real Yellow Rose of Texas," 50–56, 94, Emily West Papers, Texas State Library and Archives Commission, Austin, Texas. The word "darkey" does not appear in the current version of "The Yellow Rose of Texas." Instead, "She is the sweetest little rosebud that Texas ever knew" completes the song. See Ruthe Winegarten, *Black Texas Women: A Sourcebook, Documents, Biographies, Timeline*, 7–8, 259–60, 231 n. 4, 274.

34. Jacobs, *Incidents in the Life of a Slave Girl*, 28; Baptist, "'Cuffy,' 'Fancy Maids,' and 'One-Eyed Men.'"

35. Catherine M. Hanchett, "'What Sort of People and Families...': The Edmondson Sisters," 24; Solomon Northup, "Twelve Years a Slave: Narrative of Solomon Northup," 268; Baptist, "'Cuffy,' 'Fancy Maids,' and 'One-Eyed Men.'"

36. Jacobs, *Incidents in the Life of a Slave Girl*, 28.

37. Addie Brown to Rebecca Primus, March 30, 1862, Primus Papers, CHS; Farah Jasmine Griffin, ed., *Beloved Sisters and Loving Friends: Letters from Rebecca*

Primus of Royal Oak, Maryland, and Addie Brown of Hartford, Connecticut, 1854–1868, 29, 65–66.

38. Stevenson, *The Journals of Charlotte Forten Grimké*, 3:373; Brenda Stevenson, "Charlotte Forten (1837–1914)," 288.

39. Stevenson, *The Journals of Charlotte Forten Grimké*, 3:373. For differing interpretations of Forten Grimké's views, see Noliwe Rooks, *Hair Raising: Beauty, Culture, and African American Women*, 23; Stevenson, *The Journals*, 34, 3:300.

40. M. H. Freeman, "The Educational Wants of the Free Colored People," reproduced in *The American Negro: His History and Literature*, ed. William Loren Katz, 116–17.

41. Ibid., 119.

42. John H. Crowder (hereafter cited as JHC) to Dear Mother, April 27, 1863, John H. Crowder, Pension File #370173, Record Group 15, National Archives, Washington, DC (hereafter cited as NA). Joseph T. Glatthaar, "The Civil War through the Eyes of a Sixteen-Year-Old Black Officer: The Letters of Lieutenant John H. Crowder of the 1st Louisiana Native Guards," 205, 213.

43. JHC to Dear Mother, April 27, 1863, Crowder Pension File, NA.

44. M. E. Bingaman to Mrs. Johnson, April 21, 1860, William T. Johnson and Family Memorial Papers (hereafter cited as Johnson Papers), Louisiana and Lower Mississippi Valley Collection, Louisiana State University (hereafter cited as LSU). Thanks to Lois Virginia Meacham Gould for providing this citation. See Virginia Meacham Gould, ed., *Chained to the Rock of Adversity: To Be Free, Black, and Female in the Old South*, 12.

45. Lavina McCary to Ann Johnson, October 26, 1852, Johnson Papers, LSU; Gould, *Chained to the Rock of Adversity*, 12. The spelling of *Brustie* varies.

46. J[ames] M. Johnson to Henry, May 21, 1860, in Michael P. Johnson and James L. Roark, eds., *No Chariot Let Down: Charleston's Free People of Color on the Eve of the Civil War*, 72, 76; Michael P. Johnson and James L. Roark, *Black Masters: A Free Family of Color in the Old South*, 202.

47. J. M. Johnson to Henry, May 21, 1860, in Johnson and Roark, *No Chariot Let Down*, 72. Emphasis in original.

48. Carter G. Woodson, ed., *The Mind of the Negro as Reflected in Letters Written During the Crisis, 1800–1860*, 541–42.

49. J. M. Johnson to Henry, May 30, 1860, in Johnson and Roark, *No Chariot Let Down*, 80.

50. Frances Ellen Watkins [Harper], *Poems on Miscellaneous Subjects*, 20–21. See Frances Ellen Watkins Harper, "The Two Offers."

51. See Mary Anne Dickerson Jones Album, LCP; Lapsansky, "Afro-Americana: Meet the Dickersons," 17.

52. Rebecca Jackson, *Gifts of Power: The Writing of Rebecca Jackson, Black Visionary, Shaker Eldress*, 11, 86.

53. Ibid., 86.

54. Philip S. Foner, ed., *Frederick Douglass on Women's Rights*, 55, 59, 69; "Irish Ladies' Anti-Slavery Society," 69; Sealander, "Antebellum Black Press Images of Women," 166–67.

55. "Miscellaneous," *The Liberator*, June 9, 1837.

56. Sarah Mapps Douglass to Mary Anne Dickerson, November 14, 1846, Album, LCP (emphasis added).

57. Young, *Antebellum Black Activists*, 145; Sterling, *We Are Your Sisters*, 132.

58. Zilpha Elaw, "Memoirs of the Life, Religious Experience, Ministerial Travels and Labours of Mrs. Zilpha Elaw, An American Female of Colour: Together with Some Account of the Great Religious Revivals in America [Written by Herself]," 61.

59. "Miscellaneous," *The Liberator*, June 9, 1837.

60. G. Brustie to Kind Mda [Ann Johnson], February 14, 1858, LSU. It is not clear when Mrs. Brustie returned to New Orleans, but letters written June 19, 1858, and June 26, 1858, to Ann Johnson indicated that "all" of her family was well (V. Brustie to Dear friend, June 26, 1858, LSU). See also Gould, *Chained to the Rock of Adversity*, 28–29; "Miscellaneous," *The Liberator*, June 9, 1837; Laura F. Edwards, "Law, Domestic Violence, and the Limits of Patriarchal Authority in the Antebellum South," 733–70.

61. Brustie to Kind Mda, February 14, 1858, LSU; Gould, *Chained to the Rock of Adversity*, 28–29.

62. [John K. Furman, ed.,] "A Faithful Report of the Trial of Doctor William Little, on an indictment for an assault and battery, committed on the body of his lawful wife, Mrs. Jane Little, A Black Lady," in Paul Finkelman, ed., *Free Blacks, Slaves and Slaveowners in Civil and Criminal Courts: The Pamphlet Literature*, series 6, 1:103–13. For discussions of family discord among enslaved and emancipated women, see Brenda Stevenson, "Distress and Discord in Virginia Slave Families, 1830–1860," 103–24; Sterling, *We Are Your Sisters*, 338–41.

63. [Furman,] "A Faithful Report," 115.

64. Women in colonial Louisiana under Spanish rule received land grants and held property in their own names. See Nancy Isenberg, *Sex and Citizenship in Antebellum America*, 172–86, for a discussion of women's property rights elsewhere in the United States.

65. See Nancy Lewis Ruffin (hereafter cited as NLR) to George W. Ruffin (hereafter cited as GWR), November 12, 1858, undated letter, Heslip-Ruffin Collection, Amistad Research Center (hereafter cited as ARC); Sterling, *We Are Your Sisters*, 219.

66. NLR to GWR, November 18, 1858, December 16, 1859, ARC; Sterling, *We Are Your Sisters*, 219.

67. NLR to GWR, November 18, 1858; NLR to GWR, February 18, 1859, December 16, 1859, ARC (emphases added); Sterling, *We Are Your Sisters*, 219–20.

68. NLR to GWR, February 18, 1859, ARC.

69. NLR to GWR, November 18, 1859, December 16, 1859, ARC; Sterling, *We Are Your Sisters*, 219–20.

70. "Miscellaneous," *The Liberator*, June 9, 1837. See Donna Elizabeth Sedevie, "The Prospect of Happiness: Women, Divorce and Property," 189–206.

71. Victoria Bynum, *Unruly Women: The Politics of Social and Sexual Control in the Old South*, 58–68.

72. Suzanne Lebsock, *Free Women of Petersburg: Status and Culture in a Southern Town, 1784–1860*, 100, 103, 104. See also Beverly Greene Bond, "'The Extent of the Law': Free Women of Color in Antebellum Memphis, Tennessee," 19;

Loren Schweninger, "Property Owing Free African-American Women in the South, 1800–1870," 263.

73. Michael P. Johnson and James L. Roark, "Strategies of Survival: Free Negro Families and the Problem of Slavery," 91–93.

74. For discussions of infant mortality and morbidity among enslaved children, see Wilma King, *Stolen Childhood: Slave Youth in Nineteenth-Century America*, 9–12; Robert A. Margo and Richard H. Steckel, "The Heights of American Slaves: New Evidence on Slave Nutrition and Health," *Social Science History* (hereafter cited as *SSH*), 516–38; Richard H. Steckel, "A Peculiar Population: The Nutrition, Health, and Mortality of American Slaves from Childhood to Maturity," 721–41; Richard H. Steckel, "A Dreadful Childhood: The Excess Mortality of American Slaves," *SSH*, 427–65.

75. Martina Dickerson Jones Album, LCP; Cheryll Ann Cody, "Naming, Kinship, and Estate Dispersal: Notes on Slave Family Life on a South Carolina Plantation, 1786 to 1833," 192–211.

76. "To my dear Willie," Mary Ann Dickerson Jones Album, LCP.

77. Tryphena Blanche Holder Fox, Civil War Diary Transcript, April 2, 1863, Tryphena Blanche Holder Fox Papers, Mississippi Department of Archives and History, Jackson, Mississippi (hereafter cited as MDAH); Nancy Schrom Dye and Daniel Blake Smith, "Mother Love and Infant Death, 1750–1920," 330.

78. Wilma King, " 'Suffer with them till death': Slave Women and Their Children in Nineteenth-Century America"; Frederick Douglass, *My Bondage and My Freedom*, 56; Lucy A. Delaney, "From The Darkness Cometh the Light or Struggles for Freedom," 15–16; William Wells Brown, "Narrative of William Wells Brown, a Fugitive Slave," 187–88.

79. James Thomas Flexner, *The Young Hamilton: A Biography*, 16–27.

3. The Pursuit of Happiness: Work and Well-Being

1. Marilyn Richardson, ed., *Maria W. Stewart, America's First Black Woman Political Writer: Essays and Speeches*, 38–39. See Gayle T. Tate, "Political Consciousness and Resistance among Black Antebellum Women," 67–89; Loren Schweninger, "Property Owning Free African-American Women in the South, 1800–1870," 253–79.

2. Cyprian Clamorgan, *The Colored Aristocracy of St. Louis*, 14.

3. Ibid., 16.

4. Leon F. Litwack, *North of Slavery: The Negro in the Free States, 1790–1860*, 162–63; Leonard P. Curry, *The Free Black in Urban America, 1800–1850: The Shadow of the Dream*, 20–21; John Harold Sprinkle Jr., " 'Let Their Situation at Least Engage Our Sympathy, if We can Afford Them No Relief': Patterns of Occupation and Residence among Free Blacks in Early Nineteenth-Century Wilmington, Delaware," Delaware Public Archives, Hall of Records, Dover, Delaware, 5; Noel Ignatiev, *How the Irish Became White*, 100; Gayle T. Tate, *Unknown Tongues: Black Women's Political Activism in the Antebellum Era, 1830–1860*, 66. For discussions regarding free black women heads of households, see Suzanne Lebsock, *Free Women of Petersburg: Status and Culture in a Southern Town, 1784–1860*, 100, 103, 104; Michael P. Johnson and James L. Roark, "Strategies of Survival: Free

Negro Families and the Problem of Slavery," 91–93; George Blackburn and Sherman L. Ricards. "The Mother-Headed Family among Free Negroes in Charleston, South Carolina, 1850–1860," 11–25.

5. "Lucy Stone and Senator Douglas," *Douglass' Monthly* (October 1859): 147; Judith Sealander, "Antebellum Black Press Images of Women," 163.

6. Philip S. Foner, ed., *Frederick Douglass on Women's Rights*, 19; "Lucy Stone and Senator Douglas," 147; Sealander, "Antebellum Black Press Images of Women," 163.

7. See chapter 1 regarding the avenues to freedom. See also Tate, *Unknown Tongues*, 66; Judith K. Schafer, "'Open and Notorious Concubinage': The Emancipation of Slave Mistresses by Will and the Supreme Court in Antebellum Louisiana," 165–82; Loren Schweninger, "Prosperous Blacks in the South, 1790–1880," 34–35; Susan M. Socolow, "Economic Roles of the Free Women of Color of Cap Francais," 292; Kimberly S. Hanger, "'The Fortunes of Women in America': Spanish New Orleans's Free Women of African Descent and Their Relations with Slave Women," 153.

8. Juliet E. K. Walker, *The History of Black Business in America: Capitalism, Race, Entrepreneurship*, 129.

9. Joan H. Geismar, *The Archaeology of Social Disintegration in Skunk Hollow: A Nineteenth-Century Rural Black Community*, 48.

10. *Register of Trades of the Colored People in the City of Philadelphia and Districts*, 3–8; Walker, *History of Black Businesses*, 130; Sharon Harley, "Northern Black Female Workers: Jacksonian Era," 10; Tate, "Political Consciousness and Resistance," 68; Thomas Dublin, *Transforming Women's Work: New England Lives in the Industrial Revolution*, 159–60; George Blackburn and Sherman L. Ricards, "The Mother-Headed Family among Free Negroes in Charleston, South Carolina, 1850–1860," 23; Marion B. Lucas, *A History of Blacks in Kentucky*, 1:111–12. See T. Stephen Whitman, *The Price of Freedom: Slavery and Manumission in Baltimore and Early National Maryland*, 141; Tate, "Political Consciousness and Resistance," 72–73. For references to free blacks scattered throughout petitions submitted by whites to southern legislatures, see Loren Schweninger, ed., *A Guide to the Microfilm Edition of Race, Slavery, and Free Blacks: Series I, Petitions to Southern Legislatures, 1777–1867*.

11. Lebsock, *The Free Women of Petersburg*, 99; List of Free Negroes Licensed, Dexter Tiffany Papers, Missouri Historical Society (hereafter cited as MHS), St. Louis, Missouri.

12. See Whittington B. Johnson, "Free African-American Women in Savannah, 1800–1860: Affluence and Autonomy Amid Adversity," 261–63, 265.

13. Addie Brown (hereafter cited as AB) to My Dear Sister ([Rebecca Primus] hereafter cited as RP), January 16, 1866, Primus Papers, CHS; Karen V. Hansen, "'No *Kisses* is Like Youres': An Erotic Friendship Between Two African-American Women During the Mid-Nineteenth Century," 7–8. For discussion of women in Baltimore performing "men's work," see Barbara Elizabeth Wallace, "'Fair Daughter of Africa': African American Women in Baltimore, 1790–1860," 124–25.

14. Lynn Marie Hudson, "When Mammy Became a Millionaire: Mary Ellen Pleasant, an African American Entrepreneur," 46–47; John W. Blassingame, ed., *Slave Testimony: Two Centuries of Letters, Speeches, Interviews, and Autobiographies*,

454–55; Lois Virginia Meacham Gould, "In Full Enjoyment of Their Liberty: The Free Women of Color of the Gulf Ports of New Orleans, Mobile, and Pensacola, 1769–1860," 54; L. Virginia Gould, "Urban Slavery—Urban Freedom: The Manumission of Jacqueline Lemelle," 303–4; Robert Olwell, "'Loose, Idle and Disorderly': Slave Women in the Eighteenth-Century Charleston Marketplace," 99–102; Gary B. Nash, *Forging Freedom: The Formation of Philadelphia's Black Community, 1720–1840,* 74–75; Deborah L. Newman, "Black Women in the Era of the American Revolution in Pennsylvania," 211–24; Shane White, "'We Dwell in Safety and Pursue Our Honest Callings': Free Blacks in New York City, 1783–1810," 458. See Socolow, "Economic Roles of the Free Women of Color of Cap Francais," 282; Loren Schweninger, "Slave Independence and Enterprise in South Carolina, 1780–1865," 101; Loren Schweninger, "The Underside of Slavery: The Internal Economy, Self-Hire, and Quasi-Freedom in Virginia, 1780–1865," 5–6; Walker, *The History of Black Business,* 131–33; Alex Lichtenstein, "'That Disposition to Theft, With Which They Have Been Branded': Moral Economy, Slave Management, and the Law," 413–40.

15. See *Register of Trades of the Colored People in the City of Philadelphia and the Districts;* Registry of Free Persons of Color, 1832–1864, Baldwin County, Probate Court, Milledgeville, Georgia; Susan Strasser, *Never Done: A History of American Housework,* 104–24; Shane White, *Somewhat More Independent: The End of Slavery in New York City, 1770–1810,* 165.

16. Dorothy Sterling, ed., *We Are Your Sisters: Black Women in the Nineteenth Century,* 131; David Roediger, *The Wages of Whiteness: Race and the Making of the American Working Class,* 144–46; Christine Stansell, *City of Women: Sex and Class in New York, 1789–1860,* 157. See William Still, *The Underground Rail Road. A record of facts, authentic narratives, letters, & c. . . . ,* 755–56; Frances Smith Foster, ed., *A Brighter Coming Day: A Frances Ellen Watkins Harper Reader,* 8; Amanda Smith, *An Autobiography: The Story of the Lord's Dealings with Mrs. Amanda Smith . . . ,* 27; Nancy Prince, *A Black Woman's Odyssey Through Russia and Jamaica: The Narrative of Nancy Prince,* 5–7; Richardson, *Maria W. Stewart,* xv; Zilpha Elaw, "Memoirs of the Life, Religious Experience, Ministerial Travels, and Labours of Mrs. Elaw," 53, 79; Jerena Lee, "The Life and Religious Experience of Jarena Lee," 27.

17. Strasser, *Never Done,* 164–65; Roediger, *The Wages of Whiteness,* 145; Stansell, *City of Women,* 156–57.

18. Lloyd A. Hunter, "Slavery in St. Louis, 1804–1860," 241–42; Gould, "In Full Enjoyment of Their Liberty," 58; Luther Porter Jackson, *Free Negro Labor and Property Holding in Virginia, 1830–1860,* 91–92; Lebsock, *The Free Women of Petersburg,* 99; Michael P. Johnson and James L. Roark, *Black Masters: A Free Family of Color in the Old South,* 173. See Robert Olwell, "'Loose, Idle and Disorderly': Slave Women in the Eighteenth-Century Charleston Marketplace," 97–110.

19. Stansell, *City of Women,* 158.

20. Harriet Jacobs, *Incidents in the Life of a Slave Girl: Written by Herself,* 168, 174, 176, 181, 183; Eliza Potter, *A Hairdresser's Experience in the High Life,* 21–26.

21. Tate, *Unknown Tongues,* 10–11, 31, 37.

22. AB to RP, October 16, 1866, Primus Papers, CHS.

23. Strasser, *Never Done,* 131–32.

24. Hudson, "When Mammy Became a Millionaire," 47; Lynn M. Hudson,

The Making of "Mammy Pleasant": A Black Entrepreneur in Nineteenth-Century San Francisco, 33; Prince, *A Black Woman's Odyssey,* 6–7; Stansell, *City of Women,* 159.

25. AB to RP, June 3, 1866, Primus Papers, CHS; Farah Jasmine Griffin, ed., *Beloved Sisters and Loving Friends: Letters from Rebecca Primus of Royal Oak, Maryland, and Addie Brown of Hartford, Connecticut, 1854–1868,* 27–28.

26. Wallace, "'Fair Daughter of Africa,'" 116; Seventh Census of the U.S., 1850, Population Schedule, Leon County, Florida, NA; Seventh Census of the U.S., 1850, Population Schedule, Duval County, Florida, NA; Eighth Census of the U.S., 1860 Population Schedule, Leon County, Florida, NA; Eighth Census of the U.S., 1860 Population Schedule, Duval County, Florida, NA; List of Free Negroes Licensed by the County Court of St. Louis County, 1841–1859, Tiffany Papers, MHS; Society of Friends, *A Statistical Inquiry,* 18. For a more expansive list of occupations for black Philadelphians in 1838, see Walker, *Black Business History,* 130, especially table 5.1.

27. For a discussion of laundering clothes, see Strasser, *Never Done,* 104–24.

28. T. O. Madden with Ann L. Miller, *We Were Always Free: The Maddens of Culpeper County, Virginia, A 200-Year Family History,* 30–31, 176–77. See Tera W. Hunter, "Domination and Resistance: The Politics of Wage Household Labor in New South Atlanta," 345; Loren Schweninger, "A Slave Family in the Antebellum South."

29. Tryphena Blanche Holder Fox (hereafter cited as TBHR) to Anna Rose Holder (hereafter cited as ARH), March 29, 1861, July 15, 1865, Fox Papers, MDAH.

30. Sharon G. Dean attributes the expression "a humble pose" to Frederick Douglass. See Potter, *A Hairdresser's Experience,* xlvi; Leon Litwack, *North of Slavery: The Negro in the Free States, 1790–1860,* 180; Madden, *We Were Always Free,* 36. See also Bertram Wyatt-Brown, "The Mask of Obedience: Male Slave Psychology in the Old South," 1228–52; Mary Boykin Chesnut, *A Diary from Dixie,* 38.

31. Walker, *Black Business,* 129. See Patricia K. Hunt, "The Struggle to Achieve Individual Expression through Clothing and Adornment: African American Women Under and After Slavery," 231–32.

32. Litwack, *North of Slavery,* 184–85; Patricia K. Hunt, "Clothing as an Expression of History: The Dress of African-American Women in Georgia, 1880–1915," 460. For a general discussion of clothes about women labeled as a "wretched slave" to fashions, see Potter, *A Hairdresser's Experience,* 62–63. See also Nancy Reynolds Davidson, "E. W. Clay: American Political Caricaturist of the Jacksonian Era," 214–15; Nash, *Forging Freedom,* 255–58.

33. Elizabeth Keckley, *Behind the Scenes; or Thirty Years a Slave, and Four Years in the White House,* 64–65, 76, 77–78, 88–90; Jennifer Fleischner, *Mrs. Lincoln and Mrs. Keckly: The Remarkable Story of the Friendship Between a First Lady and a Former Slave,* 133, 145–48, 183–84, 194; Juliet E. K. Walker, "Racism, Slavery, and Free Enterprise: Black Entrepreneurship in the United States before the Civil War," 369; Prince, *A Black Woman's Odyssey,* 32.

34. Keckley, *Behind the Scenes,* 78–79, 82; Fleischner, *Mrs. Lincoln and Mrs. Keckly,* 200.

35. Keckley, *Behind the Scenes,* 80.

36. Potter, *A Hairdresser's Experience,* 73–74, 287.

37. AB to RP, April 29, 1866, Primus Papers, CHS.

38. Potter, *A Hairdresser's Experience*, 26, 27, 44. Note that the *Register of Trades*, 6–7, includes hairdressers, but the greater number of them are male rather than female. See Wilma King, "Eliza Johnson Potter: Traveler, Entrepreneur, and Social Critic," 91–104; Cheryl Fish, "Voices of Restless (Dis)continuity: The Significance of Travel for Free Black Women in the Antebellum Americas," 475–95.

39. Potter, *A Hairdresser's Experience*, xlviii-xlix, li, 38, 173.

40. Sterling, *We Are Your Sisters*, 96; Walker, *The History of Black Business in America*, 141–43; Schweninger, "Property Owning Free African-American Women," 256.

41. Martha Ward, *Voodoo Queen: The Spirited Lives of Marie Laveau*, 73; Potter, *A Hairdresser's Experience*, 80, 162, 166.

42. Ward, *Voodoo Queen*, 4, 7–8, 73, 75, 80. See Potter, *A Hairdresser's Experience*, 163–66.

43. Walker, *The History of Black Business in America*, 129; [Phillip S. Lapsansky], "Afro-Americana: Meet the Dickersons," 17; Constance McLaughlin Green, *The Secret City: A History of Race Relations in the Nation's Capital*, 16; Schweninger, "Property Owning Free African American Women," 256–57; Koger, *Black Slaveowners*, 91; Jacobs, *Incidents in the Life of a Slave Girl*, 12. See Joshua D. Rothman, "'Notorious in the Neighborhood': An Interracial Family in Early National and Antebellum Virginia," 73–114.

44. Walker, *The History of Black Business*, 136; Koger, *Black Slaveowners*, 91, 150–51.

45. Hudson, "When Mammy Became a Millionaire," 46–47.

46. Walker, *The History of Black Business*, 143; Lois Brown, "Memorial Narratives of African American Women in Antebellum New England," 50; James Oliver Horton and Lois E. Horton, *Black Bostonians: Family Life and Community Struggle in the Antebellum North*, 16; James Oliver Horton, *Free People of Color: Inside the African American Community*, 31–32; White, *Somewhat More Independent*, 175; Curry, *The Free Black in Urban America*, 49; Tate, "Political Consciousness and Resistance," 74. For a discussion of boarders, see David Brody, *Steelworkers in America: The Nonunion Era*, 96–111; Sprinkle, "'Let Their Situation at Least Engage Our Sympathy,'" 11–18.

47. *Nashville City and Business Directory*, 61, 233, Tennessee Department of State Library and Archives, Nashville, Tennessee. Jonathan M. Atkins, "Party Politics and the Debate over the Tennessee Free Negro Bill, 1859–1860," 250; Schweninger, "Property Owning Free African-American Women," 257.

48. See Lewis Cecil Gray, *History of Agriculture in the Southern United States to 1860* for details regarding cash crops.

49. See Nell Irvin Painter, *Sojourner Truth: A Life, a Symbol*, 164–78, for a discussion regarding the construction of the "Ar'n't I a Woman?" speech. Although plowing is considered a man's job, references to women plowing exist in the WPA narratives.

50. John B. Cade, "Out of the Mouths of Ex-Slaves," 320; Johnson and Roark, *Black Masters*, 14–15, 23; Koger, *Black Slaveowners*, 130–37. For a discussion regarding the formation of a "network" among enslaved women at work, see Deborah Gray White, *Ar'n't I a Woman? Female Slaves in the Plantation South*, 119–20, 121, 128, 129.

51. Koger, *Black Slaveowners*, 120–22, 124.

52. Ibid., 28, 122. For tables showing the annual rice yields in All Saints Parish and the number of pounds per slave for a comparison with the Harris slaves, see Charles Joyner, *Down by the Riverside: A South Carolina Slave Community*, 19–20.

53. Walker, "Racism, Slavery, and Free Enterprise," 350, 354–55; Eighth Census of the U.S., 1860 Population, Plaquemines Parish, Louisiana, NA. See Kimberly S. Hanger, "Patronage, Property, and Persistence: The Emergence of a Free Elite in Spanish New Orleans," 44–64.

54. Virginia Meacham Gould, ed., *Chained to the Rock of Adversity: To Be Free, Black, and Female in the Old South*, 28; TBHF to ARH, December 27, 1857, MDAH.

55. Mills, *The Forgotten People*, 77–80; Mills, "Coincoin," 220–21; Hanger, "'The Fortunes of Women,'" 166–68; Ross M. Robertson, *History of the American Economy*, 117–21. See successions of Marie Rose and Suzanne Metoyer, Parish Clerk, Natchitoches, Louisiana (hereafter cited as PCNLA).

56. Betsy Sompayrac, "Last Will and Testament"; "Succession of Betsy Sompayrac, Petition," PCNLA.

57. Sompayrac, "Last Will and Testament," PCNLA; Sworn Statement, mss. 182, Folder #485, Cane River Collection (hereafter cited as CRC), Historic New Orleans (hereafter cited as HNO).

58. Sompayrac, "Last Will and Testament," PCNLA.

59. Sworn Statement, July 1837, Folder #485, CRC, HNO; Daniel L. Schafer, *Anna Madgigine Jai Kingsley: African Princess, Florida Slave, Plantation Owner*, 129–31; Berlin, *Slaves Without Masters*, 272, 277. See Adrienne D. Davis, "The Private Law of Race and Sex: An Antebellum Perspective," 240. Thanks to Daniel L. Schafer for providing a copy of Anna Kingsley's will.

60. De Bow, *Statistical View*, 63; Carter G. Woodson, *Free Negro Owners of Slaves in the United States in 1830: Together with Absentee Ownership of Slaves in the United States in 1830*; Koger, *Black Slaveowners*, 20–21. See David L. Lightner and Alexander M. Ragan, "Were African American Slaveholders Benevolent or Exploitative? A Quantitative Approach," 545, 549.

61. Tate, "Political Consciousness and Resistance," 67–69.

62. Glenda Riley, *Inventing the American Woman: An Inclusive History*, 1:66–67; Harley, "Northern Black Female Workers," 5–16, 119–21; Noel Ignatiev, *How the Irish Became White*, 97–98; Sterling, *We Are Your Sisters*, 134–35.

63. Helen Tunnicliff Catterall, ed., *Judicial Cases Concerning American Slavery and the Negro*, 1:233; Johnson, "Free African-American Women," 265; William C. Dawson, *Compilation of the Laws of the State of Georgia*, 412; Adele Logan Alexander, *Ambiguous Lives: Free Women of Color in Rural Georgia, 1789–1879*, 37; Dorothy Provine, "The Economic Position of the Free Blacks in the District of Columbia, 1800–1860," 65–66; Letitia Woods Brown, *Free Negroes in the District of Columbia, 1790–1846*, 135–36; Dan Durett, "Free Blacks in Selected Georgia Cities, 1820–1860," 16, 37–38; Frances LaJune Johnson Powell, "A Study of the Structure of the Freed Black Family in Washington, DC, 1850–1880," 52; Curry, *The Free Black in Urban America*, 16–20.

64. See Petitions to the General Assembly, 1856, North Carolina, reel 7, in Schweninger, *Microfilm Petitions*.

65. Janet Duitsman Cornelius, *When I Can Read My Title Clear: Literacy, Slavery, and Religion in the Antebellum South*, 33; June Purcell Guild, *Black Laws of*

Virginia: A Summary of the Legislative Acts of Virginia Concerning Negroes from Earliest Times to the Present, 175–76; Dawson, *Compilation of the Laws of the State of Georgia*, 413; R. I. Brigham, "Negro Education in Ante Bellum Missouri," 412–13; Tate, "Political Consciousness and Resistance," 75. See Lewis C. Lockwood, ed., *Two Black Teachers During the Civil War: Mary S. Peake, the Colored Teacher at Fortress Monroe, and Charlotte Forten, Life on the Sea Islands;* Albert S. Broussard, *African-American Odyssey: The Stewarts, 1853–1963*, 16, 18.

66. Prince, *A Black Woman's Odyssey*, xvi–xvii, xxvii.

67. Harriet E. Wilson, *Our Nig; or, Sketches from the Life of a Free Black in a Two-Story White House, North. Showing that Slavery's Shadows Fall Even There*, xi, xxv; Beth Maclay Doriani, "Black Womanhood in Nineteenth-Century America: Subversion and Self-Construction in Two Women's Autobiographies," 199–222; Foster, *Written by Herself*, 87.

68. Wilson, *Our Nig*, xxx; Painter, *Sojourner Truth*, 185–99. See Nell Irvin Painter, "Representing Truth: Sojourner Truth's Knowing and Becoming Known," 461–92; Painter, *Sojourner Truth*, 185–99; Carla L. Peterson, *"Doers of the Word": African-American Women Speakers and Writers in the North (1830–1880)*, 76–77.

69. Potter, *A Hairdresser's Experience*, xlvii.

70. AB to My Dear Sister, January 16, 1866, Primus Papers, CHS.

71. Register of Prostitutes, City Archives, Philadelphia, Pennsylvania (hereafter cited as CAPPA); White, *Somewhat More Independent*, 165. See Jackson, *Free Negro Labor*, 93; Jeffrey S. Adler, "Streetwalkers, Degraded Outcasts, and Good-for-Nothing Huzzies: Women and the Dangerous Class in Antebellum St. Louis," 737–55; Richard Tansey, "Prostitution and Politics in Antebellum New Orleans," 449–79; Carroll Smith-Rosenberg, "Beauty, the Beast, and the Militant Woman: A Case Study in Sex Roles and Social Stress in Jacksonian America," 562–84; Patricia Cline Cohen, "Unregulated Youth: Masculinity and Murder in the 1830s City," 33–52; White, *Somewhat More Independent*, 165.

72. Bynum, *Unruly Women*, 81–82.

73. White, "'We Dwell in Safety,'" 459; White, *Somewhat More Independent*, 165; Stansell, *City of Women*, 171; Walker, *The History of Black Business*, 130.

74. Adler, "Streetwalkers, Degraded Outcasts, and Good-for-Nothing Huzzies," 741–42. See Berlin, *Slaves Without Masters*, 265.

75. Leslie Patrick-Stamp, "Numbers That Are Not New: African Americans in the Country's First Prison, 1790–1835," 95–128; "Female Convict Docket, 1838–1866," CAPPA; House Executive Report, 22nd Cong., 2 Sess., Doc. 49, Ser. 234; House Executive Report, 24th Cong., 1 Sess., Doc. 81, Ser. 288; House Executive Report, 25th Cong., 2 Sess., Doc. 140, Ser. 326, NA; Litwack, *North of Slavery*, 95–96.

76. Ralph Clayton, *Slavery, Slaveholding, and the Free Black Population of Antebellum Baltimore*, 52–53; Berlin, *Slaves Without Masters*, 335; John Hope Franklin and Loren Schweninger, *Runaway Slaves: Rebels on the Plantation*, 195–96; Curry, *The Free Black in Urban America*, 89, 115, 116, 118.

77. Aggy Watts Petition, October 9, 1841 (2E773), and Clarissa Bartlett Petition, December 6, 1837, Natchez Trace Collection, Center for American History, University of Texas, Austin, Texas; Lizzie Jones Petition, January 31, 1859 (1859-55–05), South Carolina Department of Archives and History; Schweninger, *A Guide to the Microfilm Edition of Race, Slavery, and Free Blacks*, 107. Thanks to

Charmaine A. Flemming for citations regarding free black women requesting to indenture or enslave themselves. See Victoria E. Bynum, *Unruly Women: The Politics of Social and Sexual Control in the Old South,* 102–3.

78. Petitions of Lucy Andrews, 11:0069, 11:0752, 11:0765, South Carolina; Petition of Kissiah Trueblood, 7:0601, North Carolina; Petition of Sally Scott, 7:0624, North Carolina; Petition of Eliza Hassell, 7:0598, North Carolina; Petition of W. P. Hill regarding Elizabeth, 11:0684, South Carolina, in Schweninger, *Microfilm Petitions;* Committee on Colored Population Response (ND-2534-01), House of Representatives, December 3, 1859 (ND 2534-01), SCDAH.

79. "Guardians of the Poor Alm House Hospital Register," March 9, 1846, CAPPA. See Curry, *The Free Black in Urban America,* 127.

80. See Alms House Female Register 1803–1887; Alms House Hospital Register; Female Convict Docket, 1838–1866, CAPPA.

81. Petitions, 1857–16–01, SCDAH.

82. Stephanie J. Shaw, "Black Club Women and the Creation of the National Association of Colored Women," 10–25; Tate, *Unknown Tongues,* 68–69. See Shirley J. Yee, *Black Women Abolitionists: A Study in Activism, 1828–1860,* 74–78; Harry Reed, *Platform for Change: The Foundations of the Northern Free Black Community, 1775–1865,* 76–77, 85–91.

83. Sterling, *We Are Your Sisters,* 106, 107; Daughters of Africa Order Book, March 1, 1824, May 1, 1827, Historical Society of Pennsylvania, Philadelphia, Pennsylvania; Yee, *Black Women Abolitionists,* 80.

84. Claude F. Jacobs, "Benevolent Societies of New Orleans Blacks During the Late Nineteenth and Early Twentieth Centuries," 22; Diane Batts Morrow, *Persons of Color and Religious at the Same Time: The Oblate Sisters of Providence, 1828–1860,* 21–22.

85. Friendly Moralist Society Minutes, January 17, 1842, Special Collections, College of Charleston, South Carolina (hereafter cited as SPCC); Michael P. Johnson and James L. Roark, "'A Middle Ground': Free Mulattoes and the Friendly Moralist Society in Antebellum Charleston," 248; Robert L. Harris Jr., "Charleston's Free Afro-American Elite: The Brown Fellowship Society and the Humane Brotherhood," 289–310.

86. Friendly Moralist Society Minutes, September 18, 1846, June 14, 1847, SPCC. For added insight about the Friendly Moralist Society's financial constraints, see Johnson and Roark, "'A Middle Ground,'" 253–60.

87. Friendly Moralist Society Minutes, June 21, 1847, September 13, 1849, SPCC.

88. Richardson, *Maria W. Stewart,* 38.

4. "Knowledge is power": Educational and Cultural Achievements

1. Marilyn Richardson, ed., *Maria W. Stewart, America's First Black Woman Political Writer: Essays and Speeches,* 30, 46, 47. For an unusual account of a woman gaining literacy and its relationship to her spiritual freedom, see Rebecca Jackson, *Gifts of Power: The Writings of Rebecca Jackson, Black Visionary, Shaker Eldress,* ed. Jean McMahon Humez.

2. See Janet Duitsman Cornelius, *When I Can Read My Title Clear: Literacy, Slavery, and Religion in the Antebellum South;* Janet Cornelius, "We Slipped and

Learned to Read: Slave Accounts of the Literacy Process, 1830–1865," 171–85; Wilma King, *Stolen Childhood: Youth in Bondage in Nineteenth-Century America*, 67–80; Ira Berlin, *Slaves Without Masters: The Free Negro in the Antebellum South*, 74–78; Gayle T. Tate, *Unknown Tongues: Black Women's Political Activism in the Antebellum Era, 1830–1860*, 152–54, 199–200; Gayle T. Tate, "Political Consciousness and Resistance among Black Antebellum Women," 76, 80–81; Darlene Clark Hine and Kathleen Thompson, *A Shining Thread of Hope: The History of Black Women in America*, 123.

For references to the use of education as a social responsibility or way to uplift the race, see Fanny Jackson-Coppin, *Reminiscences of School Life, and Hints on Teaching*, 17; Julie Winch, "'You Have Talents—Only Cultivate Them': Philadelphia's Black Female Literary Societies and the Abolitionist Crusade," 103; Dorothy Sterling, ed., *We Are Your Sisters: Black Women in the Nineteenth Century*, 267, 277; Brenda Stevenson, ed., *The Journals of Charlotte Forten Grimké*, 1:70–71, 140; Brenda Stevenson, "Charlotte Forten," 289; Linda Perkins, "Black Women and Racial 'Uplift' Prior to Emancipation," 324, 325–27; Linda M. Perkins, "The Impact of the 'Cult of True Womanhood' on the Education of Black Women," 18; Linda M. Perkins, "Heed Life's Demands: The Educational Philosophy of Fanny Jackson Coppin," 181–90; Shirley J. Yee, *Black Women Abolitionists: A Study in Activism, 1828–1860*, 61–66, 73–74.

3. Richardson, *Maria W. Stewart*, 29; Jane A. Crouch, "Autobiography," unpublished, undated, Early Summer School Files, Hampton University Archives (hereafter cited as HUA), 1–3.

4. Thomas Jefferson, *Notes on the State of Virginia*, ed. William Peden, 139–40; William J. Cooper Jr. and Thomas E. Terrill, *The American South: A History*, 251.

5. Nell Irvin Painter, *Sojourner Truth: A Life, A Symbol*, 125; C. Peter Ripley, ed., *Witness for Freedom: African American Voices on Race, Slavery, and Emancipation*, 102. See Albert Deutsch, "The First U.S. Census of the Insane (1840) and Its Use as Pro-Slavery Propaganda," 469–77. Thanks to Dashiel Guyen for bringing this citation to my attention.

6. Richardson, *Maria W. Stewart*, 36, 41.

7. Ibid., 30, 35. For arguments related to uplifting the race by free blacks, especially women, see Martin R. Delany, *The Condition, Elevation, Emigration, and Destiny of the Colored People of the United States*, 199, 205.

8. Linda K. Kerber, *Women of the Republic: Intellect and Ideology in Revolutionary America*, 283, 285; Nancy Cott, *The Bonds of Womanhood: "Woman's Sphere" in New England, 1780–1835*, 104–106; Gerda Lerner, *The Creation of Feminist Consciousness*, 213–16, 218; Glenda Riley, *Inventing the American Woman: A Perspective on Women's History*, 50; Michelle Nichole Garfield, "'The Pen is ours to Wield': Black Literary Society Women in 1830s Philadelphia," 127–28.

9. Richardson, *Maria W. Stewart*, 37. See Linda M. Perkins, "The Impact of the 'Cult of True Womanhood' on the Education of Black Women," 17–28.

10. Theresa A. Rector, "Black Nuns as Educators," 237–38, 240–41; Sister M. Reginald Gerdes, "To Educate and Evangelize: Black Catholic Schools of the Oblate Sisters of Providence, 1828–1880," 187; Thaddeus J. Posey, "Praying in the Shadows: The Oblate Sisters of Providence, a Look at Nineteenth-Century Black Catholic Spirituality," 16, 18. See Diane Batts Morrow, *Persons of Color and Religious at the Same Time: The Oblate Sisters of Providence, 1828–1860*; Diane Batts

Morrow, "'Our Convent': The Oblate Sisters of Providence and Baltimore's Antebellum Black Community," 27–47.

11. Posey, "Praying in the Shadows," 17–19; Rector, "Black Nuns as Educators," 240; Morrow, "Our Convent," 39, 41–42; Perkins, "Black Women and Racial 'Uplift,'" 327–28; Morrow, *Persons of Color and Religious*, 84–85.

12. Gerdes, "To Educate and Evangelize," 189; Morrow, "Our Convent," 46.

13. *David Walker's Appeal, in Four Articles: Together with a Preamble, to the Coloured Citizens, But in Particular, and Very Expressly, to those of The United States of America*, ed. Charles M. Wiltse, x, 25–26.

14. June Purcell Guild, ed., *Black Laws of Virginia: A Summary of the Legislative Acts of Virginia Concerning Negroes from Earliest Times to the Present*, 175–76; Cornelius, *When I Can Read My Title Clear*, 33. Missouri passed a law prohibiting the instruction of blacks in 1847 (R. I. Brigham, "Negro Education in Ante Bellum Missouri," 412–13; John Hope Franklin, *The Free Negro in North Carolina, 1790–1860*, 169).

15. Berlin, *Slaves Without Masters*, 304, 306; Sister Audrey Marie Detiege, *Henriette DeLille, Free Woman of Color*, 6; Peter W. Clark, "'The Greatest Gift of All': A Pictorial Biography...," Sisters of the Holy Family Archives, New Orleans, Louisiana; Emily Clark and Virginia Meacham Gould, "The Feminine Face of Afro-Catholicism in New Orleans, 1727–1852," 409–48.

16. Mary Niall Mitchell, "'A Good and Delicious Country': Free Children of Color and How They Learned to Imagine the Atlantic World in Nineteenth-Century Louisiana," 123–44; Molly Mitchell, "'After the War I Am Going to Put Myself a Sailor': Geography, Writing, and Race in Letters of Free Children in Civil War New Orleans," 26–37.

17. See Miss Susan Paul, *Memoir of James Jackson: The Attentive and Obedient Scholar, Who Died in Boston, October 31, 1833, Aged Six Years and Eleven Months.*

18. Brown, *Memoir of James Jackson*, 52–53, 88–89.

19. Wilma King Hunter, "Coming of Age: Hollis B. Frissell and the Emergence of Hampton Institute, 1893–1917," 5; Dan Durett, "Free Blacks in Selected Georgia Cities, 1820–1860," 30; Lewis C. Lockwood to the American Missionary Association (hereafter cited as AMA), March 9, 1862, AMA Microfilm; Mary Peake to AMA, undated (HI#4364), AMA Microfilm; Guild, *Black Laws of Virginia*, 175–176; Robert F. Engs, *Freedom's First Generation: Black Hampton, Virginia, 1861–1890*, 12–13; Lewis C. Lockwood, ed., *Two Black Teachers During the Civil War: Mary S. Peake, the Colored Teacher at Fortress Monroe, and Charlotte Forten, Life on the Sea Islands*, 31–35.

20. Crouch, "Autobiography," 1–3, 5, HUA; Luther Porter Jackson, *Free Negro Labor and Property Holding in Virginia, 1830–1860*, 19–20. Crouch mentions three schools in Alexandria operated by blacks in the 1840s, and her contemporary, the slave-born Ida R. Morris, mentions schools run by blacks in the city during the Civil War in Ida R. Morris, "Autobiography" (undated, unpublished), Early Summer School Files, HUA.

21. Crouch, "Autobiography," 8, HUA.

22. John B. Reid, "'A Career to Build, a People to Serve, a Purpose to Accomplish': Race, Class, Gender, and Detroit's First Black Women Teachers, 1865–1916," 303–04, 307, 310; Ruffin-Helsip Papers, Amistad Research Center, Tulane University, New Orleans, Louisiana (hereafter cited as ARC).

23. Sterling, *We Are Your Sisters*, 180; Leon F. Litwack, *North of Slavery: The Negro in the Free States, 1790–1860*, 114–16.

24. Tate, *Unknown Tongues*, 153; Susan D. Greenbaum, "A Comparison of African American and Euro-American Mutual Aid Societies in 19th Century America," 100–101; Robert E. Cray Jr., "White Welfare and Black Strategies: The Dynamics of Race and Poor Relief in Early New York, 1700–1825," 273–89; R. J. Young, *Antebellum Black Activists: Race, Gender, and Self*, 134; Morrow, "Our Convent," 34–35, 38.

25. Theodore Hershberg, "Free-Born and Slave-Born Blacks in Antebellum Philadelphia," 408.

26. Sterling, *We Are Your Sisters*, 138; Gloria Oden, "The Black Putnams of Charlotte Forten's Journal," 244; Stevenson, *The Journals*, 17; Dorothy Burnett Porter, "The Remonds of Salem, Massachusetts: A Nineteenth-Century Family Revisited," 281.

27. Sterling, *We Are Your Sisters*, 187–88 (emphasis in the original).

28. Stephen Kendrick and Paul Kendrick, *Sarah's Long Walk: The Free Blacks of Boston and How Their Struggle for Equality Changed America*, 238; Oden, "The Black Putnams," 244; Leonard P. Curry, *The Free Black in Urban America: The Shadow of the Dream*, 167.

29. Leonard W. Levy and Harlan B. Philips, "The Roberts Case: Source of the 'Separate by Equal' Doctrine," 514.

30. Kendrick and Kendrick, *Sarah's Long Walk*, 176–77.

31. Ibid., 257.

32. Stevenson, *The Journals*, 1:140; Brenda Stevenson, "Charlotte Forten (1837–1914)," 286–87; Porter, "The Remonds of Salem," 282.

33. Maritcha Lyons, "Memories of Yesterday, All of Which I Saw and Part of Which I Was: An Autobiography," reel 1, pp. 7, 15, Williams Collection, Schomburg Center for Research, New York, New York; Sterling, *We Are Your Sisters*, 188–89.

34. Lyons, "Memories of Yesterday," 15; Sterling, *We Are Your Sisters*, 189.

35. Stevenson, *The Journals*, 1:140.

36. See Steven M. Stowe, "The Not-So-Cloistered Academy: Elite Women's Education and Family Feeling in the Old South," 92–93; Steven M. Stowe, "The THING Not Its Vision": A Woman's Courtship and Her Sphere in the Southern Planter Class," 115–18; Carroll Smith-Rosenberg, "The Female World of Love and Ritual: Relations between Women in Nineteenth-Century America."

37. Amanda Smith, *An Autobiography: The Story of the Lord's Dealings with Mrs. Amanda Smith . . .* , 28–29.

38. David Sheinin, "Prudence Crandall, Amistad, and Other Episodes in the Dismissal of Connecticut Slave Women from American History," 132–33. See Edmund Fuller, *Prudence Crandall: An Incident of Racism in Nineteenth-Century Connecticut*.

39. See John L. Rury, "The New York African Free School, 1827–1836: Conflict over Community Control of Black Education," 187–97, for a discussion of blacks fighting for autonomy over the New York African Free School.

40. Gerda Lerner, ed., *Black Women in White America: A Documentary History*, 85. The PFASS had established its own school following an 1834 assessment of the public education for black children under the tutelage of New Englander Rebecca Buffum. When she left in 1838, Sarah Mapps Douglass assumed leadership.

41. Rury, "The New York African Free School," 192–93.

42. Ibid., 195–96.

43. John H. Hewitt, "The Search for Elizabeth Jennings, Heroine of a Sunday Afternoon in New York," 400, 403–4. See Diane Ravitch, *The Great School Wars: A History of the New York City Public Schools*.

44. Jean R. Soderlund, "The Philadelphia Female Anti-Slavery Society," 76–77.

45. Ibid., 77; Sterling, *We Are Your Sisters*, 129. The PFAAS held its meetings in the schoolroom and paid a portion of the rent until 1849.

46. Lerner, *Black Women in White America*, 85–86; Gerda Lerner, "Sarah Mapps Douglass," 352.

47. Fannie Jackson-Coppin, *Reminiscences of School Life and Hints on Teaching*, 19–20.

48. H. Amelia Loguen to Lewis Douglass, April 10, 1862, in Carter G. Woodson, ed., *The Mind of the Negro as Reflected in Letters Written During the Crisis, 1800–1860*, 541. See Lyons, "Memoirs of Yesterday," 6–7; Sarah Margru Kinson to My Dear Mr. Whipple, #F1–5812, AMA, ARC.

49. Lerner, *Black Women in White America*, 76; Sterling, *We Are Your Sisters*, 189–90.

50. Sterling, *We Are Your Sisters*, 191–93, 201. Oberlin became a college in the 1850s.

51. Ellen N. Lawson and Marlene Merrill, "Antebellum Black Coeds at Oberlin College," 828; James Oliver Horton, "Black Education at Oberlin College: A Controversial Commitment," 77.

52. Ellen N. Lawson and Marlene Merrill, "The Antebellum 'Talented Thousandth': Black College Students at Oberlin before the Civil War," 151; Lawson and Merrill, "Antebellum Black Coeds," 831; Perkins, "The Impact of the 'Cult of True Womanhood,'" 20.

53. Lawson and Merrill, "The Antebellum 'Talented Thousandth,'" 145, 146.

54. Ellen Nickenzie Lawson and Marlene D. Merrill, *The Three Sarahs: Documents of Antebellum Black College Women*, 13:11–12; Howard Jones, *Mutiny on the Amistad: The Saga of a Slave Revolt and Its Impact on American Abolition, Law, and Diplomacy*, 3–26.

55. Miss S. Kinson to Friend [Lewis] Tappan, Esq., May 2, 1847, AMA, ARC.

56. Lawson and Merrill, "The Antebellum 'Talented Thousandth,'" 145.

57. Jackson-Coppin, *Reminiscences of School Life*, 11.

58. Ibid., 15, 17; Perkins, "Heed Life's Demands," 181.

59. Stevenson, "Charlotte Forten," 287–88.

60. William Cheek and Aimee Lee Cheek, *John Mercer Langston and the Fight for Black Freedom, 1829–65*, 302–306.

61. Elizabeth Martin and Vivian Meyer, *Female Gazes: Seventy-Five Women Artists*, 46; Kirsten P. Buick, "The Ideal Works of Edmonia Lewis: Invoking and Inverting Autobiography," 195, 201.

62. S[arah] M[apps] D[ouglass] to Martina Dickerson, November 3, 1843, Martina Dickerson Album, Library Company of Philadelphia, Philadelphia, Pennsylvania (hereafter cited as LCP).

63. Ellen N. Lawson, "Sarah Woodson Early: 19th Century Black Nationalist 'Sister,'" 815–19.

64. Ibid., 819–20.

65. Tate, *Unknown Tongues,* 152; Hewitt, "Search for Elizabeth Jennings," 407, 410.

66. Lawson and Merrill, "Antebellum Black Coeds at Oberlin College," 829–31; Coppin, *Reminiscences of School Life,* 13, 18.

67. Stevenson, *The Journals,* 34–37.

68. Sterling, *We Are Your Sisters,* 194.

69. Nellie Y. McKay, "Nineteenth-Century Black Women's Spiritual Autobiographies: Religious Faith and Self-Empowerment," 145.

70. Jefferson, *Notes on the State of Virginia,* 140.

71. Stevenson, *The Journals,* 1:71, 1:92.

72. Ibid., 1:70–71; Julie Winch, "'You Have Talents—Only Cultivate Them': Philadelphia's Black Female Literary Societies and the Abolitionist Crusade," 102; Kwando Mbiassi Kinshasa, "Free Blacks' Quest for a National Identity: Debates in the African American Press on Assimilation and Emigration, 1827–1861," 88–89. See [Joseph Willson] *Sketches of the Higher Class of Colored Society in Philadelphia by a Southerner,* 93–116; Dorothy B. Porter, "The Organized Educational Activities of Negro Literary Societies, 1828–1846," 555–76.

73. James Oliver Horton and Lois E. Horton, *Black Bostonians: Family Life and Community Struggle in the Antebellum North,* 31; [Willson], *Sketches of the Higher Class,* 108–9.

74. Winch, "'You Have Talents—Only Cultivate Them,'" 101–3, 107–8; [Willson] *Sketches of the Higher Class,* 107–9.

75. Rebecca F. Peterson to Martina Dickerson, July 11, 1840, Martina Dickerson Album, LCP.

76. [Willson], *Sketches of the Higher Class,* 108; Porter, "The Organized Educational Activities," 559–60.

77. Harry Reed, *Platform for Change: The Foundations of the Northern Free Black Community, 1775–1865,* 76–76, 85–91. See Julie Winch, "'You Have Talents—Only Cultivate Them.'"

78. Catharine Johnson Diary, May 10, 1864, William T. Johnson and Family Memorial Papers, Louisiana and Lower Mississippi Valley Collections, Louisiana State University, Baton Rouge, Louisiana (hereafter cited as LSU); Virginia Meacham Gould, ed., *Chained to the Rock of Adversity: To Be Free, Black, and Female in the Old South,* 69.

79. Johnson Diary, August 2, 1865, LSU; Gould, *Chained to the Rock,* 71.

80. Frances Ellen Watkins [Harper], *Poems on Miscellaneous Subjects,* 13–14. See Frances Smith Foster, ed., *A Brighter Coming Day: A Frances Ellen Watkins Harper Reader,* 54–55, 63.

81. Jane H. Pease and William H. Pease, *They Who Would Be Free: Blacks' Search for Freedom, 1830–1861,* 124–25; Donald Yacovone, "The Transformation of the Black Temperance Movement, 1827–1854: An Interpretation," 285; Garfield, "'The Pen is ours to Wield,'" 127–28.

82. Francis Ellen Watkins Harper, "The Two Offers," 21–30; Frances Smith Foster, *Written by Herself: Literary Production by African American Women, 1746–1892,* 90–92.

83. Watkins [Harper], *Poems on Miscellaneous Subjects,* 20–21; Harper, "The Two Offers," 21–22; Melba Joyce Boyd, *Discarded Legacy: Politics and Poetics in the Life of Frances E. W. Harper, 1825–1911,* 118; Foster, *A Brighter Coming Day,* 105–17.

84. "Female Anti-Slavery Society," *The Liberator,* July 14, 1832.

85. Watkins [Harper], *Poems on Miscellaneous Subjects,* 9–11; Frances Smith Foster, *A Brighter Coming Day,* 9–11.

86. Watkins, *Poems on Miscellaneous Subjects,* 8; William Still, *The Underground Rail Road. A record of facts, authentic narratives, letters, & c. . . . ,* 755.

87. For a discussion of the slave interviews and narratives, see Randall M. Miller and John David Smith, eds., *Dictionary of Afro-American Slavery,* 365–68, 515–19; Gilbert Osofsky, ed., *Puttin' On Ole Massa: The Slave Narratives of Henry Bibb, William Wells Brown, and Solomon Northup,* 10–44; George P. Rawick, ed., *The American Slave: A Composite Autobiography,* Supplement, series 1, *Alabama Narr.,* 1:ix–lvi; Rawick, *The American Slave: A Composite Autobiography,* Supplement, series 2, *Texas Narr.,* 2:1, xxiii–xxix.

88. Foster, *Written by Herself,* 78–80.

89. Harriet Jacobs, *Incidents in the Life of a Slave Girl: Written by Herself,* 1–2, 77; Foster, *Written by Herself,* 96.

90. Jacobs, *Incidents in the Life of a Slave Girl,* xxiv–xxv.

91. Jane Rhodes, *Mary Ann Shadd Cary: The Black Protest in the Nineteenth Century,* 73–74; Alexander L. Murray, "*The Provincial Freeman:* A New Source for the History of the Negro in Canada and the United States," 126–27.

92. J. William Snorgrass, "Pioneer Black Women Journalists from the 1850s to the 1950s," 592.

93. Rhodes, *Mary Ann Shadd Cary,* 99.

94. Sterling, *We Are Your Sisters,* 191.

5. *"Whom do you serve, God or man?": Spiritualists and Reformers*

1. Zilpha Elaw, "Memoirs of the Life, Religious Experience, Ministerial Travels, and Labours of Mrs. Elaw, an American Female of Colour; Together with Some Account of the Great religious Revivals in America [Written by Herself]," 89–90. For a broader analysis of religious women and their search for authorization in the face of obstacles, see Catherine A. Brekus, *Female Preaching in America: Strangers and Pilgrims, 1740–1845;* Catherine A. Brekus, " 'Let Your Women Keep Silence in the Churches': Female Preaching and Evangelical Religion in America, 1740–1845"; Gerda Lerner, *The Creation of Feminist Consciousness: From the Middle Ages to Eighteen Seventy;* Bettye Collier-Thomas, *Daughters of Thunder: Black Women Preachers and Their Sermons.*

2. Lerner, *The Creation of Feminist Consciousness,* 106. See Maria W. Stewart, "Productions of Mrs. Maria W. Stewart"; Julia A. J. Foote, "A Brand Plucked from the Fire: An Autobiographical Sketch by Mrs. Julia A. J. Foote"; Olive Gilbert, ed., *Narrative of Sojourner Truth: A Bondswoman of Olden Time. . . .*

3. R. J. Young, *Antebellum Black Activists: Race, Gender, and Self,* 137. Thanks to Jacqueline McLeod for her introduction to the concepts of a socially and spiritually constructed self.

4. William Andrews, ed., *Sisters of the Spirit: Three Black Women's Autobiographies of the Nineteenth Century,* 3. Relevant discussion can be found in Lerner, *The Creation of Feminist Consciousness,* 138–66.

5. See Elizabeth, "Memoir of Old Elizabeth, a Coloured Woman"; Jarena

Lee, "The Life and Religious Experience of Jarena Lee"; Zilpha Elaw, "Memoirs of the Life"; Julia A. J. Foote, "A Brand Plucked from the Fire"; Rebecca Jackson, *Gifts of Power: The Writings of Rebecca Jackson, Black Visionary, Shaker Eldress.* See also Jean M. Humez, " 'My Spirit Eye': Some Functions of Spiritual and Visionary Experience in the Lives of Five Black Women Preachers, 1810–1880," 129–30.

The sanctification of and call to preach for Amanda Berry Smith (1837–1915) came after the Civil War; therefore, she is not a significant part of this discussion. Her narrative, *An Autobiography: The Story of the Lord's Dealings with Mrs. Amanda Smith . . .* , is useful for a later period.

6. Sylvia R. Frey and Betty Wood, *Come Shouting to Zion: African American Protestantism in the American South and British Caribbean to 1830,* 64; Norrece T. Jones Jr., *Born a Child of Freedom, Yet a Slave: Mechanisms of Control and Strategies of Resistance in Antebellum South Carolina,* 131.

7. William D. Piersen, *Black Yankees: The Development of an Afro-American Subculture in Eighteenth-Century New England,* 51–52; Arthur Zilversmit, *The First Emancipation: The Abolition of Slavery in the North,* 7–9; Jones, *Born a Child of Freedom,* 131. See Jean E. Friedman, *The Enclosed Garden: Women and Community in the Evangelical South, 1830–1890;* Mechal Sobel, *Trabelin' On: The Slave Journey to an Afro-Baptist Faith.*

8. Frank Lambert, " 'I Saw the Book Talk': Slave Readings of the First Great Awakening," 190; Piersen, *Black Yankees,* 65–73.

9. Lambert, "I Saw the Book Talk," 190; John C. Shields, ed., *The Collected Work of Phillis Wheatley,* 22; Piersen, *Black Yankees,* 68–69.

10. Albert J. Raboteau, *Slave Religion: The "Invisible Institution" in the Antebellum South,* 131; Piersen, *Black Yankees,* 67.

11. Raboteau, *Slave Religion,* 137–40.

12. Ibid., 163–64.

13. Andrews, *Sisters of the Spirit,* 5. See Brekus, *Female Preaching in America,* 133–34; Carol V. R. George, *Segregated Sabbaths: Richard Allen and the Emergence of Independent Black Churches, 1740–1840;* Gary B. Nash, *Forging Freedom: The Formation of Philadelphia's Black Community, 1720–1840,* 118–19.

14. Thelma Marie Townsend, "Spiritual Autobiographies of Religious Activism by Black Women in the Antebellum Era," 17–19. See Ephesians 5:22–24; I Timothy 2:11–13. See Barbara Welter, "The Cult of True Womanhood, 1820–1860," 151–74.

15. Marilyn Richardson, ed., *Maria W. Stewart, America's First Black Woman and Political Writer: Essays and Speeches,* 8–9, 19 (emphasis added); Carla L. Peterson, *"Doers of the Word": African-American Women, Speakers and Writers in the North (1830–1880),* 57, 59.

16. Richardson, *Maria W. Stewart,* 14–17, 68; Nellie Y. McKay, "Nineteenth-Century Black Women's Spiritual Autobiographies: Religious Faith and Self-Empowerment," 142–43, 151; Townsend, "Spiritual Autobiographies," 46, 57.

17. Nell Irvin Painter, *Sojourner Truth: A Life, a Symbol,* 29. For other discussions and examples of conversion experiences, see Clifton H. Johnson, ed., *God Struck Me Dead: Religious Conversion Experiences and Autobiographies of Ex-slaves;* Charles Joyner, *Down by the Riverside: A South Carolina Community,* 168; Ollie Alho, *The Religion of the Slaves: A Study of the Religious Tradition and Behavior of Plantation Slaves in the United States 1830–1865,* 182–83; Friedman, *The Enclosed*

Garden, 72; Susan Hill Lindley, *You Have Stept Out of Your Place: A History of Women and Religion in America*, 179–80; Emery Battis, *Saints and Sectaries: Anne Hutchinson and the Antinomian Controversy in the Massachusetts Bay Colony*, 33. See Lerner, *The Creation of Feminist Consciousness*, especially chapters 4 and 5, for a related discussion of visions and dreams.

18. Elaw, "Memoirs of the Life," 56–57, 66–67; Foote, "A Brand Plucked from the Fire," 180–81, 185–87 (emphasis added).

19. See Acts 9:1–43.

20. Elaw, "Memoirs of the Life," 66–67; Lindley, *You Have Stept Out of Your Place*, 180.

21. Lee, "The Life and Religious Experience," 39–40; Foote, "A Brand Plucked from the Fire," 180–81; Acts 9:1–18.

22. Isaiah 61:1 (emphasis in the original). The Bible verse found on the title page of "Memoir of Old Elizabeth, a Coloured Woman," should be Galatians 3:28 rather than 3:25 as cited.

23. Lee, "The Life and Religious Experience," 27; Foote, "A Brand Plucked from the Fire," 208 (emphasis added).

24. Elaw, "Memoirs of the Life," 160 (emphasis added).

25. Painter, *Sojourner Truth*, 20, 25, 73–74; Gilbert, *Narrative of Sojourner Truth*, 100–101; Lerner, *Creation of Feminist Consciousness*, 105–7.

26. Elizabeth, "Memoir of Old Elizabeth," 5–9.

27. Humez, "'My Spirit Eye,'" 132; Foote, "A Brand Plucked from the Fire," 196.

28. Foote, "A Brand Plucked from the Fire," 190, 196, 217–18.

29. Lee, "The Life and Religious Experience," 40.

30. Elaw, "Memoirs of the Life," 61–62, 84.

31. Jackson, *Gifts of Power*, 17–18, 145, 219; McKay, "Nineteenth-Century Black Women's Spiritual Autobiographies," 148.

32. Jackson, *Gifts of Power*, 146–47, 253–55.

33. Ibid., 163–64.

34. Ibid., 5–6; Foote, "A Brand Plucked from the Fire," 217; Andrews, *Sisters of the Spirit*, 5; McKay, "Nineteenth-Century Black Women's Spiritual Autobiographies," 144, 150; Lerner, *The Creation of Feminist Consciousness*, 107. See Darlene Clark Hine, "Lifting the Veil, Shattering the Silence: Black Women's History in Slavery and Freedom," 7; Townsend, "Spiritual Autobiographies," 183.

35. Lee, "The Life and Religious Experience," 39.

36. Elaw, "Memoirs of the Life," 73, 75, 76, 83; Jackson, *Gifts of Power*, 6.

37. Elizabeth, "Memoir of Old Elizabeth," 9, 12–13, 15, 17.

38. Lee, "The Life and Religious Experience," 36, 37; Frances Smith Foster, *Written by Herself: Literary Production by African American Women, 1746–1892*, 57–58. In the introduction to *An Autobiography: The Story of The Lord's Dealings with Mrs. Amanda Smith*, xxxi, the year for the request to preach under the auspices of the African Methodist church is 1809.

39. Lee, "The Life and Religious Experience," 36. See Joel 2:28: "And it will come to pass afterward, *that* I will pour out my spirit on all flesh; and your sons and daughters will prophesy, your old men will dream dreams, your young men will see visions." See also Lerner, *The Creation of Feminist Consciousness*, 157.

40. Lee, "The Life and Religious Experience," 36–37. Both Zilpha Elaw and Rebecca Cox Jackson desired more education to enhance their ministry, and each saw her desire fulfilled through her religious beliefs. See Foote, "A Brand Plucked from the Fire," 182; Jackson, *Gifts of Power*, 107.

41. Lee, "The Life and Religious Experience," 37.

42. Joanne M. Braxton, *Black Women Writing Autobiography: A Tradition within a Tradition*, 58.

43. Lee, "The Life and Religious Experience," 37; Brekus, *Female Preaching in America*, 246.

44. Foote, "A Brand Plucked from the Fire," 209; Richardson, *Maria W. Stewart*, 19; Romans 16:1–3; Philippians 4:3.

45. Lerner, *The Creation of Feminist Consciousness*, 140; Lee, "The Life and Religious Experience," 36–38; Foote, "A Brand Plucked from the Fire," 208–9, 227.

46. Jackson, *Gifts of Power*, 86.

47. Foote, "A Brand Plucked from the Fire," 209; 1 Corinthians 11:3–12; Romans 16:1–3. Selective use of 1 Corinthians 11 yields data to support either argument. For example, 1 Corinthians 11:8 says, "For man does not originate from woman, but woman from man." The following verse asserts that "man was not created for the woman; but woman for the man." Verse 10 asserts that the woman ought to have a symbol of authority on her head because of the angels. Other verses, including 1 Corinthians 11:11–12, balance power positions between women and men.

48. Foote, "A Brand Plucked from the Fire," 221–23; Collier-Thomas, *Daughters of Thunder*, 60–61, 64–65.

49. Painter, *Sojourner Truth*, 135.

50. Esther 1; Daniel Noel Freedman, ed., *The Anchor Bible Dictionary*, 2:633.

51. Esther 1:16–22.

52. Herbert Lockyer, *All the Women of the Bible: The Life and Times of All the Women of the Bible*, 166.

53. Maryemma Graham, ed., *Complete Poems of Frances E. W. Harper*, 98–100.

54. Elaw, "Memoirs of the Life," 62; Painter, *Sojourner Truth*, 135–36.

55. Foote, "A Brand Plucked from the Fire," 205–6.

56. Ibid., 206–7.

57. Ibid., 207, 208.

58. Ibid., 227.

59. Elaw, "Memoirs of the Life," 124.

60. Jackson, *Gifts of Power*, 103, 105–6.

61. Ibid., 150.

62. Ibid., 154; Lerner, *The Creation of Feminist Consciousness*, 101–2.

63. Jackson, *Gifts of Power*, 27, 37–38, 92–93, 145.

64. Ibid., 220.

65. Ibid., 181–82; Lerner, *The Creation of Feminist Consciousness*, 110.

66. Jackson, *Gifts of Power*, 32; Braxton, *Black Women Writing*, 58.

67. Jackson, *Gifts of Power*, 274.

68. Lee, "The Life and Religious Experience," 28–29; Foster, *Written by Herself*, 67. Sojourner Truth was aware of the differences between the treatment she received and that meted out to others at the Kingdom of Matthias which touted

egalitarianism, yet she did not base her complaints on racial distinctions (Painter, *Sojourner Truth*, 55–57).

69. Nash, *Forging Freedom*, 132–33, 192–93.

70. Painter, *Sojourner Truth*, 39; Lee, "The Life and Religious Experience," 28; Nash, *Forging Freedom*, 191–92.

71. Elaw, "Memoirs of the Life," 85–86; Acts 17:26, Psalms 68:31.

72. Jackson, *Gifts of Power*, 277.

73. Carroll Smith-Rosenberg, "The Female World of Love and Ritual: Relations between Women in Nineteenth-Century America," 1; Jackson, *Gifts of Power*, 9. See Nancy F. Cott, "Passionlessness: An Interpretation of Victorian Sexual Ideology, 1790–1850," 219–36.

74. Jackson, *Gifts of Power*, 9 n. 10.

75. Ibid., 88, 219 (emphasis in the original); Cott, "Passionlessness," 220, 222; Lerner, *The Creation of Feminist Consciousness*, 88.

76. See Lerner, *The Creation of Feminist Consciousness*, 109.

77. Peterson, "*Doers of the Word*," 74–75.

78. Emily Clark and Virginia Meacham Gould, "The Feminine Face of Afro-Catholicism in New Orleans, 1727–1852," 409–48.

79. Tracy Fessenden, "The Sisters of the Holy Family and the Veil of Race," 191, 193; Fichter, "The White Church and the Black Sisters," 37. See discussion of *placage* in chapter 1.

80. Sister Mary Bernard Deggs, *No Cross, No Crown: Black Nuns in Nineteenth-Century New Orleans*, xxxii–xxxiv; Joseph H. Fichter, "The White Church and the Black Sisters," 40; Fessenden, "The Sisters of the Holy Family," 194.

81. Fichter, "The White Church and the Black Sisters," 40–41; Fessenden, "The Sisters of the Holy Family," 202.

82. Lerner, *The Creation of Feminist Consciousness*, 106.

83. Sojourner Truth did not preach while affiliated with the Kingdom of Matthias since Robert Matthias deemed it "out of bounds for women" (Painter, *Sojourner Truth*, 54).

84. Gilbert, *Narrative of Sojourner Truth*, 100–101, 105; Painter, *Sojourner Truth*, 86–87.

85. Painter, *Sojourner Truth*, 87, 89, 93, 95; Lerner, *The Creation of Feminist Consciousness*, 106.

86. Painter, *Sojourner Truth*, 116, 119.

87. Ibid., 119–20.

88. Ibid., 164.

89. Ibid., 152–60, 164, 169. See pages 164–78 for a full discussion of Gage's account of the "Ar'n't I a Woman?" speech.

90. Jacquelyn Grant, "A Refusal to Be Silenced," 23.

91. See Neil A. Patten, "The Nineteenth Century Black Woman as Social Reformer: The 'New' Speeches of Sojourner Truth," 4.

92. Elaw, "Memoirs of the Life," 91, 92, 93, 98. The biblical reference to Greek slaveowner Philemon and his slave Onesimus comes from the epistle of Paul to Philemon (16) urging Philemon to receive Onesimus "not now as a servant, but above a servant, a brother beloved."

93. Elaw, "Memoirs of the Life," 90; Brekus, *Female Preaching in America*, 249.

94. Diane Batts Morrow, *Person of Color and Religious at the Same Time: The Oblate Sisters of Providence, 1828–1860*, 69, 116–17; Fessenden, "The Sisters of the Holy Family," 196.

95. Esther 8:11, 9:22; Painter, *Sojourner Truth*, 136.

96. Painter, *Sojourner Truth*, 136.

97. Gilbert, *Narrative of Sojourner Truth*, 66–68; Painter, *Sojourner Truth*, 30.

6. *"Female sympathy in the cause of freedom and humanity"*: Activists and Abolitionists

1. Marilyn Richardson, ed., *Maria W. Stewart, America's First Black Woman Political Writer: Essays and Speeches*, 45.

2. Frances Anne Kemble, *Journal of a Residence on a Georgian Plantation in 1838–1839*, 7.

3. Leon F. Litwack, *North of Slavery: The Negro in the Free States, 1790–1860*, viii-ix; Leonard Curry, *The Free Black in Urban America: The Shadow of the Dream*, 82–83. See "Our Free Colored Population," *Douglass' Monthly* (August 1859): 125; Dan Durett, "Free Blacks in Selected Georgia Cities, 1820–1860," 2–3; Juliet E. K. Walker, "The Legal Status of Free Blacks in Early Kentucky, 1792–1825," 382–95; Julie Winch, " 'You Have Talents—Only Cultivate Them': Philadelphia's Black Female Literary Societies and the Abolitionist Crusade," 103.

4. Convention of Colored People," *The North Star*, October 20, 1848. For discussions of black abolitionists, see Benjamin Quarles, Black Abolitionists; Waldo E. Martin Jr., *The Mind of Frederick Douglass*.

5. See Harriet Jacobs, *Incidents in the Life of a Slave Girl: Written by Herself*, 95–105; Dickson D. Bruce Jr., *Archibald Grimké: Portrait of a Black Independent*, 14–15, 16; Benjamin Quarles, *Frederick Douglass*, 90; Gayle T. Tate, "Political Consciousness and Resistance among Black Antebellum Women," 78–84.

6. Dorothy Burnett Porter, "The Remonds of Salem, Massachusetts: A Nineteenth-Century Family Revisited," 282; Litwack, *North of Slavery*, viii, 64–66, 97; Curry, *The Free Black in Urban America*, 90–95; *The Revised Statutes of the State of Missouri*, 754–57.

7. Dorothy Sterling, ed., *We Are Your Sisters: Black Women in the Nineteenth Century*, 130; Julia A. J. Foote, "A Brand Plucked from the Fire," 167.

8. Zelmire, "Unnatural Distinction," *The Liberator* (July 28, 1832): 118.

9. See chapter 5 above. See also John Harold Sprinkle Jr., " 'Let Their Situation at Least Engage Our Sympathy, if We can Afford Them No Relief': Patterns of Occupation and Residence among Free Blacks in Early Nineteenth-Century Wilmington, Delaware," 6.

10. Sterling, *We Are Your Sisters*, 187.

11. John H. Hewitt, "The Search for Elizabeth Jennings, Heroine of a Sunday Afternoon in New York City," 389, 391–92; Vincent Harding, *There Is a River: The Black Struggle for Freedom in America*, 194.

12. Porter, "The Remonds of Salem," 282–83.

13. "The Black Swan, Alias Miss Elizabeth Greenfield," in Philip S. Foner, ed., *The Life and Writings of Frederick Douglass: Pre-Civil War Decade, 1850–1860*, 2: 239–40; Philip S. Foner, ed., *Frederick Douglass on Women's Rights*, 19, 149 n. 19.

14. Julia A. J. Foote, "A Brand Plucked from the Fire," 222.

15. Brenda Stevenson, ed., *The Journals of Charlotte Forten Grimké*, 2:230. For further discussions of race relations, see Litwack, *North of Slavery*, 109–12; Ira Berlin, *Many Thousands Gone: The First Two Centuries of Slavery in North America*, 187–88.

16. See David J. McCord, ed., *The Statutes at Large of South Carolina*, 352–65; *Acts of the General Assembly of the State of South Carolina*, 28–49; *Laws of Kentucky*, 297–98; William C. Dawson, *A Compilation of the Laws of the State of Georgia*, 412–14.

17. Petition "To the Honorable Senate and House of Representatives of the State of Delaware," January 6, 1816, in Schweninger, *Microfilm Petitions*. See "To the Legislature of the State of Delaware," 1:0335, Delaware; "An Act Respecting Free Negroes and Free Mulattoes," 1:0339, Delaware; "The Petitioners seek Repeal," 1:0347, Delaware; in Schweninger, *Microfilm Petitions*.

18. *The Revised Statutes of Missouri*, 756–57; *Laws of the State of Missouri*, 66–68; *The Revised Laws of Indiana*, 375–76; *Laws of the State of Indiana*, 60; *The Statutes of Iowa*, 69–70; *Territorial Laws of Michigan*, 635; Salmon P. Chase, ed., *Statutes of Ohio and the Northwest Territory from 1788 to 1833*, 1:68, 79–81, 393; *Laws of Illinois; General Laws of the State of Illinois*, 57–60; Litwack, *North of Slavery*, 35–36, 68–70; Curry, *The Free Black in Urban America*, 83–89. See Edgar F. Love, "Registration of Free Blacks in Ohio: The Slaves of George C. Mendenhall," 38–47; Frances LaJune Johnson Powell, "A Study of the Structure of the Freed Black Family in Washington, DC, 1850–1880," 50, 51–52.

19. See "To the Legislature of the State of Delaware," December 1815, 1:0335; "To the Senate and House of Representatives of the State of Delaware," January 9, 1816, 1:0347; Schweninger, *Microfilm Petitions*.

20. See Schweninger, *Microfilm Edition*. For a discussion related to the ostensible dependency of women, see Laura F. Edwards, "Law, Domestic Violence, and the Limits of Patriarchal Authority in the Antebellum South," 733–70.

21. See Drew Gilpin Faust, ed., *The Ideology of Slavery: Proslavery Thought in the American South, 1830–1860*, 9; Charles M. Wiltse, ed., *David Walker's Appeal, in Four Articles; Together with a Preamble, to the Coloured Citizens of the World, But in Particular, and Very Expressly, to Those of the United States of America*; Curry, *The Free Black in Urban America*, 110.

22. Plea of Elvira Jones, 18:0402, Schweninger, *Microfilm Petitions*; Loren Schweninger, "Property Owning Free African American Women in the South, 1800–1870," 264.

23. Paul Finkelman, ed., *State Slavery Statutes: Guide to State Slavery Statutes*, viii–ix; Berlin, *Slaves Without Masters*, 146–47. See Finkelman, *State Slavery Statutes* (microfiche [hereafter cited as Finkelman]) for "Virginia Statutes, 1814," 148; "Virginia Statutes, 1827," 120–21; "Virginia Statutes, 1828," 156–57; "Virginia Statutes, 1829," 134; "Virginia Statutes, 1832," 198; "Virginia Statutes, 1835," 392–94.

24. "An act for the benefit of Amelia Saulsbury," February 1, 1859, Enrolled Bills, 1:81, Delaware Public Archives, Hall of Records, Dover, Delaware; Pleas of Ann Caldwell, 3:0621, 0624, Mississippi, Schweninger, *Microfilm Petitions*; Plea of Sookey, 7:0485, North Carolina, Schweninger, *Microfilm Petitions*; Durett, "Free Blacks in Selected Georgia Cities," 4–5, 7; *The Revised Statutes of the State of Missouri*, 755–56; *Laws of Mississippi*, 253; Jonathan M. Atkins, "Party Politics and the Debate over the Tennessee Free Negro Bill, 1859–1860," 252–53.

25. Suzanne Lebsock, *The Free Women of Petersburg: Status and Culture in a Southern Town, 1784–1860*, 87–88. See Dawson, *A Compilation of the Laws of the State of Georgia*, 412, 413; Michael P. Johnson and James L. Roark, *Black Masters: A Free Family of Color in the Old South*, 47–48; Durett, "Free Blacks in Selected Georgia Cities, 1820–1860," 35; Curry, *The Free Negro in Urban America*, 89; Finkelman, "Alabama Statute, 1822," 61.

26. Berlin, *Slaves Without Masters*, 334.

27. Durett, "Free Blacks in Selected Georgia Cities," 35; Berlin, *Slaves Without Masters*, 334. See Myra C. Glenn, "The Naval Reform Campaign Against Flogging: A Cast Study in Changing Attitudes Toward Corporal Punishment, 1830–1850," 408–25; "Whipping and Castration as Punishments for Crime," 371–86.

28. "To the honorable, the Representatives of South Carolina," 1794, 8:0354, Schweninger, *Microfilm Petitions;* Johnson and Roark, *Black Masters*, 42–43, 164; Dawson, *A Compilation of the Laws of the State of Georgia*, 40, 410–11; John Hope Franklin and Alfred A. Moss Jr., *From Slavery to Freedom: A History of Negro Americans*, 170–71.

In 1809, South Carolina granted relief from the poll tax required of all free persons of color "except such as shall be clearly proven to the collector to be incapable, from maims or otherwise, of providing their livelihood" (Herbert Aptheker, "South Carolina Poll Tax, 1737–1895," 132–37).

29. Berlin, *Slaves Without Masters*, 146–48, 288, 311–12, 327–31; Durett, "Free Blacks in Selected Georgia Cities," 9, 38–39; Anita Didt Guy, *Maryland's Persistent Pursuit to End Slavery, 1850–1864*, 17; Carl Lane and Rhoda Freeman, "John Dipper and the Experience of the Free Black Elite, 1816–1836," 508–11; Powell, "A Study of the Structure of the Freed Black Family in Washington, DC, 1850–1880," 52; Curry, *The Free Black in Urban America*, 94, 104–5; Atkins, "Party Politics and the Debate over the Tennessee Free Negro Bill," 261, 263. See Joshua D. Rothman, "'Notorious in the Neighborhood': An Interracial Family in Early National and Antebellum Virginia," 73–114.

30. Randolph B. Campbell, *An Empire for Slavery: The Peculiar Institution in Texas, 1821–1865*, 110; Ruthe Winegarten, *Black Texas Women: A Sourcebook, Documents, Biographies, Timeline*, 1, 274.

31. Mary Madison Memorial and Petition #251, Texas State Library and Archives Commission, Austin, Texas. Thanks to Ruthe Winegarten for providing the Madison citation and documents about free black women in Texas.

32. Ibid.

33. Ibid.

34. John S. Mbiti, *African Religions and Philosophy*, 203.

35. Peter P. Hinks, "'Frequently Plunged into Slavery': Free Blacks and Kidnapping in Antebellum Boston," 16; Carol Wilson, *Freedom at Risk: The Kidnapping of Free Blacks in America, 1780–1865*, 103.

36. See Sterling, *We Are Your Sisters*, 227–32; Berlin, *Slaves Without Masters*, 99–101.

37. Alfred H. Kelly, Winfred A. Harbison, and Herman Belz, *The American Constitution: Its Origins and Development*, 254–55; Joseph Nogee, "The Prigg Case and Fugitive Slavery, 1842–1850," 190–91. See Paul Finkelman, "The Kidnapping of John Davis and the Adoption of the Fugitive Slave Law of 1793," 397–422.

38. Paul Finkelman, ed., *Slavery in the Courtroom: An Annotated Bibliography of American Cases*, 60–64.

39. Kermit L. Hall, William M. Wiecek, and Paul Finkelman, eds., *American Legal History: Cases and Materials*, 202; Stanley I. Kutler, ed., *The Supreme Court and the Constitution: Readings in American Constitutional History*, 145.

40. Kutler, *The Supreme Court and the Constitution*, 146–47. See Article IV, Section 2, U.S. Constitution.

41. Nogee, "The Prigg Case and the Fugitive Slave," 198.

42. Jane H. Pease and William H. Pease, *They Who Would Be Free: Blacks' Search for Freedom, 1830–1861*, 207.

43. Jacobs, *Incidents in the Life of a Slave Girl*, 95–105; Jean Fagan Yellin, *Harriet Jacobs: A Life*, 45–47, 49–62.

44. Leonard W. Levy, "The 'Abolition Riot': Boston's First Slave Rescue," 85.

45. Ibid., 86–87.

46. Ibid., 88–89; Sterling, *We Are Your Sisters*, 221; Quarles, *Black Abolitionists*, 205.

47. See Jane H. Pease and William H. Pease, *The Fugitive Slave Law and Anthony Burns: A Problem in Law Enforcement*, 6, 14; Sterling, *We Are Your Sisters*, 227–32. See also Stanley W. Campbell, *The Slave Catchers: Enforcement of the Fugitive Slave Law, 1850–1860*.

48. Pease and Pease, *The Fugitive Slave Law*, 25–54.

49. Stevenson, *The Journals*, 1:60.

50. Ibid., 1:60.

51. "Equal Rights of All Classes in the Cars," *The Liberator* (February 25, 1842): 32; James Oliver Horton and Lois E. Horton, *Black Bostonians: Family Life and Community Struggle in the Antebellum North*, 76; Donald M. Jacobs, ed., *Courage and Conscience: Black and White Abolitionists in Boston*, xiv; Pease and Pease, *The Fugitive Slave Law*, 27; Donald M. Jacobs, "David Walker and William Lloyd Garrison: Racial Cooperation and the Shaping of Boston," 1–20. See Stephen Kendrick and Paul Kendrick, *Sarah's Long Walk: The Free Blacks of Boston and How Their Struggle for Equality Changed America*.

52. Sarah Bradford, *Harriet Tubman: The Moses of Her People*, 120; Sterling, *We Are Your Sisters*, 223; Jacobs, "David Walker and William Lloyd Garrison: Racial Cooperation and the Shaping of Boston Abolition," 7; Catherine Clinton, *Harriet Tubman: The Road to Freedom*, 136–39; Jean M. Humez, *Harriet Tubman: The Life and Life Stories*, 40–41; Kate Clifford Larson, *Bound for the Promised Land: Portrait of an American Hero*, 179–83. See "A Fugitive Slave Case in Troy—Rescue of the Fugitive," *Douglass' Monthly* (June 1860): 282, for a related discussion.

53. Sterling, *We Are Your Sisters*, 222; Tate, "Political Consciousness and Resistance," 74–75.

54. Sterling, *We Are Your Sisters*, 221–22; Pease and Pease, *They Who Would Be Free*, 207.

55. Roderick W. Nash, "William Parker and the Christiana Riot," 24, 26, 28; Paul Finkelman, *Slavery in the Courtroom: An Annotated Bibliography of American Cases*, 95–96; W. U. Hensel, *The Christiana Riot and the Treason Trials of 1851*, 20–26; Ella Forbes, "'By my own Right Arm': Redemptive Violence and the 1851 Christiana, Pennsylvania Resistance," 164. See "The Freedman's Story, In two Parts," 276–95.

56. Hensel, *The Christiana Riot*, 30, 105, 114.

57. Ibid., 121; Nash, "William Parker and the Christiana Riot," 29–30.

58. Olivia Mahoney, "Black Abolitionists," 33.

59. See Clinton, *Harriet Tubman*, 85–89, 98–108; Humez, *Harriet Tubman*, 19–43, 189–90; Larson, *Bound for the Promised Land*, 136–37, 251, 254–55.

60. Eliza Potter, *A Hairdresser's Experience in the High Life*, 17–19.

61. Johnson and Roark, *Black Masters*, 162–63. See Atkins, "Party Politics and the Debate over the Tennessee Free Negro Bill," 245–78.

62. *Arkansas State Gazette and Democrat*, June 19, 1858, 2, 5.

63. Ibid., July 31, 1858, 3:2.

64. Billy D. Higgins, "The Origins and Fate of the Free Black Community," 439–40; J. D. B. DeBow, *Statistical View of the United States, being a Compendium of the Seventh Census*, 66; Eighth Census of the United States, 1860; Finkelman, "Arkansas Statute," 175–78.

65. "Circular by Frances Ellen Watkins Harper for Arkansas Free Blacks, January 1860," in C. Peter Ripley, ed., *Black Abolitionist Papers*, 5:54–57. Thanks to Ronnie Nichols for this citation.

66. Lizzie Jones Petition to the State of South Carolina Laurins District (1859–55–05), South Carolina Department of Archives and History, Columbia, South Carolina; Reenslavement Petitions, Auditor of Pubic Accounts, reel 1320, Library of Virginia, Richmond, Virginia; Johnson and Roark, *Black Masters*, 165–66. See Michael P. Johnson and James L. Roark, ed., *No Chariot Let Down: Charleston's Free People of Color on the Eve of the Civil War*, 129 n. 5; Jos. C. G. Kennedy, *Preliminary Report of the Eighth Census, 1860*, 134; Thomas D. Morris, *Southern Slavery and the Law, 1619–1860*, 32. See also Finkelman, "Alabama Statutes, 1860," 63–64; Finkelman, "Virginia Statutes, 1860," 492–93.

67. Lucy A. Delaney, "From The Darkness Cometh the Light or Struggles for Freedom," 15–16, 19. See Eugene D. Genovese, "The Treatment of Slaves in Different Countries: Problems in the Applications of the Comparative Method," 158–72.

68. Solomon Northup, "Twelve Years a Slave: Narrative of Solomon Northup," 388–89, 394–95, 406. The Anne Hampton Northup memorial appears in Solomon Northup, *Twelve Years a Slave: Narrative of Solomon Northup . . .*, appendix B, 325–27.

69. Petition of Rebecca Conch, May 23, 1838, Natchez Trace Collection (2E773), Center for American History, University of Texas, Austin, Texas. A large number of petitions submitted to southern legislatures are charges of enslavement based upon false claims (Schweninger, *Microfilm Edition*).

70. William D. Valentine Diary, November 27, 1852, Southern Historical Collection, University of North Carolina, Chapel Hill, North Carolina.

71. Johnson and Roark, *Black Masters*, 161.

72. See Janice Sumler-Lewis, "The Fortens of Philadelphia: An Afro-American Family and Nineteenth-Century Reform," 25–26, for a discussion of James Forten's response to the American Colonization Society's attempts to garner his support. See also Randall M. Miller, "Georgia on Their Minds: Free Blacks and the African Colonization Movement in Georgia," 349–62; Mia Bay, *The White Image in the Black Mind: African-American Ideas about White People, 1830–1925*, 22–26.

73. See Curry, *The Free Black in Urban America*, 96–111; Rebecca Jackson, *Gifts of Power: The Writings of Rebecca Jackson, Black Visionary, Shaker Eldress*, 14–15;

David Grimsted, "Rioting in Its Jacksonian Setting," 361–97; Emma Jones Lapsansky, "'Since They Got Those Separate Churches': Afro-Americans and Racism in Jacksonian Philadelphia," 54–78; Noel Ignatiev, *How the Irish Became White,* 131.

74. Lois Virginia Meacham Gould, "In Full Enjoyment of Their Liberty: The Free Women of Color of the Gulf Ports of New Orleans, 1769–1860," 102; "The free colored population," *Douglass' Monthly* (June 1859): 92. See Sarah L. Jones McNeal, "Biography of Zachariah Morgan," Morgan Family Papers, Bentley Library, University of Michigan, Ann Arbor, Michigan.

75. See Mary Niall Mitchell, "'A Good and Delicious Country': Free Children of Color and How They Learned to Imagine the Atlantic World in Nineteenth-Century Louisiana," 123–44; Molly Mitchell, "'After the War I Am Going to Put Myself a Sailor': Geography, Writing, and Race in Letters of Free Children in Civil War New Orleans," 26–37.

76. Jane Rhodes, *Mary Ann Shadd Cary: The Black Press and Protest in the Nineteenth Century,* 1–24, 43–50; Paul A. Cimbala, "Mary Ann Shadd Cary and Black Abolitionism," 20. See Shirley J. Yee, "Finding a Place: Mary Ann Shadd Cary and the Dilemmas of Black Migration to Canada, 1850–1870," 1–16; Jason H. Silverman, "Mary Ann Shadd and the Search for Equality," 4:1261–74.

77. Randall Miller, ed., *"Dear Master": Letters of a Slave Family,* 106; Miller, "Georgia on Their Minds," 361.

78. Sterling, *We Are Your Sisters,* 125; Hewitt, "The Search for Elizabeth Jennings," 398–99.

79. Sterling, *We Are Your Sisters,* 124–25; Sumler-Lewis, "The Fortens of Philadelphia," 40–41.

80. Sarah M. Douglass, "[Speech] Delivered before the Female Literary Society of Philadelphia, Pennsylvania [June 1832]," in C. Peter Ripley, *The Black Abolitionist Papers: The United States, 1830–1846,* 3:116–17; Sterling, *We Are Your Sisters,* 126–27.

81. Waldo E. Martin Jr., *The Mind of Frederick Douglass,* 25; William Still, *The Underground Rail Road. A record of facts, authentic narratives, letters, & c. . . . ,* 757; Yee, *Black Women Abolitionists,* 60; Rhodes, *Mary Ann Shadd Cary,* 7–12, 14–15; Melba Joyce Boyd, *Discarded Legacy: Politics and Poetics in the Life of Frances E. W. Harper, 1825–1911,* 36–37; J. Marcus Mitchell, "The Paul Family," 73, 75; Sterling, *We Are Your Sisters,* 187; Robert L. Hall, "Massachusetts Abolitionists Document the Slave Experience," 82; James Oliver Horton, "Generations of Protest: Black Families and Social Reform in Ante-Bellum Boston," 245–46.

82. James Oliver Horton and Lois E. Horton, *Black Bostonians: Family Life and Community Struggle in the Antebellum North,* especially chapter 2; Yee, *Black Women Abolitionists,* 12–39; Tate, "Political Consciousness and Resistance," 67–89.

83. Janice Sumler-Lewis, "The Forten-Purvis Women of Philadelphia and the American Anti-Slavery Crusade," 284. See Emma Jones Lapsansky, "Feminism, Freedom, and Community: Charlotte Forten and Women Activists in Nineteenth-Century Philadelphia," 3–19.

84. Deborah Bingham Van Broekhoven, "'Let Your Names Be Enrolled': Method and Ideology in Women's Antislavery Petitioning," 179–99; Jean Fagan Yellin and John C. Van Horne, eds. *The Abolitionist Sisterhood: Women's Political Culture in Antebellum America,* 12–13.

85. "Free Produce Store," *The North Star,* October 20, 1848, October 27, 1848.

86. "Editorial Remarks," *The Liberator,* April 23, 1831; Paul W. Gates, *The Farmer's Age: Agriculture 1815–1860,* 3:128; Michelle Nichole Garfield, "'The Pen is ours to Wield': Black Literary Society Women in 1830s Philadelphia," 94–95, 98. For discussions about the cultivation of sugar cane, see Sidney W. Mintz, *Sweetness and Power: The Place of Sugar in Modern History;* J. Carlyle Sitterson, *Sugar Country: The Cane Sugar Industry in the South, 1753–1950;* Walter Prichard, "Routine on a Louisiana Sugar Plantation Under the Slavery Regime," 168–78; Lewis Cecil Gray, *History of Agriculture in the Southern United States to 1860.*

87. Still, *The Underground Rail Road,* 759.

88. Margaret Hope Bacon, "By Moral Force Alone: The Antislavery Women and Nonresistance," 281; Garfield, "'The Pen is ours to Wield,'" 94.

89. Phillip Lapsansky, "Graphic Discord: Abolitionist and Antiabolitionist Images," 205–6; Lee Chambers-Schiller, "'A Good Work among the People': The Political Culture of the Boston Antislavery Fair," in Jean Fagan Yellin and John C. Van Horne, eds., *The Abolitionist Sisterhood: Women's Political Culture in Antebellum America,* 251; Sumler-Lewis, "The Fortens of Philadelphia," 99–100; Stevenson, *The Journals,* 1:115.

90. Willi Coleman, "Architects of a Vision: Black Women and Their Antebellum Quest for Political and Social Equality," 28; Shirley J. Yee, "Organizing for Racial Justice: Black Women and the Dynamics of Race and Sex in Female Antislavery Societies, 1832–1860," 48. See Yee, *Black Women Abolitionists,* 112–36.

91. Richardson, *Maria W. Stewart,* 8, 9, 20.

92. Ibid., 57.

93. Ibid., 12, 18–19; Walker, *David Walker's Appeal,* 2.

94. Richardson, *Maria W. Stewart,* 22, 72, 73.

95. See R. J. M. Blackett, *Beating Against the Barriers: The Lives of Six Nineteenth-Century Afro-Americans,* 87–90.

96. M[ary] A[nn] S[hadd] Cary to Thomas F. Cary, n.d., Moorland-Spingarm Research Center, Mary Ann Shadd Cary Papers, Howard University, Washington, DC.

97. Lynn M. Hudson, *The Making of 'Mammy Pleasant': A Black Entrepreneur in Nineteenth-Century San Francisco,* 24–43; Clinton, *Harriet Tubman,* 128–32; Humez, *Harriet Tubman,* 32–35, 38–39; Larson, *Bound for the Promised Land,* 157–60, 174–75.

98. Frances Smith Foster, ed., *A Brighter Coming Day: A Frances Ellen Watkins Harper Reader,* 49–50. See page 48 for a November 14, 1859, letter by Watkins to Mary Brown, wife of John Brown, in which she enclosed a "few dollars as a token of my gratitude, reverence and love."

99. Michael P. Johnson, *Abraham Lincoln, Slavery, and the Civil War: Selected Writings and Speeches,* 108, 111, 115; Henry Steele Commager, ed., *Documents of American History,* 386, 388; John Niven, *The Coming of the Civil War, 1837–1861,* 141.

100. Still, *The Underground Rail Road,* 765; James M. McPherson, *Ordeal by Fire: The Civil War and Reconstruction,* 157–58. President Lincoln countermanded Fremont's order, which had horrified Unionists who declared they would defect to the Confederates if the order stood.

101. Still, *The Underground Rail Road,* 765; Richardson, *Maria W. Stewart,* 45.

7. The Civil War and Emancipation: Freedom for All

1. See Leon F. Litwack, *Been in the Storm So Long: The Aftermath of Slavery*, 64–103.

2. Joseph T. Glatthaar, *Forged in Battle: The Civil War Alliance of Black Soldiers and White Officers*, 3, 6–7; Thomas Wentworth Higginson, *Army Life in a Black Regiment*, 27, 35. See James M. McPherson, *Ordeal by Fire: The Civil War and Reconstruction*, 349.

3. McPherson, *Ordeal by Fire*, 350–51; John Hope Franklin and Alfred A. Moss Jr., *From Slavery to Freedom: A History of Negro Americans*, 227; James G. Hollandsworth Jr., *The Louisiana Native Guards: The Black Military Experience During the Civil War*, 70.

4. Eighth Census of the United States, 1850 Population Schedule, National Archives, Washington, DC; Eric Foner, *Reconstruction: America's Unfinished Revolution, 1863–1877*, 1.

5. Dorothy Sterling, ed., *We Are Your Sisters: Black Women in the Nineteenth Century*, 243; Brenda Stevenson, ed., *The Journals of Charlotte Forten Grimké*, 3: 428–30; Brenda Stevenson, "Charlotte Forten (1837–1914)," 291; Susie King Taylor, *Reminiscences of My Life in Camp With the 33d United States Colored Troops Late 1st S.C. Volunteers*, 18; Foner, *Reconstruction*, 1–2.

6. Dudley H. Miles, ed., *The Photographic History of the Civil War, in Ten Volumes*, 9:176, 178.

7. Dudley Taylor Cornish, *The Sable Arm: Negro Troops in the Union Army, 1861–1865*, 229–30; McPherson, *Ordeal by Fire*, 360; Jim Cullen, "'I's a Man Now': Gender and African American Men," 82. See Iver Bernstein, *The New York City Draft Riots: Their Significance for American Society and Politics in the Age of the Civil War;* Matthew Frye Jacobson, *Whiteness of a Different Color: European Immigrants and the Alchemy of Race*, 52–56; David Roediger, *The Wages of Whiteness: Race and the Making of the American Working Class*, 173–74.

8. See Leslie M. Harris, "From Abolitionist Amalgamators to 'Rulers of the Five Points': The Discourse of Interracial Sex and Reform in Antebellum New York City," 191–212; Bernstein, *New York City Draft Riots*, 30–31.

9. Maritcha Remond Lyon, "Memories of Yesterday All of Which I Saw and Part of Which I Was: An Autobiography," 8–9 Williamson Collection, Schomburg Center for Research in Black Culture, New York, New York; Sterling, *We Are Your Sisters*, 232; McPherson, *Ordeal by Fire*, 360; Bernstein, *New York City Draft Riots*, 6–8, 10, 25–29; Fanny Jackson-Coppin, *Reminiscences of School Life, and Hints on Teaching*, 18.

10. Sterling, *We Are Your Sisters*, 233.

11. Bernstein, *New York City Draft Riots*, 28–30; Glatthaar, *Forged in Battle*, 140; Sterling, *We Are Your Sisters*, 233. See Robyn Wiegman, "The Anatomy of Lynching."

12. Glatthaar, *Forged in Battle*, 140; Edwin S. Redkey, ed., *A Grand Army of Black Men: Letters from African-American Soldiers in the Union Army, 1861–1865*, 28.

13. Ella Forbes, *African American Women During the Civil War*, 3; Foner, *Reconstruction*, 8; McPherson, *Ordeal by Fire*, 355.

14. Jane Rhodes, *Mary Ann Shadd Cary: The Black Press and Protest in the Nineteenth Century*, 153–54; Sterling, *We Are Your Sisters*, 258; Jason H. Silverman,

"Mary Ann Shadd and the Search for Equality," 1271; Paul A. Cimbala, "Mary Ann Shadd Cary and Black Abolitionism," 36.

15. McPherson, *Ordeal by Fire,* 254, 271; Edward L. Pierce, "The Contrabands at Fortress Monroe," 632, 633–35; Forbes, *African American Women,* 10–11.

16. Victor B. Howard, "The Civil War in Kentucky: The Slave Claims His Freedom," 246–57; C. Peter Ripley, "The Black Family in Transition, 1860–1865," 375.

17. Ira Berlin and Leslie S. Rowland, eds., *Families and Freedom: A Documentary History of African-American Kinship in the Civil War Era,* 97.

18. Howard P. Nash Jr., *Stormy Petrel: The Life and Times of General Benjamin F. Butler, 1818–1893,* 184–85; Leslie A. Schwalm, *A Hard Fight for We: Women's Transition from Slavery to Freedom in South Carolina,* 90; Noralee Frankel, "The Southern Side of 'Glory': Mississippi African-American Women During the Civil War," 335–39; Jane E. Schultz, "Race, Gender, and Bureaucracy: Civil War Army Nurses and the Pension Bureau," 47.

19. Howard, "The Civil War in Kentucky," 251; Herbert G. Gutman, *The Black Family in Slavery and Freedom, 1750–1925,* 371–73. See Berlin and Rowland, *Families and Freedom,* 102–7, 110–14; Richard Sears, "John G. Fee, Camp Nelson, and Kentucky Blacks, 1864–1865," 29–45.

20. Glatthaar, *Forged in Battle,* 169–70; Schwalm, *A Hard Fight for We,* 141. See Redkey, *A Grand Army of Black Men,* 229–31; James M. McPherson, *The Negro's Civil War: How American Blacks Felt and Acted During the War for the Union,* 193–203.

21. Joseph T. Glatthaar, "The Civil War through the Eyes of a Sixteen-Year-Old Black Officer: The Letters of Lieutenant John H. Crowder of the 1st Louisiana Native Guard," 204–5; Glatthaar, *Forged in Battle,* 171–72; Hollandsworth, *The Louisiana Native Guards,* 28. Stars's name is also spelled "Starrs."

22. John H. Crowder, Lieut (hereafter cited as JHC) to Dear Mother, February 6, 1863, May 1, 1863, May 4, 1863, May 5, 1863, May 15, 1863, John H. Crowder, File #370173, Record Group 105, National Archives (hereafter cited as NA); Glatthaar, "The Civil War," 211, 214–15.

23. JHC to Dear Mother, May 1, 1863, May 4, 1863, May 5, 1863, Crowder Pension File, NA; Mother's Brief #193580, Crowder Pension File, NA; Glatthaar, "The Civil War," 214–15.

24. Redkey, *A Grand Army of Black Men,* 2; Glatthaar, *Forged in Battle,* 169–73 (emphasis added).

25. See Drew Gilpin Faust, "'Trying to Do a Man's Business': Slavery, Violence, and Gender in the American Civil War," 197–214; Redkey, *A Grand Army of Black Men,* 237, 243. See also LeeAnn Whites, *The Civil War as a Crisis in Gender, Augusta, Georgia, 1860–1890.*

26. Glatthaar, *Forged in Battle,* 173; Cullen, "'I's a Man Now,'" 83; Redkey, *A Grand Army of Black Men,* 229–30.

27. Glatthaar, *Forged in Battle,* 175; Redkey, *A Grand Army of Black Men,* 242–44.

28. Ira Berlin et al., eds., *Freedom: A Documentary History of Emancipation, 1861–1867* Series 2: *The Black Military Experience,* 659, 714; Frankel, "The Southern Side of 'Glory'," 339; Noralee Frankel, *Freedom's Women: Black Women and Families in Civil War Era Mississippi,* 31–35, 39–40; Schwalm, *A Hard Fight for We,* 103; Taylor, *Reminiscences of My Life,* 16.

29. McPherson, *The Negro's Civil War,* 135, 136–39.

30. Elizabeth Keckley, *Behind the Scenes, or Thirty Years a Slave, and Four Years in the White House*, 47, 105; Ervin L. Jordan Jr., *Black Confederates and Afro-Yankees in Civil War Virginia*, 119; Forbes, *African American Women During the Civil War*, 196–97. See Jennifer Fleischner, *Mrs. Lincoln and Mrs. Keckly: The Remarkable Story of the Friendship Between a First Lady and a Former Slave*, 87–88.

31. Keckley, *Behind the Scenes*, 112–14. See Forbes, *African American Women*, 196–97.

32. Keckley, *Behind the Scenes*, 114–16; Sterling, *We Are Your Sisters*, 250; McPherson, *The Negro's Civil War*, 138–39. See Robert W. Schoeberlein, "A Fair to Remember: Maryland Women in Aid of the Union," for a discussion of general relief efforts.

33. Taylor, *Reminiscences*, iv, 8–9, 11, 26.

34. Taylor, introduction to *Reminiscences*.

35. C. Peter Ripley, Roy E. Finkenbine, Michael F. Hembree, and Donald Yacovone, eds., *Witness for Freedom: African American Voices on Race, Slavery, and Emancipation*, 245 (emphasis in the original); Sterling, *We Are Your Sisters*, 259–60; Catherine Clinton, *Harriet Tubman: The Road to Freedom*, 164–68; Jean M. Humez, *Harriet Tubman: The Life and the Life Stories*, 56–61; Kate Clifford Larson, *Bound for the Promised Land: Harriet Tubman, Portrait of an American Hero*, 212–17.

36. Lisa Y. King, "In Search of Women of African Descent Who Served in the Civil War Union Navy," 302–9.

37. Catharine Johnson, Diary, August 16, 1864, William T. Johnson and Family Memorial Papers, Louisiana and Lower Mississippi Valley Collections, Louisiana State University, Baton Rouge; Virginia Meacham Gould, ed., *Chained to the Rock of Adversity: To Be Free, Black, and Female in the Old South*, 70–71.

38. Jordan, *Black Confederates and Afro-Yankees*, 216–17; Ira Berlin, *Slaves Without Masters: The Free Negro in the Antebellum South*, 386–87; Michael P. Johnson and James L. Roark, *Black Masters: A Free Family of Color in the Old South*, 301–2, 305–7.

39. Johnson and Roark, *Black Masters*, 306, 307.

40. Carter G. Woodson, ed., *The Mind of the Negro as Reflected in Letters Written during the Crisis, 1800–1860*, 544.

41. Stevenson, *The Journals*, 4:494.

42. Ibid.; Benjamin Quarles, *The Negro in the Civil War*, 17; John Crimprich and Robert C. Mainfort Jr., "The Fort Pillow Massacre: A Statistical Note," 830.

43. Stevenson, *The Journals*, 4:495.

44. Sarah Bradford, *Harriet Tubman: The Moses of Her People*, 97; Sterling, *We Are Your Sisters*, 259; Larson, *Bound for the Promised Land*, 221; Humez, *Harriet Tubman*, 62; Taylor, *Reminiscences*, 31–32.

45. Schultz, "Race, Gender, and Bureaucracy," 48, 55. See *General Orders Affecting the Volunteer Force. Adjutant General's Office, 1864*, 6. See Civil War Pension files for Rebecca Albert, File #52844; Catherine Anderson, File #780473; Diana Benton, File #71023; Mary E. Green, File #542652; Abby Harris, File #161519; Pattie Manning, File #822862; Sarah F. Prichard, File #436683; Lucy A. Roberts, File #167701; and Sophia Shears, File #103486, Record Group 15, National Archives, Washington, DC.

46. Schultz, "Race, Gender, and Bureaucracy," 53, 55.

47. See John Cimprich, "The Fort Pillow Massacre: Assessing the Evidence," 150–68.

48. Ibid., 155–56, 164–65; Cimprich and Mainfort, "The Fort Pillow Massacre," 835–36; McPherson, *The Negro's Civil War*, 220–26; Franklin and Moss, *From Slavery to Freedom*, 241–42.

49. John Hope Franklin, *The Emancipation Proclamation*, 20–21, 106.

50. Booker T. Washington, *Up from Slavery: An Autobiography*, 24–26.

51. Leslie A. Schwalm, " 'Sweet Dreams of Freedom': Freedwomen's Reconstruction of Life and Labor in Lowcountry South Carolina," 9.

52. See Kent Anderson Leslie, *Woman of Color, Daughter of Privilege: Amanda America Dickson, 1849–1893*, 52, 57–58, 64, 70–72, 104; Leland Winfield Meyer, *The Life and Times of Colonel Richard M. Johnson of Kentucky*, 311, 317–23; Wilma King, "Within the Professional Household: Slave Children in the Antebellum South," 525, 532–33, 539–40.

53. Michael P. Johnson and James L. Roark, *Black Masters: A Free Family of Color in the Old South*, 14–15, 101–6.

54. See Sharon Ann Holt, "Making Freedom Pay: Freedpeople Working for Themselves, North Carolina, 1865–1900," 229–62.

55. Washington, *Up from Slavery*, 20–21; James D. Anderson, *The Education of Blacks in the South, 1860–1935*, 5–78. See Stevenson, *The Journals*; Elizabeth Hyde Botume, *The First Days amongst the Contrabands*; Elizabeth Jacoway, *Yankee Missionaries in the South: The Penn School Experiment*.

56. See Ellen N. Lawson and Marlene Merrill, "Antebellum Black Coeds at Oberlin College," 18–21; Wilma King Hunter, "Three Women at Tuskegee, 1882–1925: The Wives of Booker T. Washington," 76–81.

57. Charlotte Forten, At Sea, Monday, October 27, 1862, Charlotte Forten Grimké Papers, Moorland-Spingarn Collection, Howard University, Washington, DC; Stevenson, *The Journals*, 3:391; Stevenson, "Charlotte Forten," 3:290.

58. Charlotte Forten, "Life on the Sea Islands," Part 1, 593–94; Stevenson, *The Journals*, 3:402.

59. Stevenson, *The Journals*, 3:422, 4:499; Tryphena Blanche Holder Fox to Anna Rose Holder, June 24, 1860, Fox Papers, MDAH.

60. Addie Brown to My Dear Sister, January 16, 1866, Primus Family Papers, CHS.

61. Rebecca Primus to Family, April 20, 1867, May 18, 1867, PFP.

62. Stevenson, *The Journals*, 3:402, 406.

63. Frankel, *Freedom's Women*, 96; Harriet Jacobs, *Incidents in the Life of a Slave Girl: Written by Herself*, 11. See Laura Fair, "Dressing Up: Clothing, Class, and Gender in Post-Abolition Zanzibar."

64. Forbes, *African American Women*, 113.

65. Stevenson, *The Journals*, 3:403.

66. Whittington B. Johnson, "A Black Teacher and Her School in Reconstruction Darien: The Correspondence of Hettie Sabattie and J. Murray Hoag, 1868–1869," 90–105.

67. Johnson, "A Black Teacher and Her School," 100–101.

68. RP to Dear Parents & Sister, March 10, 1867, Primus Papers, CHS.

69. RP to Dear Parents & Sister, April 7, 1866, Primus Papers, CHS.

70. RP to Family, March 23, 1867, Primus Papers, CHS.

71. Sterling, *We Are Your Sisters*, 354–55.

72. "Memphis Riots and Massacres," Report No. 101, House of Representatives, 39th Cong., 1st sess. (July 25, 1866), 13–19; Beverly Greene Bond, " 'Till Fair Aurora Rise'; African-American Women in Memphis, Tennessee, 1840–1915," 69–71, 89–92; Hannah Rosen, "Not That Sort of Women: Race, Gender, and Sexual Violence during the Memphis Riot of 1866," 267–93.

73. Susan Brownmiller, *Against Our Will: Men, Women, and Rape*, 32, 37–38; Sterling, *We Are Your Sisters*, 355; Catherine Clinton, "Bloody Terrain: Freedwomen, Sexuality, and Violence During Reconstruction," 139, 147.

74. Frances Smith Foster, ed., *Minnie's Sacrifice, Sowing and Reaping, Trial and Triumph: Three Rediscovered Novels by Frances E. W. Harper*, 85.

75. Elsa Barkley Brown, "Negotiating and Transforming the Public Sphere: African American Political Life in the Transition from Slavery to Freedom," 109, 119, 121–24; Elsa Barkley Brown, "To Catch the Vision of Freedom: Reconstructing Southern Black Women's Political History, 1865–1880," 72–73.

Women were among the September 19, 1868, crowd of Republican politicians in Camilla, Georgia, when a rally on the courthouse square ended in pandemonium. Whites fired into the crowd killing nine of the rally-goers. Included among this number was at least one black woman. Intimidation was so great it kept all blacks away from the Camilla polls on election day. See Lee Formwalt, "Petitioning Congress for Protection: A Black View of Reconstruction at the Local Level," 305–22; Lee Formwalt, "The Camilla Massacre of 1868: Racial Violence as Political Propaganda," 399–426.

76. Frances E. W. Harper, *Sketches of Southern Life*; Sterling, *We Are Your Sisters*, 369–70.

77. RP to My Dear Parents & Sister, April 7, 1866, Primus Papers, CHS.

78. Keckley, *Behind the Scenes*, 139.

Bibliography

Newspapers

Arkansas State Gazette and Democrat
Douglass' Monthly
The Liberator
The North Star

Official Records

Adams County Courthouse, Natchez, Mississippi
    William Barland, Last Will and Testament
    B. F. Conner, Last Will and Testament
    Alexander Parker, Last Will and Testament
    Sarah Robinson, Last Will and Testament
Baldwin County Probate Court, Milledgeville, Georgia
    Registry of Free Persons of Color, 1832–1864
City Archives, Philadelphia, Pennsylvania
    Alms House Female Register, 1803–1887
    Alms House Hospital Register
    Female Convict Docket, 1838–1866
    Guardians of the Poor Alms House Hospital Register
    Prostitute's Register
Georgia Department of Archives and History, Atlanta, Georgia
    Register of Free Persons of Color, Camden County, 1818
    Register of Free Persons of Color, Chatham County, 1826–1835
    Register of Free Persons of Color, Columbia County, 1819–1836
    Register of Free Persons of Color, Talliferro County 1829–1861
Kentucky Department for Libraries and Archives, Frankfort, Kentucky
    Order Books, Jefferson County

National Archives, Washington, DC
     Civil War Pension Files
          Record Group 15
          Rebecca Albert File #52844
          Catherine Anderson File #780473
          Diana Benton File #71023
          John H. Crowder File #370173
          Mary E. Green File #542652
          Abby Harris File #161519
          Pattie Manning File #822862
          Sarah F. Prichard File #436683
          Lucy A. Roberts File #167701
          Sophia Shears File #103486
     House of Representatives Record, "Memphis Riots and Massacres,"
          Report No. 101, 39th Cong., 1st sess. (July 25, 1866), 13–19.
Parish Clerk, Natchitoches, Louisiana
     Last Will and Testament of Betsy Sompayrac
     Succession of Betsy Sompayrac
     Succession of Marie Rose Metoyer
     Succession of Suzanne Metoyer
*Population of the United States in 1860: Compiled from Original Returns of
     the Eighth Census by Joseph C. G. Kennedy.* Washington, DC: Govern-
     ment Printing Office, 1864.
Preliminary Report on the Eight Census, 1860 by Jos. C. G. Kennedy. Washing-
     ton, DC: Government Printing Office, 1862.
State Slavery Statutes. Edited by Paul Finkelman. Frederick, MD: Univer-
     sity Publications of America Academic Edition, 1989. Microfiche.

State Statutes

The Code of Mississippi. Jackson: Price and Fall, 1848.
The Code of Virginia. 2nd ed. Westport, CT: Negro Universities Press, 1970.
General Laws of the State of Illinois. Springfield: Lanphies and Walker, 1853.
Laws of Illinois. Vandalia: Robert Blackwell, 1831.
Laws of Kentucky. Frankfort: Hodges, 1851.
Laws of the State of Indiana. Indianapolis: J. P. Chapman, 1853.
Laws of the State of Missouri. Jefferson City: Allen Hammond, 1843.
The Revised Code of Mississippi. Jackson: E. Barksdale, 1857.
The Revised Laws of Indiana. Indianapolis: Douglass and Maguire, 1831.

The Revised Statutes of the State of Missouri. St. Louis: J. W. Dougherty, 1845.

The Statutes of Iowa. Dubuque: Russell and Reeves, 1839.

Statutes of Ohio and the Northwest Territory from 1788 to 1833. Vol. 1. Cincinnati: Corey and Fairbank, 1833.

Territorial Laws of Michigan. Lansing: W. George, 1825.

Census

DeBow, J. D. B. *Statistical View of the United States, being a Compendium of the Seventh Census.* Washington, DC: A. O. P. Nicholson, 1854.

Eighth Census of the U.S., 1860 Population Schedule, Duval County, Florida.

Eighth Census of the U.S., 1860 Population Schedule, Leon County, Florida.

Eighth Census of the U.S., 1860 Population Schedule, Plaquemines Parish, Louisiana.

Seventh Census of the U.S., 1850, Population Schedule Duval County, Florida.

Seventh Census of the U.S., 1850, Population Schedule, Leon County, Florida.

Manuscripts

Amistad Research Center, Tulane University, New Orleans, Louisiana
    American Missionary Association Archives
    Ruffin-Helsip Collection
Arkansas History Commission, Little Rock, Arkansas
Bentley Library, University of Michigan, Ann Arbor, Michigan
    Morgan Family Papers
Center for American History, University of Texas, Austin, Texas
    Natchez Trace Collection (2E773)
College of Charleston, Charleston, South Carolina
    Friendly Moralist Society Minutes
    Special Collections
Connecticut Historical Society, Hartford, Connecticut
    Manus Papers, #83542
    Primus Family Papers (microfilm)

Delaware Public Archives, Hall of Records, Dover, Delaware
    Enrolled Bills (microfilm)
    General Reference #706, Negroes Kidnapped
    John Harold Sprinkle Jr., "'Let Their Situation at Least Engage Our
        Sympathy, if We Can Afford Them No Relief': Patterns of
        Occupation and Residence among Free Blacks in Early Nine-
        teenth Century Wilmington, Delaware"
Hampton University Archives, Hampton, Virginia
    American Missionary Association Microfilm
    Early Summer School Files
Historic New Orleans, New Orleans, Louisiana
    Cane River Collection
Historical Society of Pennsylvania, Philadelphia, Pennsylvania
    Order Book, Daughters of Africa
Library Company of Philadelphia, Philadelphia, Pennsylvania
    Cogdell-Sanders Papers
    Dickerson Family Papers
Library of Congress, Washington, DC
    Frederick Douglass Papers
    Thomas Sewall Papers
    Enoch Tucker Papers
Library of Virginia, Richmond, Virginia
    Auditor of Public Accounts, Reel 1320
Louisiana and Lower Mississippi Valley Collections, Louisiana State
        University, Baton Rouge, Louisiana
    William T. Johnson and Family Memorial Papers
    Katharine Johnson Diary
Mississippi Department of Archives and History, Jackson, Mississippi
    Tryphena Blanche Holder Fox Papers
Missouri Historical Society, St. Louis, Missouri
    Dexter Tiffany Collection
Moorland-Spingarn Collection, Howard University, Washington, DC
    Mary Ann Shadd Cary Papers
    Charlotte Forten Grimké Papers
Ohio Historical Society, Columbus, Ohio
    Polly Case
Schomburg Center for Research in Black Culture, New York, New York
    Williamson Collection
Sisters of the Holy Family Archives, New Orleans, Louisiana
    "'The Greatest Gift of All': A Pictorial Biography"

South Carolina Department of Archives and History, Columbia, South
    Carolina
    Barnwell County Judge of Probate Manumission Book, 1803–1845
        (typewritten transcription, Works Progress Administration
        Project 65–33–118, 1938)
    General Assembly Papers
    Legislative Committee Reports
    Petitions
Southern Historical Collection, University of North Carolina, Chapel
    Hill, North Carolina
    Silas Everett Fales Papers
Special Collection, College of Charleston, Charleston, South Carolina
    Friendly Moralist Society Minutes
Tennessee Department of State Library and Archives, Nashville, Tennessee
    Nashville City and Business Directories
Texas State Library and Archives Commission, Austin, Texas
    Mary Madison Memorial
    Emily West Papers
University of South Carolina, Columbia, South Carolina
    Lawton Family Papers
University of Texas, Austin, Texas
    Natchez Trace Collection, Center for American History
Virginia State Library, Richmond, Virginia
    Auditor of Public Accounts, Reel 1320

Unpublished Manuscripts

Bogger, Tommy Lee. "The Slave and Free Black Community in Norfolk,
    1775–1865." PhD diss., University of Virginia, 1976.
Bond, Beverly Greene. "'Till Fair Aurora Rise'; African-American Women
    in Memphis, Tennessee, 1840–1915." PhD diss., University of Mem-
    phis, 1996.
Brekus, Catherine A. "'Let Your Women Keep Silence in the Churches':
    Female Preaching and Evangelical Religion in America, 1740–1845."
    PhD diss., Yale University, 1993.
Davidson, Nancy Reynolds. "E. W. Clay: American Political Caricaturist
    of the Jacksonian Era." PhD diss., University of Michigan, 1980.
Diaz, Arlene J. "'Ciudadanas' and 'Padres de Familia': Gender Conflicts
    in the Early Venezuelan Republic." American Bar Foundation Work-
    ing Paper #9412, Department of History, University of Minnesota.

Durett, Dan. "Free Blacks in Selected Georgia Cities, 1820–1860." Atlanta University, M.A. thesis, 1973.

Garfield, Michelle Nichole. "'The Pen is ours to Wield': Black Literary Society Women in 1830s Philadelphia." PhD diss., Duke University, 2002.

Gould, Lois Virginia Meacham. "In Full Enjoyment of Their Liberty: The Free Women of Color of the Gulf Ports of New Orleans, Mobile, and Pensacola, 1769–1860." PhD diss., Emory University, 1991.

Hansen, Karen V. "'No *Kisses* is Like Youres': An Erotic Friendship Between Two African-American Women During the Mid-Nineteenth Century."

Hudson, Lynn Maria. "When 'Mammy' Becomes a Millionaire: Mary Ellen Pleasant, an African American Entrepreneur." PhD diss., Indiana University, 1995.

Hunter, Wilma King. "Coming of Age: Hollis B. Frissell and the Emergence of Hampton Institute, 1893–1917." PhD diss., Indiana University, 1982.

Kinshasa, Kwando Mbiassi. "Free Blacks' Quest for National Identity: Debates in the African American Press on Assimilation and Emigration." PhD diss., New York University, 1983.

McNeil, Sarah L. Jones. "Biography of Zachariah Morgan." Morgan Family Papers. Bentley Library, University of Michigan, Ann Arbor, Michigan.

Montesano, Philip. "Some Aspects of the Free Negro Question in San Francisco, 1849–1870." Thesis, University of San Francisco, 1967.

Powell, Frances LaJune Johnson. "A Study of the Structure of the Freed Black Family in Washington, DC, 1850–1880." D.A. thesis, Catholic University of America, 1980.

Reidy, Joseph Patrick. "Master and Slave Planters and Freedmen: The Transition from Slavery to Freedom in Central Georgia, 1820–1880." PhD diss., Northern Illinois University, 1982.

Ribiansky, Nicole. "Property Owning Free African American Women." Seminar in African American History Paper, HST 870, presented April 26, 1995, Michigan State University, East Lansing, Michigan.

Schweninger, Loren, ed. *Microfilm Edition of Race, Slavery, and Free Blacks: Series I, Petitions to Southern Legislatures, 1777–1867.* Bethesda: University Publications of America, 1999.

Sprinkle, John Harold, Jr. "'Let Their Situation at Least Engage Our Sympathy, if We Can Afford Them No Relief': Patterns of Occupation and Residence among Free Blacks in Early Nineteenth-Century

Wilmington, Delaware." Delaware Public Archives, Hall of Records, Dover, Delaware.

Sumler-Lewis, Janice. "The Fortens of Philadelphia: An Afro-American Family and Nineteenth-Century Reform." PhD diss., Georgetown University, 1978.

Townsend, Thelma Marie. "Spiritual Autobiographies of Religious Activism by Black Women in the Antebellum Era." PhD diss., Michigan State University, 1992.

Wallace, Barbara Elizabeth. "'Fair Daughters of Africa': African American Women in Baltimore, 1790–1860." PhD diss., University of California, Los Angeles, 2001.

Wares, Lydia Jean. "Dress of the African American Woman in Slavery and Freedom: 1500 to 1935." PhD diss., Purdue University, 1981.

Wells, Donna M. "Frederick Douglass and the Power of Photograph: Annotated Bibliography." Undated working paper.

Published Primary Sources

Adams, Charles Francis. *Familiar Letters of John Adams and His Wife Abigail Adams, During the Revolution With a Memoir of Mrs. Adams.* Freeport, NY: Books for Libraries Press, 1970.

Barksdale, Richard, and Keneth Kinnamon, eds. *Black Writers of America: A Comprehensive Anthology.* New York: Macmillan Company, 1972.

Berlin, Ira, Thavolia Glymph, Steven F. Miller, Joseph P. Reidy, Leslie S. Rowland, and Julie Saville, eds. *Freedom: A Documentary History of Emancipation, 1861–1867.* Series 1, vol. 3: *The Wartime Genesis of Free Labor.* Cambridge: Cambridge University Press, 1990.

Berlin, Ira, Joseph P. Reidy, Leslie S. Rowland, eds. *Freedom: A Documentary History of Emancipation, 1861–1867.* Series 2: *The Black Military Experience.* Cambridge: Cambridge University Press, 1982.

Berlin, Ira, and Leslie S. Rowland, eds. *Families and Freedom: A Documentary History of African American Kinship in the Civil War Era.* New York: New Press, 1997.

Blassingame, John W., ed. *Slave Testimony: Two Centuries of Letters, Speeches, Interviews, and Autobiographies.* Baton Rouge: Louisiana State University Press, 1977.

Botume, Elizabeth Hyde. *The First Days amongst the Contrabands.* New York: Arno Press and New York Times, 1968.

Brown, William Wells. "Narrative of William Wells Brown, a Fugitive

Slave." In *Puttin' On Ole Massa: The Slave Narratives of Henry Bibb, William Wells Brown, and Solomon Northup.* Edited by Gilbert Osofsky, 173–223. New York: Harper Torchbooks, 1969.

Bruns, Roger, ed. *Am I Not a Man and a Brother: The Antislavery Crusade of Revolutionary America, 1688–1788.* New York: Chelsea House Publishing, 1977.

Butterfield, L. H., Wendell D. Garrett, and Marjorie E. Sprague, eds. *Adams Family Correspondence.* Vol. 1: *December 1761–May 1776.* Cambridge: Belknap Press, 1963.

Catterall, Helen Tunnicliff, ed. *Judicial Cases Concerning American Slavery and the Negro.* 5 vols. Washington: Carnegie Institute of Washington, 1926.

Chesnut, Mary Boykin. *A Diary from Dixie.* Edited by Ben Ames Williams. Boston: Houghton Mifflin, 1950.

Clamorgan, Cyprian. *The Colored Aristocracy of St. Louis.* St. Louis: n.p., 1858.

Commager, Henry Steele, ed. *Documents of American History.* 6th ed. New York: Appleton-Century-Crofts, 1958.

Crane, Elaine Foreman, ed. *The Diary of Elizabeth Drinker.* Boston: Northeastern University Press, 1991.

Dawson, William C. *A Compilation of the Laws of the State of Georgia.* Milledgeville: Grantland and Orme, 1831.

Delaney, Lucy A. "From the Darkness Cometh the Light or Struggles for Freedom." In *Six Women's Slave Narratives.* Edited by Henry Louis Gates Jr. New York: Oxford University Press, 1988.

Douglass, Frederick. *Life and Times of Frederick Douglass, Written by Himself: His Early Life as a Slave, His Escape from Bondage, and His Complete History.* New York: Collier Books, 1962.

———. *My Bondage and My Freedom.* New York: Dover Publications, 1969.

———. *Narrative of the Life of Frederick Douglass: An American Slave Written by Himself.* In *Frederick Douglass: The Narrative, and Selected Writings.* Edited by Michael Meyer. New York: Random House, 1984.

Elaw, Zilpha. "Memoirs of the Life, Religious Experience, Ministerial Travels, and Labors of Mrs. Zilpha Elaw." In *Sisters of the Spirit: Three Black Women's Autobiographies of the Nineteenth Century.* Edited by William L. Andrews. Bloomington: Indiana University Press, 1986.

Elizabeth. "Memoir of Old Elizabeth, a Colored Woman." In *Six Women's Slave Narratives: The Schomburg Library of Nineteenth-Century Black Women Writers.* Edited by Henry Louis Gates Jr. New York: Oxford University Press, 1988.

Finkelman, Paul, ed. [John K. Furman]. "A Faithful Report of the Trial of Doctor William Little, on an indictment for an assault and battery, committed upon the body of his lawful wife, Mrs. Jane Little, A Black Lady." In *Free Blacks, Slaves, and Slaveowners in Civil and Criminal Courts: The Pamphlet Literature*, 103–11. Series 6, vol. 1. New York: Garland, 1988.

———. *Slavery in the Courtroom: An Annotated Bibliography of Cases.* Washington: Library of Congress Government Printing Office, 1985.

Foner, Philip S., ed. *Frederick Douglass on Women's Rights.* Westport: Greenwood Press, 1976.

———. *The Life and Writings of Frederick Douglass: Pre–Civil War Decade, 1850–1860.* New York: International Publishers, 1950.

Foote, Julia A. J. "A Brand Plucked from the Fire: An Autobiographical Sketch by Mrs. Julia A. J. Foote." In *Sisters of the Spirit: Three Black Women's Autobiographies of the Nineteenth Century.* Edited by William L. Andrews. Bloomington: Indiana University Press, 1986.

Forten, Charlotte. "Life on the Sea Islands." *Atlantic Monthly* Part I (May 1864): 587–96.

Foster, Frances Smith, ed. *A Brighter Coming Day: A Frances Ellen Watkins Harper Reader.* New York: Feminist Press, 1990.

Freeman, M. H. "The Educational Wants of the Free Colored People." *The Anglo-African Magazine* 1 (April 1859). In William Loren Katz, ed., *The American Negro: His History and Literature*, 116–17. New York: Arno Press and New York Times, 1968.

General Orders Affecting the Volunteer Force. Adjutant General's Office, 1864. Washington, DC: Government Printing Office, 1865.

Gilbert, Olive, ed. *Narrative of Sojourner Truth: A Bondswoman of Olden Time, Emancipated by the New York Legislature in the Early Part of the Present Century; with a History of her Labours and Correspondence Drawn from her "Book of Life."* Battle Creek: published by the author, 1878.

Gould, Virginia Meacham, ed. *Chained to the Rock of Adversity: To Be Free, Black, and Female in the Old South.* Athens: University of Georgia Press, 1998.

Griffin, Farah Jasmine, ed. *Beloved Sisters and Loving Friends: Letters from Rebecca Primus of Royal Oak, Maryland, and Addie Brown of Hartford, Connecticut, 1854–1868.* New York: Alfred A. Knopf, 1999.

Guild, June Purcell, ed. *Black Laws of Virginia: A Summary of the Legislative Acts of Virginia Concerning Negroes from Earliest Times to the Present.* Richmond: Whittet and Snepperson, 1936.

Harper, Frances E. W. *Sketches of Southern Life.* http://www.etext.lib.virginia
.edu/toc/modeng/public/HarLife.html.

Higginson, Thomas Wentworth. *Army Life in a Black Regiment.* New York:
Collier Books, 1962.

Hogan, William Ransom, and Edwin Adams Davis, eds. *William Johnson's
Natchez: The Ante-Bellum Diary of a Free Negro.* Baton Rouge: Louisiana State University Press, 1951.

Jackson, Rebecca. *Gifts of Power: The Writings of Rebecca Jackson, Black
Visionary, Shaker Eldress.* Edited by Jean McMahon Humez. Amherst:
University of Massachusetts Press, 1981.

Jackson-Coppin, Fannie. *Reminiscences of School Life, and Hints on Teaching.* Philadelphia: A. M. E. Book Concerns, 1913.

Jacobs, Harriet. *Incidents in the Life of a Slave Girl: Written by Herself.* Edited
by Jean Fagan Yellin. Cambridge: Harvard University Press, 1987.

[Jacobs, John]. "A True Tale of Slavery." *The Leisure Hour: A Family Journal
of Instruction and Recreation* (London) 476 (February 7, 1861): 85–87;
(February 14, 1861): 108–110; (February 21, 1861): 125–27; (February
28, 1861): 139–41.

Jefferson, Thomas. *Notes on the State of Virginia.* Edited by William Peden.
New York: W. W. Norton, 1982.

Johnson, Clifton H., ed. *God Struck Me Dead: Religious Conversion Experiences and Autobiographies of Ex-slaves.* Philadelphia: Pilgrim Press,
1969.

Johnson, Michael P., ed. *Abraham Lincoln, Slavery, and the Civil War: Selected
Writings and Speeches.* Boston: Bedford/St. Martin, 2001.

Johnson, Michael P., and James L. Roark, eds. *No Chariot Let Down:
Charleston's Free People of Color on the Eve of the Civil War.* New York:
W. W. Norton, 1984.

Keckley, Elizabeth. *Behind the Scenes; or, Thirty Years a Slave, and Four Years
in the White House.* New York: Oxford University Press, 1988.

Kemble, Frances Anne. *Journal of a Residence on a Georgian Plantation in
1838–1839.* Athens: University of Georgia, 1984.

King, Wilma, ed. *A Northern Woman in the Plantation South: Letters of
Tryphena Blanche Holder Fox, 1856–1876.* Columbia: University of
South Carolina Press, 1993.

Lee, Jarena. "The Life and Religious Experience of Jarena Lee." In *Sisters
of the Spirit: Three Black Women's Autobiographies of the Nineteenth Century.* Edited by William L. Andrews. Bloomington: Indiana University Press, 1986.

Littlefield, Daniel F., ed. *The Life of Okah Tubbee.* Lincoln: University of
Nebraska Press, 1988.

Lockwood, Lewis C., ed. *Two Black Teachers During the Civil War: Mary S. Peake, the Colored Teacher at Fortress Monroe, and Charlotte Forten, Life on the Sea Islands.* New York: Arno Press and New York Times, 1969.

Miller, Randall, ed. *"Dear Master": Letters of a Slave Family.* Ithaca: Cornell University Press, 1978.

Northup, Solomon. *Twelve Years a Slave: Narrative of Solomon Northup, a Citizen of New York, Kidnapped in Washington City in 1841, and Rescued in 1853, From a Cotton Plantation Near the Red River in Louisiana.* Auburn: Derby and Miller, 1853.

———. "Twelve Years a Slave: Narrative of Solomon Northup." In *Puttin' On Ole Massa: The Slave Narratives of Henry Bibb, William Wells Brown, and Solomon Northup.* Edited by Gilbert Osofsky. New York: Harper Torchbooks, 1969.

Norton, Mary Beth, and Ruth M. Alexander, eds. *Major Problems in American Women's History.* 2nd ed. Lexington, MA: D. C. Heath, 1996.

Paul, Miss Susan. *Memoir of James Jackson: The Attentive and Obedient Scholar, Who Died in Boston, October 31, 1833, Aged Six Years and Eleven Months.* Edited by Lois Brown. Cambridge: Harvard University Press, 2000.

Perdue, Charles L., Jr., Thomas E. Barden, and Robert K. Phillips, eds. *Weevils in the Wheat: Interviews with Virginia Ex-Slaves.* Bloomington: Indiana University Press, 1980.

Potter, Eliza. *A Hairdresser's Experience in the High Life.* New York: Oxford University Press, 1991.

Prince, Nancy. *A Black Woman's Odyssey through Russia and Jamaica: The Narrative of Nancy Prince.* New York: Markus Wiener Publishing, 1990.

Rawick, George P., ed. *The American Slave: A Composite Autobiography.* 24 vols. Westport: Greenwood Press, 1972.

———. *The American Slave: A Composite Autobiography.* Supplement, series 1, 12 vols. Westport: Greenwood Press, 1977.

———. *The American Slave: A Composite Autobiography.* Supplement, series 2, 10 vols. Westport: Greenwood Press, 1979.

Redkey, Edwin S., ed. *A Grand Army of Black Men: Letters from African-American Soldiers in the Union Army, 1861–1865.* New York: Cambridge University Press, 1992.

"Register of Free Blacks Augusta County, Virginia," part 1. http://jefferson.village.edu/vshadow2/govdoc/fblack.html.

"Register of Free Negroes and Mulattoes in the Corporation of Staunton (Virginia)." http://jefferson.village.edu/vshadow2/govdoc/fblack.html.

Register of Trades of the Colored People in the City of Philadelphia and the Districts. Philadelphia: Merrihew and Gunn, 1838.

Richardson, Marilyn, ed. *Maria W. Stewart, America's First Black Political Writer: Essays and Speeches*. Bloomington: Indiana University Press, 1987.

Ripley, C. Peter, Roy E. Finkenbine, Michael F. Hembree, and Donald Yacovone, eds. *Witness for Freedom: African American Voices on Race, Slavery, and Emancipation*. 4 vols. Chapel Hill: University of North Carolina, 1993.

Ripley, C. Peter, ed. *The Black Abolitionist Papers: The United States, 1830–1846*. Chapel Hill: University of North Carolina Press, 1991.

Rose, Willie Lee, ed. *A Documentary History of Slavery in North America*. New York: Oxford University Press, 1976.

Schweninger, Loren, ed. *The Southern Debate over Slavery: Petitions to Southern Legislatures, 1778–1864*. Urbana: University of Illinois Press, 2001.

Shields, John C., ed. *The Collected Works of Phillis Wheatley*. New York: Oxford University Press, 1988.

Smith, Amanda Berry. *An Autobiography: The Story of the Lord's Dealings with Mrs Amanda Smith, Colored Evangelist; Containing an Account of her Life Work of Faith, and her Travels in America, England, Ireland, Scotland, India, and Africa, as an Independent Missionary*. Chicago: Afro-American Press, 1969.

Sterling, Dorothy, ed. *We Are Your Sisters: Black Women in the Nineteenth Century*. New York: W. W. Norton, 1984.

Stevenson, Brenda, ed. *The Journals of Charlotte Forten Grimké*. New York: Oxford University Press, 1988.

Stewart, Maria W. "Productions of Mrs. Maria W. Stewart." In *Spiritual Narratives*. New York: Oxford University Press, 1988.

Still, William. *The Underground Rail Road. A record of facts, authentic narratives, letters, & c., narrating the hardships, hairbreadth escapes and death struggles of the slaves in their efforts for freedom, as related by themselves and others, or the largest stockholders, and most liberal aiders and advisers, of the road*. Philadelphia: Porter and Coats, 1872.

Taylor, Susie King. *Reminiscences of My Life in Camp with the 33d United States Colored Troops Late 1st S.C. Volunteers*. Boston: published by author, 1992.

Truth, Sojourner. *Narrative of Sojourner Truth*. Edited by Margaret Washington. New York: Vintage Books, 1993.

———. *Narrative of Sojourner Truth: A Bondswoman of Olden Time Emancipated by the New York Legislature in the Early Part of the Present Century With a History of Her Labors and Correspondence Drawn from her Book of Life*. Chicago: Johnson Publishing, 1970.

Veney, Bethany. "The Narrative of Bethany Veney, A Slave Woman." In *Collected Black Women's Narratives*. Edited by Henry Louis Gates Jr. New York: Oxford University Press, 1988.

Walker, David. *David Walker's Appeal, in Four Articles: Together with A Preamble, to the Coloured Citizens of the World, but In Particular, and Very Expressly, to those of The United States of America*. Edited by Charles M. Wiltse. New York: Hill and Wang, 1965.

Washington, Booker T. *Up from Slavery: An Autobiography*. New York: Bantam, 1967.

[Willson, Joseph]. *Sketches of the Higher Class of Colored Society in Philadelphia by a Southerner*. Philadelphia: Merrihew and Thompson, Printers, 1841.

Woodson, Carter G., ed. *The Mind of the Negro as Reflected in Letters Written during the Crisis, 1800–1860*. New York: Russell and Russell, 1969.

Secondary Sources

Abzug, Robert H. "The Black Family During Reconstruction." In *Key Issues in Afro American Experience*, vol. 2: *Since 1865*. Edited by Nathan I. Huggins, Martin Kilson, and Daniel M. Fox, 26–43. New York: Harcourt, Brace, and Jovanovich, 1971.

Alexander, Adele Logan. *Ambiguous Lives: Free Women of Color in Rural Georgia, 1789–1879*. Fayetteville: University of Arkansas Press, 1991.

Alho, Ollie. *The Religion of the Slaves: A Study of the Religious Tradition and Behavior of Plantation Slaves in the United States 1830–1865*. Helsinki: Academia Scientiarum Fennica, 1976.

Anderson, James D. *The Education of Blacks in the South, 1860–1835*. Chapel Hill: University of North Carolina Press, 1988.

Ashcraft-Eason, Lillian. "Freedom among African American Servants and Slaves in the Seventeenth-Century British Colonies." In *Women and Freedom in Early America*. Edited by Larry D. Eldridge, 62–79. New York: New York University Press, 1997.

Bacon, Margaret Hope. "By Moral Force Alone: The Antislavery Women and Nonresistance." In *The Abolitionist Sisterhood: Women's Political Culture in Antebellum America*. Edited by Jean Fagan Yellin and John C. Van Horne, 275–97. Ithaca: Cornell University Press, 1994.

Bailyn, Bernard. *The Ideological Origins of the American Revolution*. Cambridge: Belknap Press, 1967.

Ball, Edward. *The Sweet Hell Inside: A Family History*. New York: William Morrow, 2001.

Battis, Emery. *Saints and Sectaries: Anne Hutchinson and the Antinomian Controversy in the Massachusetts Bay Colony.* Chapel Hill: University of North Carolina Press, 1962.

Bay, Mia. *The White Image in the Black Mind: African-American Ideas about White People, 1830–1925.* New York: Oxford University Press, 2000.

Bearden, Jim, and Linda Jean Butler. *Shadd: The Life and Times of Mary Shadd Cary.* Toronto: N. C. Press, 1977.

Bedini, Silvio A. *The Life of Benjamin Banneker.* New York: Charles Scribner's Sons, 1972.

Berlin, Ira. *Many Thousands Gone: The First Two Centuries of Slavery in North America.* Cambridge: Belknap Press of Harvard University Press, 1998.

————. *Slaves Without Masters: The Free Negro in the Antebellum South.* New York: Oxford University Press, 1981.

Bernstein, Iver. *The New York City Draft Riots: Their Significance for American Society and Politics in the Age of the Civil War.* New York: Oxford University Press, 1990.

Blackett, R. J. M. *Beating Against the Barriers: Biographical Essays in Nineteenth-Century Afro-American History.* Baton Rouge: Louisiana State University Press, 1986.

Blassingame, John W. *Black New Orleans, 1860–1880.* Chicago: University of Chicago Press, 1973.

Blewett, Mary H. *Men, Women, and Work: Class, Gender, and Protest in the New England Shoe Industry, 1780–1910.* Urbana: University of Illinois Press, 1988.

Bogger, Tommy L. *Free Blacks in Norfolk, Virginia, 1796–1860: The Darker Side of Freedom.* Charlottesville: University of Virginia Press, 1997.

Bond, Beverly Greene. "'The Extent of the Law': Free Women of Color in Antebellum Memphis, Tennessee." In *Negotiating Boundaries of Southern Womanhood: Dealing with the Powers That Be.* Edited by Janet L. Coryell, Thomas H. Appleton Jr., Anastatia Sims, and Sondra Gioia Treadway, 7–26. Columbia: University of Missouri Press, 2000.

Boyd, Melba Joyce. *Discarded Legacy: Politics and Poetics in the Life of Frances E. W. Harper, 1825–1911.* Detroit: Wayne State University, 1994.

Boydston, Jeanne. *Home and Work: Housework, Wages, and the Ideology of Labor in the Early Republic.* New York: Oxford University Press, 1990.

Bradford, Sarah. *Harriet Tubman: The Moses of Her People.* New York: Corinth Books, 1961.

Braxton, Joanne M. *Black Women Writing Autobiography: A Tradition within a Tradition.* Philadelphia: Temple University Press, 1989.

Braxton, Joanne M., and Sharon Zuber. "Silences in Harriet 'Linda Brent' Jacobs' *Incidents in the Life of a Slave Girl.*" In *Listening to Silences: New Essays in Feminist Criticism.* Edited by Elaine Hedges and Shelley Fisher Fishkin, 146–68. New York: Oxford University Press, 1994.

Breen, T. H., and Stephen Innes. *"Myne Owne Ground": Race and Freedom on Virginia's Eastern Shore, 1640–1676.* New York: Oxford University Press, 1980.

Brekus, Catherine A. *Female Preaching in America: Strangers and Pilgrims, 1740–1845.* Chapel Hill: University of North Carolina Press, 1999.

Brody, David. *Steelworkers in America: The Nonunion Era.* Cambridge: Harvard University Press, 1960.

Broussard, Albert S. *African-American Odyssey: The Stewarts, 1853–1963.* Lawrence: University of Kansas Press, 1998.

Brown, Elsa Barkley. "To Catch the Vision of Freedom: Reconstructing Southern Black Women's Political History, 1865–1880." In *African American Women and the Vote, 1837–1965.* Edited by Ann D. Gordon, Bettye Collier-Thomas, John H. Bracey, Arlene Voski Avakian, and Joyce Avrech Berkman, 66–99. Amherst: University of Massachusetts Press, 1997.

Brown, Kathleen M. *Good Wives, Nasty Wenches, and Anxious Patriarchs: Gender, Race, and Power in Colonial Virginia.* Chapel Hill: University of North Carolina Press, 1996.

Brown, Letitia Woods. *Free Negroes in the District of Columbia, 1790–1846.* New York: Oxford University Press, 1972.

Brownmiller, Susan. *Against Our Will: Men, Women, and Rape.* New York: Simon and Schuster, 1975.

Bruce, Dickson D., Jr. *Archibald Grimké: Portrait of a Black Independent.* Baton Rouge: Louisiana State University Press, 1993.

Buckley, Thomas E., S. J. "Unfixing Race: Class, Power, and Identity in an Interracial Family. In *Sex, Love, Race: Crossing Boundaries in North American History.* Edited by Martha Hodes, 164–90. New York: New York University Press, 1999.

Buick, Kirsten P. "The Ideal Works of Edmonia Lewis: Invoking and Inverting Autobiography." In *Reading American Art.* Edited by Marianne Doezema and Elizabeth Milroy, 190–207. New Haven: Yale University Press, 1998.

Burton, Orville Vernon. *In My Father's House Are Many Mansions: Family and Community in Edgefield, South Carolina.* Chapel Hill: University of North Carolina, 1985.

Bynum, Victoria. *Unruly Women: The Politics of Social and Sexual Control in the Old South.* Chapel Hill: University of North Carolina Press, 1992.

Campbell, Randolph B. *An Empire for Slavery: The Peculiar Institution in Texas, 1821–1865.* Baton Rouge: Louisiana State University Press, 1989.

———. *The Slave Catchers: Enforcement of the Fugitive Slave Law, 1850–1860.* Chapel Hill: University of North Carolina Press, 1970.

Carby, Hazel V. *Reconstructing Womanhood: The Emergence of the Afro-American Woman Novelist.* New York: Oxford University Press, 1987.

Cheek, William, and Aimee Lee Cheek. *John Mercer Langston and the Fight for Black Freedom, 1829–65.* Urbana: University of Illinois Press, 1989.

Cimbala, Paul A. "Mary Ann Shadd Cary and Black Abolitionism." In *Against the Tide: Women Reformers in American Society.* Edited by Paul A. Cimbala and Randall M. Miller, 19–40. Westport, CT: Praeger, 1997.

Cimprich, John. "The Fort Pillow Massacre: Assessing the Evidence." In *Black Soldiers in Blue: African American Troops in the Civil War Era.* Edited by John David Smith, 150–68. Chapel Hill: University of North Carolina, 2002.

Clayton, Ralph. *Slavery, Slaveholding, and the Free Black Population of Antebellum Baltimore.* Bowie: Heritage, 1993.

Clinton, Catherine. "Bloody Terrain: Freedwomen, Sexuality, and Violence During Reconstruction." In *Half Sisters of History: Southern Women and the American Past.* Edited by Catherine Clinton, 136–53. Durham: Duke University Press, 1994.

———. *Harriet Tubman: The Road to Freedom.* New York: Little, Brown, 2004.

———. *The Plantation Mistress: Woman's World in the Old South.* New York: Pantheon Books, 1982.

Coleman, Willi. "Architects of a Vision: Black Women and Their Antebellum Quest for Political and Social Equality." In *African American Women and The Vote, 1837–1965.* Edited by Ann D. Gordon, Bettye Collier-Thomas, John H. Bracey, Arlene Voski Avakian, and Joyce Avrech Berkman, 24–40. Amherst: University of Massachusetts Press.

Collier Thomas, Bettye. *Daughters of Thunder: Black Preaching Women and Their Sermons, 1850–1979.* San Francisco: Jossey-Bass, 1998.

Cooper, William J., Jr., and Thomas E. Terrell. *The American South: A History.* New York: Alfred A. Knopf, 1990.

Cornelius, Janet Duitsman. *When I Can Read My Title Clear: Literacy, Slavery, and Religion in the Antebellum South.* Columbia: University of South Carolina Press, 1991.

Cornish, Dudley Taylor. *The Sable Arm: Negro Troops in the Union Army, 1861–1865.* New York: Longman, Green, 1956.

Corrigan, Mary Beth. "'It's a Family Affair': Buying Freedom in the District of Columbia, 1850–1860." In *Working Toward Freedom: Slave Society and Domestic Economy in the American South.* Edited by Larry E. Hudson Jr., 163–91. Rochester: University of Rochester Press, 1994.

Cott, Nancy. *The Bonds of Womanhood: "Woman's Sphere" in New England, 1780–1835.* 2nd ed. New Haven: Yale University Press, 1997.

Cullen, Jim. "'I's a Man Now': Gender and African American Men." In *Divided Houses: Gender and the Civil War.* Edited by Catherine Clinton and Nina Silber, 76–91. New York: Oxford University Press, 1992.

Curry, Leonard P. *The Free Black in Urban America, 1800–1850: The Shadow of the Dream.* Chicago: University of Chicago Press, 1981.

Davis, David Brion. *The Problem of Slavery in Western Culture.* Ithaca: Cornell University Press, 1970.

Davis, Edwin Adams, and William Ransom Hogan. *The Barber of Natchez.* Baton Rouge: Louisiana State University Press, 1954.

Davis, H. P. *Black Democracy: The Story of Haiti.* New York: Dodge Publishing Company, 1936.

Deggs, Sister Mary Bernard. *No Cross, No Crown: Black Nuns in Nineteenth-Century New Orleans.* Edited by Virginia Meacham Gould and Charles E. Nolan. Bloomington: Indiana University Press, 2001.

Delany, Martin R. *The Condition, Elevation, Emigration, and Destiny of the Colored People of the United States.* Baltimore: Black Classic Press, 1993.

Detiege, Sister Audrey Marie. *Henriette DeLille, Free Woman of Color.* New Orleans: Sisters of the Holy Family, 1976.

Dominguez, Virginia R. *White by Definition: Social Classification in Creole Louisiana.* New Brunswick: Rutgers University Press, 1994.

Dublin, Thomas. *Transforming Women's Work: New England Lives in the Industrial Revolution.* Ithaca: Cornell University Press, 1994.

Faust, Drew Gilpin, ed. *The Ideology of Slavery: Proslavery Thought in the American South, 1830–1860.* Baton Rouge: Louisiana State University Press, 1991.

Ferrell, Robert H. *American Diplomacy: A History.* New York: W. W. Norton, 1975.

Fick, Carolyn E. *The Making of Haiti: The Saint Domingue Revolution from Below.* Knoxville: University of Tennessee Press, 1990.

Fields, Barbara Jeanne. *Slavery and Freedom on the Middle Ground: Maryland During the Nineteenth Century.* New Haven: Yale University Press, 1985.

Finkelman, Paul. "Crimes of Love, Misdemeanors of Passion: The Regulation of Race and Sex in the Colonial South." In *The Devil's Lane:*

Sex and Race in the Early South. Edited by Catherine Clinton and Michele Gillespie, 124–35. New York: Oxford University Press, 1997.

———. *Dred Scott v. Sandford: A Brief History with Documents*. Boston: Bedford Books, 1997.

———. *An Imperfect Union: Slavery, Federalism, and Comity*. Chapel Hill: University of North Carolina Press, 1981.

———. *Slavery in the Courtroom: An Annotated Bibliography of American Cases*. Union, NJ: Lawbook Exchange, 1998.

———. *State Slavery Statutes: Guide to State Slavery Statutes*. Frederick, MD: University Publications of America, 1989.

Fleischner, Jennifer. *Mrs. Lincoln and Mrs. Keckly: The Remarkable Story of the Friendship Between a First Lady and a Former Slave*. New York: Broadway Books, 2003.

Flexner, James Thomas. *The Young Hamilton: A Biography*. Boston: Little, Brown, 1978.

Foner, Eric. *Reconstruction: America's Unfinished Revolution, 1863–1877*. New York: Harper and Row, 1988.

Forbes, Ella. *African American Women During the Civil War*. New York: Garland, 1998.

Foreman, P. Gabrielle. "Manifest in Signs: The Politics of Sex and Representation in *Incidents in the Life of a Slave Girl*." In *Harriet Jacobs and Incidents in the Life of a Slave Girl: New Critical Essays*. Edited by Deborah M. Garfield and Rafia Zafar, 76–99. New York: Cambridge University Press, 1996.

Foster, Frances Smith, ed. *Minnie's Sacrifice, Reaping and Sowing, Trial and Triumph: Three Rediscovered Novels by Frances E. W. Harper*. Boston: Beacon Press, 1994.

———. *Written By Herself: Literary Production by African American Women, 1746–1892*. Bloomington: Indiana University Press, 1993.

Fox-Genovese, Elizabeth. *Within the Plantation Household: Black and White Women of the Old South*. Chapel Hill: University of North Carolina, 1988.

Frankel, Noralee. *Freedom's Women: Black Women and Families in Civil War Era Mississippi*. Bloomington: Indiana University Press, 1999.

———. "From Slave Women to Free Women: The National Archives and Black Women's History in the Civil War Era." *Prologue: Quarterly of the National Archives and Records Administration* 29 (Summer 1997): http://www.nara.gov/publications/prologue/frankel.html.

———. "The Southern Side of 'Glory': Mississippi African-American Women During the Civil War." In *"We Specialize in the Wholly Impos-*

sible": *A Reader in Black Women's History.* Edited by Darlene Clark Hine, Wilma King, and Linda Reed, 335–43. Brooklyn: Carlson Publishing, 1995.

Franklin, John Hope. *The Free Negro in North Carolina, 1790–1860.* New York: W. W. Norton, 1971.

Franklin, John Hope, and Alfred A. Moss Jr. *From Slavery to Freedom: A History of Negro Americans.* 8th ed. New York: McGraw Hill, 2000.

Franklin, John Hope, and Loren Schweninger. *Runaway Slaves: Rebels on the Plantation.* New York: Oxford University Press, 1999.

Freehling, William W. "The Founding Fathers, Conditional Antislavery, and the Nonradicalism of the American Revolution." In *Annual Editions, American History: Pre-Colonial Through Reconstruction.* 15th ed. Edited by Robert James Maddox. Sluice Dock: Duskin/McGraw-Hill, 1999.

Freeman, Daniel Noel, ed. *The Anchor Bible Dictionary,* vol. 2. New York: Doubleday, 1992.

Frey, Sylvia R., and Betty Wood. *Come Shouting to Zion: African American Protestantism in the American South and British Caribbean to 1830.* Chapel Hill: University of North Carolina Press, 1998.

Friedman, Jean E. *The Enclosed Garden: Women and Community in the Evangelical South, 1830–1900.* Chapel Hill: University of North Carolina Press, 1985.

Fuller, Edward. *Prudence Crandall: An Incident of Racism in Nineteenth-Century Connecticut.* Middletown: Wesleyan University Press, 1971.

Gates, Paul W. *The Farmer's Age: Agriculture 1815–1860.* Vol. 3: *The Economic History of the United States.* New York: Holt, Rinehart, and Winston, 1960.

Geismar, Joan H. *The Archaeology of Social Disintegration in Skunk Hollow: A Nineteenth-Century Rural Black Community.* New York: Academic Press, 1982.

Genovese, Eugene D. *In Red and Black: Marxian Explorations in Southern and Afro-American History.* New York: Pantheon Books, 1971.

George, Carol V. R. *Segregated Sabbaths: Richard Allen and the Emergence of Independent Black Churches, 1740–1840.* New York: Oxford University Press, 1973.

Glatthaar, Joseph T. *Forged in Battle: The Civil War Alliance of Black Soldiers and White Officers.* New York: Free Press, 1990.

Gordon-Reed, Annette. *Thomas Jefferson and Sally Hemings: An American Controversy.* Charlottesville: University of Virginia Press, 2000.

Gould, L. Virginia. "Urban Slavery—Urban Freedom: The Manumission of Jacqueline Lemelle." In *More Than Chattel: Black Women and Slavery in the Americas.* Edited by David Barry Gaspar and Darlene Clark Hine, 298–314. Bloomington: Indiana University Press, 1996.

Graham, Maryemma, ed. *Complete Poems of Frances E. W. Harper.* New York: Oxford University Press, 1988.

Gray, Lewis Cecil. *History of Agriculture in the Southern United States to 1860.* 2 vols. Gloucester: Peter Smith, 1958.

Green, Constance McLaughlin. *The Secret City: A History of Race Relations in the Nation's Capital.* Princeton: Princeton University Press, 1967.

Guillory, Monique. "Under One Roof: The Sins and Sanctity of the New Orleans Quadroon Balls." In *Race Consciousness: African-American Studies for the New Century.* Edited by Judith Jackson Fossett and Jeffrey A. Tucker. New York: New York University Press, 1997.

Gutman, Herbert G. *The Black Family in Slavery and Freedom, 1750–1925.* New York: Vintage Books, 1977.

Guy, Anita Didt. *Maryland's Persistent Pursuit to End Slavery, 1850–1864.* New York: Garland, 1997.

Hall, Kermit L., William M. Wiecek, and Paul Finkelman, eds. *American Legal History: Cases and Materials.* New York: Oxford University Press, 1991.

Hall, Robert L. "Massachusetts Abolitionists Document the Slave Experience." In *Courage and Conscience: Black and White Abolitionists in Boston.* Edited by Donald M. Jacobs, 75–100. Bloomington: Indiana University Press, 1993.

Hamer, Judith A., and Martin J. Hamer, eds. *Centers of the Self: Short Stories by Black American Women from the Nineteenth Century to the Present.* New York: Hill and Wang, 1994.

Hanger, Kimberly S. *Bounded Lives, Bounded Places: Free Black Society in Colonial New Orleans, 1769–1803.* Durham: Duke University Press, 1997.

———. " 'The Fortunes of Women in America': Spanish New Orleans's Free Women of African Descent and Their Relations with Slave Women." In *Discovering the Women in Slavery: Emancipating Perspectives on the American Past.* Edited by Patricia Morton, 153–78. Athens: University of Georgia Press, 1996.

———. "Patronage, Property, and Persistence: The Emergence of a Free Black Elite in Spanish New Orleans." In *Against the Odds: Free Blacks in the Slave Societies of the Americas.* Edited by Jane G. Landers, 44–64. London: Frank Cass, 1996.

Harding, Vincent. *There Is a River: The Black Struggle for Freedom in America.* New York: Vintage Books, 1983.

Harley, Sharon. "Northern Black Female Workers: Jacksonian Era." In *The Afro-American Woman: Struggles and Images.* Edited by Rosalyn Terborg-Penn, 5–16. Port Washington, NY: Kennikat Press, 1978.

Harper, Frances Ellen (Watkins). "The Two Offers." In *Centers of the Self: Short Stories by Black American Women From the Nineteenth Century to the Present.* Edited by Judith A. Hammer and Martin J. Hammer. New York: Hill and Wang, 1994.

Harper, F[rances] E[llen] (Watkins). *Poems on Miscellaneous Subjects.* Philadelphia: Rhistoric Publications, 1969.

Harris, Leslie M. "From Abolitionist Amalgamators to 'Rulers of the Five Points': The Discourse of Interracial Sex and Reform in Antebellum New York City." In *Sex, Love, Race: Crossing Boundaries in North American History.* Edited by Martha Hodes, 191–212. New York: New York University Press, 1999.

Hensel, W. U. *The Christiana Riot and the Treason Trials of 1851.* New York: Negro Universities Press, 1969.

Hershberg, Theodore. "Free-Born and Slave-Born Blacks in Antebellum Philadelphia." In *Race and Slavery in the Western Hemisphere.* Edited by Stanley Engerman and Eugene D. Genovese, 395–426. Princeton: Princeton University Press, 1975.

Hershberg, Theodore, and Henry Williams. "Mulattoes and Blacks: Intragroup Color Differences and Social Stratification in Nineteenth-Century Philadelphia." In *Philadelphia: Work, Space, Family, and Group Experience in the Nineteenth Century.* Edited by Theodore Hershberg. New York: Oxford University Press, 1981.

Higginbotham, A. Leon, Jr. *In the Matter of Color: Race and the American Legal Process, the Colonial Period.* New York: Oxford University Press, 1978.

Hine, Darlene Clark. "Lifting the Veil, Shattering the Silence: Black Women's History in Slavery and Freedom." In *Hind Sight: Black Women and the Re-Construction of American History.* Bloomington: Indiana University Press, 1994.

———. "Rape and the Inner Lives of Black Women: Thoughts on the Culture of Dissemblance." In *Hind Sight: Black Women and the Re-Construction of American History,* 37–47. Brooklyn: Carlson Publishing, 1994.

Hinton, Richard J. *John Brown and His Men: With Some Account of the Roads They Traveled to Reach Harper's Ferry.* New York: Funk and Wagnalls, 1894.

Hodes, Martha. *White Women, Black Men: Illicit Sex in the Nineteenth-Century South*. New Haven: Yale University Press, 1997.

Hogan, William R., and Edwin A. Davis, eds. *The Barber of Natchez*. Baton Rouge: Louisiana State University Press, 1954.

Hollandsworth, James G., Jr. *The Louisiana Native Guards: The Black Military Experience During the Civil War*. Baton Rouge: Louisiana State University, 1995.

Honour, Hugh. *The Image of the Black in Western Art: From the American Revolution to World War I, Black Models and White Myths*, vol. 4. Cambridge: Harvard University Press, 1989.

Horton, James Oliver. *Free People of Color: Inside the African American Community*. Washington: Smithsonian Institution Press, 1993.

Horton, James Oliver, and Lois E. Horton. *Black Bostonians: Family Life and Community Struggle in the Antebellum North*. New York: Holmes and Meier, 1979.

———. *Black Bostonians: Family Life and Community Struggle in the Antebellum North*. New York: Holmes and Meier, 1999.

Hudson, Lynn M. *The Making of "Mammy Pleasant": A Black Entrepreneur in Nineteenth-Century San Francisco*. Urbana: University of Illinois Press, 2003.

Humez, Jean M. *Harriet Tubman: The Life and Life Stories*. Madison: University of Wisconsin Press, 2003.

———. "'My Spirit Eye': Some Functions of Spiritual and Visionary Experience in the Lives of Five Black Women Preachers, 1810–1880." In *Women and the Structure of Society: Selected Research from the Fifth Berkshire Conference on the History of Women*. Edited by Barbara J. Harris and JoAnn K. McNamara, 129–43. Durham: Duke University Press, 1984.

Hunt, Alfred N. *Haiti's Influence on Antebellum America: Slumbering Volcano in the Caribbean*. Baton Rouge: Louisiana State University, 1988.

Hunt, Patricia K. "The Struggle to Achieve Individual Expression through Clothing and Adornment: African American Women Under and After Slavery." In *Discovering the Women in Slavery: Emancipating Perspectives on the American Past*. Edited by Patricia Morton, 227–40. Athens: University of Georgia Press, 1996.

Hunter, Tera W. "Dominion and Resistance: The Politics of Wage Household Labor in New South Atlanta." In *"We Specialize in the Wholly Impossible": A Reader in Black Women's History*. Edited by Darlene Clark Hine, Wilma King, and Linda Reed, 343–58. Brooklyn: Carlson Publishing, 1995.

Ignatiev, Noel. *How the Irish Became White*. New York: Routledge, 1995.

Isenberg, Nancy. *Sex and Citizenship in Antebellum America*. Chapel Hill: University of North Carolina Press, 1998.

Jackson, Luther Porter. *Free Negro Labor and Property Holding in Virginia, 1830–1860*. New York: Atheneum, 1969.

Jacobson, Matthew Frye. *Whiteness of a Different Color: European Immigrants and the Alchemy of Race*. Cambridge: Harvard University Press, 2000.

James, C. L. R. *The Black Jacobins: Toussaint L'Ouverture and the San Domingo Revolution*. 2nd ed. New York: Vintage Books, 1963.

Johnson, Michael P., and James L. Roark. "Strategies of Survival: Free Negro Families and the Problem of Slavery." In *In Joy and in Sorrow: Women, Family, and Marriage in the Victorian South, 1830–1900*. Edited by Carol Bleser, 88–102, 288–93. New York: Oxford University Press, 1991.

———. *Black Masters: A Free Family of Color in the Old South*. New York: W. W. Norton, 1984.

Johnson, Walter. *Soul by Soul: Life Inside the Antebellum Slave Market*. Cambridge: Harvard University Press, 1999.

Johnson, Whittington B. *Black Savannah, 1788–1864*. Fayetteville: University of Arkansas Press, 1996.

———. "Free African-American Women in Savannah, 1800–1860: Affluence and Autonomy Amid Adversity." In *"We Specialize in the Wholly Impossible": A Reader in Black Women's History*. Edited by Darlene Clark Hine, Wilma King, and Linda Reed. Brooklyn: Carlson Publishing, 1995.

Jones, Howard. *The Course of American Diplomacy: From the Revolution to the Present*. New York: Franklin Watts, 1985.

———. *Mutiny on the Amistad: The Saga of a Slave Revolt and Its Impact on American Abolition, Law, and Diplomacy*. New York: Oxford University Press, 1987.

Jones, Norrece T., Jr. *Born a Child of Freedom, Yet a Slave: Mechanisms of Control and Strategies of Resistance in Antebellum South Carolina*. Hanover: Wesleyan University Press, 1990.

Jordan, Ervin L., Jr. *Black Confederates and Afro-Yankees in Civil War Virginia*. Charlottesville: University of Virginia Press, 1995.

Joyner, Charles W. *Down by the Riverside: A South Carolina Community*. Urbana: University of Illinois Press, 1984.

Kelly, Alfred H., Winfred A. Harbison, and Herman Belz. *The American Constitution: Its Origins and Development*. 6th ed. New York: W. W. Norton, 1983.

Kendrick, Stephen, and Paul Kendrick. *Sarah's Long Walk: The Free Blacks of Boston and How Their Struggle for Equality Changed America*. Boston: Beacon Press, 2004.

Kerber, Linda K. *Women of the Republic: Intellect and Ideology in Revolutionary America*. New York: W. W. Norton, 1986.

King, Wilma. "Eliza Johnson Potter: Traveler, Entrepreneur, and Social Critic." In *Ordinary Women, Extraordinary Lives: Women in American History*. Edited by Kriste Lindenmeyer, 91–104. Wilmington, DE: Scholarly Resources, 2000.

———. "'Out of Bounds': Emancipated and Enslaved Women in Antebellum America." In *Free Women of Color in Slave Societies of the Americas*. Edited by David Gaspar and Darlene Clark Hine, 127–44. Urbana: University of Illinois Press, 2005.

———. *Stolen Childhood: Slave Youth in Nineteenth-Century America*. Bloomington: Indiana University Press, 1995.

———. "'Suffer with them till death': Slave Women and Their Children in Nineteenth-Century America." In *More than Chattel: Black Women and Slavery in the Americas*. Edited by Darlene Clark Hine and David Barry Gaspar, 147–68. Bloomington: Indiana University Press, 1996.

Klein, Herbert S. "African Women in the Atlantic Slave Trade." In *"We Specialize in the Wholly Impossible": A Reader in Black Women's History*. Edited by Darlene Clark Hine, Wilma King, and Linda Reed, 67–75. Brooklyn: Carlson Publishing, 1995.

Koger, Larry. *Black Slaveholders: Free Black Slave Masters in South Carolina*. Jefferson, NC: McFarland, 1985.

Korngold, Ralph. *Citizen Toussaint*. Boston: Little, Brown, 1945.

Kutler, Stanley I., ed. *The Supreme Court and the Constitution: Readings in American Constitutional History*. 2nd ed. New York: W. W. Norton, 1977.

Landers, Jane G. *Black Society in Spanish Florida*. Urbana: University of Illinois Press, 1997.

Lapsansky, Phillip. "Graphic Discord: Abolitionist and Antiabolitionist Images." In *The Abolitionist Sisterhood: Women's Political Culture in Antebellum America*, 201–30. Ithaca: Cornell University Press, 1994.

[———]. "Afro-Americana: Meet the Dickersons." *The Library Company of Philadelphia, 1993 Annual Report*, 17–24. Philadelphia: Library Company of Philadelphia, 1993.

Lapsansky, Phillip S. "Afro-Americana: Family Values, in Black and White." *The Library Company of Philadelphia, 1991 Annual Report*, 26–40. Philadelphia: Library Company of Philadelphia, 1991.

Larson, Kate Clifford. *Bound for the Promised Land: Portrait of an American Hero*. New York: Ballantine Books, 2004.

Lawson, Ellen N. "Sarah Woodson Early: 19th Century Black Nationalist 'Sister.'" In *Black Women in United States History*. Edited by Darlene Clark Hine, Elsa Barkley Brown, Tiffany R. L. Patterson, and Lillian S. Williams, 3:815–26. Brooklyn: Carlson Publishing, 1990.

Lawson, Ellen Nickenzie, and Marlene D. Merrill. "Antebellum Black Coeds at Oberlin College." In *Black Women in United States History*. Edited by Darlene Clark Hine, Elsa Barkley Brown, Tiffany R. L. Patterson, and Lillian S. Williams, 3:827–35. Brooklyn: Carlson Publishing, 1990.

———. *The Three Sarahs: Documents of Antebellum Black College Women*, vol. 13. New York: Edwin Mellen Press, 1984.

Lebsock, Suzanne. *The Free Women of Petersburg: Status and Culture in a Southern Town, 1784–1860*. New York: W. W. Norton, 1984.

Lerner, Gerda. *Black Women in White America: A Documentary History*. New York: Vintage Books, 1973.

———. *The Creation of Patriarchy*, vol. 1. New York: Oxford University Press, 1986.

———. *The Creation of the Feminist Consciousness: From the Middle Ages to Eighteenth Seventy*, vol. 2. New York: Oxford University Press, 1993.

———. "Sarah Mapps Douglass." In *Black Women in America: An Historical Encyclopedia*. Edited by Darlene Clark Hine, Elsa Barkley Brown, and Rosalyn Terborg-Penn, 351–53. Brooklyn: Carlson Publishing, 1993.

Leslie, Kent Anderson. *Woman of Color, Daughter of Privilege: Amanda America Dickson*. Athens: University of Georgia Press, 1995.

Lindley, Susan Hill. *You Have Stept Out of Your Place: A History of Women and Religion in America*. Louisville: Westminster John Knox Press, 1995.

Litwack, Leon F. *Been in the Storm So Long: The Aftermath of Slavery*. New York: Vintage Books, 1980.

———. *North of Slavery: The Negro in the Free States, 1790–1860*. Chicago: University of Chicago Press, 1961.

Lockyer, Herbert. *All the Women of the Bible: The Life and Times of All the Women of the Bible*. Grand Rapids: Zondervan Publishing House, 1995.

Lott, Eric. *Love and Theft: Blackface Minstrelsy and American Working Class*. New York: Oxford University Press, 1993.

Lucas, Marion B. *A History of Blacks in Kentucky*, vol. 1. Frankfort: Kentucky Historical Society, 1992.

Madden, T. O., Jr., with Ann L. Miller. *We Were Always Free: The Maddens of Culpeper County, Virginia, A 200-Year Family History.* New York: W. W. Norton, 1992.

Martin, Elizabeth, and Vivian Meyer. *Female Gazes: Seventy-Five Women Artists.* Toronto: Second Story Press, 1997.

Martin, Waldo E., Jr. *The Mind of Frederick Douglass.* Chapel Hill: University of North Carolina Press, 1984.

McKay, Nellie Y. "Nineteenth-Century Black Women's Spiritual Autobiographies: Religious Faith and Self-Empowerment." In *Interpreting Women's Lives: Feminist Theory and Personal Narratives.* Edited by the Personal Narrative Group, Joy Webster Barbre, Amy Farrell, Shirley Nelson Garner, Susan Geiger, Ruth-Ellen Boetcher Joeres, Susan M-A Lyons, Mary Jo Maynes, Pamela Mittlefehldt, Riv-Ellen Prell, and Virginia Steinhagen, 139–54. Bloomington: Indiana University Press, 1989.

McLeRoy, Sherrie S., and William R. McLeRoy. *Strangers in Their Midst: The Free Black Population of Amherst County, Virginia.* Bowie, MD: Heritage Books, 1993.

McPherson, James M. *The Negro's Civil War: How American Negroes Felt and Acted During the War for the Union.* New York: Ballantine Books, 1991.

———. *Ordeal by Fire: The Civil War and Reconstruction.* New York: Alfred A. Knopf, 1982.

Melish, Joanne Pope. *Disowning Slavery: Gradual Emancipation and "Race" in New England, 1780–1860.* Ithaca: Cornell University Press, 1998.

Meyer, Leland Winfield. *The Life and Times of Colonel Richard M. Johnson of Kentucky.* New York: Columbia University Press, 1932.

Miles, Dudley H., ed. *The Photographic History of the Civil War, in Ten Volumes.* Vol. 9: *Poetry and Eloquence of Blue and Gray.* New York: Trow Press, 1911.

Mills, Gary B. *The Forgotten People: Cane River's Creoles of Color.* Baton Rouge: Louisiana State University, 1977.

Mintz, Sidney W. *Sweetness and Power: The Place of Sugar in Modern History.* New York: Penguin, 1986.

Mitchell, Molly. "'After the War I Am Going to Put Myself a Sailor': Geography, Writing, and Race in Letters of Free Children in Civil War New Orleans." In *Children and War: A Historical Anthology.* Edited by James Marten, 26–37. New York: New York University Press, 2002.

Morgan, Edmund S. *American Slavery—American Freedom: The Ordeal of Colonial Virginia.* New York: W. W. Norton, 1975.

Morris, Thomas D. *Southern Slavery and the Law, 1619–1860*. Chapel Hill: University of North Carolina, 1996.

Morrow, Diane Batts. "'Our Convent': The Oblate Sisters of Providence and Baltimore's Antebellum Black Community." In *Negotiating Boundaries of Southern Womanhood: Dealing with the Powers That Be*. Edited by Janet L. Coryell, Thomas H. Appleton Jr., Anastatia Sims, and Sondra Gioia Treadway, 27–47. Columbia: University of Missouri Press, 2000.

———. *Persons of Color and Religious at the Same Time: The Oblate Sisters of Providence, 1828–1860*. Chapel Hill: University of North Carolina Press, 2002.

Morton, Patricia. *Disfigured Images: The Historical Assault on Afro-American Women*. New York: Greenwood Press, 1991.

Murray, Pauli. *Proud Shoes: The Story of an American Family*. New York: Harper and Row, 1987.

Nagel, Joane. *Race, Ethnicity, and Sexuality: Intimate Intersections, Forbidden Frontiers*. New York: Oxford University Press, 2003.

Nash, Gary B. *Forging Freedom: The Formation of Philadelphia's Black Community, 1720–1840*. Cambridge: Harvard University Press, 1988.

———. *Race and Revolution*. Madison, WI: Madison House, 1990.

———. *Red, White, and Black: The Peoples of Early North America*. 4th ed. Upper Saddle River, NJ: Prentice Hall, 2000.

Nash, Howard P., Jr. *Stormy Petrel: The Life and Times of General Benjamin F. Butler, 1818–1893*. Cranbury: Associated University Presses, 1969.

Newman, Deborah L. "Black Women in the Era of the American Revolution in Pennsylvania." In *"We Specialize in the Wholly Impossible": A Reader in Black Women's History*. Edited by Darlene Clark Hine, Wilma King, and Linda Reed, 211–24. Brooklyn: Carlson Publishing, 1995.

Niven, John. *The Coming of the Civil War, 1837–1861*. Arlington Heights: Harlan Davidson, 1990.

Olwell, Robert. "'Loose, Idle and Disorderly': Slave Women in the Eighteenth-Century Charleston Marketplace." In *More Than Chattel: Black Women and Slavery in the Americas*. Edited by David Barry Gaspar and Darlene Clark Hine, 97–110. Bloomington: Indiana University Press, 1996.

Painter, Nell Irvin. *Sojourner Truth: A Life, a Symbol*. New York: W. W. Norton, 1996.

Pease, William, and Jane H. Pease. *The Fugitive Slave Law and Anthony Burns: A Problem in Law Enforcement*. Philadelphia: Lippincott, 1995.

———. *They Who Would Be Free: Blacks' Search for Freedom, 1830–1860*. New York: Atheneum, 1974.

Perkins, Linda. "Black Women and Racial 'Uplift' Prior to Emancipation." In *Black Women in the United States*. Edited By Darlene Clark Hine, Elsa Barkley Brown, Tiffany R. L. Patterson, and Lillian S. Williams, 3:1077–94. Brooklyn: Carlson Publishing, 1990.

Peterson, Carla L. *"Doers of the Word": African-American Women Speakers and Writers in the North (1830–1880)*. New York: Oxford University Press, 1995.

Phillips, Ulrich B. *American Negro Slavery: A Survey of the Supply, Employment, and Control of Negro Labor as Determined by the Plantation Regime*. Baton Rouge: Louisiana State University Press, 1966.

Piersen, William D. *Black Yankees: The Development of an Afro-American Subculture in Eighteenth-Century New England*. Amherst: University of Massachusetts Press, 1988.

Powers, Bernard E., Jr. *Black Charlestonians: A Social History, 1822–1885*. Fayetteville: University of Arkansas Press, 1994.

Quarles, Benjamin. *Black Abolitionists*. New York: Oxford University Press, 1969.

———. *Frederick Douglass*. Washington, DC: Associated Publishers, 1948.

Raboteau, Albert J. *Slave Religion: The "Invisible Institution" in the Antebellum South*. New York: Oxford University Press, 1978.

Reed, Harry. *Platform for Change: The Foundations of the Northern Free Black Community, 1775–1865*. East Lansing: Michigan State University Press, 1994.

Reid, John B. "'A Career to Build, a People to Serve, a Purpose to Accomplish': Race, Class, Gender, and Detroit's First Black Women Teachers, 1865–1916." In *"We Specialize in the Wholly Impossible": A Reader in Black Women's History*. Edited by Darlene Clark Hine, Wilma King, and Linda Reed, 303–20. Brooklyn: Carlson Publishing, 1995.

Rhodes, Jane. *Mary Ann Shadd Cary: The Black Press and Protest in the Nineteenth Century*. Bloomington: Indiana University Press, 1998.

Riley, Glenda. *Inventing the American Woman: An Inclusive History*. 2nd ed. Vol. 1 to 1877. Wheeling, IL: Harlan Davidson, 1995.

Robertson, Ross M. *History of the American Economy*. 2nd ed. New York: Harcourt, Brace, and World, 1964.

Roediger, David. *The Wages of Whiteness: Race and the Making of the American Working Class*. Revised ed. London: Verso, 1999.

Rooks, Noliwe. *Hair Raising: Beauty, Culture, and African American Women*. New Brunswick: Rutgers University Press, 1996.

Rosen, Hannah. "Not That Sort of Women: Race, Gender, and Sexual Violence during the Memphis Riot of 1866." In *Sex, Love, Race: Crossing Boundaries in North American History*. Edited by Martha Hodes, 267–93. New York: New York University Press, 1999.

Schafer, Daniel L. *Anna Madgigine Jai Kingsley: African Princess, Florida Slave, Plantation Owner*. Gainesville: University Press of Florida, 2003.

Schwalm, Leslie A. *A Hard Fight for We: Women's Transition from Slavery to Freedom in South Carolina*. Urbana: University of Illinois Press, 1997.

Schweninger, Loren, ed. *A Guide to the Microfilm Edition of Race, Slavery, and Free Blacks: Series I, Petitions to Southern Legislatures, 1777–1867*. Bethesda: University Publications of America, 1999.

———. *James T. Rapier and Reconstruction*. Chicago: University of Chicago Press, 1978.

Sheinin, David. "Prudence Crandall, Amistad, and Other Episodes in the Dismissal of Connecticut Slave Women from American History." In *Discovering the Women in Slavery: Emancipating Perspectives on the American Past*. Edited by Patricia Morton, 129–52. Athens: University of Georgia Press, 1996.

Silverman, Jason H. "Mary Ann Shadd and the Search for Equality." In *Black Women in United States History*. Edited by Darlene Clark Hine, Elsa Barkley Brown, Tiffany Patterson, and Lillian Williams, 4:1261–74. Brooklyn: Carlson Publishing, 1990.

Sitterson, J. Carlyle. *Sugar Country: The Cane Sugar Industry in the South, 1753–1950*. Lexington: University of Kentucky Press, 1953.

Snorgrass, J. William. "Pioneer Black Women Journalists from the 1850s to the 1950s." In *Black Women in United States History*, vol. 10. Edited by Darlene Clark Hine, Elsa Barkley Brown, Tiffany R. L. Patterson, Lillian S. Williams, 591–607. Brooklyn: Carlson Publishing, 1990.

Sobel, Mechal. *Trabelin' On: The Slave Journey to an Afro-Baptist Faith*. Princeton: Princeton University Press, 1988.

Society of Friends. *A Statistical Inquiry into the Condition Of The People of Colour, of the City and District of Philadelphia*. Philadelphia: Kite and Walton, 1849.

Socolow, Susan M. "Economic Roles of the Free Women of Color of Cap Francais." In *More than Chattel: Black Women and Slavery in the Americas*. Edited by David Barry Gaspar and Darlene Clark Hine, 279–97. Bloomington: Indiana University Press, 1996.

Stansell, Christine. *City of Women: Sex and Class in New York, 1789–1860*. New York: Alfred A. Knopf, 1986.

Stevenson, Brenda. "Charlotte Forten (1837–1914)." In *Portraits of American Women: From Settlement to the Present*. Edited by G. J. Barker-Benfield and Catherine Clinton, 279–97. New York: St. Martin's Press, 1991.

———. "Distress and Discord in Virginia Slave Families, 1830–1860." In *In Joy and in Sorrow: Women, Family, and Marriage in the Victorian South, 1830–1900*. Edited by Carol Bleser, 103–24. New York: Oxford University Press, 1991.

Stowe, Harriet Beecher. *Uncle Tom's Cabin; or, Life Among the Lowly*. Edited by Ann Douglas. New York: Penguin Classics, 1986.

Stowe, Steven M. "The Not-So-Cloistered Academy: Elite Women's Education and Family Feeling in the Old South." In *The Web of Southern Social Relations: Women, Family, and Education*. Edited by Walter Fraser Jr. Athens: University of Georgia Press, 1985.

Strasser, Susan. *Never Done: A History of American Housework*. New York: Pantheon Books, 1982.

Tate, Gayle T. *Unknown Tongues: Black Women's Political Activism in the Antebellum Era, 1830–1860*. East Lansing: Michigan State University, 2003.

Thompson, Vincent Bakpetu. *The Making of the African Diaspora in the Americas, 1441–1900*. London: Longman, 1989.

Thurber, Cheryl. "The Development of the Mammy Image and Mythology." In *Southern Women: Histories and Identities*. Edited by Virginia Bernhard, Betty Brandon, Elizabeth Fox-Genovese, and Theda Perdue, 87–108. Columbia: University of Missouri Press, 1992.

Van Broekhoven, Deborah Bingham. "'Let Your Names Be Enrolled': Method and Ideology in Women's Antislavery Petitioning." In *The Abolitionist Sisterhood: Women's Political Culture in Antebellum America*. Edited by Jean Fagan Yellin and John C. Van Horne, 179–200. Ithaca: Cornell University Press, 1994.

Vandervelde, Isabel. *Other Free People in Early Barnwell District*. Aiken, SC: Art Studio Press, 2001.

Wade, Richard. *Slavery in the Cities: The South 1820–1860*. New York: Oxford University Press, 1964.

Walker, Juliet E. K. *The History of Black Business in America: Capitalism, Race, Entrepreneurship*. New York: Twayne Publishers, 1998.

Ward, Martha. *Voodoo Queen: The Spirited Lives of Marie Laveau*. Jackson: University Press of Mississippi, 2004.

Wesley, Charles H. *Negro Labor in the United States*. New York: Vanguard, 1927.

White, Deborah Gray. *Ar'n't I a Woman? Female Slaves in the Plantation South*. New York: W. W. Norton, 1985.

White, Shane. *Somewhat More Independent: The End of Slavery in New York City, 1770–1810*. Athens: University of Georgia Press, 1991.

Whitman, T. Stephen. *The Price of Freedom: Slavery and Manumission in Baltimore and Early National Maryland*. Lexington: University of Kentucky, 1997.

Williamson, Joel. *New People: Miscegenation and Mulattoes in the United States*. Baton Rouge: Louisiana State University Press, 1980.

Wilson, Carol. *Freedom at Risk: The Kidnapping of Free Blacks in America, 1780–1865*. Lexington: University Press of Kentucky, 1994.

Wilson, Harriet E. *Our Nig: or, Sketches from the Life of a Free Black in a Two-Story White House, North, Showing that Slavery's Shadows Fall Even There*. New York: Vintage Books, 1983.

Winch, Julie. " 'You Have Talents—Only Cultivate Them': Philadelphia's Black Female Literary Societies and the Abolitionist Crusade." In *The Abolitionist Sisterhood: Women's Political Culture in Antebellum America*. Edited by Jean Fagan Yellin and John C. Van Horne, 101–18. Ithaca: Cornell University Press, 1994.

Winegarten, Ruthe. *Black Texas Women: A Sourcebook, Documents, Biographies, Timeline*. Austin: University of Texas, 1996.

Woodson, Carter G. *Free Negro Heads of Families in the United States in 1830: Together With a Brief Treatment of the Free Negro*. New York: Negro Universities Press, 1925.

———. *Free Negro Owners of Slaves in the United States in 1830: Together with Absentee Ownership of Slaves in the United States in 1830*. Washington, DC: Association for the Study of Negro Life and History, 1924.

Wright, James M. *The Free Negro in Maryland, 1834–1860*. New York: Columbia University Press, 1921.

Wyatt-Brown, Bertram. *Southern Honor: Ethics and Behavior in the Old South*. New York: Oxford University Press, 1982.

Yee, Shirley J. *Black Women Abolitionists: A Study in Activism, 1828–1860*. Knoxville: University of Tennessee Press, 1992.

———. "Organizing for Racial Justice: Black Women and the Dynamics of Race and Sex in Female Antislavery Societies, 1832–1860." In *Black Women in America*. Edited by Kim Marie Vaz. Thousand Oaks, CA: Sage, 1995.

Yellin, Jean Fagan. *Harriet Jacobs: A Life*. New York: Basic Civitas Books, 2004.

Yellin, Jean Fagan, and John C. Van Horne, eds. *The Abolitionist Sisterhood: Women's Political Culture in Antebellum America*. Ithaca: Cornell University Press, 1994.

Young, R. J. *Antebellum Black Activists: Race, Gender, and Self*. New York: Garland, 1996.

Zilversmit, Arthur. *The First Emancipation: The Abolition of Slavery in the North*. Chicago: University of Chicago Press, 1967.

Periodicals

Adler, Jeffrey S. "Streetwalkers, Degraded Outcasts, and Good-for-Nothing Huzzies: Women and the Dangerous Class in Antebellum St. Louis." *Journal of Social History* 25 (Summer 1992): 737–55.

Aptheker, Herbert. "South Carolina Poll Tax, 1737–1895." *Journal of Negro History* 31 (April 1946): 131–39.

Atkins, Jonathan M. "Party Politics and the Debate over the Tennessee Free Negro Bill, 1859–1860." *Journal of Southern History* 71 (May 2005): 245–78.

Baptist, Edward E. " 'Cuffy,' 'Fancy Maids,' and 'One-Eyed Men': Rape, Commodification, and the Domestic Slave Trade in the United States." *American Historical Review* 106 (December 2001): 1619–50.

Berlin, Ira. "The Structure of the Free Negro Caste in the Antebellum United States." *Journal of Social History* 9 (Spring 1976): 297–318.

Blackburn, George, and Sherman L. Ricards. "The Mother-Headed Family among Free Negroes in Charleston, South Carolina, 1850–1860." *Phylon* 42 (March 1981): 11–25.

Brigham, R. I. "Negro Education in Ante-Bellum Missouri. *Journal of Negro History* 30 (October 1945): 405–20.

Brown, Elsa Barkley. "Negotiating and Transforming the Public Sphere: African American Political Life in the Transition from Slavery to Freedom." *Public Culture* 7 (Fall 1994): 107–46.

Brown, Lois. "Memorial Narratives of African American Women in Antebellum New England." *Legacy* 20 (2003): 38–61.

Burton, Orville Vernon. "Anatomy of an Antebellum Rural Free Black Community: Social Structure and Social Interaction in Edgefield District, South Carolina, 1850–1860." *Southern Studies* 21 (Fall 1982): 294–325.

Cade, John B. "Out of the Mouths of Ex-Slaves." *Journal of Negro History* 20 (July 1935): 294–337.

Carlson, Becky. " 'Manumitted and Forever Set Free': The Children of

Charles Lee Younger and Elizabeth, a Woman of Color." *Missouri Historical Review* 96 (October 2001): 16–31.

Cimprich, John, and Robert C. Mainfort Jr. "The Fort Pillow Massacre: A Statistical Note." *Journal of American History* 76 (December 1989): 830–37.

Clark, Emily, and Virginia Meacham Gould. "The Feminine Face of Afro-Catholicism in New Orleans, 1727–1852." *William and Mary Quarterly* 59 (April 2002): 409–48.

Cody, Cheryll Ann. "Naming, Kinship, and Estate Dispersal: Notes on Slave Family Life on a South Carolina Plantation, 1786 to 1833." *William and Mary Quarterly* 39 (January 1982): 192–211.

Cohen, Patricia Cline. "Unregulated Youth: Masculinity and Murder in the 1830s City." *Radical History Review* 52 (1992): 33–52.

Cohen, William. "Thomas Jefferson and the Problem of Slavery." *Journal of American History* 56 (December 1969): 503–26.

Cornelius, Janet. "We Slipped and Learned to Read: Slave Accounts of the Literacy Process, 1830–1865." *Phylon* 44 (September 1983): 171–85.

Crane, Virginia Glenn. "Two Women, White and Brown, in the South Carolina Court of Equity, 1842–1845." *South Carolina Historical Magazine* 96 (July 1995): 198–220.

Cray, Robert E., Jr. "White Welfare and Black Strategies: The Dynamics of Race and Poor Relief in Early New York, 1700–1825." *Slavery and Abolition* 7 (1986): 273–89.

Deutsch, Albert. "The First U. S. Census of the Insane (1840) and Its Use as Pro-Slavery Propaganda." *Bulletin of the History of Medicine* 15 (May 1944): 469–82.

Davis, Adrienne D. "The Private Law of Race and Sex: An Antebellum Perspective." *Stanford Law Review* 51 (January 1999): 221–88.

Diedrich, Maria. "'My Love is Black As Yours is Fair': Premarital Love and Sexuality in the Antebellum Slave Narrative." *Phylon* 47 (September 1986): 238–47.

Doriani, Beth Maclay. "Black Womanhood in Nineteenth-Century America: Subversion and Self-Construction in Two Women's Autobiographies." *American Quarterly* 43 (June 1991): 199–222.

Dye, Nancy Schrom, and Daniel Blake Smith. "Mother Love and Infant Death, 1750–1920." *Journal of American History* 73 (September 1986): 329–53.

Edwards, Laura F. "Law, Domestic Violence, and the Limits of Patriarchal Authority in the Antebellum South." *JSH* 65 (November 1999): 733–70.

Ergood, Bruce. "The Female Protection and the Sun Light: Two Contemporary Negro Mutual Aid Societies." *Florida Historical Quarterly* 50 (July 1971): 25–38.

Fair, Laura. "Dressing Up: Clothing, Class, and Gender in Post-Abolition Zanzibar." *Journal of African History* 39 (1998): 63–94.

Faust, Drew Gilpin. "'Trying to Do a Man's Business': Slavery, Violence, and Gender in the American Civil War." *Gender and History* 4 (Summer 1992): 197–214.

Fessenden, Tracy. "The Sisters of the Holy Family and the Veil of Race." *Religion and American Culture: A Journal of Interpretation* 10 (Summer 2000): 187–224.

Fichter, Joseph H. "The White Church and the Black Sisters." *U.S. Catholic Historian* 12 (Winter 1994): 31–48.

Fields, Barbara J. "Slavery, Race, and Ideology in the United States of America." *New Left Review* 181 (May/June 1990): 95–118.

Finkelman, Paul. "The Kidnapping of John Davis and the Adoption of the Fugitive Slave Law of 1793." *Journal of Southern History* 56 (August 1990): 397–422.

Fish, Cheryl. "Voices of Restless (Dis)continuity: The Significance of Travel for Free Black Women in the Antebellum Americas." *Women Studies* 26 (1997): 475–95.

Fogel, Robert William, and Stanley L. Engerman. "Philanthropy at Bargain Prices: Notes on the Economics of Gradual Emancipation." *Journal of Legal Studies* 3 (June 1974): 377–401.

Foley, William E. "Slave Freedom Suits before Dred Scott: The Case of Marie Jean Scypion's Descendants." *Missouri Historical Review* 79 (October 1984): 1–23.

Forbes, Ella. "'By my own Right Arm': Redemptive Violence and the 1851 Christiana, Pennsylvania Resistance." *Journal of Negro History* 83 (Summer 1998): 159–67.

Formwalt, Lee, ed. "The Camilla Massacre of 1868: Racial Violence as Political Propaganda." *Georgia Historical Quarterly* 71 (Fall 1987): 399–426.

———. "Petitioning Congress for Protection: A Black View of Reconstruction at the Local Level." *Georgia Historical Quarterly* 73 (Summer 1989): 305–22.

Franklin, John Hope. "The Free Negro in the Economic Life of Ante-Bellum North Carolina." *North Carolina Historical Review* 19 (July 1942 and October 1942): 239–59, 359–75.

———. "Slaves Virtually Free in Ante-Bellum North Carolina." *Journal of Negro History* 28 (1943): 284–310.

"The Freedman's Story, In Two Parts." Part 2. *Atlantic Monthly* 17 (March 1866): 276–95.

Gamber, Wendy. "A Precarious Independence: Milliners and Dressmakers in Boston, 1860–1890." *Journal of Women's History* 4 (Spring 1992): 60–88.

Gerdes, Sister M. Reginald. "To Educate and Evangelize: Black Catholic Schools of the Oblate Sisters of Providence (1828–1880)." *U. S. Catholic Historian* 7 (Spring/Summer, 1988): 183–200.

Glatthaar, Joseph T. "The Civil War through the Eyes of a Sixteen-Year-Old Black Officer: The Letters of Lieutenant John H. Crowder of the 1st Louisiana Native Guards." *Louisiana History* 35 (Spring 1994): 201–16.

Glenn, Myra C. "The Naval Reform Campaign Against Flogging: A Cast Study in Changing Attitudes Toward Corporal Punishment, 1830–1850." *American Quarterly* 35 (Autumn 1983): 408–25.

Grant, Jacquelyn. "A Refusal to Be Silenced." *Sojourners* (December 1986): 23–24.

Greenbaum, Susan D. "A Comparison of African American and Euro-American Mutual Aid Societies in 19th Century America." *Journal of Ethnic Studies* 19 (Fall 1991): 95–119.

Grimsted, David. "Rioting in Its Jackson Setting." *American Historical Review* 77 (April 1972): 361–97.

Hagler, D. Harland. "The Ideal Woman in the Antebellum South: Lady or Farmwife?" *Journal of Southern History* 46 (August 1980): 405–18.

Halliburton, R., Jr. "Free Black Owners of Slaves: A Reappraisal of the Woodson Thesis." *South Carolina Historical Magazine* 76 (July 1975): 129–42.

Hanchett, Catherine M. "'What Sort of People and Families...': The Edmondson Sisters." *Afro-Americans in New York Life and History* 6 (July 1982): 21–37.

Harris, Robert L., Jr. "Charleston's Free Afro-American Elite: The Brown Fellowship Society and the Humane Brotherhood." *South Carolina Historical Magazine* 82 (October 1981): 289–310.

Hewitt, John H. "The Search for Elizabeth Jennings, Heroine of a Sunday Afternoon in New York City." *New York History* 71 (October 1990): 387–415.

Higgins, Billy D. "The Origins and Fate of the Free Black Community." *Arkansas Historical Quarterly* 54 (Winter 1995): 427–43.

Hinks, Peter P. "Frequently Plunged into Slavery": Free Blacks and Kidnapping in Antebellum Boston." *Historical Journal of Massachusetts* 20 (1992): 16–31.

Holt, Sharon Ann. "Making Freedom Pay: Freedpeople Working for Themselves, North Carolina, 1865–1900." *Journal of Southern History* 60 (May 1994): 229–62.

Horton, James Oliver. "Black Education at Oberlin College: A Controversial Commitment." *Journal of Negro Education* 54 (1985): 477–99.

———. "Freedom's Yoke: Gender Conventions among Antebellum Free Blacks." *Feminist Studies* 12 (Spring 1986): 51–76.

———. "Generations of Protest: Black Families and Social Reform in Ante-Bellum Boston." *New England Quarterly* 49 (June 1976): 242–56.

Howard, Victor B. "The Civil War in Kentucky: The Slave Claims His Freedom." *Journal of Negro History* 67 (Fall 1982): 245–56.

Hunt, Patricia K. "Clothing as an Expression of History: The Dress of African-American Women in Georgia, 1880–1915." *Georgia Historical Quarterly* 76 (Summer 1992): 459–71.

Hunter, Lloyd. "Slavery in St. Louis, 1804–1860." *Missouri Historical Society Bulletin* 30 (July 1974): 233–65.

Hunter, Wilma King. "Three Women at Tuskegee, 1882–1925." *Hampton Institute Journal of Ethnic Studies* 3 (September 1976): 76–81.

Ingersoll, Thomas N. "Free Blacks in a Slave Society: New Orleans, 1718–1812." *William and Mary Quarterly* 48 (April 1991): 173–200.

Jacobs, Claude F. "Benevolent Societies of New Orleans Blacks During the Late Nineteenth and Early Twentieth Centuries." *Louisiana History* 28 (1988): 21–33.

Johnson, Michael P., and James L. Roark. "'A Middle Ground': Free Mulattoes and the Friendly Moralist Society of Antebellum Charleston." *Southern Studies* 21 (Fall 1982): 246–65.

Johnson, Walter. "The Slave Trader, the White Slave, and the Politics of Racial Determination in the 1850s." *Journal of American History* 87 (June 2000): 13–38.

Johnson, Whittington B. "A Black Teacher and Her School in Reconstruction Darien: The Correspondence of Hettie Sabattie and J. Murray Hoag, 1868–1869." *Georgia Historical Quarterly* 75 (Spring 1991): 90–105.

King, Lisa Y. "In Search of Women of African Descent Who Served in the Civil War Union Navy." *Journal of Negro History* 83 (Fall 1998): 302–9.

King, Wilma. "Within the Professional Household: Slave Children in the Antebellum South." *The Historian* 59 (Spring 1997): 523–40.

Lambert, Frank. "'I Saw the Book Talk': Slave Readings of the First Great Awakening." *Journal of Negro History* 77 (Fall 1992): 185–96.

Lane, Carl, and Rhoda Freeman. "John Dipper and the Experience of the

Free Black Elite, 1816–1836." *Virginia Magazine of History and Biography* 100 (October 1992): 485–514.

Lapsansky, Emma Jones. "Feminism, Freedom, and Community: Charlotte Forten and Women Activists in Nineteenth-Century Philadelphia." *Pennsylvania Magazine of History and Biography* 113 (January 1989): 3–19.

———. "'Since They Got Those Separate Churches': Afro-Americans and Racism in Jacksonian Philadelphia." *American Quarterly* 32 (Spring 1980): 54–78.

Lawson, Ellen N., and Marlene Merrill. "The Antebellum 'Talented Thousandth': Black College Students at Oberlin before the Civil War." *Journal of Negro Education* 52 (1983): 142–55.

Lebsock, Suzanne D. "Free Black Women and the Question of Matriarchy: Petersburg, Virginia, 1784–1820." *Feminist Studies* 2 (Summer 1983): 271–92.

Levy, David W. "Racial Stereotypes in Antislavery Fiction." *Phylon* 31 (Fall 1970): 265–79.

Levy, Leonard W. "The 'Abolition Riot': Boston's First Slave Rescue." *New England Quarterly* 25 (March 1952): 85–92.

Levy, Leonard W., and Harlan B. Philips. "The Roberts Case: Source of the 'Separate by Equal' Doctrine." *American Historical Review* 56 (April 1951): 510–18.

Lichtenstein, Alex. "'That Disposition to Theft, With Which They Have Been Branded': Moral Economy, Slave Management, and the Law." *Journal of Social History* 21 (Spring 1988): 413–40.

Lightner, David L., and Alexander M. Ragan. "Were African American Slaveholders Benevolent or Exploitative? A Quantitative Approach." *Journal of Southern History* (August 2005): 535–58

Lopez, Ian F. Haney. "The Social Construction of Race: Some Observations on Illusion, Fabrication, and Choice." *Harvard Civil Rights–Civil Liberties Law Review* 29 (Winter 1994): 1–62.

Love, Edgar F. "Registration of Free Blacks in Ohio: The Slaves of George C. Mendenhall." *Journal of Negro History* 69 (Winter 1984): 38–47.

MacDonald, Cheryl. "Last Stop on the Underground Railroad: Mary Ann Shadd in Canada." *The Beaver* 70 (February–March 1990): 32–38.

Mahoney, Olivia. "Black Abolitionists." *Chicago History* 20 (1991): 22–37.

Main, Gloria L. "Gender, Work, and Wages in Colonial New England." *William and Mary Quarterly* 51 (January 1994): 39–66.

Margo, Robert A., and Richard H. Steckel. "The Heights of American Slaves: New Evidence on Slave Nutrition and Health." *Social Science History* 6 (Fall 1982): 516–38.

Matson, Lynn R. "Phillis Wheatley—Soul Sister?" *Phylon* 33 (Fall 1972): 222–30.

Matthewson, Tim. "Jefferson and Haiti." *Journal of Southern History* 61 (May 1995): 209–48.

McClintock, Megan J. "Civil War Pensions and the Reconstruction of Union Families." *Journal of American History* 83 (September 1996): 456–80.

Miller, Randall M. "Georgia on Their Minds: Free Blacks and the African Colonization Movement in Georgia." *Southern Studies* 17 (1978): 349–62.

Mills, Gary B. "Coincoin: An Eighteenth-Century 'Liberated' Woman." *Journal of Southern History* 42 (May 1976): 203–22.

Mitchell, J. Marcus. "The Paul Family." *Old-Time New England* 63 (January–March 1973): 73–77.

Mitchell, Mary Niall. "'A Good and Delicious Country': Free Children of Color and How They Learned to Imagine the Atlantic World in Nineteenth-Century Louisiana." *History of Education Quarterly* 40 (Summer 2000): 123–44.

Murray, Alexander L. "*The Provincial Freeman*: A New Source for the History of the Negro in Canada and the United States." *Journal of Negro History* 44 (April 1959): 123–35.

Nash, Roderick W. "William Parker and the Christiana Riot." *Journal of Negro History* 46 (January 1961): 24–31.

Nicholls, Michael L. "Passing Through this Troublesome World: Free Blacks in the Early Southside." *Virginia Magazine of History and Biography* 92 (January 1984): 50–70.

———. "'The squint of freedom': African-American Freedom Suits in Post-Revolutionary Virginia." *Slavery and Abolition* 20 (August 1999): 47–62.

Nogee, Joseph. "The Prigg Case and Fugitive Slavery, 1842–1850." *Journal of Negro History* 39 (July 1954): 185–205.

Oden, Gloria. "The Black Putnams of Charlotte Forten's Journal." *Essex Institute Historical Collections* 126 (October 1990): 237–53.

Painter, Nell Irvin. "Representing Truth: Sojourner Truth's Knowing and Becoming Known." *Journal of American History* 81 (Spring 1994): 461–92.

———. "Sojourner Truth in Life and Memory: Writing the Biography of an American Exotic." *Gender and History* 1 (Spring 1990): 3–16.

Patrick-Stamp, Leslie. "Numbers That Are Not New: African Americans in the Country's First Prison, 1790–1835." *Pennsylvania Magazine of History and Biography* 119 (January–April 1995): 95–128.

Patten, Neil A. "The Nineteenth Century Black Woman as Social Reformer: The 'New' Speeches of Sojourner Truth." *Negro History Bulletin* 49 (January–March 1986): 2–4.

Patton, Phil. "Mammy, Her Life and Times." *American Heritage* (September 1993): 78–87.

Paul, Lee. "The Real Yellow Rose of Texas." *Wild West* (April 1996): 50–56, 94.

Perkins, Linda M. "Heed Life's Demands: The Educational Philosophy of Fanny Jackson Coppin." *Journal of Negro Education* 51 (1982): 181–90.

———. "The Impact of the 'Cult of True Womanhood' on the Education of Black Women." *Journal of Social Issues* 39 (Fall 1983): 17–28.

Pierce, Edward L. "The Contrabands at Fortress Monroe." *Atlantic Monthly* 8 (November 1861): 626–40.

Porter, Dorothy Burnett. "The Organized Educational Activities of Negro Literary Societies, 1828–1846." *Journal of Negro Education* 5 (October 1936): 555–76.

———. "The Remonds of Salem, Massachusetts: A Nineteenth-Century Family Revisited." *Proceedings of the American Antiquarian Society* 95 (October 1985): 259–95.

———. "Sarah Parker Remond, Abolitionist and Physician." *Journal of Negro History* 20 (July 1935): 287–93.

Posey, Thaddeus J. "Praying in the Shadows: The Oblate Sisters of Providence, a Look at Nineteenth-Century Black Catholic Spirituality." *U. S. Catholic Historian* 12 (Winter 1994).

Prichard, Walter. "Routine on a Louisiana Sugar Plantation Under the Slavery Regime." *Mississippi Valley Historical Review* 14 (September 1927): 168–78.

Provine, Dorothy. "The Economic Position of the Free Blacks in the District of Columbia, 1800–1860." *Journal of Negro History* 58 (January 1973): 61–72.

Rector, Theresa A. "Black Nuns as Educators." *Journal of Negro Education* 51 (Summer 1982): 237–53.

Reidy, Joseph P. "'Coming from the Shadow of the Past': The Transition from Slavery to Freedom at Freedmen's Village, 1863–1900." *Virginia Magazine of History and Biography* 95 (October 1987): 403–28.

Ripley, C. Peter. "The Black Family in Transition, 1860–1865." *Journal of Southern History* 41 (August 1975): 369–80.

Rosen, Hannah. "Not That Sort of Women: Race, Gender, and Sexual Violence During the Memphis Riot of 1866." In *Sex, Love, Race: Crossing Boundaries in North American History.* Edited by Martha Hodes, 267–93. New York: New York University Press, 1999.

Ross, Steven Joseph. "Freed Soil, Freed Labor, Freed Men: John Easton and the Davis Bend Experiment." *Journal of Southern History* 44 (May 1978): 213–32.

Rothman, Joshua D. "'Notorious in the Neighborhood': An Interracial Family in Early National and Antebellum Virginia." *Journal of Southern History* 67 (February 2001): 73–114.

Rury, John L. "The New York African Free School, 1827–1836: Conflict over Community Control of Black Education." *Phylon* 44 (September 1983): 187–97.

———. "Philanthropy, Self Help, and Social Control: The New York Manumission Society and Free Blacks, 1785–1810." *Phylon* 46 (September 1985): 231–41.

Russell, John H. "Colored Freemen as Slave Owners in Virginia." *Journal of Negro History* 1 (July 1916): 233–42.

Schafer, Judith Kelleher. "'Open and Notorious Concubinage': The Emancipation of Slave Mistresses by Will and the Supreme Court in Antebellum Louisiana." *Louisiana History* 28 (Spring 1987): 165–82.

Schoeberlein, Robert W. "A Fair to Remember: Maryland Women in Aid of the Union." *Maryland Historical Magazine* 90 (Winter 1995): 467–88.

Schultz, Jane E. "Race, Gender, and Bureaucracy: Civil War Army Nurses and the Pension Bureau." *Journal of Women's History* 6 (Summer 1994): 45–69.

Schwalm, Leslie A. "'Sweet Dreams of Freedom': Freedwomen's Reconstruction of Life and Labor in Lowcountry South Carolina." *Journal of Women's History* 9 (Spring 1997): 9–38.

Schwarz, Philip J. "Emancipators, Protectors, and Anomalies: Free Black Slaveowners in Virginia." *Virginia Magazine of History and Biography* 95 (July 1987): 317–38.

Schweninger, Loren. "A Negro Sojourner in Antebellum New Orleans." *Louisiana History* 20 (1979): 305–14.

———. "Property Owing Free African-American Women in the South, 1800–1870." *Journal of Women's History* 1 (Winter 1990): 13–44.

———. "Prosperous Blacks in the South, 1790–1880." *American Historical Review* 95 (February 1990): 31–56.

———. "A Slave Family in the Ante Bellum South." *Journal of Negro History* 60 (January 1975): 29–44.

———. "Slave Independence and Enterprise in South Carolina, 1780–1865." *South Carolina Historical Magazine* 93 (April 1992): 101–25.

———. "The Underside of Slavery: The Internal Economy, Self-Hire, and Quasi-Freedom in Virginia, 1780–1865." *Slavery and Abolition* 12 (September 1991): 13–44.

Sealander, Judith. "Antebellum Black Press Images of Women." *Western Journal of Black Studies* 6 (Fall 1982): 159–65.

Sears, Richard. "John G. Fee, Camp Nelson, and Kentucky Blacks, 1864–1865." *Register of the Kentucky Historical Society* 85 (Winter 1987): 29–45.

Sedevie, Donna Elizabeth. "The Prospect of Happiness: Women, Divorce, and Property." *Journal of Mississippi History* 57 (Fall 1995): 189–206.

Senese, Donald J. "The Free Negro and the South Carolina Courts, 1790." *South Carolina Historical Magazine* 68 (1967): 140–53.

Shaw, Stephanie J. "Black Club Women and the Creation of the National Association of Colored Women." *Journal of Women's History* 3 (Fall 1991): 10–25.

Smith-Rosenberg, Carroll. "Beauty, the Beast, and the Militant Woman: A Case Study in Sex Roles and Social Stress in Jackson America." *American Quarterly* 23 (October 1971): 562–84.

———. "The Female World of Love and Ritual: Relations between Women in Nineteenth-Century America." *Signs* 1 (Autumn 1975): 1–29.

Sommerville, Diane Miller. "The Rape Myth in the Old South Reconsidered." *Journal of Southern History* 61 (August 1995): 481–518.

Steckel, Richard H. "A Dreadful Childhood: The Excess Mortality of American Slaves." *Social Science History* 10 (Winter 1986): 427–65.

———. "A Peculiar Population: The Nutrition, Health, and Mortality of American Slaves from Childhood to Maturity." *Journal of Economic History* 46 (September 1986): 721–41.

Stowe, Steven M. "'The THING Not Its Vision': A Woman's Courtship and Her Sphere in the Southern Planter Class." *Feminist Studies* 9 (Spring 1983): 113–30.

Sumler-Lewis, Janice. "The Forten-Purvis Women of Philadelphia and the American Anti-Slavery Crusade." *Journal of Negro History* 66 (Winter 1981–1982): 281–87.

Sutherland, Daniel E. "A Special Kind of Problem: The Response of Household Slaves and Their Masters to Freedom." *Southern Studies* 20 (Summer 1981): 151–66.

Tansey, Richard. "Prostitution and Politics in Antebellum New Orleans." *Southern Studies* 19 (Winter 1980): 449–79.

Tate, Gayle T. "Political Consciousness and Resistance among Black Antebellum Women." *Women and Politics* 13 (1993): 67–89.

Toplin, Robert Brent. "Between Black and White: Attitudes Toward Southern Mulattoes, 1830–1861." *Journal of Southern History* 45 (May 1979): 185–200.

Velde, Lea Vander, and Sandhya Subramanian. "Mrs. Dred Scott." *Yale Law Journal* 106 (January 1997): 1033–1122.

Walker, Juliet E. K. "The Legal Status of Free Blacks in Early Kentucky, 1792–1825." *Filson Club Historical Quarterly* 57 (July 1981): 328–95.

———. "Racism, Slavery, and Free Enterprise: Black Entrepreneurship in the United States before the Civil War." *Business History Review* 60 (Autumn 1986): 343–82.

Welter, Barbara. "True Cult of True Womanhood, 1820–1860." *American Quarterly* 18 (Summer 1966): 151–74.

"Whipping and Castration as Punishments for Crime." *Yale Law Journal* 8 (June 1899): 371–86.

White, Shane. "'We Dwell in Safety and Pursue Our Honest Callings': Free Blacks in New York City, 1783–1810." *Journal of American History* 75 (September 1988): 445–70.

Whitman, Stephen. "Diverse Good Causes: Manumission and the Transformation of Urban Slavery." *Social Science History* 19 (Fall 1995): 333–70.

Wiegman, Robyn. "The Anatomy of Lynching." *Journal of the History of Sexuality* 3 (January 1993): 445–67.

Williams, Christine. "Prosperity in the Face of Prejudice: The Life of a Free Black Woman in Frontier St. Louis." *Gateway Heritage* 19 (Fall 1998): 4–11.

Woodson, Carter G. "Free Negro Owners of Slaves in the United States in 1830." *Journal of Negro History* 9 (January 1924): 6–35.

Wyatt-Brown, Bertram. "The Mask of Obedience: Male Slave Psychology in the Old South." *American Historical Review* 93 (December 1988): 1228–52.

Yacovone, Donald. "The Transformation of the Black Temperance Movement, 1827–1854: An Interpretation." *Journal of the Early Republic* 8 (Fall 1988): 283–97.

Yarbrough, Fay A. "Power, Perception, and Interracial Sex: Former Slaves Recall a Multiracial South." *Journal of Southern History* 71 (August 2005): 559–88.

Index

About the Author

Wilma King has a joint appointment in the Department of History and in Black Studies at the University of Missouri–Columbia, where she holds the Arvarh E. Strickland Distinguished Professorship in African-American History and Culture. She is the author of *Stolen Childhood: Slave Youth in Nineteenth-Century America* and editor of *A Northern Woman in the Plantation South: Letters of Tryphena Blanche Holder Fox, 1856–1876.*